A STEW OR A STORY

OTHER BOOKS BY M. F. K. FISHER

An Alphabet for Gourmets

Among Friends

The Art of Eating: Five Gastronomical Works

As They Were

The Boss Dog: A Story

The Cooking of Provincial France

Consider the Oyster

A Considerable Town

Conversations with M. F. K. Fisher

A Cordiall Water: A Garland of Odd & Old Receipts
    to Assuage the Ills of Man & Beast

Dubious Honors

The Gastronomical Me

Here Let Us Feast: A Book of Banquets

How To Cook a Wolf

Last House: Reflections, Dreams, and Observations, 1943–1991

Long Ago in France: The Years in Dijon

Map of Another Town: A Memoir of Provence with Map
    and Drawings by Barbara Westman

M. F. K. Fisher, a Life in Letters: Correspondence, 1929–1991

Not Now But Now

The Physiology of Taste, or Meditations on Transcendental Gastronomy

Serve It Forth

Sister Age

Stay Me, Oh Comfort Me: Journals and Stories, 1933–1941

The Story of Wine in California

To Begin Again: Stories and Memoirs, 1908–1929

Two Towns in Provence

A Welcoming Life: The M. F. K. Fisher Scrapbook

With Bold Knife and Fork

A STEW OR A STORY

An Assortment of Short Works by

M. F. K. FISHER

Gathered and Introduced by

JOAN REARDON

Shoemaker & Hoard

Library of Congress Cataloging-in-Publication Data
Reardon, Joan, 1930–
A stew or a story : an assortment of short works by M. F. K. Fisher /
gathered and introduced by Joan Reardon.
p. cm.
Includes bibliographical references.
ISBN-13: 978-1-59376-115-8
ISBN-10: 1-59376-115-5
1. Fisher, M. F. K. (Mary Frances Kennedy), 1908–1992
2. Women food writers—United States—Biography.
3. Food writing. I. Fisher, M. F. K. (Mary Frances Kennedy), 1908–1992 II. Title.
TX649.F5R445 2006
641.092—dc22
2006008708

Cover art: © 1989 by David Levine. Used by permission of the artist.
Book design and composition by Mark McGarry, Texas Type & Book Works
Set in Monotype Dante
Printed in the United States of America

Shoemaker & Hoard

An Imprint of Avalon Publishing Group, Inc.
1400 65th Street, Suite 250
Emeryville, CA 94608
AVALON
publishing group incorporated Distributed by Publishers Group West

10 9 8 7 6 5 4 3 2 1

I still think that one of the pleasantest of all emotions is to know that I, I with my brain and my hands, have nourished my beloved few, that I have concocted a stew or a story, a rarity or a plain dish, to sustain them truly against the hungers of the world.

—M. F. K. Fisher, *The Gastronomical Me*

CONTENTS

PREFACE

In her literary as well as personal life, M. F. K. Fisher preferred small bites—nibbles, tidbits, teasers. Her daughters, Anna and Kennedy, remember her sampling a forkful or two of smoked trout or a spoonful of caviar along with a small slice of sourdough toast and a sip of wine, and they reminisce about her simple meals—braised celery or endive in a vinaigrette sauce, hearts of romaine in a well-dressed salad, a bowl of ripe raspberries. She never subscribed to a formal procession of courses, entrées with rich sauces, or multiple side dishes, and her writings are filled with preferences for a single leftover lamb chop happily eaten at breakfast, a mug of tasty soup for lunch, and a perfectly poached egg preceded by a glass or two of sherry for dinner.

So it follows that like the tasty palate pleasers she favored during her meals, the hundreds of pieces she wrote over the course of more than fifty years were also short, stylish, concentrated in flavor, and varied in form. Above all, they were reflections of her talent to communicate the essence of a personal or culinary experience in an eminently readable short story, essay, or article often savored in one sitting.

A Stew or a Story collects more than fifty articles not republished in book form, gathers the gems not found in the dustbin, but in the magazines difficult to track down in periodical indexes, or in early "women's" magazines. For the most part lost to M. F. K. Fisher's readers, the pieces offer, in addition to their own intrinsic merit, valuable insights into her early culinary interests, her amazing sense of place, and her keen appreciation of feasts and celebrations. That she was one of the first "food writers" to pair food with wine, stress the simple anatomy of a recipe, and lightheartedly draw upon the vagaries of culinary history will all be reaffirmed in these pages.

But any recap of Fisher's publishing career must also address the evolution of her style and her predilection for certain subjects. Magazines played an important part in her attraction to short forms. From her earliest years in Whittier, California, when courtesy magazines filled the Kennedy home because her father Rex was the editor of the *Whittier News*, to the pension in Dijon, where Mary Frances and her first husband Al Fisher boarded, she eagerly read the latest copies of *Time, Ladies' Home Journal,* and *Redbook*. Magazines were her source of escape, entertainment, and emulation. And while Al Fisher labored over the lines of his epic poem, *The Ghost in the Underblows,* at the Café de Paris, Mary Frances scribbled plots of mysteries and thrillers that she thought might sell in the commercial magazine market.

Returning to the States in the midst of the Depression in 1931 did not change but only intensified her eagerness to supplement their meager income by writing for the California Automotive Club's magazine, *Westways*. In the spring of 1934, Mary Frances submitted three sketches and an article on Laguna Beach to the magazine and received $35 for her efforts. "Pacific Village" was about a fictitious community named Olas and its struggle to preserve its identity as an artists' colony rather than expand into a tourists' destination spot. Because she had known the village since her childhood and was witnessing firsthand its development into a bustling beach resort, she brought a personal perspective to the article. She also proved to others as well as to herself that she could write a publishable piece.

After Al eventually secured a position at Occidental College and the Fishers moved to Highland Park, Mary Frances' desire to publish took a different turn. Encouraged by their former Laguna neighbor Dillwyn Parrish to write wittily and knowingly about whatever caught her fancy, Mary Frances soon began to elaborate on recipes and dining scenarios she discovered in old culinary texts. A recipe for garum found in Apicius' Roman cookbook, the secrets of spices discovered by the crusaders, and the Florentine savories brought to France by Catherine de Medici's cooks became the subjects for a sequence of *amuse-gueules* she gave to Dillwyn whenever he and his wife, Gigi, dined at the Fisher home. Directing her writing to one person, she suddenly didn't think about seeking a publisher for her work. Dillwyn, however, showed them to his sister, who, in turn, sent them to her friend and editor Gene Saxton at Harper and Brothers, who offered to publish them as a book if Mary Frances would expand the number of essays that he had already seen.

In *Serve It Forth* (1937), Mary Frances juxtaposed vignettes from culinary history with personal experiences—Roman history with preparing *escargots d'or* in a Dijon kitchen, the abstinence of a medieval monk with the sensual delight of a toasted tangerine, the parable of Jacob and Esau with the fumblings of a once skillful waiter. Never dwelling on a subject for too long, her voice alternated between tongue-in-cheek humor and the celebration of appetite. The book not only introduced M. F. K. Fisher to American audiences as a self-styled "humanistic-gastronomical" writer, but it also set the format for many of her subsequent books.

What she had not quite managed successfully in *Serve It Forth*, i.e., integrating a recipe into the flow of the text, she accomplished in her second book, *Consider the Oyster* (1941), where the recipes enhanced the tales rather than interrupted the reader's attention. Writing the book to distract Dillwyn, whom she had married in 1939, from the severe pain incurred from Buerger's disease, Mary Frances focused on the oyster stew suppers of her childhood as well as on the sex life of the androgynous bivalve, and she also wrote charming essays about Oysters Rockefeller and aphrodisiacs. Unmindful of all readers except Dillwyn, she still clung to her belief that "I must always write toward somebody I love to make it seem real."

Circumstances, however, forced her to earn a living with her pen after Dillwyn's suicide in 1941, and Mary Frances began her third book, *How to Cook a Wolf* (1942), saying, "It was probably the first time I was aware of writing to pay my way." Previously she had written about how to survive in wartime in her father's paper, the *Whittier News*; in *How to Cook a Wolf* she went on to develop her thoughts about shortages, rationing, and air-raid shelter meals in a book that would ultimately become her manifesto on "living agreeably in a world full of an increasing number of disagreeable surprises."

The attention generated by *How to Cook a Wolf* led to *Look* magazine's selection of M. F. K. Fisher as one of the country's prominent career women and to Paramount's hiring her as a junior script writer. "How Not to Cook an Egg," excerpted from *How to Cook a Wolf,* appeared in the May 1942 issue of *Gourmet*. A year later, *Coronet* offered her a contract to write a monthly column called "The Pepper Pot." Her first article was "Consider the Lunch-Box," and it echoed the "balance the day, not the meal" nutritional advice she had spelled out in *How to Cook a Wolf*. The ten articles that followed also amplified many of the topics of the earlier book—sludge, scrapple, feasts, and famine. Although she had previously published two selections from *Serve It Forth* in *Harper's Monthly* and had been represented in other magazines as well, the *Coronet* contract was her first substantial writing commitment to a magazine, and she was paid $100 for each article.

The next year *House Beautiful* offered her a monthly column beginning with the June 1944 issue. Featuring a photo of Mary Frances by George Hurrell, the editors introduced the magazine's new food writer:

> She's a unique combination of writer and food connoisseur, who has mastered the mysteries of the cook stove and can translate that knowledge into provocative words to inspire novice and gourmet alike. She's a food philosopher who believes that good living and good eating are synonymous, and that good eating isn't dictated by one's purse but by the zest one brings to the planning of everyday meals. In her language there's a food poem in bread, wine and cheese, when you know which bread, wine and cheese to put together.

From the first article in the series, "June Moon, Silver Spoon," to the last, "For Supper... on a Sultry Night," in May 1945, Mary Frances followed the calendar of seasons and holidays, offered menus, and contributed recipes for two or three dishes. Unusual for the time, she sought to make wine as familiar to American tables as bread and butter. And she created moods around celebrations, always making food the centerpiece in the art of good living.

Meanwhile Mary Frances' most personally revealing book, *The Gastronomical Me*, had been published in 1943, and a version of the chapter "Define This Word" was printed in the *Atlantic Monthly* under the title "I Was Really Very Hungry." After spending the summer of 1945 in New York City with her third husband, Donald Friede, she completed *Here Let Us Feast* (1946), signed on with the Limited Editions Club to translate Brillat-Savarin's *Physiology of Taste* (1949), and wrote the novel *Not Now*

But Now (1947). Mary Frances also acquired a different literary agent, Henry Volkening, who lost no time in negotiating a contract for an abecedary of twenty-four articles for *Gourmet,* beginning with the November 1948 issue. During this time Mary Frances also contributed several pieces to *House Beautiful, Atlantic Monthly,* and *Vogue.*

The 1940s was not only the most productive decade in her career, but those ten years also revealed a subtle shift from excerpting material from her previously published books into magazine articles to writing for magazines with the intention of later reconfiguring the material into book form. After some lengthening and revision, the *Gourmet* series was published as *An Alphabet for Gourmets* in July 1949.

With the dissolution of her third marriage, the death of her mother, and the decision to return to the ranch in Whittier to help her aging father, Mary Frances turned her back on M. F. K. Fisher, the writer, and turned her attention to the education of her two young daughters and to pinch-hitting at the *Whittier News.* In the early 1950s she published only one piece, the novella "Legend of Love," in *Ladies' Home Journal.* After her father's death in 1953, she moved from Southern California to the Napa Valley and subsequently spent more than three years in the early and late 1950s in the south of France. Although she contributed articles to *Holiday, McCall's, Gourmet, Harper's Bazaar,* and *House Beautiful,* they were occasional pieces about picnics and shopping in Aix, the Foire Gastronomique in Dijon, and apéritifs abroad.

In 1961, *A Cordiall Water* initiated a varied sequence of books on wine in California, the cooking of provincial France, living in Aix and Marseilles, and revisiting tried-and-true recipes. And in 1964, *The New Yorker* offered Mary Frances a "first reading" contract. By June 1965, three of her stories and a few book reviews, including "The Full-Orbed Dinner," had been published in the magazine.

The 1960s also ushered in what came to be known as America's culinary revolution. French chefs served in the Kennedy White House, Julia Child's *French Chef* TV series brought coq au vin and *boeuf Bourguignon* into the nation's living rooms, Craig Claiborne reviewed the newest restaurants in *The New York Times,* and James Beard's cooking classes drew students from New York's elite.

Mary Frances' contract to write Time-Life's first volume in the Foods of the World series, *The Cooking of Provincial France,* during the

mid-'6os, led to a closer identification with the culinary establishment—
especially to Julia Child and Michael Field, and eventually to James
Beard and Judith Jones—than Mary Frances had had until that time. And
soon her opinions about wines, various foods, French cuisine, and
dining in America were sought by the growing number of food and
wine magazines.

Within the context of heightened interest in food, she decided to go
through her recipe file "for the real monstrosities in it," and was surprised to find too many good recipes to ignore. When Putnam offered
her a contract to write a book about how she liked to cook for the
people in her world, "the gastronomical favorites of a lifetime," she also
started to collect recipes from friends, cooks, and even close relatives
that reflected the plain days in American cooking. Under the terms of
her agreement with Putnam, *The New Yorker* acquired rights to publish
ten chapters of *With Bold Knife and Fork* before the publication date in
October 1969. The first article, "Once a Tramp, Always..." in a sequence
called "Gastronomy Recalled," appeared in the September 7, 1968, issue,
followed by articles on secret ingredients, innards, casseroles, rice, meat,
and drinks. Mary Frances' fan mail escalated.

Completing *With Bold Knife and Fork* had meant immersing herself in
memories of favorite foods and the people who provided them, and
Mary Frances began to think about writing about her childhood in
Whittier. As part of her contract with Knopf, at least six of the chapters
of the memoir *Among Friends* were published in *The New Yorker* in 1970
and 1971 under the collective title "The Enclave."

In the early 1970s, Mary Frances moved from St. Helena to a home
designed and built for her on the Bouverie Ranch in Glen Ellen. Knowing that her possessions were safe and cared for by a friendly staff, she
and her sister Norah traveled to the south of France, often staying in
either Aix or Marseille for several months. Mary Frances' account of
the mysterious attraction that Marseille had always held for her was
called *A Considerable Town* (1978), and, while written with a certain
amount of self-doubt on Mary Frances' part, it was the last book published by her that was not a collection or reconfiguration of stories and
articles previously written.

Although Fisher published over twenty-five books, including one
novel, she rarely produced a sustained narrative, but rather wrote short

sequences and pieces that her editors—Gene Saxton, Patrick Covici, William Targ, Judith Jones, and Jack Shoemaker—successfully gathered together into delightful books. To their credit, her literary agents also played no small part in the process. Beginning in 1938 with Mary Leonard Pritchett, who had a reputation for placing articles in quality magazines, Mary Frances' early work was published in *Atlantic Monthly, Town and Country, Gourmet, House Beautiful,* and *Harper's.* She was also especially well served from 1946 to 1972 by Henry Volkening, who consistently sold her books to prestigious publishers, arranged for the various editions of *The Art of Eating,* and negotiated her "right of first refusal" contracts with *The New Yorker.* After Volkening's death and her general dissatisfaction with the way his successors at Russell and Volkening were representing her, Mary Frances signed on with Robert Lescher, who encouraged the reprinting of her previously published books at North Point Press, sold foreign rights to many of them, and continued to place her work in quality periodicals. Magazine articles by her and about her sustained her reputation through nonproductive years, and they contributed to her considerable stature as the doyenne of culinary writers during her last years.

Although she often wrote disparagingly about "tapping out some more gastronomical nonsense to fill up a large hole in my checkbook," the magazine articles collected in *A Stew or a Story* are vintage Fisher. They give her style a precise definition and are visible proof that M. F. K. Fisher always had a penchant for literary *amuse-gueules* to whet the appetite, tease the palate, and concentrate the reader's attention.

JOAN REARDON

FICTION

LEGEND OF LOVE

NINI WAS DESTINED, foreordained, to be the final victim. She had everything that was needed, all the requisite virtues of a murderee—or so it seemed for a time. She was a stocky, solid little girl, about seven, and in turn and yet together she was like a turtle, like a pigeon, and like a kitten and a puppy.

She was serene, and capable of silence. She was round, blond, smooth; but she could be ruffled, and her spiritual feathers would stand up, if anything offensive to her finicking nature showed itself. Her fur likewise would stand up roughly, cat-way, if it sensed an affront to her innate gentility. And there was always ready in her, behind the fat sweet baby face and the lids blinking over her large pale eyes, a real growl, like a little dog's. She had the right instincts, that is, and she should have been able to protect herself. As it turned out, she was, with some help, although the basic fact that she could not help having people love her was both her near undoing and what saved her.

Her mother was a beautiful blond alcoholic; her father was a musician who was about thirty and looked a wan sixty; and Nini had been raised mostly in a quiet house in France, far away from the trembling hate and passion of her parents, until she came to Miss Abel's school when she was old enough.

The Turtle

One of the people at Miss Abel's school who loved Nini the most, and perhaps the quickest and with least questioning, was Janet Palmer. Mrs. Palmer watched the way they met, the first time, and from then on she felt all right about them, and about Janet's being there at the school. She saw the pulse of the girl's thin throat, and knew that if she put her hand on the delicate cage of her ribs it would be as if a bird beat against them, hard enough to break its feathers. She could have groaned in pain for Janet's fright at being here, so alone in the new place, until she saw how Nini held out her hand to the other child. Janet had her first fingers bent tightly over her middle fingers. She flushed, and shook her hands self-consciously, not looking at her mother, before she put one of them stiffly into Nini's.

"Good-bye, Mrs. Palmer. *Au revoir*," Nini said seriously.

All four of her upper front teeth were out, and she lisped, but with a pedantic clearness. The two children walked away, without a look back, unsmiling.

"There are three new kittens," Nini said. "One is rather whitish gray, and one is quite a lot more grayish white. The baby is simply gray. Do you by chance speak French also?"

Janet was very bony and long, beside Nini. She was built with an intangible obliquity, a delicate slant upward and sideward, like an El Greco saint. She'd soon put on a few pounds, Mrs. Palmer thought. She stood in the hot September air until she saw the two little figures, the tall one and the solid short Nini, drop to their knees in the shadow of the haystack by the stables, where the kittens must be in their odorous alfalfa cave. She could not hear except with her inside ear, the one that develops in a woman during pregnancy and can never be deafened again as long as she lives, and with that ear she heard Janet's low cry of pleasure as the three babies wobbled out, blinking.

She shook her hands lightly, for she, too, had braided her fingers, and then she went with a feeling of sudden happiness toward the main building, to report for duty.

It was agreeable, the way arcades held the school together. She had been long enough in California to know "good Mission" from "bad Mission," and bougainvillea from trumpet vine, and she felt contented about working in this harmonious collection of low, cool, airy buildings, white-walled, covered with splashing vines, shaded by the ever-moving eucalyptus trees. Air moved gently all about, even on this hot autumn day; it smelled of leaves and clean dust from the rolling tawny hills that rose up all around, and as Mrs. Palmer walked through the small cool patio outside Miss Abel's office fat pigeons whirred up from the edge of the fountain in the middle. She pinched off the tip of a sprawling chrysanthemum and sniffed her fingers, to hide from herself her nervousness as she opened the office door and went into the dim room.

She had been there before, when she asked for and got the job. She smiled at herself, to feel again the old panic.

"I can't help wondering what I've done wrong," she had said that morning, "to be called to the headmistress' office."

Miss Abel laughed. "It's a conditioned reflex," she said. "Once you've gone to a boarding school you're scarred for life."

"Good morning, Miss Abel," Mrs. Palmer said now, trying not to blink: the room seemed very dark at first. "Here I am."

The woman behind the desk did not stand up. She was dressed as before, in a white cotton riding shirt and a black skirt, and her small, beautiful feet crossed primly in the desk hole looked incongruous in elaborate, almost chorus-girl pumps of white suede with big buckles of black to make them even daintier. Expensive, Mrs. Palmer thought without meaning to.

"Come in, come in," Miss Abel said.

She had very large breasts, and her voice seemed to come from a deep point between them, vital and solid and strong, as warm as if it were a locket that had been hanging there in the maternal canyon.

"I still feel scared, being here...that conditioned reflex."

They laughed and shook hands, and Miss Abel absentmindedly sniffed at hers, which had caught the faint bite of chrysanthemum from the younger woman's. "Nothing like it," she murmured, "except maybe a tomato vine in the hot sun, if you brush against it. Now how about your little girl? Name is Janet, of course. Did you bring her this morning? The girls won't all be here for another three or four days. She may be lonely, being the only day girl. You still don't want to leave her with me?"

Mrs. Palmer felt a familiar panic. "No, I don't," she said as quietly as she could, while her fingers started to braid themselves, hidden in her pockets. "I told you. Janet's had a tough year, with her father's illness and then his dying. I do truly believe, Miss Abel, that it will give her a feeling of solidity to spend a lot of time with me and see how happy it makes me to have her near. She'll get plenty of companionship here. We'll stay until just before supper every day. I'll bring her out on Saturdays if you want me to. I could help with the composition papers."

Miss Abel laughed, a little teasing. "All right, all right," she said. "Don't be upset. Did you find a good place to stay?"

Mrs. Palmer shrugged. "It's all right. In an auto court the Chamber of Commerce told me about. Very new. Very clean and respectable. It takes me about sixteen minutes to get here. Janet's off with little Nini, the child you told me about. They'll speak French together. I hope that's all right."

"Good. That's fine. Nini is something. She's good medicine. Now I'll show you your classroom and the bookshelves. We should have done this before. You're going to have to order new third-year texts, I'm afraid—girls that far along eat all the time, chocolate and crumbs.... This may seem pretty casual?" she suggested to Mrs. Palmer. "But that's the way I want it. I get a lot of work out of my girls, and they never know it. Later, of course—"

Miss Abel reached for her two heavy black canes, and got painfully to her feet in their silly shoes. One of her legs seemed to have no bone in it at all, and yet it followed the other one fairly well, and somehow helped to hold upright the headmistress' overheavy body as she and Mrs. Palmer went slowly out into the patio.

Pigeons rose again from the edge of the fountain, and at the sound of the canes on the dark tiles two collies and a fat-bellied spaniel joined the women, followed them along the arcades, and then lay down with deep sighs outside the door of the French room.

Mrs. Palmer felt dismayed by the thin rows of ink-stained shabby grammars. How would she go about ordering more? Were these any good as texts, or should she hurriedly inspect others, and how would she know what ones? How many girls would she have? How do you teach French to people? she wondered dismally. She had been a fool to take this job, just to have Janet with her. *Je vois, tu vois, il voit*—like fun I do—

je ne vois rien du tout except that I'm a fool. Where is Janet? Let's run out of here.

Miss Abel deftly held both her canes in one hand, and the other one laid lightly on Mrs. Palmer's arm, above her wrist. "It'll be fine, really fine," she said, her voice rising from between her deep, heavy breasts like a warmed piece of gold, or like a plump, glossy pigeon from the edge of the sunlit fountain. "Yes, really fine," she said more softly, shifting her canes and starting again for the door.

Mrs. Palmer followed her, feeling a little resentful and foolish, like a moody mare that had just been gentled by her rider.

"I'll see if we can turn up some of the girls for you—ought to be a few around the stables."

They went slowly across the glaring gravel of the yard. At first it seemed painful, but the crippled woman plainly felt it unimportant that they must creep along and that one of her beautiful little feet dangled as if from a leg made of spent rubber, and the two collies and the spaniel ambled along in a familiar careful way, not too close to the canes but not servilely at heel.

A few tired, perspiring parents unloaded boxes of blankets and suitcases under the pepper trees by the Big Girls' dormitories. There was a quiet sound of chatter, doors banging, the scraping of newly painted drawers being pulled out. Mrs. Palmer thought of when she was young, and of the anguish of parting underneath all the excitement. It was bad enough to be a child. Now she was a parent. Now she was both. She was in pain for all the others like her, as she walked slowly and politely beside her headmistress.

"We'll have twenty-seven horses this year—have three girls coming in tomorrow from Utah with their own Arabians. I sent Truro back to manage the trailers—they'll drive out. You'll like my Truro. She's one of my girls—graduated here. Her husband's off to war. Good luck for us, anyway. There's Mr. Appert. I want you to meet Mr. Appert."

Miss Abel waved a cane toward the long, Mexican-looking stables.

"Mr. Appert," she called strongly, in a way that would have stopped a regiment at full charge, and a bent old man stood grudgingly still, at the edge of the dark munchy corridor that went through the middle of the adobe building.

They stepped into it, and it was cool as an icehouse after the blazing yard. The dogs sighed deeply again, and fell upon the soft straw underfoot. There was a feeling of many tranquil breaths going in and out, from the invisible deep-chested horses in their stalls. There was a lovely smell of clean animals and good manure.

"Mrs. Palmer, Mr. Appert." Miss Abel leaned easily against the whitewashed wall. Her short graying hair stood out in little spikes around the edges of her pate, wet from the effort of the walk.

Mrs. Palmer shook hands with the dour, bent old man. He did not smile, but she did, nervously.

He had a clown's face, with bright small blue eyes set into sockets that looked as if they had been gouged out by a woodcarver's tool, and his nose and jaw too looked like the exaggerated carving of a clumsy but happy man sitting long since in a hut in a forest, waiting for the snows to melt, keeping his hands busy. But Mr. Appert's face had pulled itself down into a clown's grimace of disgust, too real to be anything but funny.

"Mrs. Palmer is going to teach French and help me this year, Mr. Appert," Miss Abel told him.

"Hah," he said.

Mrs. Palmer kept on smiling. She could not help it, for he did look like a merry clown made up to be grumpy, and her feeling that perhaps he was not merry at all but was indeed thoroughly grumpy began to amuse her almost hysterically.

"I know a little French," he said unexpectedly. "I'm Swiss myself. Had a girl once from the Canton of Vaud."

He said *Wo* for *Vaud*, in a loud scornful way, and at that the dogs put up their ears and from the stalls came the stirring of several of the invisible beasts. Mrs. Palmer laughed out loud, helplessly.

The old man went on truculently, "But I like Visp better."

He said it *Wizb*. She laughed more. He gave her a funny peek from his deep eyes and she thought, *He is doing this to please me. He is not a mean old man at all.* Then he said "Hah" as if he were fed up with the whole thing, and went off down the dark alley between the stalls, with not a glance at either of the women.

"You must see his pigs," Miss Abel said comfortably. "He is wonderful with pigs. He's wonderful with everything. I don't think I could manage without Mr. Appert.... Is that your girl?"

At the far end of the stables Janet and Nini stood—Janet slanting a little, Nini like a little oak tree—hand in hand in the bright doorway.

Miss Abel let out her voice again. "Nini," she called strongly, and at once the children headed into the odorous darkness before them.

Mr. Appert came out of one of the stalls. "Gonta get the slops now," he said. "Wanta come? Go see what she wants first wid you."

Mrs. Palmer looked with a feeling of helpless intensity at Janet, while her eyes, accustomed now to the dimness, followed her fine child. How would all this be for her? Would she find reassurance and more love here?

As the children came near to them there was a strong smell of hotness, the unmistakable smell of little girl–bodies covered with sweat and clean dirt. Mrs. Palmer sniffed at it. Janet's was stronger than Nini's, perhaps because she had been scared, earlier, and was still not quite at ease. There was a lot of straw in her hair, and her face looked beautiful, with beads of sweat on her upper lip and temples, and delicate hollows, heat hollows, under her large purple-brown eyes.

"This is Janet," Mrs. Palmer said. "Janet, this—"

Janet made a good nick. . . . "Do a nick now, baby," her father used to say mockingly from his bed, and she always would, as if daring him.

"How do you do, Janet?" Miss Abel said in a surprisingly formal cool voice, the one for New Girls. "Nini, how are you this morning?"

"Thank you, Miss Abel; I am fine and I showed her the kittens and she met Jean-Jacques and he spat something right in our faces, but we did not care and did not pay any attention to him." Nini's flat wide face was very serious, and she lisped fastidiously, as if she were reciting a lesson with enjoyment.

"He's a white duck, really enormous, mother," Janet said. "What he needs is a wife, Mr. Appert told us. He doesn't really spit. Just hisses kind of wet. We're going to help feed the pigs."

"Slops," Nini corrected her imperturbably. "That is how you say it in English for pigs."

"Go along," Miss Abel said, her voice warm again.

The children ran away.

She put her hand lightly on Mrs. Palmer's arm, for another subtle disciplinary touch. "I imagine you feel better now. It's going to be fine."

She hobbled out into the sunlight, and sent her voice trumpeting across the big dry yard toward the swings, where several girls shouted and tossed their brown legs up higher and higher while friends pushed them.

"Girls."

The swings died down. The girls came toward them in a shy, politely obedient group.

Mrs. Palmer looked desperately at them. They would be her pupils. They would hate her, have crushes on her, stumble over *je vois* unseeingly. For nine months now she would smell them and breathe what they breathed. She moved a pace away from Miss Abel, for she could not bear to be reassured again with that gentling, that intuitive physical contact of the strong small hand upon her arm, and she knew that her panic was plain as a shout. *Here they come,* she said, and deliberately she loosened the muscles in her hidden fingers, and tasted the air that moved across the yard from the grove of cottonwoods beyond the hutches and the pasture.

The rolling yellow hills laid themselves out to the movement of her gaze, and on the farthest horizon she saw two trees. She and Janet would walk that far, some evening when it got cooler. She made a mocking bow to her convenient sentimentality.

"That's Two Trees," Miss Abel said softly. "We go up there for picnics. I go up there often—lift my eyes unto the hills. Eucalyptus—must be very old. . . . Girls, I wish to introduce you to Mrs. Palmer."

The group smiled and shuffled, all the lithe young untried legs, the innocent faces, the shy eyes tangling into a swirl of vitality. Mrs. Palmer smiled back at them.

Miss Abel said, shaking her canes like a seasoned character actress, "Now off with most of you. Some of you stay here. Mrs. Palmer needs help with those tired old Advanced French books. Nan, Sybil, Jeannine, you help. Anyone else who wants to. . . . Lunch is at twelve thirty sharp, Mrs. Palmer. We can go over the class registrations at three this afternoon in my office. Very nice little girl you have—she'll be all right."

Mrs. Palmer stood as straight as she could, until she noticed how straight the three girls were standing. Then she slumped a little, and saw how they watched the younger kids with a disconsolate air beneath their manners. Nini and Janet swerved out into the yard toward the noon shade of the grove, and the children swarmed after them, yelling meaninglessly.

"Which one of you is Nan?" Mrs. Palmer tried not to sound too brisk and bright. It was the only one of the names she could remember. She must be more attentive.

All three girls smiled eagerly, politely, and as they walked toward the classrooms Mrs. Palmer got them sorted out. Jeannine was a sweet soft one, with the kind of face that would always vanish, except for her steady blue yes. She was a senior, with the same labored French accent she had started with when she was a freshman. Sybil was somewhat younger, in the tenth grade. She was tall and haughty, in a courteous way. Her face had good, strong, coarse cheekbones, and she would photograph well. She walked like a pony. Nan, on the other hand, seemed to shamble a little, as if she were trying to. She and Sybil had both traveled to France, but she spoke with the easiness of a language learned from the scullery boy rather than the governess. She was a thin, brusque girl, with the kind of face that in fifty or five seconds could flash on and off and then on again a warm, intimate, giddying smile. She wore dark blue shorts, and a Basque shirt over her almost flat breasts, and Mrs. Palmer thought she would still look gawky in a dress.

They walked politely along with her, under a long arcade and into the classroom smelling of fresh paint.

"So you are all going to take French?"

They all were.

"Well, let's simply clean out these dirty books and see what we can salvage . . . Où est la plume de ma tante, and so on."

The girls smiled dutifully.

Mrs. Palmer began to hum, thinking of her sweaty, blissful little girl running hand in hand with Nini toward the grove. It was wonderful, all of it: the hot dry yard, Miss Abel, old Appert peeking at her from his carved eye sockets, slops for his pigs, all the unseen horses breathing so sweetly.

"This book stinks, if I may be forgiven the vulgarity," Nan said.

Jeannine looked disapproving but giggled, and Sybil giggled without looking much of anything, and they turned from Nan's daring brilliant smile to Mrs. Palmer.

"See," Nan said, and held the thing up loosely, and graham-cracker crumbs and some long horsetail hairs and a bobby pin and unidentifiable gray dust sifted from its flapping pages.

"Oh, revolting," the girls said.

Nan laughed sharply. "It stinks, that's all."

"Well, all right," the girls protested, as if enjoying their helplessness.

"Here, smell," and Nan tussled with soft Jeannine, trying to push the foul book against her face.

Sybil cried out, "Oh stop it, you two. Stop it."

They were all giggling. Then they stopped, sharp as a cut, when Mrs. Palmer said, "Books get that way." She went on, "Do you like to sing? Do you think French singing would be fun this year?"

Is that the way to act like a teacher? she wondered as she watched their strange young faces, so keen, so remote. *Will they ever really hear me? Où est la plume*—

Things were fine; they were going all right.

It was hard to know which slept the quicker, the more deeply: little thin brown child or mother. They came into the tight box of their motel cabin at night without noticing it as anything but home, and ran cool water into the short tub. After Janet put on her nightgown Mrs. Palmer spread a clean sheet on the revolting prickle of the carpet, and the girl lay there sleepily, like a minute houri...what was the name—those women Matisse used to paint?...She propped herself on one elbow, to eat whatever her mother fixed for her.

They did not talk much. Janet talked some about animals. Anything that breathed, whether it wore fur or scales or feathers, was as it were a part of her, a child from her flesh, a cell from her own blood. The cranky duck Jean-Jacques was her familiar, and she knew why the mother cat hid her kittens from the crowd of New Girls, and probably she knew where, Mrs. Palmer thought proudly without asking her.

Mr. Appert trusted her more than any other kid except Nini to stand on the fence while he fed his pigs. The sow was going to have babies, Janet said happily: she was as big as a house, and dangerous. And Truro was going to let her ride Golondrina soon. That meant she was learning a lot about horses. She probably already knew a lot more about horses than some of the kids. Janet tossed her head. If Truro would suggest, without even asking, that she might soon be riding Golondrina—hah!

"You sound like Mr. Appert," Mrs. Palmer said.

She felt clean and fine after the bath, and as she sat down on the sheet near but not touching her daughter, she was very peaceful.

"Hah," Janet said again amenably.

"It was better the first time. Tell me about Truro."

"Oh, gee, she's wonderful, just wonderful." Janet signed in a moony way, copying an Old Girl.

"How about—well, how about that Nan?" Mrs. Palmer asked.

"Oh, gee, but she's wonderful, just wonderful."

"Oh, rubbish. How about—"

"Oh, gee, she's just wonderful," Janet said, and then rolled over on the white sheet away from her mother. They felt very clean and silly.

"Finish your supper. If you knock over my glass I'll pulverize you."

Janet opened her mouth for a wide inaudible scream, and then yawned helplessly.

Everything was fine: soon she would be asleep. There were papers to correct. Mrs. Palmer thought with voluptuous chagrin of them, and she drowsed. She wanted to wonder about Truro, too . . . or Mrs. Gerwing, the music teacher. Mrs. Gerwing had not liked it when she suggested working on a group of French songs. She must be careful, more careful, in this nest of females—tread lightly.

Janet was asleep. Mrs. Palmer, deft with practice, shook her awake enough to walk, and led her to the bathroom and then to her half of the wide let-down bed. The child would not remember in the morning.

They had to leave by seven thirty. As the days grew shorter and cooler it was fun to go out onto the quiet street, under the drifting plane trees of the little hill town. They knew the service station man on the corner, the night man. He always waved sleepily to them. Often there was a light autumnal dew laid like mist on the tidy lawns. It had a good smell.

Janet always smelled good, too, to her gradually placid mother, so long tossed about but now for a time quiet. Janet smelled of toothpaste, egg and toast, now and then healthy little-girl if she had not bathed the night before. The part in her dark hair was the best place for a good secret sniff, Mrs. Palmer thought with the cunning of a sensual woman who for too long has poured all her desires into a maternal mold.

She loved the ride out to school, Janet so alive beside her.

One morning there was a turtle on the tiny square of lawn before their door. They could not believe it at first, and thought it must be a rock, but when it showed them its head and innocent pointed tail, and stuck out its flippers trustingly, Janet would have wakened all their unknown neighbors with her delight.

"Oh, Nini will love it, love it," she whispered. "Oh, gee, but it's wonderful. It's just wonderful." She crouched over it, not frightened by its cold stare at her.

Mrs. Palmer disliked the thought of picking it up, although the method was clearly indicated and safe enough, given the beast's structure. She thought at first of asking the service station man to help them.

"Oh, hurry, hurry, Mother," Janet whispered. "He might escape."

"He?"

"Yes, Mike. That's his name, Mike. He might just walk off."

"Not too fast for us," Mrs. Palmer said resolutely, and she shoved her briefcase full of uncorrected papers at Janet and picked Mike up from the rear on both sides, nearer his back legs—or were they flippers? She felt smug about how well she did it.

Janet ran ahead and opened the door of their old coupe. Mrs. Palmer put Mike up on the obsolete shelf called a glove rack or something like that, between their necks and the sloping sun-blurred rear window.

"Lean forward," she said. "He might be a snapping turtle. There are snapping turtles."

Janet screwed around blissfully. Mike just was *there*, like a rock, no head or legs or anything. He was about eight inches across, a big fellow. Mrs. Palmer had been surprised when she picked him up. She thought vaguely of turtle soup—somewhere she had read that very little of the meat was edible and very little shell was good enough for carved high combs.

"Oh, Mike," Janet moaned. The animal stuck out its head, Mrs. Palmer saw in the rearview mirror, and he and the child looked deeply at each other. "I love you, Mike."

Oh, I can't give her what she needs, Mrs. Palmer thought suddenly, as if a scar from an old deep wound had been tickled, or a thin blade had turned over in her heart. *Here she loves a turtle, a passing stranger!*

"The one I really love is Nan," Janet said.

"I thought you loved Nini."

"Oh, Nini. Of course I love Nini. But Nan—Mother, she's just wonderful."

"What's wonderful about her?" Mrs. Palmer tried not to sound cozy. Nan was one of her best students, fine at translation, not bad at verbs and suchlike. She had that bright quick smile.

Abruptly, driving along the busy curving highway toward the foothills, Mrs. Palmer realized that Nan was, subpotentially at least, an attractive human being for her. She was alluring, with the flash of teeth, the eye dazzle which came and went so unnecessarily. She was the kind of girl other girls would have crushes on, in a boarding school, because of something beyond sex in her. Mrs. Palmer berated herself. How could she have been so dull? There was this innocent powerhouse, this flash-in-the-pan budding woman, loose as all get out in a bunch of starved females like Mrs. Palmer and Mrs. Palmer the widow and Mrs. Palmer such a nice French teacher, Mrs. Palmer *et où sont les neiges d'antan de ma tante sur la table?*

"Nan is the one I really love the most," Janet said, her fine little head screwed around to watch Mike. "I love her, that's all. She's wonderful."

"What's wonderful about her?" Mrs. Palmer asked automatically, automatically irritable.

She was still astounded at her realization of the desirable potentialities of a slab-sided girl who had gawked into and out of her classes for several weeks, parroting advanced versions of *je-vois-tu-vois* neatly, rarely smiling her rare smile. How long, O Lord, how long, if this was the mete of a normal woman self-condemned to such immolation? She must quite probably live alone, except for Janet. Would she have to guard against the twisted hungers of such unwilling contacts, while she earned their living? Would thin broad shoulders and flat hips, even on a girl, taunt her chastity? Was it the restless autumn air that made her brain thus fidget?

She leaned over her little daughter. "What about Nini lately?" she asked.

"Oh, Nini. She's always the best. It's Nan I love, though."

"Well, for Pete's sake don't say she's wonderful, just wonderful," Mrs. Palmer said snappishly.

"Well, I think she is."

"I'm sorry, darling. I got cross. What's wonderful about her?"

"Oh . . . well, once she picked up one of the kids because she was mad at her and she told her to hold on and she whirled her around, you know the way, and then she let her go. It really hurt Francie, too. She never told. Nan's really strong, the strongest girl in school. She can just pick us up like feathers. If she wants to, of course. She can be really mean if she wants to."

Well, that's just lovely, just wonderful, Mrs. Palmer thought grimly. *This adolescent menace seems to have us all loopy, to put it most nicely. . . . This flat-breasted kid with the on-and-off blazing eyes has moved in on Mother and Daughter.*

She made a careful turn, giving all the proper signals. They passed the barred gates of the Y-Bar-T Ranch next to the school. The hills rolled like lions' flanks on either side of the road.

"Well, don't let her try any of that on you," she said noncommittally. "What are you going to do with Mike?"

Janet whipped clear around on the shabby seat. "Oh, Mike, Mike darling," she crooned.

"Oh, glug," Mrs. Palmer said, feeling almost all right again.

She beeped her horn down under the pepper trees by the dormitories, and a cloud of Little Girls came out, and a few Big Girls peered suspiciously through the windows.

"Look. Look. Where is Nini?" Janet shouted.

Mike was produced in a gingerly way by Mrs. Palmer. Children drew back, pressed forward, shrieked, moaned.

She walked away, unnoticed, while the turtle stuck out first his right front flipper, and then his tail, and then his reptilian head, from which he looked stonily up at Janet, who was so proud of him.

There was one of the weekly faculty meetings.

Mrs. Palmer, feeling conscious of Mrs. Gerwing's discrete animosity about the French songs, or rather about anyone's teaching them but herself, sat very quietly. She had nothing to say anyway. The new books had come promptly. They were not very good, but the girls who had used them in the old spotty crumb-filled editions seemed delighted with them, and the verbs looked and sounded much as before. The new pupils apparently did not mind saying *Bon jour* as they came into the airy classroom, and the question of whether they would ever say much more than that did not at the moment too perturb their mistress. She felt relatively peaceful.

Mrs. Gerwing sat stiffly behind her. She had a delicate goatlike face, very old. It shook from side to side, as if she kept time to an interior music, which was exactly what she did, a slow polka she had danced to when she was a fair sixteen.

There was no other school in the whole area which would hire her, but Miss Abel seemed to hear the notes of the inner rhythm that continually shook this proud old lady, and many girls had gone out from the school with something of the same heartbeat—a very good one, too, in most cases. Mrs. Gerwing seemed able to communicate it to them, not so much through the shaking of her fine, dainty, rice-powdered face as through the timbre of her voice, the imperative lift of her knobby forefinger just one beat ahead of the music. She could draw really fine sounds from the doltish girls, at Christmas and Easter and Graduation. They gaped like melodious fishes to her signals, and spewed forth. They had a somewhat windy sound, as if there were extra breath in them, but they sang gladly, and old Mrs. Gerwing listened to them with justifiable pride, her ears dulled to the little wind and catching only the harmonious whole.

She always taught them what her own teacher would have labeled somewhat superciliously "A Potpourri," which meant that for one good number they sang three bad: for one little dance by Bach they blew out three songs labeled "Oh Sweet Spring" by A. Tillerhausen, "Grandma's Surprise" by Miss Maybelle Jones-Burke, and "Butterflies" by Unknown. She believed in the common touch, as she often said. It seemed to work very well, and proud parents as well as numbed classmates sat passively through the occasional recitals Mrs. Gerwing organized.

One thing she did not believe in was having American—or rather, English-speaking—girls sing in foreign languages. She had told Miss Abel this more than once, and it saddened and shocked her to find her words unheeded, in the justifiable excitement of acquiring a charming new French teacher. She felt her head shaking like a bobbin, and put up one hand as unobtrusively as possible to steady it.

"How do you feel about this, Truro—that is, Mrs. Moorhead?" Miss Abel asked with no apparent passion from behind her desk.

There were eight or nine women sitting there in the office (Chemistry, more or less a man, was away), and Truro would gladly have got up and left the company. She felt out of place. Two years before, she had been a senior, an Old Girl, and had been hauled in for smoking in the Tree House. Now she was a married woman, except that her husband was in Texas or anywhere, and she was supposed to act like a teacher. It made her sulky and helpless.

"I don't know, Miss Abel," she said politely, looking down at her hands. Her nails looked awful, she thought dismally. She had been helping Mr. Appert paint some of the hoofs.

"What do you mean, you don't know?"

Truro thought, *She's treating me like a schoolgirl.* She straightened, and looked down the room at her friend. "I'm sorry," she said firmly. "I think Mrs. Palmer has a good idea, to get the girls who are taking French and who are taking singing to put the two together. It seems all right to me."

She breathed heavily twice, like a satisfied horse, and sat back. Sideways she saw that Miss Abel was sending her a small smile. Sideways the other way she saw that Mrs. Gerwing's head was bobbing like a cork. *Poor old broken-down mare*, she thought . . . *but she has a lot of fight in her.*

The other teachers went this way and that, listlessly. Mrs. Palmer said little: she was new. They agreed not to include French songs in the Christmas program. Mrs. Gerwing became strong and gracious, and nobody else cared one way or the other.

Miss Abel called out in her clear strong voice, not the warm one, and Jeannine and a couple of the other seniors brought in some weak coffee which was unwanted but hot.

Everything was quite gay and bustling for a few minutes: Mr.

Gerwing had come for his wife in his old orange truck, and Mrs. Palmer drove off in her coupe with little Janet asleep waiting for her, and Miss Abel waved to them with her canes in the lighted yard. A few of the older girls looked out from the farthest dormitories.

Truro helped Jeannine take out the cups and the sticky chocolate cookies the domestic science class had made that morning. She stuck a cookie in her pocket as she said good night and turned off the pantry lights. She would eat it in bed. She was going on duty at twelve in the Pink Room, so she couldn't write to Jim. Sweet talk, sweet tongue, sweet tooth. She pinched the cookie.

Miss Abel came slowly into the office where Truro stood aimless and dreaming. "Go on," she said. "I'll work for a while."

"Yes, Miss Abel."

"How are things going? Any trouble?"

"No. A little mischief now and then. Nan put a hoppie-toad in my bed. I didn't mind. I knew beforehand."

"Someone tell you, then?"

"Oh, sure. Stool pigeon."

They smiled contentedly at each other.

"I don't know if I ever told you, honey," Miss Abel said unexpectedly. "You did a fine job, bringing out the Hoskins children and those three Arabians. It was quite a job. Jim will be proud of you."

Truro felt tearful. "All I wanted to do was get far away from San Antonio and that camp," she said. "That's all. The children are nice kids. And those Arabians—we can really get them into shape for the Spring Show, Miss Abel. And the trailers look swell, too, lined up there behind the stables."

They smiled quietly again, and Truro did switch off the lights after she heard Miss Abel's canes reach the room at the end of the front hall. It was about eleven, too late to work; she was glad for that, for her friend.

In Texas, it would be about twelve, or was it one, or two? Oh, never mind. Wherever Jim was she sent him her undying love and wished she were with him.

Truro latched the big oak door, walked across the patio, turned on the night-light that showed softly along the arcades, and reached her dormitory. She walked without sound into the first of the four big rooms of sleeping children. The smallest lay quietly; Nini was snoring in her corner, for her face was too flat, Truro thought, like a pug dog's or a Pekingese's. She stood over Nini's bed for a minute, looking at the sprawled fat limbs. Nini trusted her to be the night angel. It was a good thought. She would be that way for her own kids, later.

In the other rooms older girls twisted or whispered or slept abysmally. Truro stood at the dimly lighted doorways, and said gently, "Good night." Nobody answered, but she could hear a few swallows stuck in unruly throats, and knew that here and there she had interrupted adolescent plottings. She grinned, not being too far removed from them herself, and went along to her own room in the middle of the building.

She took off her clothes, tidied herself with brief nicety in her little bathroom, and hurried to get between the sheets. There she found herself tired, and completely alone, and in spite of her resolutions she rolled into a tough springy ball, like a child, and cried hot tears that ran sideways into her nose. She did not want any of the girls to hear her snufflings. Soon she stopped. She felt ashamed, but better.

It was not until the next morning that she saw the turtle, crushed to a viscous mass, neatly on a black tin dining room tray beneath her bed. When she did she put the tray behind the shower curtain in her bathroom, threw up, and for the first time in her life knocked on Miss Abel's door before breakfast.

"What? See who it is, Marble," Miss Abel said in a mumbling way, and Truro knew she was putting in her dentures. The spaniel sniffed at the crack under the door and barked once. "Come in," Miss Abel said.

Truro opened the door and patted the fat dog, and walked into the dim, stuffy little bedroom.

The headmistress sat up lumpily in her ugly brass bed, a faded lavender jacket of crocheted wool pulled around her heavy shoulders. "What's wrong with you?" she asked sharply. "You look ill, child."

Truro then did what she firmly had not meant to, and began to weep again, and Miss Abel held out her arms and let the sickened girl come into them, in between her warm great motherly breasts. Everything was all right soon, and Truro could talk in a detached way about what she had found.

"That's little Janet's turtle," Miss Abel said in a businesslike way, as if she were consulting a card from her mind's files. "Poor child. She was very happy about it. I'll tell her. She left it here in a box last night, because her mother had to keep her up late for that meeting. Is that when it happened, while we were all busy? It must have been."

"Miss Abel, it looked as if it had been under my bed for quite a while—it was beginning to dry on the edges, I mean onto the tray. But whoever put it there knew I'd be gone and not peeking under my bed. I don't know how I did happen to find it. Looking for my slippers? It seems like something a mean boy would do. Turtles are tough. It was really crushed. Hammer, I think. It must have been a job." Truro felt sick again, but stood up from the edge of Miss Abel's bed with dignity. "I must get back and see about the children. I'll keep it out of the way until they're at breakfast and then ask Mr. Appert—They mustn't know."

"They'll have to know," Miss Abel said crossly. "Every girl in school knew that turtle. I'll tell them it got out of the box and wandered down to the stable and got stepped on in one of the stalls."

They looked, each at a poker face.

"Well," Miss Abel went on, "it's improbable, but it could happen. It did happen. And we don't need to go into details about which of the old nags put it on a tray and carried it into your room. Get along now, honey."

Truro went off buzzing with the familiar schoolgirl elation, in spite of her shock: Miss Abel had called her "honey" twice lately. Jim called her "toots." That was better, but of course not from Miss Abel.

She felt better by now. She took last night's cookie from her pocket, and ate it ravenously on the way to polish up the children. Mr. Appert would help her with the other.

Miss Abel rose wearily. It was part of being overweight and overage, she thought with wry admission. By ten o'clock she would feel livelier: she had grown used to the emerging pattern of her late middle years.

She hopped about nimbly, in spite of her heavy tiredness. Her room was small and deliberately crowded, and she did not have to try to look vertical when she was alone. She put lipstick on her mouth, knowing it would be gone after breakfast and not renewed until perhaps five o'clock. *What a fat raddled face*, she thought with detached distaste, too accustomed to its dim familiarity in the mirror to see its fine small nose, the firm lips over white teeth, and small steady eyes capable of much love.

"It is some kind of signal to us," she murmured aloud. She ran a brush through her short hair. "It's a signal, pointing. I must try to understand it."

She planned, as she readied herself for the day, to catch Janet Palmer as she and her mother got out of their car under the pepper trees. Already some of the children would have discovered that the turtle was not in his box, she felt sure. There might even be a pretended search going on: Truro was a smart girl.

Miss Abel stood at her door, firmly upright on her thick black sticks, and withdrew into herself while she said three psalms, the ones beginning, "The Lord is my shepherd," "Be thou my Judge," and "Fret not thyself because of the ungodly."

"Flee from evil, flee from evil," she repeated, faltering in the last long one, but even in her uncertainty she was strengthened by the flowing words, and went out toward the dining room with a steadier heart.

She could not catch the little Palmer girl before Assembly, so after Prayers and the usual songs she got slowly to her feet and gave her daily run over of the news on the school grounds: this and that, and then three new litters of rabbits had been born—to Candy, owned by Sue Hoskins; to Fluff, owned by Mary Ann Ord; to Bob, owned by Margie Thayer. She waited for the planned ripple of amusement to subside.

"Bob is a fine mother," she said, putting her neck down into her shoulders like a pleased fat pigeon. "She shows no surprise at her new state."

From the back of the room she saw Truro look with passionate admiration at her. She felt indomitable, at least until she got the next bit over with.

"I have unhappy news now, girls, which will be especially hard for Janet Palmer," she said.

She looked quietly at the little girl in the second row, such a slender fine child. Janet looked back at her, readying herself like a thoroughbred, Miss Abel thought resolutely, and in the back of the big room she could feel Mrs. Palmer getting ready too.

"Janet," she said, "last night your turtle wandered off. He apparently got too near an animal much bigger than himself, and got crushed.

Mr. Appert will take care of things properly. We all regret this, for Mike—Mike was his name—would have made a fine member of the company. . . . And now, Mrs. Gerwing, shall we try the new arrangement of The Lord's Prayer, by the Glee Club?"

The club, surprised at this unexpected request, shuffled hastily into a group, and began its breathy intoning.

The Little Girls sat on quietly in front. Miss Abel and Mrs. Palmer and Truro and probably several other people saw Nini try to take Janet's hand. Janet pretended not to see it at first, and her face looked pinched and surprisingly unattractive for a few long seconds. Then she put her fingers into the other child's, and they sat there politely while the Big Girls droned on, until Mrs. Gerwing came to her final triumphant crash on the Amen and all of them could go out.

Mr. Appert, who had been hovering as a longtime disbeliever in the kitchen corridor, gave Truro his high sign and they disappeared.

The children headed this way and that, toward their first classes. Nan came up gawkily to Janet and Nini, by now interlaced, and ran her hand roughly through their bangs and cuffed them a bit, like a boy, and they smiled up at her before she went on toward the French room.

Marble walked solemnly behind Miss Abel, his belly seeming almost to brush the hot ground.

Mrs. Palmer wanted to run to her child and weep for her, all over her, bitter tears that would sting. Instead she went into the classroom, still cool in the November heat, and idly straightened a glass of late zinnias that some girl had put on her desk. They were nice to her, all of them, all the people. She saw Janet walk silently into the second grade room, with Nini beside her, and she felt a physical ache in the most private parts of her, where the child had sprung from.

Later Miss Abel asked her what Janet had said. She was silent, helpless. Then she answered, "Nothing. She knew I'd heard about it. She was ten thousand miles away. Nini was her staff to lean on."

"You mustn't mind that."

"I don't. I'm thankful. But Janet did look stony."

"Has she any ideas?"

"Ideas?" Miss Abel felt that she had blundered, but before she could recoup Mrs. Palmer went on. "You mean that Mike wasn't stepped on by a horse. I never heard of that, either, and I've always been with horses.

Neither likes it. I mean horses don't like stepping on turtles. They manage to avoid doing it. They sense it, through their hoofs. Where was it?"

Miss Abel felt for a few seconds like telling, but she did not know this
younger woman well enough yet, and the fact that she admitted it made
her uneasier. She shrugged slowly down her arms onto her canes, with
a sigh, and said, "Later, I'll tell you. But it was not in the stables. And you
tell me what you can." She went off, her dainty foot dangling.

But Mrs. Palmer did not seem to have anything to tell. She asked Janet
in several different ways, at different times, what she knew about Mike's
death. Janet would close like an affrighted mollusk, something warning
her to shut herself down upon anything too sensitive to risk exposing. A
poisonous tone of anxiety in her mother's voice, a badly hidden odor of
question in the loving tide of her voice, alerted the child as if she were
an oyster in troubled waters, and she became inert, shut, untouchable.

"How do you like things out there?" Mrs. Palmer would ask, after
ascertaining that Janet's color was good, her grasp not too hot, her
breath sweet—in other words, that she was amenable to approach.

"Oh, I love it. Truro let me ride without a lead rein yesterday. She
says I'll be good. I'm good now, as a matter of fact, compared with
some of the kids. I'm a lot better than Nini. She almost fell off Golondrina yesterday, and if it hadn't been for me because I rescued her, just
pulled up Plumy and leaned over and put my hands on Nini's reins and
really saved her, she would have had a fall, Truro told me. Truro was
really proud of me."

"I'm proud of you too."

"Thank you. How about having a hamburger at a drive-in to celebrate, Mother? Just forget dinner and drive in and sit there and eat about
six hamburgers? How is our money?"

"It's fine," Mrs. Palmer said. By now she felt gay and happy, but all
the time she was wondering when would come the right moment to ask
more about Mike the turtle, and knowing well that no matter how she
asked, Janet would withdraw, and hating to have that happen when she
felt so warm and near her secret-faced darling child.

She would try this way and that, always failing.

Tonight she said, "We're rolling in money. I can only eat two, though, I bet.... Did Mr. Appert ever tell you which horse it was that did it?"

"Why?"

"I wondered, that's all."

"No."

Janet pulled herself as gently as possible into the corner of the car seat, as if not to wound her mother by too sharp a withdrawal. *She is a gracious child*, Mrs. Palmer thought helplessly: *she does not wish to point out too clearly to me my stupidity and my gaucherie. Her face is stern. Now we must start over again.*

So far there was nothing to tell Miss Abel.

"How about Sybil?" she would ask awkwardly another time.

"Who's she, Mother?"

"You know, that tall pretty girl in the tenth grade."

"Oh, she's a Big Girl," Janet would say, as if she were dismissing the subject. Then she might ask, "Why?" and Mrs. Palmer, feeling like a dolt, would say:

"I thought she might know which horse it was. She's a good rider."

"Hah," Janet would say, meaning anything at all, but mostly *Leave me alone*.

"Oh, you and Mr. Appert."

"Gosh, he works hard. Work work work he says his life is, and he's right. In and out, back and forth, all the dirtiest jobs, and if it isn't one thing it's another. He loves his pigs best, though. Nini had a big argument with him. She says her kittens, the new ones—"

"New?"

"Yes, three new ones. The others got too big all of a sudden. She says her kittens are much cuter than pigs, but he says his new pigs are cuter. There are ten of them, he says. We can't see them for days yet. Mr. Appert is just trembling with excitement, just trembling."

"How about trembling over your scrambled eggs?"

Mrs. Palmer felt that she had almost heard something, a faint shadow of truth. It was not yet enough. *Time, time*, she thought, and then pushed the panic as far out of focus as she could, reassuring herself by one glance at her child's rounding face, one thought of the sturdy good people at the school: simple Truro, subtle old Gerwing, the quiet house-mothers, Goldie the cook. . . . it was the right place for her and Janet, for a while longer. *Evil is everywhere,* she thought, *but so is good. In the spring maybe I can get a puppy. A turtle is an odd pet to love. It was an accident that brought Mike to our door and it was wrong for Janet to love him so much so quickly, and it was an accident later . . . or was it?* And off her uneasy thoughts would go again.

The Pigeon and the Pussy

Mrs. Gerwing tried not to allow herself the weakness of loving one pupil more than another. She had been a teacher too long, and should know better: it always led to pain.

Sometimes she thought her heart had ached so often that there was nothing left in it to hurt, but every year or two she found herself caught up in a helpless rush of love, and although it had happened through thick and thin, through almost half a century, she still must bow futilely before it, and confess with cynical resignation to her unfulfilled maternity.

If she had borne her own children, long ago, would she now be immune, untormented? She doubted it, and with her bitter doubt her face took on a more delicately goatlike look, and her fine white head wobbled more fiercely, between classes when she could slump over the piano keys unwatched, resting for the new batch of soft tone-deaf ado-lescents to come in and ahahah*ah*ahah*ah* to her firm guiding touch.

That Sybil sang nicely. She was doing "Hark Hark the Lark," not badly either . . . a dreamy proud girl.

Jeannine would always lead hymns. Mrs. Gerwing grinned at her foreknowledge of such docile pupils: Jeannine would make a good min-ister's wife. There were several others like her. The school had a lot of missionary children in it, destined for far lands and the dubious enjoy-ment of singing "Oh Maker of the Sea and Sky" in Mbangimbangi, sur-rounded by mosquitoes and spindling segregated offspring, piping and praying away dutifully in the jungle for papa's sake.

Mrs. Gerwing nodded, happy for a moment to doze herself uncon-scious of what was most in her shriveled but still passionate heart, her love for little Nini.

Nini had the voice of a humble toad, and the stiff unmusical fingers of a scarecrow...of a turtle? Yes, she had the voice of a turtle, inaudible but surely there, surely stiff and horny. Turtle doves...no, they could sing sweetly in their limited way—they were the pigeons on the fountain rim, gurgling and murmuring; they, too, were quiet little Nini, fat and full of trust. They had the same aura of solidity about them, near to earth and yet ready for all flight. Little loving Nini.

The door banged open, and Mrs. Gerwing straightened herself with great dignity for the next lesson. It was Pam...Jan...no...Nan—yes, Nan—a nice girl, too, not with little Nini's heart-twisting purity about her, not with the smoothest manners, it is true, but with a dash to her, a long-glanced bravado which the old lady knew from many years in schools to be potent, capable of drawing interest and even adoration from a stone. She was not a stone, God help her. She smiled primly at Pam...no, Nan...or was it Pam? Partly she hoped the lanky girl had not caught her nodding, and partly she told herself to be a teacher and not the shell of a starved woman past all nourishment.

"Nan," she said.

Nan nodded shortly. "Hi," she said. "I mean good morning, Mrs. Gerwing. I'm sorry I'm late. Gosh, I just came up from the stables. Mr. Appert's sow—he let me look at her; boy, what a litter!"

Mrs. Gerwing sniffed with basic unhappiness and plainer distaste at the studied cloud of rusticity about her pupil. This accent on farm life, Miss Abel's pet idea—

"Please go to the teachers' lavatory at the end of the hall," she said coldly, "and do what you can to come back a little fresher."

She did not blame the girl for flouncing out, and then slouching back still arrogantly soaped. They went into the ahahah*ahahah*ah.

Mrs. Gerwing hated the way Nan or whatever her name was bit at her nails. *Most girls—or at least a part of them*, she told herself wearily, *bite at their nails between the ages of six and eight and fourteen and sixteen. It can be called oral satisfaction*, she admitted with a prim nod toward her progressive vocabulary. But this Nan's fingertips were too square. They were not ladylike and therefore they were wrong. Mrs. Gerwing believed this firmly, and banged a major resolution to cinch her decision, terminating an exercise that seemed for a moment to have got deliberately out of hand, toward the end of the lesson.

"Pam," she said unfalteringly, "why do you bite your nails so much?"

The girl stared innocently at her, stuffing her half-washed hands into her pockets.

It was like that horrid day when Sybil had put so much perfume on, and where she got it nobody knew, and Mrs. Gerwing had asked her to wash it off, and she did, and down what sullied drains nobody knew, but the next day she was sullen and scentless, and for a long time unsmiling. It happened all the time, every year and one way or another, every month of the year with its tidal pulls—

Mrs. Gerwing tossed her head to hide its shaking, and to hide her dismay looked down her nose at Nan, who stood easily, insolently before her, making no reply.

"Shall we try this again?" Mrs. Gerwing asked abruptly, the *grande dame* pulling herself out of the tea party where the princess walks in naked. She would ignore her unanswered query. There was something very wrong about the nails, so unladylike, bitten past average endurance, past their quick, into the bloody numbness of protective callus. But Mrs. Gerwing was too old to ask, to tell; perhaps she was too old to face an issue. She smiled, her head bobbing less in the rush of relief at having convinced herself that it was none of her business. "Let's try this now," she said, and she let herself feel the fat gentle shadow of Nini, so different, hover blessedly above her like a pigeon. "April, April, laugh thy girlish laughter! Then the moment after . . . weeeeeep.'"

In the part of a second before Nan burst into a loud, rough, blasting guffaw Mrs. Gerwing did not hear her own voice at all, so used was she to its unselfconscious exercise. Then, as the door closed behind the swaggering girl, the old lady was as if deafened by her futile piping, so ridiculous, and she hid her face for several minutes in her knobby hands and wondered what ugly pool she had spat into, what beast of rudeness she had enraged by her finicking questioning. Finally she straightened herself, glanced from habit at the fat watch upon the piano, and got ready for the next lesson. It was with Nini. That would clear her head of the bad laughter.

Such odd things are always happening, for so many years now, she thought, *forty, fifty years now.* Three firm chords acted as a kind of shrug for her.

It was silly to try to teach Nini. She was too young for any real lessons in what Mrs. Gerwing called, somewhat fuzzily, *la vocale*. And she had no voice, no voice at all. Perhaps it was dishonest not to discourage this extra expense. But there was plenty of money, they all knew, and Miss Abel, thank God, gave her orders for the weekly meeting of the child and the old lady, a period of squeaky chants and the tinkle of little dances played almost surreptitiously, all with quiet love.

The door crashed open again. Nan What's-her-name had flung it wide for Nini and the little Palmer girl. She flashed one of her brilliant disturbing smiles at Mrs. Gerwing, and was gone, her gnawed hands still hidden.

The children came into the room. Nini walked up to the piano bench without a smile, as usual, and said, lisping meticulously, "Janet would like to hear me sing. Hello, Mrs. Gerwing. Janet would like to hear me sing with you."

"Certainly," Mrs. Gerwing said, astonished to find her hands shaking almost like her head. "Janet, you sit down over there and listen to us practice together."

The trouble was with her heart, of course, not her head or hands: it was beating like a foolish girl's, like sixty, like a lovesick virgin's. Over how many other fat, trusting little pupils had it beat before? Was it indestructible? Would it never stop its antics?

The love-ridden old lady pushed her gnarled hands down upon yet another chord, as if to hold a kind of musical vial of aromatic spirits of ammonia beneath her long reddened nose. *Postnasal drip,* she said scornfully, *calceous deposits . . . geriatrically opposed frontal senilobotomy . . . If I live to be five thousand years old—and by now it seems as if I may well do so—I shall always love every fat trusting little child who stands waiting for me to touch middle C.* Her fingers pressed down again.

Then "Wait," she said sharply. "Nini, how are your hands? You know I like nice hands. Nice hands make you sing better. Today I was going to let you practice a little duet with Pam . . . Nan . . . what's her name?"

"Nan," Janet said from the deep corner of the love seat.

"But she could not stay, she had to leave. I do not know why or what happened but she simply ran out before we had really done much at all, perhaps she felt unwell about her hands but it was too bad, because her nails—" and Mrs. Gerwing put her forehead suddenly down upon the keyboard with a minor chord.

Janet ran from the room, leaving the door wide with her voice tagging along the arcade behind her like a streamer from a kite, "Miss Abel, Miss Abel."

Nini stood a little apart from the dizzy old lady, saying softly, like a pigeon cooing, "Oh, Mrs. Gerwing. Oh, Mrs. Gerwing. Sit up, Mrs. Gerwing."

Some of the Old Girls hurried in, and before she knew it Mrs. Gerwing was lying on the couch in the Main Room with her feet up and a fine handkerchief cool with water upon her forehead. The shades were pulled down. The sounds of life in the humming school grew dim for her. She dozed, only vaguely wondering why she had felt queer.

It seemed part of the queerness, nothing to protest about, that Nini came with Janet into the hushed room and stood looking at her, smiling. Mrs. Gerwing felt a deep happiness, to have the darling near. She sent out a silent wave of love. Nini moved closer.

"Did Nan hurt you?" she asked, as if she were speaking intimately to a flower, a bird.

Mrs. Gerwing tried to say no, but she felt too tired and was asleep even as the little girls stood there.

When she awoke, heavily and some two hours later, she began to gasp as if a terrible weight were on her chest, and Truro hurried in from Miss Abel's room at the end of the low building, where she had been laying out laundry, and found that a weight did indeed press down upon the old lady, for a newly killed pigeon, its neck wrung, lay on the thin breastbone, and a little blood ran down into the dry furrows of the papery brown skin. Truro ran silently toward the study hall, and she felt diseased.

Miss Abel came as fast as she could manage to without any sign of haste, and together she and the young woman helped Mrs. Gerwing and soothed her, as if she were a horse and perforce obedient to their knowing hands. They bathed her neck.

She was very shaky and unwilling to talk, largely because she had nothing to say except that she loved Nini, and that was beside the point surely. They felt her helplessness.

Truro took her home in the station wagon, and wrote a note for Mr. Gerwing, who was irrigating his grove, and helped Mrs. Gerwing into bed.

When she got back the lights were on in the Main Room, for it was almost winter now, and late in the day. There was a wet spot on the couch, where some blood which had run down from the pigeon had been scrubbed off. Miss Abel stood by the big piano, with Marble beside her and, against all precedent, the two young collies staidly beside the spaniel on the worn carpet.

"Truro, honey," Miss Abel said, "you please call Mrs. Palmer. She'll be at her place by now. And get the rest of the teachers in here. And Goldie. I told Mr. Appert. He won't come, but he'll be here anyway." She laughed shortly, and her big breasts shook. "Something's going on, all right. Something is always going on in a community full of potential females. I can pry and talk forever and not stop much of it. But this I'll stop fast. We have to. We've got Christmas and the recital next."

She leaned on her canes, and took off over the long waxed floor toward her office.

Truro watched her with an anxiety she had first felt ten years before, a good half of her lifetime, when she was a fat little kid whose only assets were a crossbred pony and an ability to stick on it, unless you could call being an orphan an asset. Miss Abel had raised her, and taught her how to ride right, real high school dressage a lot of it was. Once or twice Miss Abel had cuffed her. Miss Abel had never slipped on the wax floors, but Truro always watched, ready to leap, to rescue her. This night the heavy woman walked more slowly, but without faltering, and Truro went after her to make the telephone calls.

She had meant to tell about being pregnant tonight, but the bloody, dimming little pigeon did away with that chance—*for the time being,* the girl said, *for the time being.*

When the staff got together, except for Mr. Appert, not much seemed to be accomplished.

Goldie the cook looked painfully unhappy at the bald statement from Miss Abel that something rotten was going on. "Ah," she protested, "these girls all seems nice enough this year, Miz Abel. They polite enough wiv me. Always ask nicelike. Never seen bad in none. Pshaw."

She rubbed her hands over her tired kind face, and sat turning her head in a sad way as the others talked, looking at one face and then another as if there, or certainly there, she would find an answer to the horrid question.

"What we must do," Miss Abel said very distinctly, as if she were try-ing not to spit out each word like a lemon pip, "is put all our recollections together and see what emerges, as a picture of something sick, and filthy, that is building up here. We must work together, whether or not we want to, against something that can harm us as human beings, and as a school, and as Christians." She steadied herself with her canes, and went on in the same hard clear voice, "I sound hysterical, perhaps. I am not. But I have lived with young girls and women for a long time, and have seen much trouble and been able to handle it. This time I need all the help you can bring yourselves to give me. It will not be pleasant. You must tell me of every small thing you hear or see or even smell—yes, smell—that may give us a clue. Think of the germs of blood poisoning—how they race through the body—"

She looked with a sudden dismal weariness at the faces before her, the dissatisfied faces of a group of aging women (except for Chemistry) who had nothing better to do than teach what they best could in a small third-rate boarding school. They were loveless, unlovely. On some she saw the mean signs of a vicarious excitement, while she told of the dead pigeon and, at last, of the secretly buried turtle. One of the teachers turned frankly to stare at young Truro. The French teacher put her hand over her eyes.

"Mrs. Gerwing will be fit as ever tomorrow," she continued firmly. "She may even think she has only had a bad dream. We know better. We must work together to see that nothing more, nothing worse, happens here. This was a signal to us, pointing... And now let us say the Lord's Prayer."

When their self-conscious murmur of the great words had ceased, Mr. Appert clumped in noisily from the corridor. Goldie brushed past him, sniffing back tears she could not control: the strong sound of Miss Abel's voice above the teachers had been too much for her.

"Come hep me git coffee," she said, but old Appert went on in, and shut the door after him, and stood glaring in the light at the group of people.

"Well, I took care of it," he said.

"Thank you. You missed the prayer," Miss Abel said. It was an old joke between them, which she could not help making even now. She chided herself by speaking more sharply. "Mr. Appert, we seem to have a sick mind at work here now, something evil, not merely mischievous. You perhaps know more than any of us, because you see the girls outside of the classrooms. Please keep in touch with me, will you? Tell me whatever you may see in your work that is not healthy. We'll find it, all right, if we all keep our eyes open and do not let ourselves be poisoned. Yes, we must think of the bacilli of blood poisoning—the way they race so fast—"

The biology teacher stiffened a little, and Miss Abel realized with amused fatigue that she was perhaps laboring the wrong point, showing her ignorance.

"All I know is that we will stop the sickness," she went on mildly, unable to miss noticing from one of the hundred corners of her eyes how the biology teacher now expressed relieved intellectual and professional integrity. "We have fine children here this year, Old Girls and the new ones too. We are healthy people," she concluded.

She limped carefully over to sit by Mrs. Palmer on the alpaca love seat, and later stood at the patio door with her and asked her if she knew whether Nini and Janet had seen anyone come into the darkened room while Mrs. Gerwing rested after her seizure.

"I don't know, I don't know," Mrs. Palmer muttered in a flighty, distracted way. "Miss Abel . . . Nini is such a dear child, I think, but she and Janet are too far away from us, a thousand miles from any of us, happiest alone really. Could they be doing things, learning things—"

Miss Abel put out one hand toward her, but the younger woman moved quickly away, untouchable, down the dimly lighted arcade.

Even with her child she is too alone, Miss Abel thought heavily.

She patted the two collies at the door, and then went to her room, Marble's toenails clicking along to the sound of her canes on the floor. They sighed, dog and woman, once her door was reached, and went to what rest they could find.

The next morning, Mrs. Gerwing was indeed at her place for the hymns, and it seemed to her as she struck firmly down upon the yellowing keys that she had never felt stronger, more able to cope with evil. Whatever naughty child had played that trick on her was a part of the nightmare side of life, she knew, the wrong side; she herself was on God's side, the right one. It was as simple as that for her, and she felt no dismay for herself.

She knew that her head shook somewhat more obviously than usual, but it did not bother her. She looked in her clear-eyed bobbing way about the room as her fingers went sturdily through "America the Beautiful," and when Nini gazed back at her without a blink from her flat wide face the old lady smiled in a small salute, so as not to intrude too far upon whatever child thoughts there might be behind the gaze, and she flipped in an extra chord, for joy to be near the darling little girl and alive at all.

The weight of the pigeon could never be completely cast off from her breast, it was true, but actuality bade her breathe anyhow. And Mr. Gerwing had been so kind last night, and had made her hot milk, a toddy really. People were good.

She swept with uncontemptuous familiarity into the Doxology, and waited for the departing shuffle of the girls to die away.

Young Truro came up to her, and was thanked graciously for helping her to get home, as if Mrs. Gerwing had been a bit tiddly on pink champagne yesterday, not pigeon's blood, something that could happen to anyone—anyone in their set, of course.

Old Appert brushed rudely past them, and toward the office. He smelled strongly of the stables.

"Well," he said when he had closed the door, "if you got time I can talk."

Miss Abel looked long at him. Seated behind the desk she was large and crisp and unruffled, like a highly intelligent hen. "You want to sit down?" she asked.

Mr. Appert shook his head. "I'm just telling you," he said dourly. "You said you wanted to hear what goes on. Well, I'm telling you dat someone's teasing my sow. She got a good litter, all doing fine. Your girls will eat plenty bacon. But she's being teased. Don't look out she'll damage herself and dem too. I want the girls to stay clear away."

Miss Abel felt that she was about to know something; she was about to understand. She breathed deeply, and ran a pen along the glue on a scratch pad before she asked, "What girls especially?"

"I'm not saying," he said. "I'm not saying, dat's all. But girls dat tack around in boys' clothes...dey want to be men dey can be men, but if dey want to turn into nice young ladies dey should act nicer."

"Mr. Appert," Miss Abel said, "you either put up or shut up about blue jeans. There's no use fussing any more about it. You know it. We've discussed it. It's considered quite proper now." *I'm losing the signal*, she thought helplessly.

"That's all right with me, then," the old man said sourly, suddenly without accent, and he slouched out.

She looked after him with discontent, at herself, at him. He stank. He was a smelly old man. She thought of the time young Mrs. Palmer had touched her hand and left the biting smell of chrysanthemum upon it.

Through the office door the fountain sounded from the patio. Today no pigeons drank upon its rim, as if in tacit punishment. She shrugged, and then with vigor attacked her books, and when Mrs. Gerwing came and then Truro, to be the first to unwind a long cord of suspicion, she was strong and ready.

There seemed no end to the ugliness in the next days, once they started to look for it. Even the girls Miss Abel loved the most turned out to be nasty: they picked their noses, or wore dirty underclothes by choice, or whispered filth into the listening dark. *Lord Jesus, help us and keep us sane*, Miss Abel prayed.

All the rocks turned over, all the slime lying in the cruel sun: it could show this or that, but so far as she could see there was no clue to what had happened and what was still to happen until about a week later, when Mr. Appert came in to tell her that his sow had killed most of her piglets, big as they were by now.

"Bit them to death," he said. "Driven to distraction."

"Oh, what do you mean?" Miss Abel felt angered by his histrionic statement. "Driven to distraction! Speak out! 'Driven to distraction,'" she mocked.

"That's what I said. That girl would come out and whirl the little kids around right over my sow's pen, and a good sow don't like that, all that screaming. The little kids would yell, and my sow just gave up, that's all. That little Nini, she raises hell out there when she gets whirled."

Miss Abel sat quietly. In her heart she knew she had found something she must know more about. "Nini?"

"The little fat one. Nice kid. She and that Janet, they're a pair. Nan whirls them around and they sure do scream bloody murder, more like they hate it than they love it, but they want more. Nan always picks beside my pigpen for it. She does it deliberate if you ask me, which you do." He sighed. "That's a good sow. But sows are highly sensitive." His accent grew thick with sudden grief or rage. "I tell you dis agin, she vass driven to distraction." He glared with bewildered truculence at Miss Abel, and slammed out.

She sighed more heavily than he. She must continue the ugly search, turn over another stone for what would show cozily on its dark underside.

She decided to ride that afternoon. She might take Sybil, a couple of the seniors, too, go up to Two Trees and breathe a better air.

It was always an event when she went down to the stables in her finely cut black jodhpurs, her beautiful little black boots, and she could not help but savor the hush that preceded her slow entry into the sweet-smelling adobe building with its ceaseless breathing from all the stalls. Girls called out to her excitedly, and crowded around her.

They were lovely creatures, she thought, so slim and sure. She limped on through their tumbling gaiety, and leaned against the high mounting block Mr. Appert had constructed for her, with its little railing, its several steps, the holes for her two canes, all of it rising a good five feet toward the heavy rafters of the barn.

She'd take out the palomino stallion Sunrise, she said, and the girls gasped with envious admiration and Sybil and Truro went to help Mr. Appert saddle him.

From down near the pasture came a steady screaming sound, almost contented in its voluptuous regular rhythm. She felt shocked to be so alone in her shock, and she asked a girl harshly, "What's going on down there?"

"Oh, that's Nan again, whirling the Little Girls, I guess.... Sunrise!" The slender creature in her fancy Western shirt and jeans moaned as if the fine horse were a movie star, Miss Abel thought crossly. *What we need around here is a few two-legged males.*

She hopped up her little stairway with deliberate dignity, and got her boneless leg properly into its stirrup, and then, with her knees as good as any rider's in the world, she became a kind of princess in the saddle, erect, awesome, beautiful.

The girls fell away, breathless with love for how she rode, and she let Sunrise prance dramatically into the yard, wanting to get down to the pasture before other riders joined her.

"Truro, you choose five or six girls and we'll go up to Two Trees," she called.

The stable babbled with excitement. The shrieking went on and on, unheard except by her: not a head turned, not a heart shook.

In the pen below the pasture fence the old sow rooted nervously, perhaps looking for the offspring she had so lately stamped and gnawed to death, perhaps enjoying her freedom from their tugs at her, certainly uneasy though, with her eyes rolling behind their thick lashes and her little hoofs trotting this way and then that way.

Above her pen Janet Palmer leaned dangerously, expectantly, from the top bar of the fence. It would be her turn next: Nan was whirling Nini on her last turn.

The little fat girl flew solidly through the air, her wrists held in Nan's strong fingers, which were white at the ends from pressure.

White and square, Miss Abel thought. Square fingers? Part of her mind asked it while the rest took in all it could of the strange exciting scene: the tall girl, with budding breasts, and flat hips in jeans worn low in the cowboy fashion Miss Abel continued to ban, and with Nini stretching out into the air like a flag, almost whistling with speed as she went round and round over the pen above the tortured sow. Her face was stretched flatter than ever with a kind of satisfied horror, and screams came with the evenness of a fine drumbeat from her lengthened little throat.

Nan's shoulders strained under her T-shirt.

"Don't let go, don't don't don't," Janet shrieked from the fence. "Nini, she'll let go I know she will. Stop, Nan, please please stop. Do it to me now."

Nan was panting. She slowed down the whirl deftly, and set Nini on the ground outside the pen. Both of them staggered.

"There you are, kiddo," she said, before they saw Miss Abel on Sunrise.

In the violent silence the old sow sounded like a troop of sows, guzzling the earth entire.

The three girls stared up at the woman so beautifully astride the sun-colored stallion, and blinked with unfocused eyes. Nan put on the swagger she had put off for the game, and looked boldly up into the headmistress' face when she could. Janet Palmer seemed embarrassed, as if she had been caught in a social blunder. Little Nini, dear tender child—Miss Abel wondered why she loved this dear tender child more than almost any other ever—Nini had the flat face of a new kitten, one subtle with all its instincts of play, of self-preservation, and she looked far up to her teacher like a dazzled tiny animal, with her eyes far apart and blank, her little teeth pointed and dry in the whistle of her spent excitement, as if she had been teased too long with catnip on a string.

The silence, except for the bereft sow's grunting, lasted a long time. Miss Abel did not know what she should say, or would, or could, and when she finally did say in a mild voice, "I wouldn't try that again, Nan," she was surprised at herself.

What she most hated was that a look of relief came on the three young faces, and she knew that they were conscious of something bad about the whirling and the shrieking, and were expecting a true punishment.

I must do something about this, she said. *This is important. Now I know. But I still have time to go to Two Trees, to breathe.*

Sunrise fretted under her. She gentled him, and let him dance off a bit, sideways.

"You girls should be up with the others," she said coldly, raising her voice above the thud of his restless feet. "Nan, you either ask Truro about riding or go up and see if Goldie needs you to take out some trash from the back porch. You Little Girls help."

"Yes, Miss Abel," they all said, their eyes down.

She wheeled, feeling good healthy power in her wrists and her knees and her spine, forgetting for a time more the dainty foot placed so properly in its unfelt stirrup. She put her hand on Sunrise, near his fine blond mane. "Boy, boy," she gentled him, turning away from the children.

The thought of their faces, one daring and one sheepish and one blank as a kitten's, stayed underneath all else, but she was able for a time, out in the pasture waiting for her riders, to ignore trouble very neatly. As the Old Girls assembled she led them on their mounts, her voice like a warm silver trumpet, in a good drill and an amusing little figure dance, before they headed for the hills. *They can ride in any horse show in the country,* she thought with a kind of ferocity. *What I'm trying to do is healthy and good. This is a good place. I am keeping it simple and plain.*

She stumbled badly, though, when she was dismounting, and walked across the yard with greater precision than usual, toward the lighted arcades and her own small cluttered room, with Marble pattering fat and old along behind her. She was dead tired.

Goldie banged and sang and bossed her helpers in the fumy kitchens: things were getting on, and the dinner bell would ring before she was out of her habit, Miss Abel thought.

She must call Nan in tomorrow, try to get some kind of hint, of signal; she must tell her to stay with her own age group, try to find out why she didn't, why she was with the Little Girls.

She must see Mr. Appert tomorrow and ask him if any new kittens were due in the barn: she would start a new scheme and give kittens definitely to this girl and that, to Janet and Nini for instance, and let them have a Junior Pet Show in the early spring—it would keep them busier.

Dear God, what if that girl had let go of Nini?

Miss Abel turned sweaty in a flash, and then frowned at her neurotic reaction and put her useless foot neatly into the jack Mr. Appert had made for her, and pulled off the beautiful black boot. She must hurry.

That night Mrs. Palmer stayed for dinner, because of the rehearsal afterward for the Christmas recital, and by the time she got to the dining room she felt bewildered and dizzy from the all-surrounding clatter of the Little Girls' dorm, where Janet was changing from her blue jeans into a clean dress.

The air was thick with countless shower baths and the enthusiastic use of inexpensive bath powder sent by loving if continuously absent parents. Five hundred drawers seemed to slam in and out and without stopping, in the hysterically bustling rooms filled with fat and skinny children in white cotton panties, white ruffled slips. Little wings stuck out from their brown backs; little stomachs bulged softly, or in the older girls sank in flatly between the widening pelvic walls. They yelled for help with their pigtails. Nini lisped comfortably in French with Janet, who sat on Nini's bed and fumbled with back buttons on her frock.

Yes, Mrs. Palmer felt bewildered and dizzy. She got out as soon as she could, thinking without really being dismal about it that Janet had not once looked at her, and that perhaps it might be wise after all to flee the boxlike apartment and come here and give Janet entirely to the other children and sleep alone in a broken-down narrow bed in a room fifty other forlorn schoolteachers had slept in. Miss Abel would understand, she thought mazedly, as she walked into the new hum of the main building.

The Old Girls named for that week dashed fussily about the dining room, pouring water into tumblers, rustling their school aprons.

There was a great clatter from the pantries, and Goldie called out, "Come on now, is Spanish rice and Spanish rice hassa be hot as—well, hot as you know," and the Old Girls laughed happily, feeling very mature.

In the Main Room old Mrs. Gerwing sat at the big piano under one lighted floor lamp, somewhat melodramatically, Mrs. Palmer thought. (She felt tired and sour from all this peeking and prying and looking for evil. She wished they could go far back to the innocent days of reading the current St. Nicholas aloud and making the kind of taffy that got gray from all the hands that pulled it. . . . *How weakly fatuous I am*, she thought angrily.) She felt almost resentful of the white hair gleaming softly in the light, and the gnarled hands seeming to wander but playing with such firm familiarity, such soft measured music with such strength beneath it.

Mrs. Gerwing's head wobbled as usual, and her remote delicate goat face showed its usual lavish dusting of rice powder. She smiled obliquely up at the other teacher.

I simply will not have her secretly rehearsing my girls in some idiotic French roundelay, she thought. *It is impertinent. I know what music is best for these girls to learn. "Le coeur de ma mie est petit, tout petit petit"— that sort of thing. Hah. I'm not worried of course. This woman is very shy. I know exactly what we will sing for the Christmas recital, my recital.*

"Good evening," she said quietly.

Mrs. Palmer stood with some peacefulness beside the piano, listening to the reassurance of the prelude she most loved. It seemed strange that Truro had seen a dead pigeon all bloody on this nice old lady's breast, and that she had been grown-up enough to go out and get help, not messily but with aplomb, and that before that her own Janet had seen the fainting and had been grown-up too. Mrs. Palmer tried to make herself think dispassionately about what must have happened inside her child then, but she could not. She shut off the quick panic in her mind, and bent almost hungrily over the knobby ancient hands that could soothe her with their skill.

The chords rose in triumph.

Miss Abel came down the room then, in a long black skirt, probably in honor of the rehearsal. The bell clanged from kitchenward, and corridors spouted famished girls.

Mrs. Palmer, her body numbed by the steamy hubbub of the dorm, her spirit soothed by Mrs. Gerwing's canny choice of music, looked with a kind of astonishment at her daughter far down toward the end of the Main Room. Janet's fine eyes, as big and dark as plums, were candid and full of trust and love, and she stood as close as politely possible to dear stumpy Nini. That was fine. Nini was good for her.

Everyone smiled at everyone, and with the customary signal of her raised stick Miss Abel walked toward the dining room, and her charges followed, with appetites repressed according to their fury as well as their cultural heritages.

Later the rehearsal went off very well. Mrs. Gerwing whipped through hours of accompaniment and direction which would have exhausted anyone half her age, leading the girls with authoritative movements of her temporarily steady head. They would sing the familiar Christmas pattern she had worked out decades and more decades before: *Music is the same, and girls are the same,* she thought without any conscious irony. Mrs. Palmer made no sign of wanting a French song. It was a strenuous and agreeable evening.

Miss Abel had put Nan in charge of the younger Old Girls who brought in hot caffeineless coffee and cocoa, and she noticed that the rough girl was beginning to take pains with herself: Her hair was soft around her handsome sulky face, and her quick smile, which transformed her so seductively and to a point of amazement from the beholder, flashed easily and often. Her gnawed hands could not be hidden, though, and faculty eyes fastened on them with a worry geared to the owners' perceptions, as the earlier appetites were geared to the age and capacity of each hungry young stomach. But the eyes were old, not young; they were not hungry for what they read.

Truro had gone off with the Little Girls, glad to escape the smell of hot cocoa. Riding tired her stretching muscles by now. She supposed she should stop, but it was good to get on a horse. She must find out when she would have the baby: she knew more about mares than about women. She kept putting off telling Miss Abel. There seemed so many other things bothering around.

Little Nini was helping Janet Palmer put her stuff in the car, and Truro tucked in a limp pair of jeans and the fancy Bar-20 boots...Janet was a spoiled kid, but sweet.

Going back to the dorm under the pepper trees, Nini put her hand in Truro's and said, "I love Janet, Truro. I really do. She loves me best too. Just best of anything." She sighed, and Truro felt without knowing how she felt it that such innocent unthinking love was beautiful.

She went comfortably into the bedtime clatter of the dorm, sure of her control of it, and then on to her bed, sure of what dreams would meet her.

Old Mrs. Gerwing, so fortunate on the other hand to be driving off with her aged husband, felt empty of dreams, but comfortably old.

"You waited long?" she shouted at him, knowing that in spite of it he would not hear her the first time.

"Eh?" he yelped out irascibly at her over the rattle of the orange truck.

"I said you have to wait long?" she shouted.

They fumed, side by side, in an irritable yet fine companionship.

"How'd it go?" he asked. "Like another one of my special toddies tonight, eh, with a little stick in it?"

He sounded mischievous. Such a good man! She patted his thin knee. She felt at home.

Mrs. Palmer, however, did not. She saw that Janet was almost asleep in the car. She pulled her extra coat down from the back of the seat, and deftly covered the nodding child. She felt full of foggy warnings, sinister nothings, rheumy incoherent intonings. Ah, she was too young, or perhaps she was too old, to live alone in the world, unlock the door herself, take in the dozing bird-thin child, pretend to be warm and alive. *I would like to find somebody like Mr. Appert, but younger,* she thought as she drove along the black highway, *somebody simple and real, who would love Janet and spank her now and then and make about three more children with me. I wouldn't mind if he smelled—not as much, of course, but a little.*

It is not known what Mr. Appert did that night, in his secret lodging place somewhere near the school (in all the years he had been there, Miss Abel had never asked him from what burrow he arose in the morning, to what dark snug bed he returned at night), but Miss Abel, the headmistress—the fourth participant, it might be said—slept peacefully, in her crowded room which was in reality a kind of enormous cane to enable her to hop all around it when she was alone, without using the real canes which leaned, ready, beside one of the many solid little tables.

She had not expected to have such quiet hours. She had felt increasingly uneasy during the rehearsal, steadily surer of where she must look. She had been forced to chide herself for an understandable but pusillanimous hysteria as she watched the blank faces of the singing girls and knew, much better than a week or even a day ago, what murky secrets lay behind this one and that one.

It was fine that she had a good rest, that night, for in the morning Mr. Appert stood at her bedroom door until she was dressed, and then told without a look at her that he had found one of Nini's gray kittens dead by the stable wall, flung like a ripe pear from the hand of a giant, he said shakenly, hurled with great speed and ferocity, crushed like a piece of fruit, whirled and whirled and then let go of.

A few minutes later the French teacher came in, sicker even than Mr. Appert from the look of her, with a sheet of paper she had found on her desk. It was ungrammatical, she said, but it was gutter French all right, most of it of such knowing filth that she could not bring herself to translate it aloud. It was a parody of the song she had wanted the Old Girls to sing for a Christmas surprise, *"Le coeur de ma mie,"* except that it no longer said *coeur.*

"Things are moving fast," Miss Abel said finally, in a cool, almost musing way. "I'll move faster yet. The recital is tomorrow night, isn't it? You invite Nini to go home with you tonight, will you? You can make room? I'll keep every girl in this school too busy with the pine boughs for any trouble. Will you find Truro for me and ask her to come right here? And will you take my place at breakfast? Just leave that paper with me."

Mrs. Palmer went out calmed by the withdrawn force of the headmistress meeting with this thing. When she found Truro, whipping around to get the Little Girls ready for the breakfast bell, buttoning dresses, tying hair bows, she helped too, and murmured her message.

"More of it?" Truro's mouth was tight on some bobby pins.

Mrs. Palmer surprised herself by putting her hand for a moment on the girl's arm, just as Miss Abel had done to her for the first day, three months before, and then she said lightly, "I can take home a girl with Janet every night until they've all been at our house."

The children sent up a shriek of excitement.

"Tonight the first turn is for Nini."

The children not named Nini or Janet groaned. Nini said with her meticulously lisping pronunciation, "That will be very nice. Thank you, Mrs. Palmer. I must pack all my things in my suitcase during rest hour, must I not, Truro?"

"Oh, gee," Janet said, her hands laced together with delight.

Truro went toward the main building, and it seemed quite natural for Mrs. Palmer to go on checking the appearance of the noisy, hungry, still-sleepy little children.

Apparently there was no worry in Nini's mind when she could not find her kitten: she was used to the comings and goings there where mares were taken off for "vacation," where buck rabbits were loaned for breeding, where mother cats looked fat and slow and then had more kittens and more kittens.

She did say, though, on the drive to the Palmers' apartment after school, "We just hate Nan."

"Oh yes, Mother, we just hate her."

Mrs. Palmer asked, clicking on her fog lights and not risking a glance toward the two little girls, "How does that happen? I thought you said you loved her."

"Oh, no, we just despise her. She's a very rough girl. She might drop us any time, she says. She might too."

"Yes," Nini said, "she is too rough, Mrs. Palmer, we have definitely decided."

"How about Sybil? Do you hate her?"

"Oh, no, we don't hate Sybil...oh, no, we don't hate Mary Anne... oh, no, we don't hate Doris," they chanted on together.

It always astonished her to rediscover how many separate worlds spun in their own orbits in the small school. Some of the Old Girls, important ones who led student-body meetings and read their compositions at Friday Assembly and held the big silk flag for the salute: the children seemed never to have heard of them, nor have seen their red or black hair...and others, the real mice, they spoke of with especial warmth—"Oh, she's darling, she's swell, we have a crush on her."

When they got home Mrs. Palmer made cocoa and toast for them and let them eat it, all soft and rich, from her two bowls. Then they strung cranberries for the school Christmas tree, until they nodded in their chairs.

Nini thought the pull-down bed was wonderful, just wonderful.

When Mrs. Palmer lay in the dark on the couch, and listened to the two children breathing so nearby, she wished, not for the first time in her life but one of the few, that she knew how to pray. She would like to pray for Miss Abel.

At about that same time Miss Abel, who knew how to very well, was praying, and for herself, upon her knees beside her bed.

Even in the stuffy little room she could smell the pine boughs and the bruised eucalyptus branches that hung everywhere about the school.

Things looked beautiful. The girls had worked hard and long—she and
Truro had seen to that. And she had talked with Nan's former schools.
She had, finally, called the parents, after she was sure she must. They
would come to the Christmas program tomorrow and then take their
poor daughter home with them.

She put her face in her hands, trying not to hear again the stiff hope-
lessness of the father's voice, the petulant exasperation in the mother's.
"Oh, not again," each said, he dully, she with vehemence.

I have done wrong, the headmistress thought. *I should have looked further before I let her come here . . . but so many girls, so many years of girls . . .*
She got up heavily, unable to calm her thoughts as a Christian needs
must, when at prayer.

She opened the door for Marble, who came in aloofly and lay at once
upon the end of the bed, with a sharp sigh. Then she got her prayer
book, feeling inadequate, and sat beside her friend, absently pulling out
burs from the soft ears while she read words "for quiet confidence" and
"for the children" and "for the recovery of a sick person."

She went back to the part, "Give us light and strength so to train
them that they may love whatsoever things are true . . . and pure . . . and
lovely and of good report."

Marble was asleep. Soon she would be.

The Sacrifice

In the morning Miss Abel felt very clear about what she must say to
Nan, and when the girl stood before her desk she asked her to sit down
and readied her papers a little more. Then she said that she and the faculty felt that Nan had not been able to adapt herself to the very restrict-
ed and perhaps narrow standards of the school.

Nan gasped, and turned it into a snorting laugh, "You mean you're
kicking me out too?" Her face was white, drained for a few seconds of
its sensual boyish beauty, so that she looked like a tired farmwoman in
labor. Her eyes glanced wildly at the headmistress. Then it was as if she
turned a valve that shot stone into her veins instead of blood, and she
straightened insolently as hard and cold as granite.

"It has to be that way with us, Nan. I've known something of your
record, of course, from the other schools, but not as much as I know
now. Schools have a way of passing some things along and not others,

saying one thing for another, or not saying it at all. Yesterday I asked blunt questions, and I got the answers, what I was already fairly sure about. You know what I am saying. I am saying that you are leaving because you do not seem able to, after several months here last year and then summer school, and three months this year, to fit yourself into the pattern of the life we try to lead, the life I always hope you and my other girls will learn to want to lead. You have at least given me fair warning, in your own way—signals—"

Nan smiled mockingly, a bright flash.

Miss Abel looked with apparent dispassion at her, thinking something vague about the dueling code, and went on, "I have said just that to your father and mother. No more. Should I say more to them?"

Nan shrugged. "Why did they let me come here?" she asked at last. "They knew about the other places."

"That was my mistake as much as theirs. I shall make sure that it does not happen again, wherever you may go. Your father is a very fine doctor, Nan. I'll talk with him."

"He'll just send me to a hospital. He told me he would, the next time. I won't go. He hates me, and she hates me," and Nan called her mother foul names, watching Miss Abel's face stonily, talking about the way she had to do her hair at home in little snail curls, and the way she wore absorbent cotton in her blouses to make herself look prettier and like a woman, and the way her mother would tease her about being a boy.

"You are not a boy," Miss Abel cried out sharply, and then she sighed and held up her small strong brown hand. "I'll have to talk with your father," she said in a noncommittal voice. "Tonight. They will come early, he said."

"Do I have to miss the recital?" Nan asked with unexpected childishness, and then as she caught the astonishment on Miss Abel's face she seized hungrily upon the lucky moment, and put her gnawed fingers over her eyes, and seemed to melt with remorse or self-pity or unhappiness or something like that.

The heavy lame woman behind the desk knew about it: she had watched it before. She felt Nan peek at her, and sat impassively, hating all callous brutality in the whole world, and hers right now more than any other. She waited.

Nan put down her hands, her eyes satisfactorily wet, adeptly tortured.

Miss Abel wanted to leap forward and hold the girl against her, give her comfort, ease whatever lost ugly loneliness there was in her. Instead she found herself able to wish for the first time in her life that she was a Catholic, to be able to hold a little rosary in the hands clenched upon her lap. It was too late—for her to find such creature solace and for Nan to turn back and be a true...pure...lovely child...of good report.

They talked quite sensibly a little longer.

"I hate it here anyway. I always have," the girl finally said. "A bunch of Christy kids. Fat you on your canes."

That did not bother Miss Abel. She knew Nan had to say it, the way someone who has a tooth knocked loose must spit blood.

There were a few other things they talked about, forwarding laundry and all that, and when they went out Nan held the door politely for Miss Abel, and smiled dazzlingly at her, and said she would not talk much with the other girls about leaving. Her clothes would be easy to pack, she said. Truro would help her, Miss Abel said.

Nan went off toward the dorms.

Miss Abel hobbled out into the little patio. Goldfish lay coldly in the bottom of the fountain, waiting for a warmer sun. The air from the hills smelled like winter, sharp with unsettled dust and the promise of frost. It was a good season.

Had she made a clean cut, a right incision? Had she rid the body of the diseased member? Had her old skill been there? She leaned against the edge of the fountain, tired, waiting for the final antisepsis, the purging. It was as if she had pricked skin above a buried cactus thorn and must wait now until it emerged, sure while she waited of the natural self-cleansing of the worried flesh around it...yes, that it seemed like, rather than an amputation. They would all be better when the poor man came for his child. Until then—

She stood up straight. She must go through the classrooms, and quietly let the faculty know what she had decided, after all the telephoning.

Truro had been her voice, her hand. There was something on the girl's mind, aside from this foul business. She was probably pregnant. Miss Abel smiled, feeling vaguely cleansed, and went off toward the French room.

The whole school was in a fever of wreaths, boughs, carols; Nan's packing seemed to go unnoticed, although it would be impossible to know what veins of whispering underlay the skin of healthy babel.

Mrs. Gerwing bobbled about happily, with the strange strength of age. She ran the Little Girls through their carols twice, and then did several rehearsals, whenever a practice room was free, of "We Three Kings of Orient Are." By now she knew that Nan would not do the part of the Second Wise Man. Miss Abel had merely said "Family matters" and Mrs. Gerwing had nodded brightly. A tenth-grader who was almost as boylike as Nan stepped into it, breathless with delight.

"Gee. Me?" she asked.

Mrs. Gerwing looked gently at her, and said, "Now we must work, work, work, my dear. You must cooperate to the fullest. The show must go on, as they say. Nan has been called away. Now! 'Frankincense to offer have I.' Make it clear and sounding proud, my dear." She led the child delicately, subtly, into the first solo of her whole life, with soft, firm, artful chords.

Things were happening so fast. It seemed only last week that the new year had begun, with the strange girls peeking shyly about the old ones swaggering. But of course time does pass more swiftly for the old, Mrs. Gerwing reminded herself. *I am the oldest one here*, she thought, *and Nini is the youngest.*

In her heart, far past interruption from the wheezing treble of Melchior, the Second Wise Man, she listened to the little girl's lisp, now squeak, now croak, and she could have laughed aloud because of the love she felt.

"Oh, oh, oh, my dear," she chided, as if to herself, "shall we not try this again? 'Prayer and *prais*ing, all men *rais*ing—'"

She would not think of that poor Nan, and what Miss Abel had not told her but what she already knew, being on God's side; it was almost Christmas, and there were so many good things—

Mrs. Palmer, listening to one of the Old Girls limp and singsong through "*Maître Corbeau sur un arbre perché*," felt wearily that time could never go quickly enough, flow fast enough to wipe off the stains.

Nan's seat was empty, and her strange brilliant smile—

The teacher suddenly went sick and clammy, wondering where anyone had ever learned the words written into the coy inane verses of the
old French love song, on her desk yesterday. There was no one, not even
Nan with her precocious sense for true phrasing, Nan racing always a
little ahead of the other pupils...no one, no one, Mrs. Palmer insisted.

She felt a personal chagrin, to have come in so freshly, with such
naïveté, to that childishly printed obscenity upon her desk. One
comfort: only she and whoever wrote it could possibly know, in the
whole school, what it did to the old innocent words.

And how had she herself learned them? What gutter dregs could she pull
up from her early marriage in France, to spell such filth and recognize it?
Had she perhaps driven out in the night, away from the little girl in her care,
to write the doggerel in a state of dreaming, for her wakeful self to find?

She twisted in fear and pain. She was too alone, too sad in soul, to
cope properly with this thing.

The class was over. The Old Girls filed out, under the bough of odor-
ous green leaves. Every door in the school was thus bedecked; Mrs.
Palmer told herself desperately that it was a pretty custom. The Little
Girls filed in, under the bough of odorous green leaves.

"*Bon jour, petites,*" she said, and smiled at them.

They climbed into the big chairs. It was fun to be with them. Her girl
and Nini she could thee-and-thou; it made her feel good, and the other
children, less self-conscious in a foreign language than the Big Girls worrying over Racine and Victor Hugo, giggled delightedly when Nini and
Janet sparkled up at her, babbling nursery talk. They all laughed and
grew flushed, filled with a growing excitement for that coming night
and the carols. She forgot her lostness, and only once when Nini dar-
ingly croaked the first line of "*Le coeur de ma mie*" did her heart falter,
and then quickly right its rhythm.

What Miss Abel had murmured to her, as Jeannine piped through the
subjunctives of *etre, pouvoir, et savoir,* she could put with comparative
calm into another part of her mind. The girl Nan was going: that was
what mattered.

She had not had time to tell Miss Abel of the possible importance of Nini's and Janet's new hatred. She should have gone out for a minute with the headmistress, to talk in less than a whisper with her. But it was plainly imperative not to put the wind up.

She sat smiling, then before the watching nubile girls, now, but more easily before the little flower faces. There would be time...and Nan would be gone before the program.

"We'll sing what Mrs. Gerwing wants, and we'll sing it the way she wants it," she said in French to Nini. "Nini, tell them what I said."

"No, I will," Janet said.

"Janet, shut up, if thee'll be so kind," her mother said in a gay way that made all the little girls laugh.

"Mrs. Gerwing is the old witch," Nini said precisely in English. It was very funny, the way she said it with her gap-toothed lisp, and the children and Mrs. Palmer began to laugh, and their noise rose into the air so that Miss Abel, tap-tapping slowly along the arcades toward the dorm where by now Nan must be packing, hoped, strangely enough, that Truro could hear it too.

Mrs. Palmer is a nice girl... Truro is a nice girl... and the English teacher... and Mrs. Gerwing... and the wispy tubercular who flitters through chemistry.

Miss Abel grinned. She had hired him for two prime qualities: he wanted to be a medical missionary, and he was sexless, at least temporarily; both requisite virtues in dealing with the two upper grades, who were either preparing to return to the Christianized jungles of their parents' choice or, immediate alternative, fall madly in love right here in the California foothills, and never mind the orchids and the mildewing prayer books. Either way, the thin-shouldered young man was a good choice for the school. He seldom came to faculty meetings, and he was unalarmed by such vicarious seduction as his pupils could practice on him. *Ignorance is bliss*, Miss Abel thought with moderate cynicism.

Right now few of her staff were ignorant, though, and none was blissful. Mrs. Gerwing knew more than she would ever betray. Mrs. Palmer was in a neurasthenic tremble. Truro was young and strong...but perhaps she knew more than anyone? *This happens, these things happen,* Miss Abel said to herself with a kind of comfort, swinging along on her canes.

She had laid out the day like an actress in a New York penthouse, or rather more like a great man's trusted secretary. Suddenly feeling childish at her simile and awed by its implications, she asked God to forgive her and went on to her office.

Goldie came in to ask for a new bread man. This one gave them yesterday's, she said hotly. Miss Abel made a note of it.

"Boughten bread's no good anyhow," Goldie said.

"So you might as well have a nice bread man, eh?"

They cackled together; Goldie cleared her throat abruptly and went out, and Miss Abel readied herself for whatever was next: she felt the sides of her fine little nose to see if they were shiny, which they were not yet on the cool December day; she felt her small pearl earrings to see if they were straight and they were; she felt the close-cut hair on the back of her neck and she felt the top of her girdle; then with her good ankle she felt expertly along the bad one; and everything was as it should be. She was in line.

In fact, everything was so orderly, with the decorations on all the doorways and the rehearsal done with and the dreadful telephone calls behind her, that she sat for a timeless spell, her soul dozing and storing up strength, and when the luncheon bell clanged she started like a horse, and pulled herself up on her sticks with a drugged feeling. It soon passed.

Between lunch and supper that night, which was to be early so that all the girls, in their party clothes, could make themselves even more beautiful before the recital, Truro was almost engulfed by sleep.

She dozed off and on in her little bedroom placed cunningly in the center of the web of children's dorms, and she would hear whisperings through her dreams and start up, and pretend to be awake and scolding. The little girls were excited. They were tiptoeing and scuffling and giggling, getting out their best socks, their ruffled panties. Truro roared familiarly at them, and they would scoot for cover, and then creep out again as intuitively as mice before a dozing tabby.

She smiled, and gradually understood the reason for her relaxation: the girl Nan would be gone, and soon, and the trouble would be over with.

As it came to light later, the whole school, or almost the whole school, snoozed or slept deeply that afternoon, in spite of the bustle about the Christmas program.

Mr. Appert was perhaps the coziest: he knew there would be no riding, so he fed the livestock early and then, as he did oftener than not and with nobody the wiser, he lay down in sweet straw at the back of one of the Hoskins kids' horse trailers and went off like a baby, heart-free except for what had been happening lately and even that in a kind of muted way. It was a nice dozy December day, all right.

The Old Girls were here and there, talking quietly, tired from the odorous tasks of all the bough hanging. They washed their hair and made pin curls for one another, and drifted about arm in arm through the rapid twilight, with the two collies trailing now this group and now that. Jeannine went into the Senior Room with some of the girls and they made tea and sat speechless and at rest, with hillbilly music almost too faint to hear on the old record player.

The teachers went their own ways, except for old Mrs. Gerwing, who played softly in the Main Room for Mrs. Palmer, and Mrs. Palmer, who half lay on the love seat listening and feeling reassurance and peace, while Mrs. Gerwing made through her subtle fingers an act of forgiveness to the sweet younger woman, for her past opposition, and as she asked for the forgiveness thought simply of how kind her dear Mr. Gerwing was to her, how good.

There was no need for light in the long plain room, beautiful now with wreaths and the little Christmas tree.

Quiet noises came form the office, doors closing, but neither of the two enraptured women heeded.

Nan's parents were there with Miss Abel.

The doctor was a thin, rumpled man, exhausted in his eyes and in his bones. His wife was politely belligerent and mocking, with a hard smile. She tried to make Miss Abel feel, by the set of her furred shoulders, how little this third-rate school meant to her and to her famous husband and to her wronged child.

Miss Abel was used to such parents, although they never ceased to trouble her for what their children had become, were becoming. She felt that by the time such a mother sent her child away she had half murdered it, willy-nilly—and it was she, the childless woman, maimed, undesired, unfertile, who must try to breathe clean breath into the little bodies, the flickering souls.

She sat up, knowing her feet to be exquisite in the desk well. "There is nothing much any of us can say," she said, and she looked long at the father, who looked back at her as one who is familiar with pain.

"Well, I do feel it's extremely unfair to take the poor child out now," the woman cried fretfully. "Doctor and I are leaving for Mexico."

He did not bother to contradict or answer or agree or even hear, but kept his weary eyes on Miss Abel's sagging fine-nosed face.

"We've had such a difficult time with her," the mother went on. Miss Abel hoped she would not cry, but it did not much matter.

He said, at last, "I hope our coming so early has not inconvenienced you, Miss Abel. I will go down to the dormitory and get her. I'll drive the car down there . . . Mother, we should take care not to disturb the other children."

It had always sounded incongruous to Miss Abel, and even obscene, to hear husbands call their wives "mother," and tonight she felt an especial shock, to hear the worn, hurt doctor speak thus to such a bad one.

The woman looked with a kind of resentful timidity at him, and then stood up, pulling her coat about her. He helped her gently with it, as if she were an incurable patient leaving his consultation room.

"I have arranged to leave Nancy Margaret with a colleague of mine, in a very quiet place near the city," he said, and at that his wife did indeed start to cry, and in her silly muddled wailing Miss Abel heard the sound of the wild mother, baffled, lost . . . the barn cat robbed of her unlicked kitten.

He held open the door onto the patio. Marble, too close against it, stumbled to his feet with a sharp yip. The doctor stepped back punctiliously while the spaniel came in, and then he and the mother left.

Miss Abel called after them, as they started down the arcade, already lighted in the early gloom, "Can I have someone help you? The girls are all dressing, or out."

"Thank you," the doctor said. "We know the way. I shall stop in at your office when everything is in order."

Their footsteps sounded loud and irritable in the quiet.

Marble lay down with his sharp sigh in the desk well, and Miss Abel rubbed her good foot delicately behind his long silk ears. She could feel, she was sure, a kind of love come up into her body from that smaller, warmer one. She put her head on her hand, and then took the hand away form her face and looked curiously at it in the soft light from the patio. It was firm and alive, and like Marble it seemed full of love to her. She wondered why she was thinking such a remote thought... Those poor parents, that poor sick child. Soon now this would be behind all of them, one way or another.

Nan's—Nancy Margaret's father—stood in the doorway. "We can't seem to find her," he said in a good doctor's quiet voice, so that at once Miss Abel thought, *The fever is mounting, the amputation is not a success, the incision must be made deeper.*

She got up slowly, matching his calm. Her alarm, however, had communicated itself in one flash to Marble, who slid out from under her foot, made for the door, and opened it. Toenails clicked hurriedly along the arcade tiles, and the dog was gone.

The man shrugged with regret. "I frightened him," he said. "My daughter is not in her dormitory, and has not been for some time. But her mother and I have put her bags and paraphernalia into the car."

"Why don't you come in and sit down? Nan will be along," Miss Abel said, conscious of an almost sickening weariness in him. She felt that now she could talk straight toward him, not around the curves and corners of general politeness, and that it was time to, even if cruel to take him at this disadvantage. "Just sit down," she said.

He closed the door after him. "I'm tired," he said simply, and he sat down across from her and put his head back against the whitened adobe wall and she saw that for about three or five minutes he did what most good doctors do, and slept, as if he were on a prolonged labor case, he on a hard couch nearby the struggling woman with some time still to go. Then he was completely awake again, and in her dark room she could see his fine thin skull against the patio light.

"You know I am sorry about Nancy Margaret," she said.

"Of course," he said, fresh and dispassionate after his rest. "It is a difficult thing. I've failed her. I know about bones and even ulcerated tissues in the human body, but the human mind... this one is unwell, and

I am helpless about it by now. I was never with her when she was a baby. Maybe I could have seen what was going to happen."

"It might not have happened, if you had been with her then. It was more love she needed."

There were long pauses between all the things they said, but this one—

Finally the doctor shifted irritably in his chair. "That's the fashionable theory now, isn't it?" he asked in a dry way. "Well, I'm just a plain old-fashioned sawbones, an average man. These things are bound to happen now and then, and in the best of families." He stood up briskly, as if to reassure himself that he still could. "A little rest with a colleague of mine, a little guidance perhaps, and Nancy Margaret will be fine, a fine, normal, healthy girl," he said.

Miss Abel knew that whatever chance she might have had to speak straight, not in curves, was gone forever: chance to save the child, chance to save the father of the child. It was far too late for her . . . and had she herself ever shown any signs of being able to help?

She felt bitterly inadequate. She did not know enough, that was it. She tried to put together the jigsaw puzzles of unknown adolescents, not knowing what shapes they had already been cut into. How could she know? It was unfair. She began to shake a little, almost overwhelmed by the sense of futility in everything about the job she had set herself. She was in despair, in a kind of panic, for a flash.

She pulled herself up and reached blindly for her canes, as if she must move with violence and speed for a moment, or else be destroyed; and the motion did indeed wash away her panic and despair and she was all right again, although as spent as if in the past seconds she had survived a long fever.

The doctor held the door open for her, and they walked slowly down the arcade toward his car, not speaking. In its lights Nan and her mother moved busily, shoving bundles and suitcases around in the backseat.

"Here she is, the naughty girlikins," the woman called in a high gay voice. "Letting her poor mummy and daddy carry out everything! What happened to her manners here, I wonder? Off with some of her little friends, saying a fond farewell, no doubt!"

Miss Abel thought how pretty Nan looked, standing in the car light. She was maturing fast, and tonight her hair was soft about her face, and she wore a dress that became her still-gawky arms and knees. She

seemed at ease, unstrained, and turned to the headmistress with no evident mockery as she said, "Thank you for everything."

Miss Abel held out her hand, but Nan jumped lightly into the backseat and closed the door, and disappeared into the crammed darkness.
Her mother, too, avoided any perfunctory noise of farewell, but tried to
sound at ease by laughing mechanically from the front seat. The doctor's handclasp was dry and resentful, and he did not speak.

As the car turned before the driveway lights, Nan flashed a last brilliant, beautiful smile through the back window at the fat woman on her
canes, and they were gone.

Miss Abel looked down the road for a few minutes, not thinking
much about anything, and then turned back toward the low lighted
buildings of her school.

The Christmas tree bulbs around the front door, little red and green
and white ones in a thick rope of evergreen, were already on. Guests
would not be coming for another hour or more, but she was glad someone had been extravagant: it looked gay and welcoming.

And someone had turned on all the lights in her office, she noticed.
She walked faster, hoping she would find Truro and be able to tell her
that everything was done with, everything right again. But it was Mrs.
Palmer, standing against the wall inside the door as if she were flattening herself, trying to disappear.

"What is the matter with you?" Miss Abel asked in a low voice, and
when Mrs. Palmer started to answer, her face twisted out of control and
her throat pulse beat as if it would escape from her body, before she
managed to say, "We can't find Janet and Nini. Anywhere."

"Well?" Miss Abel stared blankly at her, probably because she was tired
from the muted scene of Nancy Margaret's departure, and then lulled
by her slow approach to the glowing windows of the school, through
the silent cold air of the hill country...partly because she knew there
was more to come, that all was not yet right. "Well, they're playing
somewhere. Or dressing for the program."

"No," Mrs. Palmer said flatly. She moved away from the wall a little,
more in control now. "No, we looked. Truro says they didn't come in
from play. They must still be in jeans."

"Where is Truro?"

"She is helping the Little Girls get ready. But, Miss Abel, she's terribly frightened."

"What for?" Miss Abel still felt deliberately blank... until the other woman asked, in the same flat way, "Where's Nan?"

Miss Abel laughed suddenly. "She's gone," she said, smiling.

Then she became completely alive, probably more so than ever in her life before, as she remembered how Nan had left her parents to load the car for her, and then had walked prettily into the car light to end their waiting.

"You be good about this," Miss Abel muttered fiercely at Mrs. Palmer, and she gripped the young woman's arm in command, no firm gentle pressure but a kind of goad into the flesh. "No foolish business, you hear? You're old enough now to help. Go get Truro. Have her get Jeannine or one of the Old Girls to finish the Little Girls. Get her here, and hurry up about it," she snarled. "Where's Mrs. Gerwing?"

"I don't know. Or maybe resting in the Main Room. She was playing for me."

"I'll get her. You hurry up now."

Miss Abel pushed at the woman, and felt a deep pride for her as her steps went firmly and without any signal of alarm down the arcade toward the dorms. *She'll be all right*, Miss Abel thought.

She went as fast as she could, but with extra caution, as if she must let no stumble slow her now, across the long waxed floor of the Main Room.

A lighted lamp glowed softly down upon the old lady on the couch. For a minute Miss Abel felt a shock of protest, almost of anger: she must not be dead, must not have died in her sleep tonight, this night. She was needed. She slept with the almost vanished breathing of a peaceful aged person, and the bony arm laid across her chest hardly moved up and down, until Miss Abel calmed herself and grew used to the light. She looked down for a few long seconds at the fine remote face on the couch, and thought, *What a beautiful skull she will be*, and then she said softly, "Mrs. Gerwing. Mrs. Gerwing. I need you."

Without any change in the shallow breathing the old lady opened her eyes and lay looking up, not dazzled by the light as a child would be, not alarmed by the call to her, as a child would be. It was as if she had been awake all the time, playing a little game, princess in a magic slumber.

When she started to sit up, though, she wove a bit, as if she were dizzy, and Miss Abel shifted her cane with the skill of a lifetime of such juggling, and put one hand under the thin elbow.

They walked carefully, wordlessly, back into her office. Mrs. Gerwing sat down in Miss Abel's chair.

As Miss Abel said, "Nini and little Janet are gone," it sounded foolish, hysterical, a fuss about nothing, until she saw the look of terrible alarm fill Mrs. Gerwing's eyes and spill down over her face and her body. Then she knew, finally and as it were for the first time except in her mind, that something had happened somewhere.

"Where is Nan?" Mrs. Gerwing asked, as if it were the only possible question, and when Miss Abel said, "She's gone already—she left early," the old lady stood up stiffly and cried out, "How early? When?" She pressed her knobby hands together as if she would crack them off like dry twigs, and went on, not looking anywhere but inside herself, "Those children. She has hurt them. I should have stopped her. Now she's got them. It would be the best way to prove how much she could hurt us, wouldn't it? It would be the biggest thrill for her now, wouldn't it, to be away and knowing of us here in your office, wouldn't it? Nini, Nini."

"I need you." Miss Abel interrupted her with urgent compassion. "Mrs. Gerwing, people will be coming soon. The girls are coming in right now, for sandwiches before the program. Play their favorite songs, Mrs. Gerwing. Let them sing at the tables. They love that. Do anything like that."

She did not dare look again at the frail, small old body, but she knew it stiffened and once more she felt pride in human beings as she heard the short steps head for the dining room.

"I must get Mr. Appert," she said aloud, and she herself limped firmly across the patio.

It was good that the yard lights were already on, waiting for the early cars to be parked back there. They must all hurry, though, against what she did not know, to find what she did not dare contemplate.

Truro ran toward her from the Little Girls' dorm.

"Honey, find Mr. Appert for me. You look in the haymows and around the rabbit hutches," she called out firmly. "Probably just some new game," and she grumbled dramatically, unable to look directly at the solid girl she loved so much. It was urgent that she not slow her steady pace for anything, any sign of emotion from either of them. "Hurry up. Go on," she called over her shoulder.

She heard Truro run down toward the old millhouse where they kept broken tools, saddles to mend, rusted skates. "Mr. Appert. Hey, Mr. Appert," she was calling softly. Good Truro.

Miss Abel did not want things to last like this much longer, no matter what the outcome. From the kitchens she heard Goldie slamming around in the habitual excitement of getting another meal onto the tables and then off again. Shadows ran back and forth on the far lighted squares of dining room windows, Old Girls carrying platters of sandwiches—peanut butter, processed cheese, boiled ham, Miss Abel thought with a kind of comfort for herself that she could go on naming such too-familiar details. Goldie's paid helpers toted the hot cocoa, and the teachers poured it, and the sound of Mrs. Gerwing's resolute gay thumping on the dining room upright rose, muffled but insistent, above the general hungry hum of girls and plates and footsteps.

It was as if a kind of cone of safety, lighted and impenetrable, covered the school and rose to a point far above it, and outside the cone Miss Abel felt like a bug of some gigantic species, flapping clumsily around the bright empty yard, with Truro beyond her range down by the millhouse and Mr. Appert anywhere or nowhere. She wanted to call out, to know herself as herself, not as a black-and-white beetle, soundless, speechless, lost.

A door slammed, and in a kind of stupor she watched the last late Little Girl dash for the back steps of the dining room, her party dress clutched up high over her flashing knees.

Then Mrs. Palmer came out of the dorm, and walked straight toward Miss Abel. She looked all right, except that her hands were held stiffly in the pockets of her long coat, so that she moved more like a puppet than a live woman.

"Where shall we start?" she asked. "We must start right away."

"Classrooms."

They hurried across the yard toward the low buildings. Miss Abel sorted her key ring more by touch than by the dim light of the arcades as they went, and when they reached the chemistry room the door opened at her first try and they went in, calling softly for Nini and Janet. There was enough light from the windows for them to see that unless they started an even grimmer search through cupboards and the darkest, smallest places there were no little girls hiding or hidden.

They went through all the rooms that way, and when they had finished they were panting, and Miss Abel's hands shook upon her cane heads from the effort of the fast walking, and their throats ached from the low steady calling.

They went toward the yard again, and the bright December stars paled above them as they got into the brighter light. Two cars were already parked there, but fortunately empty of people. Miss Abel groaned to see them. The girls still sat at their tables, though, and the jolly thump of the piano came through the many curtains of the dining room. "Ring-dum-bully-damy-coy-meeeee," the seniors howled happily through their favorite song.

"We'll go to the stables," she said without pausing.

Halfway there she stopped, and this time it was Mrs. Palmer who gentled the older woman. She put her arm over the heavy shoulders and could feel the whole body shaking as if it would never stop, not so much from the labored heart as from a kind of continuous quaking of the marrow within the fine and in part useless bones. "My child, my child," Mrs. Palmer said without thought, and would not have been able to know if she spoke of Janet, of Nini, or of this woman beside her. One thing was sure: it was not of herself, perhaps for the first time.

As they stood there in their strange communion of fear and strength, Truro ran out from the darkness.

Miss Abel muttered, "She mustn't come with us," and then called out in her good clear voice, "Honey, look over around the horse trailers."

She pulled herself away from Mrs. Palmer's arm and started off again.

As she went she thought in a kind of groove, or rhythm, like the bug hitting again and again on a cone of impenetrable light or on a lamp chimney, about the need for vengeance in the sick of heart, and of the likeliest victims.

Nini the lovable was the logical one here, and Janet next because Nini loved her best. It would not be to hurt Nini, of course, but those who loved her. Which were the more innocent victims, the ones doomed because they loved, the one doomed because she was loved, or the one chosen because of all of them?

Nini was quiet and dogged like the turtle, now crushed. She was gentle and proud like the broken-necked dove, the pigeon with its dimming feathers. She was the wide-eyed kitten, wanting to be teased. She was, that is, the victim, the one to be sacrificed. And Janet was a part of her, the chosen comrade. They were doomed by love...doomed by the unloved.

At the dark cave of the stable door, left open until the January freeze might come, Miss Abel said, with no doubt of obedience to her command, "Stay here," and she went in like a blind person who knows every leaf in a row of trees or every pebble on a path.

Mrs. Palmer watched the flicker of the white blouse vanish, and did not even know where she was, nor care. Her eyes looked into the dark, past all the quiet horses, through to the other open end of the stable, and out onto the hills, and to the sky, and what she felt was a kind of readying herself for whatever was to come next. It was like having a child, in a way: no need now to protest, for everything was done, and the eyes would be made for brown or blue or gray, and irrevocably the nose would be shaped for this or that, in a very few minutes now. The pain itself would last longer, what with the afterbirth and then those muscular contractions, what with the healing of a wound after an accident, what with the spasms of grief diminishing and strengthening and fading and swelling after death, the death—She stood passively staring into the dark, helpless to resist what must happen to her.

From the stable came Miss Abel's cry, and the sound of her thick body thumping and stumbling up the high steps of her mounting block, and as Mrs. Palmer ran toward the noise her widened pupils saw in the gray black a small body turning now this way, now that, on a tight rope thrown over the beam above the block.

Miss Abel pulled herself to the top step and stood straight and reached up.

"Thank God thank God thank God," she cried harshly. "Marble, it's my Marble. They are all right. There wasn't time."

She was sobbing, without thought to hide either her grief or her wild relief that the small broken-necked creature swinging above her was her friend.

"They're all right," she said over and over. "You understand? There wasn't time, girl. She had to use what she could find. You understand?"

Mrs. Palmer felt spent. She could not even cry one tear. Her mouth hurt and she licked at it, not able to peer again at the hanging spaniel, clear enough now with his loppy head and the tongue out between his grinning lips. Her eyes seemed like hot lenses with lights behind them: she would see too much too clearly for the rest of her life, she thought.

"I can't get him down, I can't get him down," Miss Abel was saying, still sobbing as if she would vomit. "We must close the doors. Help me."

She slid unashamedly down her special little steps, and they found her canes and hurried toward the big doors and swung them to, first at the end leading out into the fields, and then at the yard end. In the yard several more cars were parked, and lights were snapped off and guests laughed and walked quickly through the nip in the air toward the gay lights around the entrance. The dining room windows were dark.

Truro walked out from the shadowy lot behind the haymows. "Miss Abel," she called as she came to them, "I'm just so mad. Look here."

Neither Miss Abel nor Mrs. Palmer even breathed more deeply as Nini and Janet came hand in hand toward them, laggingly, in blue jeans and with hay thick in their hair. Mr. Appert slouched behind them, like a dour clown.

"The time they gave us," Truro fretted angrily. "All the time there in one of the Hoskins' trailers. Dozing, snoozing, that's what. No consideration for us, with people coming right this minute for the recital. People coming, us looking high and low. Look at Miss Abel, you two, all dressed up and has to come clear out here looking for you."

Truro sounded ready for tears, for she felt that she had failed at an important moment in her school life, as teacher-not-pupil, with Nini and Janet not nicely into the party dresses and full of hot cocoa and "God Rest You Merry Gentlemen" by now.

"All right, honey," Miss Abel said, her voice still thick but very sure. "What's the idea, Mr. Appert?"

The old man stood there mazedly on the edge of the bright yard. "Went to sleep all right," he said sourly. "It was a sleepy day. You know good and well I don't smoke, Miss Abel, and I like dose trailers for a snooze, if I put plenty straw in'm. Woke up and here dese two kids were, so I just lay quiet and let'm sleep too."

"Well"—Nini spoke up with a self-righteous lisp—"we discovered Mr. Appert sound asleep, and we certainly did not care to disturb him."

"Mother, we just felt tired," Janet said. "Gee, were we safe in there!"

"Safe from what?" Miss Abel asked, not wanting to while Truro and all of them stood listening but feeling that she must get it settled while she could.

"Well," Nini went on stubbornly, holding Janet's hand, "Nan told me to meet her in the stables for something and she told Janet not to come, and Janet is my friend and not Nan. Nan is too big for us. And we were so mad at her we fooled her. We hate her."

"Oh," Miss Abel said.

"Hah," Mr. Appert said.

"Just because she is a big girl"—Nini labored the point—"she certainly does not need to be rude to my friend."

Mrs. Palmer felt for a quickly passing flash that she was gong to be sick, so violent was her almost cosmic amusement at the rightness of pure human instinct.

"We simply fooled her and went into Betsy Hoskins' trailer," Janet said, and then dropped her head in her oblique way, as if she had made a social blunder.

"For Pete's sake," Truro said angrily. "So you go to sleep, just when everybody's getting ready for the party. Miss Abel, I'm simply terribly sorry." She sighed with exaggerated disgust. "Come on, kids. You've got to get into your dresses. You're filthy."

She grabbed their hands and ran across the yard and ducked between two cars, and they were gone. The door of the Little Girls' dorm slammed.

More cars turned into the main driveway, and their lights glared toward the two women and the old man standing wordless, down toward the stables.

"Mrs. Palmer," Miss Abel said abruptly, "will you go and find Mrs. Gerwing right away and tell her everything is fine? She might like to lie down for a few minutes in my room before the recital. I'll be right there. Mr. Appert—"

Mrs. Palmer turned away, as she saw Miss Abel put her hand on Mr. Appert's dirty shirtsleeve. The two of them went back into the darkness, and there was such steadiness and faith in the gesture, and such a feeling of affection, that she walked toward the low lighted buildings like a newborn but full grown person, lithe and easy, and could almost have laughed to know that she would nevermore wrap her fingers one around another in the tight fear-filled darkness of whatever pocket came to hand. She would never again be as afraid as she had been that evening. Such comfort did not seem dubious or equivocal to her, but a kind of miracle instead. She had passed the point, and won.

She hurried to the dorm, and brushed Nini's hair while Truro, still pretending to be cross, did Janet's. There was not even time for more than a quick kiss before the girls ran sheepishly away. Their nails were still dirty. They smelled like sleepy colts, from the straw and the close if largely unconscious company of Mr. Appert.

Truro started to peel off her riding pants as she and Mrs. Palmer hurried toward her room in the center of the building. "No time for a shower," she murmured. "I hope I still fit my long skirt."

Mrs. Palmer put on lipstick and saw with a kind of fulfillment, as if it were the only right thing to see at the moment, that the girl was indeed with child. She wanted to embrace her, but it would be a bad idea, for the contact of the two might unloose physical reactions which would slow them past help, and do no good. Instead, as if by unspoken agreement, they ran like sisters or like Nini and Janet hand in hand up the walk toward the back door, and then sedately into the hall toward the Main Room.

The parents and friends were already seated on wavering rows of rickety folding chairs, facing the big piano and the reproductions of *The Last Supper* and *Faith-Hope-and-Charity*.

Fir boughs and dropping eucalyptus leaves and the brave little tree could not disguise the thickening of the air, and the chemistry teacher slipped about opening windows, especially far from the whitest-haired in the audience.

A giddy buzz came from the kitchen and the pantries, where every girl in the school except one with bad lunar cramps and one with an undiagnosed spot on her lip which might be impetigo stood restlessly awaiting Miss Abel's signal.

Mrs. Gerwing walked in drunkenly from the headmistress' bedroom behind the piano, and unblinking in the sudden light she smiled and slid onto the bench under the yellowing keys. She knew without looking that somewhere at the far end of the room dear Mr. Gerwing stood, deaf to her music but faithful, in his best suit. Her knobby fingers pressed down in one loud fine chord, and then she whipped into her own version, "for one piano," of "God of Our Fathers."

Mrs. Palmer thought with a very faint feeling of hysteria that it was like hearing the overture to Tannhäuser played in a small French café by two fiddles and an accordion. It sounded good. She glanced at Truro, still puffing a little from their hurry. The girl was full of trust, safe in the steadiness of familiar walls and sounds.

The thin firm melody increased, and Miss Abel and what seemed like a thousand overgrown girls crowded with practiced if confused order into the space behind Mrs. Gerwing's piano, fitting themselves like experienced sardines into their tin.

Mrs. Gerwing looked brightly over her shoulder. Miss Abel gave a little wave of her cane, and the music, which might as well have swelled from thirty violins, with the whole orchestral weight behind them, dwindled artfully to silence.

Miss Abel stepped forward slowly, and the neighboring retired professor, and the half-drunk rancher whose stallions serviced the Arabians at the school, and the relatives who had come far from the coastal cities for this night with their young folk, leaned forward at the sound of her deep, warm, breast-borne voice.

It rose as if it were ancient worked gold from the cleft in her bosom, a priceless coin upon a chain. All ears heard it, before her the waiting strangers' "and the familiars'," behind her the children's and the ears of the pitch-perfect old lady. There was no thickness of grief in it, nor any shadow of horror, and her small deep eyes were as clear as it, and as warm, as they looked slowly about the crowded room.

The whisper of the girls' silk party dresses ceased, and not a chair creaked as she said, "Good friends, good neighbors...we are happy to welcome you here once more, to share with us the songs we have learned for you for the glad Christmas season. As is our custom, the youngest of us will tell us once more, in the words of Saint Luke, of that night when Mary 'brought forth her firstborn son, and wrapped him in swaddling clothes—'"

As Miss Abel went on to the end of the verse, Nini left the girls and stood beside her, and put her grubby hand, warm and moist from Janet's, in her leader's. She settled her small square body firmly into place, looked resolutely over the heads of the faceless crowd before her, with no mother, no father for her, and took up the story without a pause or tremor.

"'And there were in the same country shepherds—'" She lisped it slowly, but with a kind of enjoyment, as if what she was telling must thrill them all as it did her, and when she came to the end of it—"'and on earth peace, good will toward men'"—she broke into a smile of such complete happiness that it was as if, in that room, the Holy Spirit had indeed touched each heart and left it cleansed, for a time purified.

Then Nini stepped back into the ranks of beruffled children, and three bigger ones came forward, Gaspar in green taffeta, and Melchior and Balthasar in white with colored ribbons. Mrs. Gerwing plunged with an almost rollicking briskness into the opening bars of the first carol.

"*We* three *kings* of *Orient are,*" the girls piped windily to the emphatic bob of her white head, and Miss Abel and then everybody there came in with a gay bellow on the long "*Ohhhh...star* of *wonder, star* of *night...*"

It was going to be a fine Christmas party...fine, really fine, Miss Abel believed.

[*Ladies' Home Journal*, 1952]

WHAT HAPPENED TO MISS BROWNING

I.

WHAT HAPPENED TO Miss Amy Browning one Saturday in 1935 and thereafter has probably not been told, until now. For a time after her vanishing, when the new term at Miss Crittenden's school had just opened the "old girls" would talk with the "new girls" about it, wearing the correct air of being somewhat scabrously titillating. Occasionally one of poor Miss Browning's colleagues thought of it, and flushed faintly behind the practical horn-rimmed glasses which she wore when her bedroom door was locked and she could slouch freely over her piles of midsemester examinations.

What of the teacher Amy Browning? Where did she go? What *could* have happened? The teacher left behind, the one who had never thought to forget duty and decency, sighed, and then looked smug in quick self-comfort. Poor Amy....

It came about very suddenly. One afternoon, Miss Browning was taking her group of girls out for their weekly treat, just as she had done every even-Saturday for the last twenty-two years, in this or that respectable finishing school; and the next thing anybody knew, she was gone, with only her sensible thick suede-cloth gloves lying on the street, to show where she had last stood.

She waited under the clock in the main hall, at five minutes to two, and wondered as she pulled on her brown winter gloves whether she would wish that she had got out the thinner, lighter ones. How many girls would she have today? She looked at her typewritten list: eight as usual, but perhaps luck would be with her and put one or two into the infirmary with cramps or indigestion or something equally harmless. It really did not matter: after chaperoning so many hundreds of girls about the shops and streets of boarding school towns, she felt able to handle fifty or sixty at a time, if necessary. She had developed a pleasant inexorable manner which may not have roused in some young females the adoration her colleagues battened on, but at least guaranteed politeness and at most a certain amount of wary friendliness. This afternoon would be neither more nor less boring than all the others.

In fact, as she saw the bushes against the hall windows shake in a gust of wind, she decided that it would be pleasant to walk down the curving street of the little town, and smell the sea. Refreshed, she might do her Monday papers a night early, and sleep well. Tomorrow then she could sew, or even read, between Chapels....

The girls came down, laughing and tapping with their street shoes against the stone steps. They quieted when they saw her, and she smiled at them, suddenly pitying their happiness at escaping from the place, escaping in neat blue uniforms like well-bred wealthy convicts, for such a short three hours. At least she could wear what she liked... or *almost* what she liked. She smoothed her brown tweed jacket over her stomach, and felt already that her hands were too hot in winter gloves.

"Oh, Miss Browning, isn't it a marvelous day?" Little Rosemary looked up at her enthusiastically. "We're so glad we got to go with *you* this time!"

Amy Browning smiled again at her, impersonally. The child was a sneak at exams, and this minute was hoping to flatter her into ignoring the forbidden lipstick that discreetly colored her soft pretty mouth.

"Thank you. I'm glad too. Yes, spring is here, I think. And now, my dears, if five are all of you, I think we'd best be on our way."

They flocked through the big door and the gate in the high white stucco wall that enclosed the grounds, the girls standing back with conditioned docility to let their chaperone lead the way.

Outside, the wind whipped and plucked at them, and sure enough they could smell the salt and the kelp. It was a cruel smell, almost like sweat. Miss Browning nodded to herself: that was a good simile. What would the girls think to hear her use a word like "sweat"? Cruel like sweat... unkind like perspiration... She smiled contentedly, and quickened all their paces as she strode energetically along toward the little town in her flat brown oxfords.

Someone spoke softly at her side.

"What?" Miss Browning asked. *Don't mumble, child,* her mind added.

"I just said, 'Lhude sing cuccu.' This lovely, *lovely* day . . ."

It was Catherine, poor dreamy yearning girl. Miss Browning felt resigned to a month or two, now, of avoiding any encouragement of her. Every spring there was at least one crush rampant in her routine, no matter how cool and impersonal she kept herself, and uncomfortably it seemed the lot of the English teacher to draw the poetical ones. This child was a nice one, with a surprising sense for the sonnet form. It would not do to hurt her.

"Oh, it's Catherine," she said heartily. "I thought Rosemary was with me."

The tall girl looked uneasily at her, and stumbled a little as she galloped almost sideways along the path. She blushed painfully.

"Rosemary was," she said. Her voice was conspiratorial, or mumbling, as you wish. "I asked her . . . that is, she'd do anything for me and . . . and I simply had to talk with you, Miss Browning. I wanted to ask you about Chaucer. And it's such a *lovely* day."

Catherine grinned suddenly, like a child, and sniffed at the wind. She looked so young, and so happy, and so clean, that Amy could not stand to be sensible with her, but instead tucked her own brown-gloved hand impulsively into the girl's bony arm.

"Isn't it? You're right, Catherine. 'Sumer is ycomen in.' Smell the sea! We'll talk about Chaucer some other day!"

They all went on toward the town, gaily. Catherine's pale face blazed with happiness as she peered down nearsightedly at her dearest teacher, and behind them the other girls giggled and chattered and slapped their shoes hungrily against the pavement, feeling free and young, although they did not know it.

Amy almost forgot, for a few minutes, that she was forty-seven and definitely thick about the hips, and that it was time to make another payment on the small annuity that she had been building ever since, sixteen years before, her mother's death had left her almost all of her salary to do with as she thought best.

It seemed to her that she had never seen such a fine exciting day, with the palm fronds whipping in the restless air, and an occasional sight of the gray tossing water far beyond the roofs reminding her from what deeps blew the salt she tasted.

She felt like pulling off her brown felt hat. Merciful heavens, she thought, mocking herself: what would the tattletales tell? But I will take off these stuffy gloves, or one of them at least. I shall simply forget to put it on again.

She stretched her fingers, and on feeling the air blow over her moist skin, she looked down at her hand as if it did not belong to her, and was unobtrusively amazed. It was white and fine, and well kept like the rest of her short sturdy body. The nails were almond shaped, and glimmered healthily from dutiful buffing with her mother's own buffer. She was proud of her nails. Sometimes in class she looked at them with detached contentment while her pupils droned on about Herrick and Thomas Hardy. When she felt that she could not stand to look into one more unformed pallid bewildered adolescent face, she rubbed her thumbs gently over the other nails on each hand, and felt their smooth crisp ovals with real comfort.

Yes, today was a pleasant day. The girls were manageable, and the air was fresh. She smiled again, and listened to Catherine without hearing her.

A little later, though, she forgot that first feeling of pleasure. She might have known that it would not last, that the day would simply be another even-Saturday in an endless chain of even-Saturdays.

"Well, girls," she said a little sharply a they huddled in front of the last of the town's four "antique" shops, which had been thoroughly invaded that afternoon, "don't any of you feel like crumpets for tea?"

"Oh, Miss Browning!" Catherine beamed adoringly at her. "I simply love to hear you say that! It sounds so English . . . like apothecary! Or lorry!"

Amy smiled perfunctorily. Why need the child remind her of England? The white cliffs, the rolling hedge-lined lanes of Devon, seemed more remote than ever as she stood in the stinging wind of this Pacific village. Would she ever see England? Would she ever finish paying for her annuity, so that at long last she could travel to the land of her dearest dreams, and stand where Shakespeare had once stood, and walk over the high hills of the lake country with the ghosts of Wordsworth and of Shelley? Would she end her life without that, teaching girls not to split infinitives and wearing the same brown tweed suit, gradually altered to fit her own gradual widening?

"I should have said baking powder biscuits, my dear. I abominate Americans who try to Anglicize their speech."

Amy was suddenly so bored that she hardly regretted the hurt look that flickered over Catherine's sensitive plain face. Her life seemed unendurable. The only thing that kept her from running over the cliff or in front of a car or headfirst against the wall was the bitter knowledge that she had felt this way before and lived. She would feel so again. At her age, she realized, such petty agonies were to be expected, and increasingly. Ah, to be a woman, now that fifty's here, she said meanly to herself.

Afterwards Amy Browning probably never thought of the tearoom again, but the five girls, recalling the last time they saw her, depicted for their listeners with tears or muted whisperings every line of the place, every buttered crumpet, every cup of horrendous cloth-bagged bitter drink.

The brew was hot and strong, and Amy absorbed it like a blotter. She wondered if ever in her long years she had felt as thirsty, not for water but for a comfort which was not here, and which she knew desperately that she must find or perish. Why did she permit herself to suffer, knowing there was no help for her? She was one of the best English teachers in private schools on the Coast. She could stay at Miss Crittenden's as long as she damned pleased. Next year she might even ask for a raise. The girls liked her; they did not love her, except for one or two a year like Catherine, and that was to be expected. But they liked her. Or anyway they did not hate her. And in another fourteen years, or was it twenty-three, she would have paid for her annuity. Then she would be free.

Free?

Miss Browning gulped at her tea. She ran her thumbs over her fingernails.

"Will you excuse me, please?" She pushed her chair back rudely, and stood up. The girls stared at her. Catherine started to rise, her face perturbed.

"No! No, I'm all right. I just remembered something." And Amy walked solidly, calmly, out into the street, on her sensible composition-rubber soles.

II.

The wind was stronger. Already a few of the small shops along the steep twisting little street had lighted their display windows. Amy looked about her with bewilderment. Had she ever been here before? Was there actually one street in the little town that she had never walked along? The curtained misty window of a little tearoom, with some girls outlined through the lighted cloth... had she seen it before, in all the years of even-Saturdays?

She hurried toward the sea. The lights were thinner, and the shopwindows hung so precariously to the steep hill that they were triangular, like pieces of a bright pie laid sideways.

A gust of wind yanked off her hat, and she stood for a minute watching it roll fast in front of her, and then disappear with an almost jaunty flip of its brown felt brim around a dark corner toward the sea. She ran her fingers through her hair, and the cold evening air felt like balm upon her temples. Casually she pulled her gloves from her coat pocket and dropped them onto the pavement, and walked on down the hill to the last lighted window.

It was some sort of curio-shop. The town was peppered with them, all with the same hideous stocks of postcards and cheap carved ivory ginger-picks and shells polished and made into souvenir pin trays. Amy stood looking into the window, but what she saw was not this bait for tourists, but herself.

There she was, reflected on the clean glass like a faked photograph of ectoplasm or a woman made of smoke. She observed herself in whole and in part, for the first time since she was seventeen and had stood naked before the glass in her mother's room, wondering if college would bring her love, not knowing that most girls who worked their way through coeducational universities in those days had little time for wooing, even when they were slim and lovely. Now she was changed. Underneath the plain brown suit and the white blouse, and the fine linen underwear she still made for herself as she had done thirty years before, she could see her body in the window. It was heavy, solid, a firm, smooth mass as clean and creamy as an old elephant tusk. And in her brown oxfords she could feel all her toes, straight and uncalloused, fastidiously tended like her beautiful fingernails.

Her face was changed too. She looked seriously at it, floating there against the darkness behind the shopwindow, reflected like a mermaid's. Her eyes were deeper in her head, and her mouth had stretched and grown thinner, in the last thirty years. She had pulled her brown hair tightly into a knot on the back of her neck, so that her hat would go on easily, and she looked like a peasant woman, with her fine wide forehead and round cheeks.

She would have made a good mother, Amy thought dispassionately of the woman in the glass. And there was something beautiful about her, perhaps even better than youth and slenderness. But no man had ever kissed her.

There was a sudden movement behind the display in the shopwindow, and then the little door crashed open, and two elderly women stepped angrily onto the steep sloping pavement. A small Japanese followed them as far as the door, and stood bowing at their stiff backs.

"Am sorry," he shouted politely above a gust of wind. "Am very sorry. But cannot afford to buy back used articles."

The women turned away, their lined faces haughty under their traveling hats of practical navy blue. Tourists, Amy thought. Retired schoolteachers, like me in a few years. She watched avidly, as if she were invisible, and indeed the two other women seemed unconscious of her, as one of them leaned suddenly against the glass of the shining window and began to sob.

Amy was horrified. She stepped closer.

"Oh dear. Oh dear," she heard the woman say. "I did so hope . . . I was a fool to buy that abalone inkwell . . . I was a fool. . . ."

The other woman patted at her awkwardly, and said in a brusk voice, "Buck up, old dear! What's fifty cents?"

"*What's fifty cents?*" And at that the poor soul leaning against the window almost howled. "Oh, I'm so tired," she cried. "I do so want some tea!"

"Well," her companion said slowly, "well . . . not tonight. But tomorrow we'll cash another check. So come along, old dear. Come along." And she pulled at the arm of the weeping woman, who followed up the steep street, blowing genteely at her pink nose.

Amy looked at the little Japanese, but he did not seem to see her. He stood watching his visitors, then quickly ran after them.

"Ladies! Ladies, please wait," she heard him call. "Ladies, have decided can use the inkwell again. Please accept the fifty cents." And he bowed and smiled and bowed again, and then hurried back, panting, to his little doorway with their package, and went into the shop. The door closed.

The two women stood uncertainly for a moment. Then the bigger one dropped the coin in her pocket and laughed heartily, like a relieved man, and put her arm over the other one's thin shoulders, and Amy saw the two of them hurry up the hill toward the far glow of the tearoom.

The shop door crashed open again, and the Japanese ran past Amy with his coat flapping behind him.

"Ladies! Ladies! Please! Ginger for your tea!" And he thrust a little green jar into their hands, and bowed and came running back again, panting harder. The door banged shut behind him.

Amy heard them above the wind, laughing. Then they hurried on up the hill. They opened the door of the tearoom, the light shining on their plain practical blue serge suits, and on their ridiculously pleased faces, and on the gleaming rich color of the little ginger jar.

She looked into the little shopwindow piled with ugly junk, and then above it at the sign *Souvenirs . . . A. Ito . . . Oriental Goods.* She pushed open the door.

The man stood at the back of the shop, smoking a cigarette. He looked quietly at her, and she was surprised to notice that his eyes, although pointed and high at the corners, were very wide. He bowed.

"Mr. Ito," Amy cried.

Then she lowered her voice politely, and continued in the calmest way she had ever spoken in her life, "Mr. Ito, you must hide me. I have run away." And she fell headlong on the floor, in a dead faint.

III.

The first thing Amy Browning thought, when she was conscious again, was that it was a pity she had never fainted before. It was probably the most delightful sensation she had ever experienced. Her head felt light and easy, and full of half-heard music, and her body lay along the floor the way flesh lies on its bone, or hair on its skull, hungrily, lovingly.

She opened her eyes.

Curtains, made of white cotton with little scarlet fans printed hit-or-miss, were pulled over the shopwindow and the window of the front door. Light shone mildly from behind a paper umbrella inverted to make a shade against the low ceiling, and Mr. Ito stood under it. His cigarette was almost finished. His strange wide eyes looked impersonally down at her.

Amy struggled to sit up, but the Japanese pushed her back gently against the floor, hissing as he did so like a solicitous woman.

"Please!" he said. "You lie quietly there, please. Now you feel better, I shall leave you for a few minutes."

Amy sighed gratefully, and went into a little doze, like a tired animal. She dreamed that she was dancing, light as a cobweb, through enormous silent rooms where the curtains at the tall windows waved and billowed to the sound of music from far behind them. On and on she danced, not bothering even to touch the floor with her tiny twinkling feet, not bothering to breathe.

"Here is some tea for you, please," Mr. Ito said softly, bowing.

She opened her eyes again, and looked up clearly at him as he stood holding a little red enamel tray by its sides with his small hands. He had good nails, rather like hers, smooth and beautifully shaped.

Amy smiled. "I must look very queer, lying here in the middle of your floor," she said composedly.

"Not at all. I have closed the window curtains, in case someone peers in without understanding, and as for myself, much prefer floor to Western chairs. Please continue to be comfortable."

He put the tray down beside her, bowed again, and then sat down slowly himself, with his legs folded with neat intricacy beneath him. His suit of cheap striped serge wrinkled and bunched awkwardly on his rather plump body, but he was too dignified to seem ridiculous.

Amy saw that he had a black moustache, large and strong, almost like a French policeman's, but that his short hair was quite gray. His nose was fine and birdlike, and his eyes still surprised her with their width, in spite of the full upper lids that reminded her of a little plaster doll from Japan which someone had sent her when she was a child.

He handed her a small tea bowl, full of hot pale liquid, and when she leaned clumsily on one elbow to drink, he asked quickly, "May I help you?"

"Oh, no, Mr. Ito. Thank you. I feel very well now. I hope you will excuse me for troubling you. That is, I . . ."

He bowed his head, and frowned slightly. "Please do not tire yourself with explanations. Does this tea please you?"

Amy nodded, and drank slowly. It did not seem necessary to talk. When she had finished, Mr. Ito took the tray away, bowing as he disappeared into the rear of the shop. Amy lay back on the floor. Her mind was empty and peaceful.

"Excuse me," Mr. Ito said, appearing above her once more like a ghost or a dream. He looked down benevolently, and he did not smile. "Now you must come to bed. Give me your hands."

Amy put her own hands into his, and he pulled her easily to her feet, and then still holding to her he led her through the back door of the shop and down a narrow dim passage.

"This is the toilet," he said, pointing to a little door. "This is the kitchen, where you must wash yourself. There is plenty of hot water always. And upstairs," he continued as he pulled her gently up the rickety steps, "it is dark, but you will be comfortable, I think."

There was a candle burning steadily at the top. It cast its small light warmly on the low roof of a kind of wareroom, where cases made of wicker and square bales covered with satiny split bamboo lay everywhere, sending up a firm dry heady smell.

Mr. Ito led Amy, surefooted as a sleepwalker, through this disarray, and there in the corner of the attic, behind a paper screen, showed her some grass mats, on which he had laid two blue quilts, padded and thick.

"They are Chinese," he said, "but they are clean and warm. And now, good night, please."

In the light of the candle, which he left for her, she saw his head disappear down the well of the staircase, his eyelids lowered and his face sad and weary.

Then, for the first time in her life, Amy Browning went to bed with all her clothes on, and slept peacefully, without dreams or tossings.

When she awoke, she felt that it was very early, and she tiptoed down the stairs to the toilet and the kitchen so that Mr. Ito would find her clean and fresh when he first saw her. But sunlight streaming through the window at the end of the long hall showed her that it must be almost noon. She felt embarrassed.

On the sink of the tiny dark kitchen was a note.

"Lady," it said, "please accept new comb and toothbrush from A. Ito. P.S. Do not answer the doorbell if it rings."

Amy accepted "new comb and toothbrush" eagerly, and locked the kitchen door upon herself for a long delightful bathing. Then she ate some bread she found in one of the clean, rather bare cupboards. She was ravenous and could have finished the loaf. Instead she went to the front part of the little building.

The curtains with scarlet fans on them were still pulled across the windows. The shop smelled of dried grass and sawdust, with spice in it. She started to open the front door to let in some air, and then stopped, trembling. What was she thinking of? What if someone saw her? She ran from the room on tiptoe, and down the long hall, her breath coming out of her mouth in loose sobbing gasps.

Where was Mr. Ito? Had he gone to tell the police about her? Had she only dreamed that he was kind, or that he lived at all? Was she in a nightmare now?

Upstairs in the attic she lit her candle, shivering. But the sight of her blue quilts, tousled, and the white paper screen about her pile of mats, was reassuring. She picked up the quilts, and folded them neatly, remembering how Mr. Ito had laid them the night before for her to lie upon and under. Then she took the candle in her hand, and walked softly about the attic, looking at things and feeling her heart gradually return to its ordinary rhythm.

The room was larger than she had thought. It was long and narrow, the shape of the little shop and the corridor and kitchen and probably Mr. Ito's room below. There was a partition across the front third of it, with a locked door, and Amy simply climbed up onto a pile of boxes and looked over the top, not feeling that she was peeking into privacy. She could see the dim shapes of more boxes, and climbed down again, satisfied.

She took off her jacket, and rolled up the sleeves of her white blouse, and began to pull the boxes and bales into neat rows. Some of them were too heavy to lift, and some of the woven wrappings looked too flimsy to be pushed about, but she managed in an hour or two to make the attic seem almost orderly.

When she finally went down to the kitchen to wash, she was sickened by the sight of her hands, which looked dirtier than she had ever seen them, with black nails, rough skin, and... how horrid! one broken thumbnail. What should she do? She could not stand it, truly she could not stand it, to have her hands suddenly so ugly.

She buried her head in them, dirt and all, and burst into a flood of noisy, wet, and extremely comforting tears.

IV.

Mr. Ito looked as if he had been standing for some time watching her, when at last she raised her head. There was amusement on his round yellow face, but also such a faint but obvious expression of distaste that Amy sprang to her feet in confusion, full of shame.

"Oh, Mr. Ito," she cried huskily. "Please excuse me! I was ... that is ..."

"Are you frightened here, Miss Browning?"

"You know my name, then?" Her voice became a squeak.

"Yes. It is in the papers this morning," he explained as if it did not matter to him. "But why are you crying, please, in my house?"

Amy began to smile, and then thrust her hands behind her. "It's my fingernails," she said finally, and laughed outright. "I can't stand to have them dirty. I'm a fool."

"No, no," he protested quickly. "I am a bad host. Please excuse me. Will bring you implements at once. All women should have beautiful hands. Take the bundles, please, and I will return at once."

Amy jumped to help him, as he stepped heavily into the kitchen. How had she not noticed that his arms were full of packages? He put them on the sink, and went away without speaking.

When he came back, she had put the vegetables he had bought into a cupboard, and was washing lettuce clumsily under the tap. He laid a small roll of black silk on the edge of the sink, bowed, and left again. It contained orangewood sticks, a file, a little knife, and a tiny pot of oily paste that smelled of roses. Amy wanted to thank him at once, but when she left the kitchen to find him she heard voices in the shop, and remembered suddenly that he was a merchant, and that she was being looked for by the police.

She tiptoed to the attic. Should she tell Miss Crittenden where she was, and what she had done? But what had she done? Of course she had deserted five girls left in her charge ... but any one of them knew the way back to the high walls of the school. Of course, she had failed to meet her classes that morning ... but the Latin teacher knew as much as she herself about English literature, and Miss Crittenden would have no trouble in finding a substitute who would cost even less to the School.

Amy's heart leaped joyfully. There was a little window in her attic! She hurried down to the far end, and there, behind one of the biggest cases, she saw the light glimmering grayly through glass. She felt happy, and the uneasy thoughts of her other life slipped from her.

It must have been a half hour before she had cleared the way to her window. The case in front of it was heavy and unwieldy, and when she finally got that out of the way, she found that the frame around the one pane of glass was stuck shut. She pulled and pounded. Suddenly it flew open, and moist fragrant air, straight from the sea, flowed almost visibly into the dark room. She stood breathing hungrily at it, smiling, and then went silently down the stairs for a broom to sweep her dusty floor, and a cloth to wipe the grime from the windowpane. Now her room was perfect, the most beautiful room she had ever seen in her life, she decided.

When everything was clean, she sat beside the window, on the floor, and rubbed her fingertips with the unguent from the little pot, and rested. She felt tired, but untroubled.

When it was dark, she went softly down to the kitchen again to wait for supper, quite forgetting after all her years of living in summer boardinghouses and in schools that there was nobody to get it except herself, or perhaps Mr. Ito. She was ashamed when he came in, looking very tired, and without comment fixed her two eggs and some lettuce and tea.

"Can you cook rice?" he asked mildly, and when she shook her head he said that she must learn. While she ate hungrily, in spite of her confusion, he sipped his bowl of tea and ate a little lettuce, as if he must do it for politeness. When she had finished he took her plate and bowl to the sink, ran water into them, and then went quietly to the door.

"Can you wash dishes?"

Amy flushed. "Of course I can," she said crossly. "I can wash anything, Mr. Ito. I *love* to wash things!"

"Then some day perhaps you will wish to help me with some porcelain? It needs gentle hands. Is very lovely, Satsuma, both old and of today."

He smiled distantly at her, and closed the kitchen door behind him. Amy heard him move softly down the dim passage, and go into his room. In a minute the sweet heavy smell of his cigarette came to her through the thin walls of the little building.

She yawned, and went up to her own room, as surely as if she knew the way from many years. That night she slept in her chemise, and dreams of rice and Satsuma (Satsuma? A boat, a fruit on a branch, a town?...) poked and nibbled at her comfort.

V.

Amy awoke early, and began the first of a long period of days which were uncounted, unnamed, and probably the most important ones thus far in her life.

She lived them almost completely alone. Mr. Ito was gone away on business, or smoking and writing in his room, and she soon learned not to fidget while the shop bell rang fruitlessly in the front part of the house.

She worked steadily and hard, and cleaned windows and scrubbed floors and stairs and the long corridor until, to her proud eyes at least, the darkness of the little building took on a kind of luminosity. She had never enjoyed herself so thoroughly. It was perhaps because for years she had done nothing more physically tiring than walk with her girls or once a year dance shyly around the decorated gymnasium with the president of the board of school trustees, that now she found a definite voluptuous pleasure in the dullest housework.

The only things she missed, and those with a kind of passive knowledge that some day they would come again, were being able to go out of doors, and having a change of underwear. However, she worked so hard, and could open the window to so much of the salty, flowing air, that she felt healthier than ever in her life before, in spite of being housebound. As for her clothes, she soon learned to wash her white slip in the mornings so that it would be dry again for a nightgown, and the other things at night. She hung them in her little attic, on her screen. It was very simple, and she felt gleeful about it, like an animal who has learned how to open a door for itself without asking for help.

Then for a few days it rained, and the things washed at night were cold and damp in the morning. Amy soon warmed them with her body, but they stayed unpleasant and sticky. One night she decided to risk leaving them in the kitchen, close to the little gas stove.

In the morning, Mr. Ito was gone, as usual, when she slipped down to retrieve them, but on the table was a package with a note stuck on it.

"Miss," it said. "A. Ito asks please to excuse him, and accept this cloth. Is sure you sew like all ladies with beautiful hands. P.S. There are some very ugly little scissors in shop, marked 'Souvenir of the Sunny Southland.' Please procure what you need. A. Ito."

Amy flushed with delight when she unrolled the cloth in the package. There was a long piece of white cotton, with green bamboo leaves and little black rosy-breasted birds printed casually here and there upon it, and then, rolled tightly within the cotton, was a piece of silk. Silk! Amy had always believed what her mother taught her so many years ago, that a real lady never let anything but the finest linen touch her skin. Now she held the cloth, which shimmered, limp like satin and yet as thin as gauze, and rubbed it caressingly against her cheek. It was the color of moonbeams. She would make a nightgown of it, a long simple shift....

So for many afternoons, when she went up to her window to rest and rub her fingernails with the paste that smelled of roses, she sewed clothes for herself, and made the nightgown, and some panties and a petticoat from the cotton, and even a shirt to wear with her tweed skirt, which made her laugh to see herself so giddy, with birds and leaves scattered over her plump boson.

But the most important part of her life, during that period of uncounted silent days, was spent in the attic, looking into the innumerable mysterious boxes, crates, tubs, bales that filled it.

She taught herself to open things as silently and expertly as a thief, and to unpack thin plates and bowls from their wrappings of rice paper without once jarring them, and then to put them back again so that not even Mr. Ito would ever know that they had been disturbed. She went through every case in the attic, on her side of the partition. She learned, almost by touch, to tell what the porcelain would look like before she carried it into the light of her window, and sometimes she would put away a little bowl or a vase and then find it so important in her mind that she would go back to its box and unwrap it again, to sit holding it lightly in her two hands for a long time, feeling its balanced perfection through her skin and her searching nerves.

Finally, one day, she realized that every plate in a set of plates, every bowl or cup in a whole crate of cups, was different from all the others like it, different not so much in its enamel or its form as in a subtle weight and an infinitesimal shaping. She was deeply excited by this discovery, and felt that at last she understood what pride a man or a family or a whole dynasty can feel in its handiwork. She knew the real meaning of the word "handmade," which could never again be a banality to her.

There were several crude wooden chests among the boxes, and these she found full of rolls of cloth. She looked at them all, and found some pieces that were beautiful or funny, paintings on silk or simply lengths like the ones Mr. Ito had given her, and also a great many that felt coarse and unimportant. None of them interested her as much as the porcelain, and she left the cloth and the occasional box of cheap souvenirs or tinny mechanical toys with real relief, to finger once more the cool perfect outlines of the bowls and pots and vases.

After many days, or perhaps it was weeks that had passed since she opened the first box, she climbed lightly over the partition into the other part of the attic, on several crates piled pyramid-like into steps. Mr. Ito was downstairs in the shop, so she made as little sound as possible on the dusty floor, and crept from side to side of the room with her heart pounding excitedly, feeling like a burglar.

There was some light, from a dirty little window rather like her own at the other end, and she saw that many things lay stacked against the walls without any wrappings to hide them. There were some vases, almost as tall as she. She rubbed their sides, and felt little grooves along the edges of their colored designs, which shone with blue and purple and rich green under the dust. Several carved chests, looking soft and velvety in their coatings of gentle dirt, lurked in the darkest corners. They were full of drawers, and Amy's fingers itched to slip each one open, and see what was within. Nearest the window, gleaming brightly in spite of all the dirt and cobwebs that hid it, was a small square chest, about three feet high and wide, which drew her like a magnet.

It was made up, like some of the others, of rows of drawers, but each one was not a flat face of wood, plain or inlaid or carved, but a piece of beautiful brass, or perhaps copper, which curved out fully, roundly, almost like the profile of a young girl's breast, so that the whole front had a full busy look. The faint light caught richly on all the curves, and made the little box so complete that Amy felt tears behind her eyes as she looked at it.

On each drawer there was a delicate knob, fashioned with perfection in a darker copper and fastened to the little warmly rounded front as if it had grown there, like a nipple. Amy pulled at one, gently. The drawer slid open.

VI.

That night Mr. Ito stopped at the kitchen door, about six thirty. In one small brown hand he held his hat, a hideous fuzzy black porkpie, and in the other a large package.

Amy put down the can of tomato soup she was dreamily thinking of opening.

"Good evening," he said, smiling distantly under his large strong moustache. "Are you doing well for yourself? I shall be out for supper. Here are some necessities, please."

He bowed, put the package on the kitchen table, and looked at her for a moment. Then he went on, "Shall no doubt come home a little drunk tonight. Am going to Tomia Restaurant with high Japanese officials." He hissed, and smiled again, again distantly.

"Japanese! Japanese!" Amy heard herself speaking crossly. "Always Japanese! Why not Chinese? Chinese are good people too. They have fine artists too. Japanese!" She threw back her head and sniffed, angry as a mule, for no reason.

Mr. Ito's fingers ran quickly around the edge of his hat brim, like a mouse. For a minute he did not look at her, and Amy felt her heart turn in her. What had come over her? Oh, she cried silently, oh speak to me again, *speak* to me, Mr. Ito!

"Yes," he said finally. "Some Chinese are good people. You are right, Miss Browning. But you do not really care. Therefore it is easy for you to be philosophical. I am a Japanese, with my great-great-grandfather on my grandmother's side, my *maternal* grandmother, a Korean. Therefore, it is very difficult for me, A. Ito, to be philosophical. But I try. I try very hard. And occasionally, as tonight, I find it pleasant to relax and not be philosophical and dine with the Japanese politicians who cannot afford be anything but patriotic. It is stupid of me. Hope you will excuse, please."

Amy looked sharply at him. This was the longest speech he had ever made to her. Was he mocking her? His face was full and flat, and his heavy lids almost covered his strange wide eyes.

He stood for a minute longer, and then turned away. His light step sounded twice in the passageway before she called to him.

"Mr. Ito," she cried, harshly.

It seemed several minutes to her before he stood again in the doorway. She looked miserably at him.

"Mr. Ito... will you sit down for a minute? There are several things...."

She waited while he sat punctiliously down on the pine chair by the table. She pushed carelessly at the soup plate and the spoon she had laid out for herself, and at the bulky parcel he had left there, and sat down facing him.

"Mr. Ito," she said earnestly, with her elbows on the clean wood of the table and her chin in her fists, "we must come to an understanding."

He looked at her, and then asked, "Why, Miss Browning? Are you unhappy?"

"No, no," she cried impatiently. "But I am a middle-aged woman. I have some money. I must get at it somehow, so that I can pay you for my food and... and...."

"Miss Browning," he said, his voice soft and patient so that she flushed as if she had been pointed out on the street corner as a dunce, "at the moment, if you desire to stay hidden, it will be impossible for you to establish yourself with your bank. Moreover," and he put his short fine fingers together with a professorial gesture, delicately, "I do not think that you lack the essentials of life. I am thoughtless, but in the end I will understand and satisfy your needs."

They sat in the little kitchen for a few minutes without speaking. Amy smiled suddenly.

"What is Satsuma?"

He looked at her unwinkingly. "Yes," he said at last. "Is time you asked. Do you read French?"

She stuttered something about reading it better than she spoke it, a reply she remembered to have heard the French teacher say was the most obvious excuse for a bad accent.

"Have several good books on our pottery," Mr. Ito went on as if she had not spoken. "They are in French. Shall give them to you in the morning. And soon, if you wish, we can get more books, many more, from the library. I regret very much, Miss Browning, that cannot speak fine English to tell you myself. In German or in French could do better. Please excuse."

"I always wanted to go to France, too," Amy said, as if she were a ghost speaking of her life on earth.

"Yes. I was at Lyon, and at the Sorbonne. Lyon is sinister, full of unhappy Chinese. But the silk there is better than in China, now."

"Mr. Ito, when may I wash your Satsuma?" Amy was surprised to hear her voice urgent, almost passionate. She sat without looking at him, under the naked light in the little room, waiting for him to reply. Finally he did.

"Can you cook rice, Miss Browning?"

She felt a little sick.

"No. At least, probably not. But I want to," she added eagerly. "I want to, Mr. Ito."

He stood up. "Tomorrow shall show you, or perhaps bring you some instructions from the library," he said. "And now I must hurry to catch my streetcar. The Tomia Restaurant is far from here, and am anticipating an evening of jingoism and hot sake. So good night, Miss Browning." He bowed, and hurried out of the room.

"Wait," she called shrilly.

When he turned back she reached into her dress, and drew from between her warm full breasts the little ivory nugget she had kept there since the afternoon, bedeviling herself. She held it out, her hand trembling.

"What is this?" she asked it more quietly, but she felt that if he snubbed her, or turned her out into the steep street for prying into his secret room, or even if he struck her, still she must know.

He opened his eyes wider than usual, more with admiration than astonishment. Then he smiled, and Amy let her hand drop weakly onto the table.

"Miss Browning, that is a *netsuke*. It is a very fine one, probably by Tomotane or Kyoto. Now in Japan the collectors use *netsuke* for conversation pieces, but some time ago gentlemen carried them on cords at the ends of their little pillboxes. Pillboxes are called *inro*. Almost all Japanese are constipated. Almost all Japanese carried *inro*. Did you find them too?"

Amy shook her head. She felt ashamed, but for some reason she could hardly keep from smiling: Mr. Ito looked so serious, with his hat under his arm and his eyes bent upon her from the doorway.

"No," she said meekly, "I only looked in the copper chest with the... the..."

"*Netsuke?* Miss Browning, the *inro*, and I have a collection of them at the moment that has been admired by the curator of the Museum of Fine Arts of Boston, Massachusetts, the *inro* are in the dark cedar chest to the left of the window. But for a time I think you must learn to cook rice and to wash tea bowls, and perhaps to read a little bit about Japanese history. You are probably well educated and intelligent?"

Amy smiled, foolishly.

"I think probably you are. Tomorrow I shall bring you books. You are curious, like all women, but you seem to understand about *netsuke*, at least that they should be kept warm and alive."

He bowed again to her. "Good night, Lady. Sleep well, please. Good night, please."

Amy sat for a few minutes after she heard him close and lock behind him the door of the shop. She thought of a thousand things she had wanted to ask, about why he sold such trashy junk and what he did with all the beautiful vases and cups in the attic and what he meant to do about her, Amy Browning, schoolteacher. But instead of running after him again, she smiled in a little while, and put the piece of ivory, which looked like a brown nut until you saw that it was three tiny crabs carved intricately into an oval, once more down between her breasts.

While the can of soup heated on the stove, and she determined to learn how to cook, she opened Mr. Ito's bundle. He had brought her some stockings, which she could tell were too short in the foot, and other things she might need, like hairpins, and a package of cheap cigarettes. She smoked one with her supper, for the first time in her life, and although she expected to feel sick she found that she enjoyed it, and felt calmer than ever.

VII.

Amy worked hard, the next few months. She still enjoyed cleaning and tidying the little building, which took more time than she realized, and then she studied all the books that Mr. Ito brought her. Occasionally she asked him questions, when he came into the kitchen from the shop, but more often she went up into the attic and hunted through the cases until she found the piece of porcelain or of jade that she was wondering about, and learned for herself. Now and then new cases would appear, and she and Mr. Ito would carry them up the steep rickety stairs without a word, each knowing that she was passionately eager to undo them, alone.

She taught herself to cook rice, and after several attempts she asked Mr. Ito to taste it. He was polite but not enthusiastic, at first. She tried many more times, and then realized that he was eating supper with her almost every night in the dark clean little kitchen instead of his room or away. She learned to cook chicken in nut oil, and to fry shrimps to look like butterflies, and to make good tea, as well as many other things. Mr. Ito never ate with what could be called gusto, but at least he ate, and he told her that the rice was excellent, and bowed sitting down as well as standing by the table.

She began to leave the little building occasionally, usually on Monday mornings when she knew that all the girls and the teachers of that place, that school she had been in, would be at classes. She would walk swiftly, lightly, along the sea cliffs, and now and then she would enter the shop by the front door, instead of through the little alley, and if there were no customers she would laugh silently at Mr. Ito's expression and walk on into the dark hallway and her own world again, feeling merry.

Once she met Catherine, the girl who had wondered about Chaucer. Catherine stood outside the Medical Building. She looked anemic. Probably she was going in to have a hypodermic injection, or some such fashionable fiddle-faddle. Amy looked at her briefly and walked on, without alarm.

The girl ran a few steps after her, and then stopped. "Oh," she said, in a choked, incredulous voice. "*Oh!* Miss Browning...I found your gloves...aren't you..."

But Amy did not stop. She knew that Catherine would never betray her. Later she remembered the encounter with a kind of impersonal gratitude that someone, at least, had recognized her without her brown felt hat, in sandals that Mr. Ito had brought her and a blouse covered with bamboo leaves and robins. But even that fleeting gratitude did not much matter, in the life that she lived now.

Mr. Ito did not talk often, but gradually he told her about his business and why he sold cheap souvenirs and toys. "We eat from what we make in the shop," he said causally. "But we live, in the brain and the heart, on what is in your attic. The poor stuff we sell is unimportant. And then upstairs, Miss Browning, you take care of the real things."

Now and then people would come to see him, and he would take them up to her room while she stayed silently in the kitchen. Sometimes they brought boxes with them, and without being told, Amy knew that they were rescuing things they respected from the harried cities of the East, and that she and Mr. Ito were guarding them. This gave her a great sense of importance. She felt more needed in the world than she ever thought she would, even by the children she still, sometimes, dreamed of as her own.

Among other things, she read enough about gardens in the books on Japan to want one, and almost before she knew it she had designed and started a strange conventional little set piece in the few square feet at the back of the building. Taller buildings loomed deeply on the three sides of it, and her own attic window looked peakedly down upon it, but there was an ash heap all ready to become the three mountains required by tradition, and in front she made a little lake with a sand-blown beach at its upper end and a broad calm beach near the hall door. Around it she put the little green plants that Mr. Ito left silently for her upon the kitchen sink, and finally, the day she found a proper stone to be the central island in the lake, she asked him to visit the garden with her and flushed like a schoolgirl when he told her solemnly that it was very beautiful, very correct. She bowed.

One day, when it was almost summer and uncomfortably warm for her in her sturdy and by now baggy tweed skirt, she found a new box in the attic, full of clothes. They were made of soft cotton, except for one of silk of a delicate green color, and all of them were cut like a Chinese woman's clothes, with trousers and long loose coats.

She took off everything, and washed herself, and then put on the green silk suit, which slipped over her fresh skin like another fresher one. It was wonderful to feel free and clean, and no more bound about by belts, straps, garters. She put some black silk slippers from the shop upon her feet, and sat placidly then by her little window, rubbing pomade on her shining almond-shaped nail tips.

She wore the green silk suit to dinner, where Mr. Ito did not seem to notice it, but instead talked of two books that they planned to write together, one about Japanese cookery and its freshness and facility, and the other about wall hangings and scrolls. Amy knew that she could write anything with Mr. Ito, who had a poor opinion of his own grammar in English, but a clear way of telling things to her.

He stood up, after supper, his face more solemn than usual, and asked to be excused. In a few minutes, though, he was back, with a little thin-necked vase and two tiny *sake* cups on a tray, and a bottle under his arm.

"Miss Browning," he said, and then hesitated until she asked courteously, "Yes?"

"Miss Browning, will you please drink a glass of hot wine with me? This is an important evening in my life. I shall probably get a little drunk. Not here. Oh, never, please! But not at the Tomia Restaurant either. No. Oh . . . am very much upset!"

He drew air hissingly under his moustache, and put the tray down upon the table without looking at her. Amy wondered if he felt ill. His face was pale and tight looking, and she saw with a kind of embarrassment that his hands, usually so sure and firm, were shaking. She felt a great rush of tenderness toward this polite, thoughtful little man.

"Oh, Mr. Ito," she said warmly, and then cleared her throat as if she had not meant it and asked practically, "May I help you?"

He shook his head, still without looking at her.

"Thank you. Thank you. But wish to prepare this. I warm the cups under the hot water tap, and in the meantime the wine heats in this little pan . . ."

He puttered nervously about the kitchen.

Amy knew that there was nothing she could do but sit. She sat, then, enjoying the cool intimate touch of the unfamiliar silk upon her skin, and looking without really seeing them at her surprising trousered legs and the free full out-thrust of her breasts.

Finally Mr. Ito brought her a cup of the hot *sake*, his hand as steady now as stone, and the two of them drank silently. Amy liked it, and would have welcomed another cup, but Mr. Ito picked up the pan full of steaming wine, and the little tray, and bowed to her as he flicked out the door. She heard his own door close quickly behind him, down the hall.

"Well," she said, almost provoked and cross. "What's wrong with him, I wonder?"

She put out the light, and went softly up the stairs to her room. The little bit of wine had made her warm, and she felt mirthful and like a child. She opened the window and knelt before it a long time, listening to the sly whisper of the waves far below.

There was a sound in the kitchen.

She tiptoed to the head of her stairs, and looked down.

Mr. Ito, in a black kimono with silver threads glinting in it, almost like his hair, came softly from the kitchen and disappeared down the passage toward his own room.

Amy heard his door close again. She waited a few minutes, and then, without a sound in her silk slippers, went down to the kitchen to see what on earth had got into the man.

There on the sink was a note, the first she had found from him for many days.

"Miss Browning," it said. "Do not think I am inspired by wine, since it is too soon. I beg you to accept my offer of marriage, which will not be honorable in the eyes of your former associations but will always be honored by A. Ito. P.S. You are a woman ripe and intelligent, so you will excuse me. P.P.S. Am older than appearances, but am a thoughtful lover."

Amy stood without a sound, for a long time, under the mean light in the kitchen where she had so much lived during the last few months. She thought, like a drowning woman, of all the cold hollowness of her life until the day she had fallen swooning at the feet of this kind gracious man. She thought of many small past things, like the first meal at a new school, when all the girls watched her, intuitive harpies, for a weak move, a chink in her armor of hard-won impersonality. She thought of putting shoe polish on the tips of her last-year's gloves to make them brown again. But she never once thought of what might lie ahead of her, if she went back to her old life.

Instead, she walked quietly down the ugly narrow hall to Mr. Ito's door, and opened it without knocking.

She had never seen the room before. It was larger than she had expected, and lined with Western books and rolls of oriental paintings on wide shelves. There was a big roll-top desk. There was also a carved dark idol in front of a little picture on silk.

Mr. Ito stood by the bed, which was low and wide. He looked at her with his large dark eyes and then sighed sharply.

Amy went in, and shut the door after her, and Mr. Ito touched her green silk shoulders tenderly, and later proved to her that he was a indeed a thoughtful lover, and that she was a ripe woman, even a rich one.

And the two of them lived happily ever after, until they were instantly killed in a bus wreck near Penzance, in Cornwall, full of honors, in their old age.

[*The Carleton Miscellany,* 1967]

A POSSIBLE POSSESSION

EARLIER TODAY, I could have written more forcibly about the influence drifting through the house. By now, with her gone, it is vanishing, and with its fog of magic and evil, and my thoughts drift apart, away.

When she is here, everyone is very aware of her. I am. I watch her eyes, showing white above the dilated pupils, so strangely turned down and sideways, and her mouth, which can be tender or vulgar, and her hair in all shades of red-blue-henna-purple. I wonder about her life with her children, with lovers, with her students at a conservatory. I watch almost every move she makes, because I know she is loaded like a Molotov cocktail and that she hates it. I feel she is aware at some levels of how evil she may be, and the more innocent sides of her are afraid of this. She is a fine artist. What is more, she has learned to be articulate, and her opinions are mostly acute and well phrased.

She is a force that is at once blameless and sick and wicked, I believe—at times very alluring, and at times coarse-faced or blanched or haggard. Once last night when she was crouched in front of the hearth she looked like a piece of bone, dried of all human blood.

That was after the small Franklin stove seemed to spew out its logs, which rolled against her back. Never had such a thing happened before in my house, and perhaps it never will again until this same woman sits there in front of her rare wooden lirofassa, tinkling on its keys and talking about old instruments, and waiting to die or live. She was waiting all night, but she always has been.

I sat too far away to help, and I watched the scene as if I were in a theater, but with an animal curiosity as to whether she would flame like a torch or turn into ash. She was dressed less outlandishly than usual, in a thickly embroidered Turkish vest lined with smelly lamb or goat pelts, over a flammable red turtleneck and beige slacks, and her many-colored hair hung loose—and yes, she could have gone up in one burst of brightness. The other people in the room screamed and beat at her furs and leather and hair and kicked at the blazing bits of hot wood, and she pushed the ancient lyre away and sat there while they all struck at her. Her face was withdrawn, not frightened, and I watched it, trapped by distance and perhaps ennui, and recognized her welcoming of the incident.

She has told me that she is disaster-prone. I think of Malcolm Lowry, who seemed to invite holocaust. I think of the books of Charles Fort. Yes, it is logical, when there is a peculiar force like this woman. She does not invoke forces: she is one.

She is frightening, and I was relieved today to wave her a truly affectionate and concerned good-bye. "She is *gone*," I said. "Now I can light a lamp, or the stove, or especially the hearth, without risking all our lives."

At times, she is aware of her peculiar power to attract destruction. The odd thing is that she never really does—she skirts it, so that her own body, a room, a building, a busload of children, a freighter she rides on are all of them in imminent danger and are often damaged, but *she* emerges pale and shocked with the shaken survivors, and they feel grateful to each other, and unaware of anything but how close they have come to pure horror.

Many interruptions in both time and space, and my conviction that this person has supernatural power has grown less sure. I realize that she herself put the suspicion into my mind several years ago when she came here and flitted in and out, up the canyon, once wearing bound around her waist and hanging from her belt long strands of moss pulled from the old trees. Her hair was frowzy. Her eyes were mostly vacant, and her mouth, with its fine pearly teeth, wore a remote smile. I wondered how much she could be acting a part. I did not think more about it, although a man who met her that evening said he would never eat anything she cooked, because of the potions she would put into it. She gave the impression of casting a spell, plainly, and now I think seriously of the incident of the Franklin stove and wonder if she is an agent or is herself possessed of supernatural powers, no matter how innocently.

I considered this a few minutes ago when I rubbed my right forearm and felt an unfamiliar bump there. It was a small deep gouge my cat

Charles made last night through the sleeve of my jacket. It is the first time he has ever drawn blood from me. It is now mildly infected but seems to be healing. Charles, I noticed, in my almost clinical watching of the woman, was impertinent—taunting and malicious. His tail switched furiously even when nobody appeared to be noticing him. Never has he seemed as evil as when this woman is here, last night and before. This early morning, instead of coming softly to the door of my bathroom when he heard I was in there readying myself for the day, he yowled loudly right by the bed, and then paced outside, and yowled even more unreasonably at the other bathroom door and then at my bedroom door—all a nervous, vicious, defiant protest of something I could not know about. In the tub of the guest bathroom were two blobs of blood and spleen: two small animals dragged through his little door and past the woman's bed and into the tub to be eaten. Sometimes there is one such signal of Charlie's hunting, but two?

One time when she was here, she sat by the fire—she crouches and squats in a lithe way, so that other people wish they were there with her on the floor, and sometimes they do get down with her, always by the crackling fire—and she was teasing Charles. It made a beguiling picture. But his tail lashed back and forth ferociously, and finally I murmured to her, under the talk of several people, that he was growing too excited. She kept on teasing him (or he her?). Then she unwound herself and left the room, and he went outside. Later, I went into her bathroom and found it quite bloodied: a wet stained towel hidden in a corner of the long sink, another bloodier one on the laundry basket, a fresh roll of toilet paper that had been used as a kind of blotter on a gash or cut. I cleaned up the place and returned to the fireside where she was sitting. She looked pale and beautiful, and I saw she had put Band-Aids and Kleenex on claw cuts on one arm and on one leg. I said nothing. That night, Charles never came back through his door, and I did not see him until after she left, about noon.

Last night, though, she was aware of his menace, and when she started to play with him—another "picture" of the two of them so lithe and alluring with the firelight—she looked up at me and said, "I remember that you told me to watch his tail for danger." She pushed him away and he stalked over to me and sank one claw into my forearm, and then left the house. It was an odd turn of the wheel, I thought.

When the logs rolled onto her back as if they were pushed from behind or almost as if they jumped toward her, I thought vaguely of Charles, of the power generated willy-nilly between him and her. "Just get the hot ones off the rug," I said calmly, mildly. "Kick them onto the tiles—don't worry." I felt foolish, but knew that I must not interfere in any way—*any* way. If I did, she might suddenly go up in flames. This was a fact.

Neither she nor the lirofassa was hurt. Soon after she had played a couple of old melodies on it while it was still by the fire, she closed the lid and leaned back toward the cooling hearth, where I had finally put a fire screen that should perhaps have been there from the beginning, and across the room from me she looked like a ghost. Her face was chalk white, with deep eye pits. She was exhausted. But she moved the strange instrument to the opposite side of the room for the night.

I thought of the time she wandered over the land here, draped with garlands of moss. Then she had told me she felt doomed to terrible disasters and catastrophes. Wherever she went, she said, accidents followed her. No, they did not happen to her but to other people. She would be in a car and make a strange skid, and behind her an unfamiliar car would go off the road and kill three occupants. She would go to the fortieth floor in an elevator, and on its way down it would crash and kill several people. She would go to a restaurant and eat a good dinner and read the next day that twenty-six people had been hospitalized for violent poisoning from the same dish she had eaten in the same place. She was doomed. I told her she must break the spell, go to another clime. To my surprise I learned that she did—to Italy—and that when she returned she was very strong and blooming and creative. We communicated by letters now and again, and a few times she drove here with a friend or two to see me. She looked well: somewhat zany clothes, increasingly grotesque dyed hair, an indefinable helplessness about her manner in spite of her almost lifelong experience of being before an audience as a musical prodigy.

Last night and this morning, I was very aware of her supernatural power. I know she was sometimes aware of it, too, and I think that she exploits it to add to her appeal as a creative lovely being. It is frightening. But how can one call the local sheriff and say, "A witch is loose!"

Meanwhile, I am glad to be alone. Charles is withdrawn. My arm hurts a little but not enough to worry about. I hear the thin, almost wheezy sound of the old instrument, and watch with curiosity as logs roll out of the Franklin stove and people leap in horror to keep her from burning like a torch.

[*The New Yorker,* 1978]

PERSONAL GASTRONOMY

THE TEN MOST IMPORTANT
FOOD BOOKS OF ALL TIME

PROBABLY the best thing about an article like this is that nine out of nine possible readers will say, "Oh yeah...what about...?" and then start making their own lists. I feel the same way. I know the list I think I ought to give to be impressive. And I think I know the list I would give if I were naming the ten "food books" most important to me.

Of course if I am even pretending to name books about food which have influenced the very meals we eat today, I must pull great words out of my hat. There was Horace, who satirized the absurd refinements of his contemporaries at table, and discussed wittily the wines, eggs, mushrooms, oysters served to him at their dinners. There was Plinius Secundus, who knew not only wines but the fine art of bread making. There were three Roman gourmets named Apicius: one wrote a lot of recipes for cakes and sauces, and another a book called *De Re Coquinaria* which I mention because it is the correct thing to do. And then there were scientists, even as today, who write of the right way to live, of the effects of botany and *material medica* on the much-scourged human stomach. Theophrastus and Dioscorides are two of the more important of these intestinal philosophers. There were the great Frenchmen, cooks and scholars: Vatel, Audot, Careme, Grimod de La Reyniere....

For myself, I think people will always eat, and even learn the basic rules of how to do so, without books. Therefore it is the writers who can turn eating into an esthetic delight, make its intrinsic grossness delicate, who please me most and who will always do so.

First, of course, I name Brillat-Savarin's *Physiology of Taste*. It is like the music of Bach, a constant reassurance of balance and wit and profundity. After it the others on my list are numberless, an affectionate hodge-podge, which by this time next year will have changed.

Ellwanger's *Pleasures of the Table* is fun to read; it is like eating a good plum cake, stuffed full of heady flavors. *The Art of Dining* by Walker and Saintsbury's *Notes on a Cellar Book* have something of the sturdy fineness of my prime favorite. As for the great *Guide Culinaire* of Escoffier, I use it and admire it, but for pure enjoyment would rather read its fat pompous shadow, Ranhofer's *Epicurean,* with its wonderful engravings of how to carve a duck for twenty-six Russian princes (old style) and a prima donna. I like *The Art of Cookery Made Plain and Easy,* mainly because in it Mrs. Glasse said, "First catch your hare . . . ," but I find Marion Harland's *Common Sense in the Household* more honest on this side of the Atlantic, and perhaps just as important to the small wifely kitchen. And I like Ali-Bab's *Practical Gastronomy,* because it really is. And for just the opposite reason I like all of Paul Reboux's crazy books.

And that makes the prescribed ten, and the list is only born. Oh waily waily . . . it is like eating one crisp tantalizing nut and then another, to start naming favorite books about the table that is set within the mind, set a hundred times a day, for this love, that hate. Who can say, coldly and sensibly, what are the ten most important food books of all time? Not I.

[*The Chicago Daily News,* 1943]

SHALL IT BE ... EATING OR DINING?

ONCE ON A TIME and long ago...yes it must be at least three weeks since then...an old waiter stood beside my table in a restaurant in San Francisco. He talked about the Fire. He was already a waiter at the Palace then, and as he gossiped in the flat, nervous, sardonic way of his kind, I thought he'd probably looked just about the same in 1900 as he did in 1944: exhausted, ageless.

He hated the hurry now, he said, even though he was making big money in tips. "People eat five times as fast, now. That means five tips to the old one," he said. He sounded glum, and scornful, too. "People don't dine anymore. They just eat."

It was true, I thought, as I looked at the men and women at the other tables. They ate hungrily, hurriedly, with no gleam of interest in their worried faces. They were performing a necessary function, but they were performing it without any grace.

It seemed a pity, there in the old-fashioned room with fancy gilded curlicues on the high ceiling, and the smell of fresh crab legs and Rex sole...and it is a pity anywhere.

Perhaps it is the saddest at home, and most discouraging. I am certain that if I had to cook even one meal a day that was eaten without comment or appreciation or any sign of faint excitement, I'd wonder what to do to bring my board to life again.

The most obvious remedy is to break away from routine and serve new things to tease the palate. I'd do that, always in moderation to preserve my familiars from a shocked rebellion, for nothing can bring out reactionary tendencies at the table as too stiff a dose of exotic dishes.

I think I'd change the order of a meal, rather than its content. I'd recall the way a dinner *seemed* exciting, somehow, at Madam Duflos', a students' café in Paris, even when it had nothing extraordinary about any part of it. Then I'd decide that if meat and potatoes tasted good enough to dream about at Madam Duflos' Golden Snail, meat and potatoes could still taste that way in my home.

I'd serve them in the finest Duflos fashion... and because I'd want the meal to be fun, and charming, it would be. The people who ate it would come alive again, willynilly. Suddenly we'd not be eating another routine meal. We'd be dining....

The hors d'oeuvres would be as simple as possible: thin slices of salami, some sardines, bitter wrinkled olives, perhaps a bowl of pickled mushrooms, or cucumbers in cream. The wine (an unpretentious sturdy one) would taste at its best with those flavors and the crusty bread.

The steak, well hung even though perhaps not one of the nobler cuts, would have lain at room temperature for several hours, and for the last hour in a bath of strong, plain French dressing with plenty of garlic in it. At the last it would be patted dry, and then slapped onto a grill as hot as hell-fire and as searing. No turning-fork would ever prick it, and when it would finally be carved into long thin slices at the table, its juices would gush from it the color of garnets.

The piles of watercress on the platter would be tossed in the cooling juices, and then served with the steak. And there would be the bread... the wine... and no potatoes!

That, I think, is one trick of Madam Duflos' which we could copy oftener here at home: to serve potatoes or vegetables in a separate course. It makes the meal last longer, all to the good in this over-hurried life. It adds an almost ceremonious note to a very simple menu. It dignifies a dish which too often is eaten from habit alone, without appreciation of its flavor or its style.

For this dinner, then, the dinner to prove to myself and my chosen circle that a banal menu can be stimulating and amusing and full of poise, I would make a soufflé of the good old mashed potatoes which otherwise would trot humbly along beside the steak, and I would serve it on clean hot plates after the meat course had been cleared away, and only the bread and wine stayed faithfully on the table.

And after that, as naturally as if we all were really back at the Golden Snail instead of sitting in unaccustomed mellow ease at our own table suddenly grown jollier, would come a bowl of chilled grapes and pears and figs, and a plate of some gentle cheese: a Monterey Jack or a Port Salut, to blend with the ripe fruits and the last bite of bread, the last swallow of wine.

And then coffee ... and I think the magic would have happened, and we'd sit for a long time with our elbows on the table, talking easily, hearing and seeing more than we had for some time because of the way we'd *tasted more.*

[*House Beautiful,* 1944]

LOVE IN A DISH

BRILLAT-SAVARIN, who amused himself in his old age by writing *The Physiology of Taste*, a book which, after almost 125 years of near idolatry and countless imitators, remains the wittiest and wisest of its kind, concerned himself mightily with the problem of married bliss. He wrote many paragraphs and pages on the importance of gastronomy in love, and told a dozen anecdotes which in one or another of his slyly subtle ways proved the point, put bluntly, that happiness at table leads to happiness in bed.

A mutual enjoyment of the pleasures of the table, he said over and over, has an enormous influence on the felicity that can and should be found in marriage. A couple, he went on, who can share this enjoyment, "have at least once every day, a delightful reason to being together, for even those who sleep in separate beds (and there are many such in 1825) at least eat at the same table; they have an unfailing subject of conversation; they can talk not only of what they are eating, but also of what they have eaten before and will eat later, and of what they have noticed in other dining rooms, of fashionable new recipes and dishes, etc., etc.: everyone knows that such intimate chit-chat is full of its own charms."

Brillat-Savarin felt, and said so strongly, that a man and woman who share any such basic need as the one for food will be eager to please and amuse each other in the satisfying of that need, and will do what they can do to make the basically animal process enjoyable. "And the way in which mealtimes are passed," he wrote firmly, "is most important to what happiness we find in life."

Of course, this observation was not original with the old French lawyer. Chinese philosophers made it in much the same words three thousand years ago, and any thoughtful psychiatrist will make it today, when our boulevards are lined with an infinity of bad eating houses filled with dead-faced people placed like mute beasts in their stalls; today, when one out of every three marriages ends in divorce.

It seems incredible that normal human beings not only tolerate the average American restaurant food, but actually prefer it to eating at home. The only possible explanation for such deliberate mass poisoning, a kind of suicide of the spirit as well as the body is that meals in the intimacy of the dining room or kitchen are unbearable.

At a drugstore counter, backed by trusses wrapped in cellophane and faced by wavy-haired young men dressed like dental assistants, conversation is unnecessary if not quite impossible.

Nagging and whining are temporarily shut off, and a married man and woman can sit side by side like strangers.

At home, fatigue and boredom would sour the words they spoke and the food they ate, and the words would be hateful and the food would be dull as ditchwater and drearily served forth. The monotony of preparing meals which evoke no sign of pleasure would have knocked the woman into a rut of glum can-opening, the man into dour acceptance. Anything is better than being penned together in one room, having to chew and breathe in unison, they feel. And they go, in a kind of wordless dread of being alone, to this Broiler, that Chili-Heaven.

And having failed so completely to satisfy in harmony one of their three basic needs, it cannot be wondered that the other two, for love, and shelter, are increasingly unfulfilled. There can be no warm, rich home life anywhere else if it does not exist at table, and in the same way there can be no enduring family happiness, no real *marriage,* if a man and woman cannot open themselves generously and without suspicion one to the other over a shared bowl of soup as well as a shared caress.

I do not know many people very well, but I am on terms of close friendship with at least three families, this very minute, who worry me greatly because they are increasingly unhappy at table—and therefore, everywhere. It is true that things have conspired against them to make the quiet little dinners of courtship impossible: Children and wars and worries have pushed the candlelight and the leisure far into the past. But it seems to me that lack of understanding on the part of the husbands is the real trouble.

The wives, whether consciously or not, have remembered the French adage that good cooking is like love, needing both tact and variety. They have tried, not always too successfully, to make meals that were exciting and amusing. The response from their husbands, almost unfailingly, has been "What's all this fancy stuff? Give me good plain food, will you? I'm strictly a steak-and-potato boy, honey! And for God's sake remember it!"

Once spoken to this way, a woman, who feels instinctively that cooking is one of her last resorts as a creative outlet, withdraws rebuffed and hurt. She still manages to make something of a reputation for herself as a "party cook" and serves elaborate curries and heavily flavored desserts which annoy her politely silent mate. In between "company" she sincerely believes that she is trying to please him by a monotonous series of steak-and-potato dinners, although there is increasing resentment in her subconscious mind against his noncommittal acceptance of what he must surely know is boring to her.

He, on his part, may sense a disappointment in her, may feel that he has let her down in some way which he does not bother to analyze, and he covers his uncomfortable self-doubt by added silence. The result is that meals for the two of them grow more and more strained. He never comments on the food, because he knows just what there will be and what it will taste like, and if he is Anglo-Saxon he has probably been raised to think of such conversation as bad manners or at least foolish.

She, knowing that she can expect no fine fillip of a compliment, takes less interest everyday in ordering and preparing the food, and finally grows so revolted by it and all it has come to stand for in her feeling toward her husband that she cannot eat properly. She grows nervous and tires easily.

Finally, with unspoken relief, they begin to dine oftener in public places, where at first the unaccustomed noise and movement and the new flavors make meals seem a pleasure again. They talk and drink and eat gaily, and go home to more happiness than for a long time.

Soon, though, they become accustomed to one or two restaurants, where they always order the same things and are served by the same waiters. They have less and less to say. The man eats hungrily at his steak, satisfying his need for nourishment in a way which he has been led to believe is a proof of his virility, or at least masculinity. "No fancy stuff for me," he says. "Good meat, that's all a man needs—good meat and potatoes and plenty of it, and you can have these sauces, and courses and this and that. Take too much time! All right for parties, I guess...."

If he sees that his wife, sitting across from him in the café, has the blank, peaked look on her face which he has come to dread in bed, he may worry about her and tell her she should eat more honest-to-God food, instead of all those salads. She may smile at him. And she may not.

Perhaps the two of them should read or reread Brillat-Savarin's book. In it he would make clear to them that a healthy interest in the pleasures of the table, the gastronomical art, can bring much happiness. They would see the stupidity of asserting one's virility by a diet limited to the needs of a dog or lion, and the silliness of proving one's interest in exotic living by over-spiced indigestible messes.

In Richardson Wright's *Bed-Book of Eating and Drinking*, he wrote in a discussion of the delights of supping in the kitchen that more meals served on oilcloth by the stove might be one way to "stabilize our American marital status. I hold to the lowly belief," he went on, "that a man never knows the sureness of being happily married until he has... cooked a meal himself."

Brillat-Savarin believed much the same thing, and made it plain that gentlemen of unquestioned masculinity among his friends found added vigor and zest for life's pleasures in the kitchen, where they could pit their skill and intelligence against the laws of nature and more often than not emerge triumphantly with a roasted quail or a soufflé to prove their point.

I shiver with sadness for my drifting friends when I read the *Bed-Book* (Mr. Wright has but paraphrased the old Frenchman, which is almost inevitable in anything connected with gastronomy) "The first sign of marital trouble is when a man or woman finds it distasteful to face each other at table....I am convinced that a man and wife with congenial appetites and a knowledge of foods and cooking have the basis for lasting happiness."

The French have perhaps written more than any people but the Chinese know about food as well as love. (Another of them has said, "A man is captured through his heart, but is held captive forever through his stomach!") But it is not a Gallic prerogative and I have as much right as any other thoughtful and affectionate person to decide for my friends that if they were happier at table they would be happier elsewhere.

Any such state can be attained deliberately, if done with intelligence, but once attained it must be nurtured with constant attention. The man must try to understand what it is about making a curry or a bouilla-baisse that lightens his wife's face and heart. The woman must try to understand why a husband needs to bolster his preconceptions of virili-ty now and then with a bit of reactionary conservatism. He must use his brain at home as well as at his office, and decide that cultivating his palate is at least as important as perfecting his golf stroke. She must read and think, until she can conclude for herself that a heavy hand with the condiments is no guarantee of a culinary escape from boredom.

Only then will they find that they can face each other gaily across the table again, and that even steak-and-potatoes, when they have been pre-pared with a shared interest and humor and intelligence, can be one great pleasure which leads to another, and perhaps—who knows—an even greater one.

[*House Beautiful*, 1948]

GOURMETS ARE MADE—NOT BORN

THE MAKING OF a gourmet, if the theory is accepted that a gourmet can be made, is a tricky thing which depends on all the circumstances and accidents of time, place, and perhaps the stars. I am convinced that it can be done, given one supreme requisite: good taste.

I do not mean the kind of taste which is one of the five or six physical senses. Almost every normal human being has this sense, in some degree. The people in whom it is most highly developed are naturally the most fortunate, if they wish to become gourmets. Those who are truly tasteblind and cannot understand even the differences between sweet and sour would be hard put to it to know, for instance, whether they were eating a Béchamel or a Velouté sauce.

I use the phrase good taste as it is used in girls' boarding schools, in fashion magazines, and in Brillat-Savarin's book on the pleasures of the table, which has become a kind of gourmets' primer. Good taste is an innate thing, a natural and inherent perception of right and wrong. It stretches from knowing what shoes or tie to wear with what dress or suit, to how to behave in bed.

The lack of it produces a multitude of sins, of both omission and commission. Not the least of these are gastronomical. There is no education, no determination to *know*, which can cover up this basic necessity in the making of a gourmet, and it does not matter how much money or time a person spends on a fine dinner if he cannot sense what is in good taste and what is merely stylish or showy or impressive.

There are, of course, many fortunate people who have never read a book about gastronomy in their lives (when one superlatively good cook was asked why she did not keep a shelf of kitchen manuals, she said, "It clutters up my head too much!"), and who can and do know, as unerringly as a well-trained dog with God-given scent will point a bird, how to serve forth a gourmet's meal, a good meal.

There are still others, even more fortunate, who have this same instinct, this natural good taste, and who also know what they strive for: to learn all they can, to read and experiment and discuss, and finally to become one kind or another of gastronome.

It is not at all necessary to be either a scientist or an artist of gastronomy to be a true gourmet. There must be a keen interest, surely, and an enthusiasm. Above all there must be *good taste*. And given this heaven-sent thing, anyone can figure himself among the gods' favorites, no matter what the limitations of his purse.

He can *read* the classics on the subject of eating, from state libraries and secondhand bookstalls and private collections, from *The Closet of Sir Kenelm Digby, Knight*, and *Notes on a Cellar-Book* by George Saintsbury, and the back pages of last month's *Ladies' Home Companion*.

He can *cook*, beginning with a perfectly boiled egg and ending with anything at all that is incredibly complicated...say a *bombe aux ananas flambés au kirsch*.

Above all, a man can *eat:* he has to, anyway, in order to exist, and he might as well have fun doing it!

He can eat thoughtfully, deliberately, innocently, cruelly, subtly, generously—never with boredom, never without reason. He can believe that it is as important to satisfy this one of his three basic hungers, the one for food, in an artful and intelligent way as it is important to build a beautiful house to shelter himself, or to make love well in order to find himself some bliss.

He can consider the dictates of planning a meal in good taste, any meal at all from breakfast with his small daughter to dinner with three world-conference delegates; diplomacy is as important in one repast as in the other, and in both of them sex, politics, and even religion play their usual complex roles.

The breakfast, for instance, it would be bad taste to serve something too highly spiced for the young lady's palate, like link sausages

simmered in ale (which the father *loves*), but on the other hand it would
be equally unfortunate to point up her tender years by a bowl of pallid
pap and a plate of graham crackers (which she perforce endures). A nice
compromise must be made, so that her instinctive femaleness will blossom with pleasure at sharing food with a man, and none of her vanity
will suffer at having to seem like a sexless infant. Some such dish as this
might do, on an early summer morning.

Eggs for the Infanta

4 fresh eggs
4 slices toast
3 tablespoons butter
1 tablespoon finely chopped parsley

Use what is called a "poacher," the kind that really steams the eggs.
Butter the four little round pans. Have the water boiling underneath,
break an egg into each pan, cover, and cook until just done, firm but not
hard.

Meanwhile toast four pieces of good bread, and cut each into a star
or a round—anything but an ordinary day-to-day square.

Heat the butter until it begins to color. Add the parsley, shake well,
put an egg on each star, pour the butter over, and serve at once.

This dish is very easily eaten (except for cutting the toast, which the
young lady's father may do for her without seeming *too* fatherly) and
digested. The rapid cooking of the eggs takes care of that, and the
father can discreetly give himself his rightfully major share of the butter, and a dash of pepper. And, above all, it is *fun*, because of the special
shape of the eggs and the toast. It is easy to make, and any man who
tries it can sit back well fed and happy in the company of an admiring
girl-child who will suddenly seem even more delightful to him than
before.

The dinner is but an enlargement of this morning exercise in diplomacy. Religion and politics can be preeminent here, as was sex at breakfast. Two of the three delegates are from Turkey, say, or one is a Catholic
and it is Friday—or all three of them have spent enough time in prison
camps to have lost their ability to eat rich food. A host who is also a

gourmet, actual or only in the making, will discover as many such facts as possible, and ponder on them as he plans his feast.

When in doubt, a gourmet's instinctive feeling that simplicity is best will come to his aid. He will figure that his guests have endured countless, lengthy, complicated state banquets. This reasoning will help justify his seemingly rather lazy decision to serve a light simple supper to them, most probably built around fish and not too definite in flavor, as for example a curry would be.

For dessert the delegate-ridden host would be safe with almost any citizen of the Western or the Eastern worlds to offer:

A Honey-Bowl

1 large tin of whole apricots
1 large tin of pineapple "chunks"
1 or 2 large tins of other fruits
½ cup brandy or
1 cup sweet vermouth
1 cup honey, preferably dark
2 to 3 cups liquid from fruits
2 sticks whole cinnamon
slivered peel of 1 orange

Drain all the fruit well, and then arrange apricots and plums-grapes-nectarines-or-whatever in a pretty layer on the bottom and sides of a large clear, glass bowl. Pile the pineapple in the center. Pour the brandy or vermouth carefully over all the fruit, and let it stand. Bring the honey, fruit juice, cinnamon, and orange peel to a boil together and let simmer for about ½ an hour or until the peel is tender. Let cool a little and pour gently into the fruit bowl. It should cover the fruits fairly well without seeming soupy, if they have been well drained and then closely packed together.

Let stand in the refrigerator at least six hours; overnight is better. Serve from the bowl, and use large dessert spoons because the juice is so good. A cup of grated coconut can be used in the honey-syrup. Obviously the amount of fruit in the bowl dictates the amount of syrup to be made. If anything accompanies this dish it should be the simplest of small cookies, but nothing is best!

Such a dessert, sweet enough for the Oriental tongue and fresh enough for tired Western palates, might not prove forever to the host who served it that he could count himself a gourmet. But it would prove, at least to his own satisfaction, that he had the making of one in him, and that some day, if he read and cooked and *ate* enough, he might become one. It might prove, that is, that gourmets can indeed be made, not born—if they be born with good taste!

[*House Beautiful*, 1948]

THE GREAT GOOD SENSE
AND COMFORT OF THE FORK SUPPER

ONE OF THE many phenomena peculiar to this one period of this one century, I think, may be what is currently referred to as "the fork supper."

I doubt that my parents would recognize the term, and ten years from now perhaps my children won't. But today, in almost every part of America, it means an evening meal, usually fairly to completely informal, which is served from a buffet table, usually by the guests themselves, and which is eaten standing up or sitting willy-nilly on stairs, the floor or chair-arms, usually in moderate-to-great discomfort.

Fork suppers are irrevocably adapted to our small apartments, small kitchens, and the almost total lack of both servants and proper furnishings for entertaining more than a handful of people, that, whether we like them or not, we must bow to their disadvantages in order to break bread now and then with any number exceeding six of our close friends. Fortunately we are a young and malleable people, as a society, and our manners have improved enormously since the day when any normally virile man hated to balance a plate upon his knee, and any woman of average coquetry shuddered at the thought of flirting on a love seat over baked beans and brown bread, or barbecued spareribs.

I do not know if current authorities on American etiquette have yet laid down many laws for such basically untidy feastings, but I should think the field would be practically limitless. I can think of many very pertinent dicta in my own unwritten primer of the Dos and Don'ts of Dining.

The first, for me, is never to serve anything that must be cut with a knife, or even with a fork, since such an operation is either impossible or highly dangerous.

This perforce narrows the culinary boundaries: no steaks or chops, no sliced meats more than paper thick, no mushrooms bigger than one decent mouthful, no breast of guinea hen. In reverse, it suggests things that can be picked up *nicely*, in the old-fashioned sense of that word: crisply fried small chicken legs (I have always wanted to serve a monumental platter of nothing else, piled like unwrapped wine flasks in an Italian vineyard, the drumsticks all pointing inward), little croquettes, grilled ribs for a very informal supper, and discreet adaptations of a hundred Near East and Middle East tidbits, the kind eaten by Arabs with their fingers, by Chinese with chopsticks.

That, in turn, suggests my second rule: nothing that drips or dribbles should ever enter the picture.

It means no thin sauces and very judiciously served thick ones! It means that if you serve little rolled pancakes (called anything from cannelloni to blintzes) with any kind of filling, the filling should be solid enough and flavorful enough to stay where it belongs and still taste adequate. It means, too, that fried things should be properly drained, and that barbecued or grilled things should not be doused too lavishly with the various juicy bastings which many hosts consider necessary.

The next rule follows easily: plates should be large and easy to hold in one hand—no heavy porcelains—and they should have a well-defined edge or rim to take care of teeterings and swayings.

In the same way, the silver should be light and simple, and the napkins should be large and, of course, never starched. Glasses, stemmed or not, should be short and solid.

There will, of course, be no knives to drop, which leads to the rule about breads: they should be served in neatly manageable forms, small enough to be put on the one plate necessary for each guest. Naturally they should be served buttered.

It is bad enough to have to eat as uncomfortably as most such guests are forced to. They should not be further harassed by a series of dishes which are either too banal or too exotic (creamed sweetbreads in patty-shells versus an East Indian rystaffel). They should, being tired, tense, restless, and/or worried citizens, be given discreetly stimulating and interesting food, the kind that both pleases and nourishes them without demanding a tiresome flow of compliments and the unspoken prospect of future doses of bismuth.

They should be given a limited, rather than extravagant, choice of dishes, but those few in lavish quantity. If you serve sauerkraut and wieners, they should be superlative, and apparently cooked in a magic pot with no bottom. In the same way, if you serve Beluga caviar, it, too, should, like the sauerkraut, appear delightfully, luxuriously inexhaustible.

Another good rule, I regret to say, is to avoid most leafy green salads. They are not only difficult to eat for many people who are forced to tackle them while standing with one foot on the fireplace fender and half an elbow on the piano, but they wilt all too soon, grow watery, and look drably unappetizing. On the other hand, cold mousses, mayonnaises with fresh lobster, and suchlike, and macedoines of fine, freshly cooked vegetables are always both easy to handle and popular.

One I like especially is my own highly unorthodox version of the classical Salade Demi-Deuil, which I call Half-Mourning Salad, More or Less.

Half-Mourning Salad, More or Less

1 medium-size can peeled truffles (about 5–7)
their juice
1 cup dry white wine
5–7 cups diced, boiled potatoes
2 tablespoons mild prepared mustard
salt, black pepper
1 tablespoon strong vinegar or lemon juice
1½ to 2 cups good fresh cream
tender salad greens (Bibb, Oak Leaf, Romaine,
  Garden lettuce)
½ to 1 cup simple French dressing (salt, pepper,
  vinegar, olive oil)

Slice truffles very thin and put with juice into white wine. Soak one hour, or while potatoes are boiling in their jackets. Peel the potatoes when done cut into ¾ inch cubes (or a little smaller). While they cool, make a cream dressing by mixing the mustard, salt, pepper, and vinegar and then gradually adding the cream, stirring steadily. While the potatoes are still tepid, mix them, the dressing, and the truffle-and-wine mixture in a large bowl. Let it stand in a cool place 4–5 hours, stirring up gently once or twice. To serve: tear salad greens into fairly small pieces (1 inch or so), toss at the last minute with the French dressing—just enough to coat the leaves lightly; and then turn out the bowl of salad upon this generous green bed.

When I serve this, I first have cups of hot or chilled consommé according to the season, served from a big tureen and to be drunk without benefit of spoon after or during the presupper cocktails, according to my guests' tastes. I find that more and more people, if given the chance, will gratefully accept a cup of some refreshing broth, rather than a drink—or a *second* drink. Such broths should be clear or at least thin, potent but not highly seasoned, and preferably "lifted" with at least one generous tablespoon of good, dry sherry to each cup. (Another good combination: one part chicken consommé, one part clam juice, one part dry white wine, or any variation on this theme.)

With the Half-Mourning Salad, I will serve something crisp like potato chips—something salty to cut the suavity of the dish itself.

Dessert, after this salad, should not be too creamy or too rich. If it is little fruit tarts, they should be easy to eat with a fork; if it is cheeses, they should be mild to the point of delicacy, so as not to destroy the lurking delight of truffle still upon the tongue.

The coffee should be even stronger and hotter and better than usual, if that is possible. It should, needless to say, be poured, like everything else liquid, into receptacles that are sturdy and squat, and in this case, well behandled—not dainty demitasses to teeter on their saucers and tip onto ladies' laps or into gentlemen's pockets!

And this, to my way of thinking, would make up a very soul-satisfying, even elegant, repast. It would be stimulating (Everyone knows what truffles are *supposed* to do!), and interesting (Very few people slice them as lavishly as tonight!), and good. It would, given common sense and a bit of thoughtfulness for other people's comfort on the hostess' part, even be enjoyable, which is more than can be said of most such crowded cluttered gatherings.

[*House Beautiful*, 1949]

LITTLE MEALS WITH GREAT IMPLICATIONS

IT HAS long been an amusing trick, played by such gastronomical wits as Paul Reboux, for instance, to plan menus for imagined occasions: A May-Day Luncheon for Six Nubile Virgins About To Be Queened, A Light Midnight Supper for Three Stage-door Johnnies and an Actress Called Frankie, or An Intimate Dinner Prepared in the Full of the Moon by an Aging Private Secretary for her Boss.

All such ambiguously labeled meals are, of course, concocted with one end in view, whether on paper or in reality. They must, by their combinations of flavor and color, light and shade, lead to the accomplishment of some desired fact. There is no doubt in my mind that they will, for I believe firmly that hearts as well as heads can be turned through subtle cookery.

This is a frightening thought, for such power, like any other which influences men's actions and emotions, can be most dreadfully misused. Even so, I think we should, if we remember always to respect our weapons, try much more often than we do to sway our guests this way and that, to lead them toward what *we* want, by the food and drink we put before them. Our goals may be very simple. We may want nothing more, on such and such a night, than to see a loved one's taut, sallow face turn smooth and young. We may want only to know that sweet sleep will follow close upon the supper we have made. On the other hand, we may cry for the moon and a new contract at 30 percent annual increase and a three-year option, or something like that. Whatever the goal, I think it can be reached, if a few very practical rules are followed in serving "little meals with great implications," as one knowing modern woman refers to them.

Of course, the main thing is to know very clearly and candidly what you want. Then, once you have decided, you must know something of the people who can most directly help you.

You must, even though you have never met all of the guests who will lunch or dine at your table, find out what you can about them, what they have done in the world, if possible how they look, where they spend most of their time. From there you figure why they have done what they have done, why they have thin faces or fat, white hair or flaming pink with purple undertones, and why they live in New York or Hollywood but, whenever they can, flee with apparent anguish to Bermuda or Palm Springs, as opposed to Atlantic City or La Jolla.

This form of snooping can usually be done without much trouble. If it proves impossible, the only sure course to steer is a completely personal one. Imagine that *you* are the cymbidium orchid grower you want to please, or the home freezer manufacturer, or even the editor of *House Beautiful,* and then plan a menu that *you* would be won by if you were any of these fabulous figures.

Such a personal approach has most often been my own, because of my nature mainly, and because of that very nature I have kept my "little meals with great implications" very simple indeed. The truth is that more often than not my basic simplicity has made me quite unconscious, until much later, that there *were* any great implications in this luncheon or that supper.

I must confess that almost *every* meal I ever plan, cook, and serve (say, between fourteen and seventeen thousand in the past twenty years), is deeply important to me, and an unending challenge to everything I know and feel about eating, about drinking, about the people I have asked to share my knowledge, and most of all about myself. I am undoubtedly very fortunate to be able to say this, for I have almost always cooked for people I liked or respected or loved.

The thought of doing it for ones I do not like is actively sickening to me, and the very few times I have had to entertain such strangers, for professional reasons, I have frightened myself by blacking out, so that the next day I could not remember one single thing about the dinner party, in spite of the compliments paid me, then and later, too. Such self-protection is destructive and dangerous and a stupid waste of precious time, and it should be shunned like the pox—which is why I shun the people who cause it.

I cook for people I like, because I like to, and, if they are strangers when they first come to my table, I make sure beforehand that I stand a reasonable chance of finding them interesting, charming, attractive, stimulating. That is why for me every meal has its own Great Implications, whether it be for my two little daughters tonight, or for my publisher, his unknown wife, and two of their friends who plan to stop here for lunch tomorrow.

Tonight will be cold. Anne and Kennedy and I are making valentines. Kennedy must go to bed first, but I don't want her to feel left out, so on the play table by the fire, on the red and white cloth, I'll put material for one valentine on each of our napkins, blunt scissors beside our soup spoons, and a red geranium sticking out of the paste pot in the center. (This sounds a bit whimsical, but it won't be, for I'll not do it condescendingly, and I'll have as much fun as they.)

While we put together our valentines, we will drink soup slowly from solid little brown casseroles which cannot possibly tip over, and sip cool milk from silver mugs. And for dessert each will eat a heart-shaped open sandwich of dark, moist whole-grain bread, sweet butter, and red currant jelly. Then Kennedy will be falling off her chair, from sleepiness, and I'll put her to bed while Anne remains at the table listening to Burl Ives records. After she and I have cleared the plates away, we'll build one or two more extra fancy valentines together.

It sounds very nice indeed. I look forward to it. I think, quite sincerely, that it has Great Implications—in peacefulness, in shared pleasure, in the gracious eating of good simple food. Perhaps in the unknown but suspected chaos of the future, two women, so small now, may find some old hidden strength in the memory of the supper I plan for their bodies and their souls tonight by the fire.

The soup I will make is a very flexible adaptation of the classical Potage Bonne Femme (of germiny or sorrel). It depends on what herbs I have at hand, what soup stock, and most of all what ages my guests will admit to! Tonight it should more properly be called Potage Bon Enfant.

I will use a rather meager soup stock, less butter than my basic recipe calls for, three eggs instead of four, and top-milk instead of cream, to prevent collie-wobbles in the night, and I will pour it into the bowls over the crusts from the valentine sandwiches, to make it easier for small hands to carry in small spoons to small mouths.

Potage Bonne Femme

3 tablespoons butter
5 good sprigs parsley
4 leaves of green lettuce
1 small onion
1 pint (or less) of sorrel
dash of salt, pepper, grated nutmeg
2 tablespoons flour
2 quarts good veal stock
a little chervil if possible
4 egg yolks
1 cup cream, heated

Melt butter in generous kettle, add finely chopped parsley, lettuce, onion, sorrel, and add seasonings. Cover closely, and let wilt ten minutes without scorching. Add the flour, mix well, and gradually add the boiling stock. Add the chopped chervil if available, cover, and let boil moderately for another ten minutes. Meanwhile beat the egg yolks, gradually add the heated cream, and stir well. Add this liaison to the soup, taking care that it does not boil, and serve at once, either as it is or strained through a fine sieve.

(We like it as it is, but it is of course more elegant, as well as more classically germiny or sorrel, when strained.)

Then tomorrow—tomorrow it will be warm at noon, a good day for lunching in the patio. That always pleases people from the East, especially since mine has no flies, no gusts of dry wind up here in the sagey hills in February, and the sunlight falls slantingly enough now to feel kind.

I have met the publisher twice. Both times I was scared silly, and he was very courteous and warm over the restaurant table, while his brain tried coldly to figure me out. I hear his wife is charming. I feel confident that the man and woman they are bringing with them will be interesting, and probably pleasant. (In other words, I am almost completely ignorant of my guests!)

I shall serve Martinis or sherry and toasted ribbons of coconut, and then with luncheon a gamy rosé from the Santa Cruz mountains in Northern California. It will be slightly chilled. I have found it a reliable friend in such social quandaries. People who think they do not care for wine, or are even afraid of it, enjoy this light "safe" one without mistrust, and the ones who do recognize its goodness are pleased at my serving it to them, especially in the middle of the day.

We will eat a large salad made of about one part of tender watercress leaves to two of tiny fresh spinach hearts, tossed with ¼ pound of fresh grated mushrooms and a plain French dressing containing ½ teaspoonful of good curry powder for one cup of the dressing, instead of pepper. This salad wilts almost as soon as the dressing is added, and should be very cold and crisp when it is put upon the table (and much bigger than you would think necessary because it shrinks). I always chill the bowl, put the dressing in the bottom, add the salad, and mix it at the table.

With it I shall serve something that we have not yet named properly, although they have been a "specialité de la maison" for years. Now and then someone calls them scones, but they are not proper ones. Perhaps cheese crumpets might be more correct.

Cheese Crumpets

2 cups Bisquick or facsimile
1 cup good cream
¾ cup grated Parmesan or other dry cheese
½ cup mixed butter and olive oil

Mix biscuit flour and cream, stir in cheese, and beat lightly. Drop from spoon into melted butter and oil in generous pan, and bake in preheated oven at 450° for about twelve minutes or until lightly brown and done. Serve hot, wrapped in a napkin.

The cheese should be finely grated and *good*. If it is not dry, it will make the dough soggy.

The mixture of butter and olive oil makes a fine golden crust on the bottoms of these rather flat rough-looking "crumpets." People *love* them.

And that is all I shall have, tomorrow. There will be no dessert, but small cups of very fine freshly ground Santos coffee, jewel-brown and tantalizingly fragrant.

My guests have a long and probably hot drive to face when they leave me, and I want them to feel well, and fresh, and alive, not stunned and sleepy. I doubt if they will be hungry before dinnertime, for the salad they will have eaten from generous plates is a very refreshing and nourishing one, and the "crumpets" are rich and satisfying to the point of heaviness, a fine contrast to the dish that goes with them. And if my people do have to stop at Pinon Flats for a hot dog, or at La Quinta for a cup of tea, they will at least be able to wish that I had given them more, instead of cursing me for serving too much!

As for the Great Implications: they may never materialize into the book I hope to write for my publisher, or even the new friends I would like to make, because of the Little Meal I plan for this seduction. But I will have satisfied myself, at least: I will have used all my wits and all my skills to make the lunch tomorrow a pleasant causal one, and one that it is quite possible my somewhat overworked and harried visitors will remember gratefully, next week in New York or even next year anywhere at all.

And then, of course, there is tomorrow night! Now what shall I devise for that? Who will be here? What kinds of humans will we be, gathered together to eat, tomorrow night? And with what mysterious *implications?*

[*House Beautiful*, 1950]

IF THIS WERE MY PLACE

IT IS AS impossible to say what is The Perfect Restaurant as The Perfect Mate. A man will swear he wants women tall and quiet and then fall profoundly in love with a five-foot flibbertigibbet. In the same way, what I am convinced I now want when I eat in public has no connection with where I may blissfully find myself tomorrow, fork in hand.

This is for now, though. This is what I fume about *now*, when I must submit myself to the dubious delights of dining abroad, in a restaurant run for my theoretical pleasure and the owner's possible profit. This is, as well, what seems best, most proper, most thoroughly enjoyable, about the rite of nonprivate nourishment. This is, in brief, what I would want if I were running this place.

I like quiet. I hate a hysterical hubbub, whether it be of voices or of clashed plates. On the other hand, a hush which makes anything more than whispers a social outrage is equally distressing to me—or perhaps more so, because it too often smacks of ostentation and pretense: the fake crystal chandeliers, the gliding muted "captains," of a hinterland Ritz.

Modern soundproofing, strange square pancakes glued to any old kind of walls and ceilings, performs miracles indeed. So, much more expensively, do eager young architects with Ideas: they break up a barn of a place into three or four well-related rooms, seemingly no bigger than cubbyholes, and there you are, sitting cozily before a cut off the joint and a pint of Old-and-Bitter (such reformed mausoleums seem to lean toward the tweedy side, for some reason—or is it the young architects who do?), not quite certain just who is behind you in the rationed dark, nor even who may be coming through the door from the paneled bar, and not caring at all because of the general feeling of intimacy and quiet.

That sounds fine, and so it can be. It can also be oppressively quaint and soundless. You can drink and eat and even try to talk in a kind of superartful vacuum, until finally you wonder if anyone else in the room is still breathing. You begin to feel that everything human about you except your dwindling appetite has been sucked out in a kind of discreet and decorative catharsis, until as a gentle proof that you still live you are handed a synthetic clay churchwarden's pipe, with your name tagged on it, male or even female.

This is, generally, a discouraging ritual, and you are inclined to go to the nearest chili hut the next time you consider risking, with any seriousness, the hazards of such whimsy. I do not like the clay-pipe, rough-brick, crackling-hearth style of modern "restauraterie."

Perhaps one good reason (or rather two reasons) for my innate distrust of such nutritional balderdash is that I *love* the two extremes of American pubs: Joe's All-Nite Diner and the Chambord... la Buvette de la Gare and Foyot's....

I love, as much as diners, the beautifully suave, knowing, experienced restaurants, the kind that perforce can exist only in great cities where desirable women and intelligent worldlings live. The last one I was in, too long ago, gave me great satisfaction, as did the delightful hats of most of the women in it and the flicked cuffs and the child-blue boutonnieres of their escorts. I liked it all... the flames under the gleaming dishes, and the murmur of fluty Easter voices, and the finnan haddie I ate, the best in my life, to lay the ghost of all the bad I had eaten in my childhood.

But such a restaurant must be good, and honest, and real, as well as suave and knowing. There are a dozen places within call of me, this minute, with the appearances of such gastronomical grandeur, but with nothing, nothing at all, to bolster them, beyond the ornate chafing dishes and the eager supercilious stewards and the too hot plates, and all the diners pretending this is almost as good as the real thing. I hate such restaurants even more than I hate the greedy English-inn type of chophouse.

I think now, willy-nilly, of the most dismal restaurant in the American world, to my mind, the small-town coffee shop. I have been in hundreds of them, and I firmly believe that until their windows grow steamy and the waitress lets her hair fall vaguely out of place and the coffee machine sends off little pops of extra steam which the café manager frowns on because of Waste, they are just about the most horrid holes ever invented for such a decent ceremony as that of nourishing our poor tired puzzled bodies.

There are slabs of bad pie behind a piece of smeared plate glass. There are used dishes in a streamlined and doubtless antiseptic sink beneath the counter. There are tables complete with paper napkins in chromed dispensers and with tasteless pepper and medicated salt in inadequate shakers. There are chairs that rattle against the hard sanitary floors. There is, perhaps, canned music from a jukebox, dependent upon desperately cheerful diners or five-cent profligacy of the manager. Such hellholes of gastronomy need a *lot* of steam on the windows, a *very* healthy fine-pated waitress, and a really energetic coffee machine, to make them anything but hell.

It is understandable that many of us, tossed onto the endless roads of this continent, head in our wanderings for the low-brow diners, rather than these so-called coffee shops—the kind Hemingway and many a lesser giant have written about, the long, narrow real-or-imitation railroad cars, warm, bright, easy to enter and leave, redolent of other people's cigarettes and rain-flecked jackets, of coffee and hot soup. Where else can a hungry traveler go, once having spurned the "shops," but to these metamorphosed cars?

I have read almost every guide made available to the general public, I imagine, about American eating places. The memorable meals I have found in small-town hotels I can count only too easily on one hand, although I have traveled fairly widely and have carried with me, along with my normal number of fingers and thumbs, my "curious nose," first asset of even the most amateurish gastronomer.

The guides I have most trusted have led me, almost invariably, to tea-roomy places and, although I myself dislike them I can understand why most travelers prefer their fairly honest regional cooking (hot biscuits, Ladies' Aid desserts, Mrs. Frazee's Famous Chicken Puff) to the alternatives of shoddy Ritz or pool hall. Dietetically they are safe, or at least safer than the steam table Béchamel of one and the iridescent corned beef of the other. Their calories may be high—all that whipped cream on the pecan pie on Thursdays!—but the ptomaine mortality is very low indeed, and their canaries do sing so sweetly, innocent of juke.

Once in a Western state I followed the recommendations of a best-selling gastronomical guide and went to a fantastically dirty hole and ate the best barbecued spareribs of my life. And once in Georgia I obeyed the same mentor and went grudgingly to the local Waldorf, there called the Poinsettia, I think, and was rocked where I sat to have the chef, yes the *chef*, read my order and then send me a glass of properly chilled dry sherry, when I was wondering with understandable grimness if a double Martini would see me through the evening. (He came in later, and we shared a bottle of excellent wine from Maryland under the dusty fly-specked "electroliers").

But such accidents are rare. In general the mobile gourmets of the country have a very tough time indeed. I suffer for them.

I do so vicariously at this period in my life, for I am stationary and at least five hundred miles form the nearest decent eating place. I know that such a statement is blatantly intolerant and unfair. The great Henri Charpentier now runs a little and good restaurant near Redondo Beach—but when I go there I want to sleep in a motel nearby, rather than drive three hundred miles through smog, round trip. There is a place on La Cienega where deft waiters in scarlet coats move in the light from Georgian silver candelabra—but the Yorkshire pudding is burned and lead-heavy. There is an old house in San Juan Capistrano beside the shallow stream where crayfish live—but tacos give me a stomach-ache.

San Francisco, only *five* hundred miles away, has good places for the civilized nourishment of the human body. I can think, this minute, of a dozen, where I could walk in, sit down, and have the ancient Yugoslav waiter snarl amicably at me and then flap across my knees a real napkin, although the prices would indicate paper; where I could order anything I wanted, based on fresh cracked crab, bay shrimps, or lobster; where I could see the man slouch to the big icebox at the end of the dining room and pull out a perfectly chilled bottle of the proper wine.

If I were running this place, *this* place, I'd leave it just as it is, cluttered and fumy and right—right for now, that is: a bottle of cold light white wine, sizzling crab-legs meunière, crisp bread on an ugly thick white plate, and beyond them the fog and the sound of harbor horns. But last week another place was right, a lunch of pure fantasy, of equally fantastic expense and "restauraterie," in a beautifully appointed and beautifully managed and beautifully dishonest Beverly Hills hash house. And far back in my mind is that light high-voiced subtle room in New York, where the champagne and the finnan haddie were so completely right.

If I were running this place, the mythical Perfect Restaurant, I'd try to be honest and fantastic and artful, so that I could serve forth what would be, at a given moment, the essential food, the nourishment most needed in a man's Design for Living.

[*Atlantic Monthly,* 1950]

HONEST IS GOOD

MANY PEOPLE think that gourmets, true connoisseurs of eating and drinking, must possess great wealth. I do not believe this. The wealthy are gourmets, if so, in spite of their riches. It is much easier to eat honestly if one is *poor*, and eats food prepared by cooks who must, at least occasionally, use their wits and their skills rather than the truffles and rare condiments of princely kitchens.

I think now of some of the best meals in my life, and almost without exception they have been so because of the superlative honesty of "poor fare," rather than sophistication. I admire and often even *like* what is now called the Classical Cuisine . . . the intricate sauces of great chefs, and the complexities of their sweets and their pastries. But for strength, both of the body and of the spirit, I turn without hesitation to the simplest cooks. . . .

I remember the best sauce I ever ate.

It was not at Foyot's, in the old days in Paris. It was in a cabin with tar paper walls on a rainswept hillside in Southern California. The air was heavy with the scent of wet sage from outside and the fumes of a cheap kerosene stove within. Three or four children piped for more, more, from the big bowl of steaming gravy in the center of the heavy old round table crowded between the family's cots. We ate it from soup plates, the kind you used to get free with labels from cereal packages. It was made from a couple of young cottontails, and a few pulls of fresh herbs from the underbrush, and spring water and some "Red Ink" from the bottom of Uncle Johnnie's birthday jug . . . and a great deal of love. It was all we had, with cold flapjacks left from breakfast to scoop it up. It was *good*, and I knew that I was indeed fortunate to have driven up the hill that night in the rain and to have friends who would share with me.

I remember the best stew I ever ate, too.

It was not a *bouillabaisse* at Isnard's in Marseille. It was made, further south on the Mediterranean at Cassis, by a very old small woman, for a great lusty batch of relatives and other people she loved. Little grand-nephews dove for equally young octopi and delicate sea eggs, and older sons sent their rowboats silently up the dark *calanques* for rockfish lurking among the sunken German U-boats from the First War, and grizzling cousins brought in from the deep sea a fine catch of rays and other curious scaly monsters. Little girls and their mothers and great-aunts went up into the bone-dry hills for aromatic leaves and blossoms, and on the way home picked up a few bottles of herby wine from the tiny vineyards they worked in the right seasons.

The very old woman cooked and pounded and skinned and ruminated, and at about noon, two days later, we met in her one-room house and spent some twenty more hours, as I remember, eating and eating... and talking and singing and then eating again, from seemingly bottomless pots of the most delicious stew in my whole life. It had been made with love.

And from a beautiful odorous collection of good breads in my life I still taste, in my memory, the *best*.

There have been others that smelled better, or looked better, or cut better, but this one, made by a desolately lonesome Spanish-Greek Jewess for me when I was about five, was the *best*. Perhaps it was the shape. It was baked in pans just like the big ones we used, but tiny, perhaps one by three inches. And it rose just the way ours did, but tinily. (Many years later, when I read *Memoirs of a Midget* and suffered for the difficulties of such a small person's meals, I wished I could have taken to her, from time to time and wrapped in a doll's linen napkin, a fresh loaf from my friend's oven....)

Yes, that was and still is the best bread. It came from the kitchen of a very simple woman, who knew instinctively that she could solace her loneliness by the ritual of honest cooking. It taught me, although I did not understand it then, a prime lesson in survival. I must eat to live; I want to live well; therefore I must eat well. And in these days of spurious and distorted values, the best way to eat is simply, without affectation or adulteration. Given honest flour, pure water, and a good fire, there is really only one more thing needed to make the best bread in the world, fit for the greatest gourmet ever born: and that is honest love.

[*Good Cooking—The Complete Cooking Companion,* 1950]

MADE, WITH LOVE, BY HAND

PERHAPS the most basic form of preparing food for loved people, after breaking an egg, is to bake bread. It is also one of the most therapeutic in a culture increasingly mechanized. The enforced rhythm of natural processes, like fermentation, and the rise and fall, and the time to catch them all, the shaping of the loaves, and then the baking, and then the eating: all this can bring a kind of renaissance to a harried soul. It is a Favorite Prescription.

A telephone will seem relatively worth ignoring if it rings at the worst possible moment for scraping the soft dough off of fingers, wrists, arms. Eyeglasses seem almost unnecessary if they slide down the nose at the same moment. A cigarette can wait.... And there will be a beneficent fatigue, most of which will disappear during the whole process of waiting for the dough to rise, for the loaves then to rise, for the loaves to bake, for them to cool....

By the time one sits down smugly to watch worthy friends break bread together, peace has come, dictated by an inner clock more potent than any pill or portion yet invented by desperate Man. There is serenity, and it does not matter how deliberately it has been wooed, once won. The hands can lie quietly for a time.

Hands, our hands... a man's, a woman's, mine, yours... are made to feed both soul and body. Through their trained skill, music is drawn from wood and ivory and the stretched guts and skins of animals. And when the musician feels love as well as pure *maîtrise*, his hands will sing of it no matter what notes he follows, just as the painter will send passion or gentle innocence through the wooden stick with hairs for its tip onto paper-silk-stone-sailcloth, and the sculptor will hack or pour or mold, according to the life that flows through his fingers.

Hands can give love as well as accept it. They can communicate, and that is said to be a dangerously rare thing in this world. And if it is true, as I believe it to be, that there is a direct ratio between experience and appreciation, then it will also be true that the more one learns how to live through one's hands, the more one lives inwardly.

When I hold an egg lightly in the palm of my hand, there need be nothing but the texture, the shape, going irrefutably, without conscious effort, from my nerve ends up through my arm to my brain, there to be changed at will into sensation, even thought. There need be no muted sounds of drums, flutes, cacklings. I need not sniff the shape to know that it came from some kind of feathered female. I cannot taste it to prove that it exists without destroying it. And surely I need not look at it, for my hand, no matter how calloused, will tell me what I am holding. And in truth, I will know it faster and even more fully if I be blindfolded by God or man, for the sense of touch is plainly heightened without the sight that so often bolsters and dulls it.

Such a moment of what amounts to communication between a human being and an object is ready for almost all of us, and I believe that it can deepen our enjoyment of more outward, obvious touchings.

An egg is perhaps the most primeval of the forms we live with. But there are also things like potatoes. A potato, when picked up and allowed to make itself felt in the hand, is something that makes me smile to think of: sturdy, jolly, a bluff good-natured joke! Or how about the cool weight of a firm young head of cabbage, so promising within its graceful skirts?

To communicate is, in some lexicons, to commune, and that is an act more needed now than perhaps ever before on this planet. And I think it can be done in kitchen as well as in chapel, at the sink or table as well as in the theater or the redwood forest. There can be a withdrawal from strife for a time, a renewal of one's reserves of self-control, a facing of one's faults and their remedies, whether one kneels in a sanctuary or contemplates three eggplants and five tomatoes on a table in a quiet kitchen.

The eggplants will be peeled rhythmically, placed thus and so. They are beautiful, like cool satin dyed for an ancient emperor's favorite lady.

The tomatoes, too, are regal, smooth in a different way, more overtly filled with seeds to promise a surer future. They are full to bursting with the silent vivid needs of summer harvest. Sliced, they lie in a kind of familiarity over the more discreet fertility of the other vegetables. And the hands that have wordlessly used them have grown less tense and hurried in the silence of the pungent air. There has been a form of communing. Withdrawal from tactile activity used to be a status symbol. The more fragile and unawakened the fingertips, the more servants were there to protect them from even a touch of common life....By now, people who once might have lived this way are forced, willy-nilly, to sweep their own weekend hideaways and beat their own pancake batter. They go to expensive and generally entertaining cooking classes to learn how to make an omelet, and a gentleman-chef has told me that the first and hardest lesson in his very successful school is to force his students to break several eggs into a bowl, thumb each half-shell, and then squeeze the yokes and whites together into a proper mixture for what he and even I would call *oeufs brouillis*, first step toward culinary stardom.

Once the newcomers have overcome their conditioned repugnance to getting their hands "dirty," they will tackle sticky dough up to the elbows, sinksful of spinach to be washed leaf by leaf, and, through the new knowledge in their hands, they will find a way to commune, in peace.

Hands must be used everywhere in life, if it be real and full of love. One of the quickest ways, and the most direct, is in preparing food to be shared.

[*McCall's*, 1971]

LEARN TO TOUCH ... TO SMELL ... TO TASTE

THE QUESTION is simple: why do many American women seem to dislike to taste-feel-smell things?

I am often asked this, and I am an American woman. It makes me wonder, because I myself do not shun such sensual involvement and identification, but rather seek it out.

Usually people refer to *food,* and cooking and eating it, when they talk with me, because they know that I am interested in its intrinsic part in human love. They are speaking about the physical nourishment of their associates and companions and dear ones and, of course, of their own.

I think one of the reasons many women, my compatriots, shun contact with food as such is that they continue to try to live like eighteenth-century aristocrats when actually most of them have no servants and no decent human substitutes and therefore must pretend to be helpless. They call in caterers, for even four guests. They go regularly to restaurants where they have established a rapport with the headwaiter. And they must be on diets. (The logic for this rule is that diets eliminate such bothersome things as getting breakfast, and even lunch if one can skip board meetings and suchlike.)

Thus there is no need to cope with anything but occasional contact with such realities, all done by telephone, as fresh vegetables, ribboned beef, plums pearly from the tree. All these can be found, even in a megalopolis; but it is true that many Americans choose to stay away from them, whether they know it or not, because of the sensual thrust of their obvious existence, the honest call to impulses that ladies have been taught to keep at bay. And food must be cleaned, washed, peeled, stored. (So what about all the messy nastiness of it, and getting one's fingernails into a ripe tomato, and having to skin things, for God's sake? And then all that juice and mucking around with spices and Burt's special low-cholesterol butter substitute, and then the *cleaning up*.)

I know of one of my peers who got rid of her whole *batterie de cuisine*, a fantastic and beautiful supply of every pot and pan and skillet for a good kitchen, because the utensils had handles that were not recommended for her electric dishwasher.

And I know another woman, know her well enough for the two-cheeks salute anyway, who derides and even grows shrill about any given page from Julia Child's modern kitchen lexicon, because once she followed directions and used twenty-seven utensils for one dish! The result was superb, she admits, but not worth losing a slob of a cleaning woman who quit *flat out* when she saw the kitchen the next morning (typical of Modern Domestics, and also of Lady Cooks).

There is a prettier side to the coin, though, and many American women who would in other days have had their own chefs and their own staffs of trained servants now enjoy, and consciously and deliberately, an intelligent participation in practicing the arts of the kitchen and table.

And there is an increasing number of women who indulge earnestly in baking bread weekly for their families and friends. Some of the results are pitiable (or at least Old Testament); but by the time a loaf has been sliced (or sawed or hacked through), any honest woman is so blandly proud and relaxed that its inedibility cannot really matter. The atavistic magic of kneading and waiting and finally producing has taken place again, and more than one interesting nugget of soy/rye/wheat germ/blackstrap-molasses has been conceived, no matter how innocently, on an analyst's couch, with canny approval from the doctor.

An elderly friend who had not touched hand to kitchen bowl for several decades told me that when she tried to make an old-fashioned Viennese Twist for a grandson who was threatening to resign from the family because it had lost all its traditions, she lost three rings in the dough and had to send them to the local Tiffany's to be cleaned, once they had been dug out. It was a bore, she said, and went back to her neighborhood bakery.

This sounds nonsensical, but it proves that there must be some basic rapport between the materials and the user of them. If a woman is willing to plunge her clean bare hands in a sticky floury mess, it is because *she knows why*. She does not dibble and dabble. That is impossible in the making of honest food.

A master chef I know, who gives cooking classes for the classiest of dames, says that he has had to develop a brutally subtle technique, from his word "Go!" at the first lesson, to make his ladies touch anything but the outer edges of an egg. (First he strips them of their rings and bracelets and suchlike and sniffs sadistically if their nails are too long.) They conquer the trick of actually breaking an egg into a bowl, their fingers pulling back from the cracked sides like the outraged petals of a sea anemone. Then he orders blandly that they "thumb" the empty shells to push out any clinging albumen. They shriek or moan, drop what they are holding, have to fish it up from the bowl.

Gradually they obey: the lessons cost a fortune and they have promised to learn how to make an omelet even if it means two boring trips a week, all winter, to the other end of town.... And once they have cracked ten eggs into each bowl, gradually falling into a comparatively giddy rhythm about the whole revolting caper, they find that they have to make a smooth mixture of the yolks and whites, *by hand*.

Some either leave the room never to return or leave and come back in a few minutes, tight-lipped, and worth their salt. And my friend the master chef says that once this has happened, the rest is plain and even wonderful sailing. Beautiful omelets flip casually through the air and land where they should... and *then* comes the first plunge into gluey bread dough, and gradually the fingers so long conditioned to hate sticky and slippery and generally "nasty" textures understand the satin of a fresh mushroom and the velvet of a peach.

It seems strange that all this has to be taught. It should come from a natural awareness. But our culture is increasingly unnatural. We have been pushed out of focus, and it is often costly and painful to get in again... not only in special classes called cookery and college courses called sensitivity therapy but personally, *alone*.

And I believe that through touch, or perhaps because of its agents, other senses regain their first strengths. A broken egg has its own perfume when it is fresh, and of course, like all decadent matter, its stench when it is rotten. Only a few animals, and then at certain times in their lives, choose to eat carrion willingly ("high" game for the more sophisticated of the Hunting Set... a long-dead seal for an equally fastidious pair of Great Danes on a remote Pacific beach...). By nature none of us likes to become involved in the touch-taste-smell of anything that has faded or wilted or gone sour...gone plain *bad*.

But there, too, is the other side of the coin! Newness, which in all sane entities means freshness, is irresistible if we ourselves are even hopefully healthy and have still kept our human wits about us. A new fine baby smells good. So does a basketful of Bibb lettuce. Of course, one is edible and one is not, but at least they are *there*, to touch most respectfully and, in my own case with a good child, to nibble with infinite tenderness, the back of the neck, perhaps, or the tip of a finger. Lettuces are perhaps more vulnerable, being more fleeting; but they, too, should be treated with delicate care.

And as for smell, Lukas' will be different from John's, just as Bibb from a Kentucky farm will smell different, more pungent, from any grown in a sun-box in Southern California. Lukas will have a firm feel, like hand-spun Indian cotton; and John will be like damask woven in Lyons two hundred years ago, refined and still strong. And just as the two new people have different textures, so will the lettuces born of the same seed.

Day before yesterday, at least as time now flies, I read a review of a theatrical evening, a great success in New York as well as in Los Angeles. It was mostly about touch therapy. The critic wrote at length of the various kinds of "release" it gave him and said it was definitely "inspired by a non-ideological, non-theological yearning for transcendence."

This may be true. It had not occurred to me that I might seek and find transcendence in a dark room filled with strangers. All I know now is that I am pleased that a lot of my sisters, of every age, are relearning part of the art of life by touching an egg yolk, smelling a fresh lettuce leaf or berry, tasting either the product of their own hands, such as a fresh loaf of bread, or a fresh body. This may be the answer to more than one question.

[*Vogue*, 1972]

HOW VICTORIA SET THE AMERICAN TABLE

IT ALL HAPPENED here in the nineteenth century, and perhaps one of the most important influences was the reign of Queen Victoria, who never set foot on our soil. The millions of American women who slavishly and often unwittingly followed her example of dutiful wifehood were not even her subjects, but every aspect of their lives, from their ample and rigidly corseted waistlines to their religious principles, was organized as much as possible in imitation of the Queen.

Of course, there were other elements to be absorbed into our national pattern. Countless refugees from war, disease and famine in Europe flowed in a mounting tide toward America, past its eastern shores and westward to the rich prairie. The Civil War split the country bloodily, and after it a new opulence sent the first wave of settlers back to buy Italian paintings and French rugs and gaudy Germanic furnishings for the parvenu marble palaces. Blondin, a tightrope walker from Paris, ate an omelet high above Niagara Falls. The transcontinental railway was built, with a resultant breed of iron and steel tycoons, and thousands of Chinese laborers stayed on in the Far West, drinking tea and playing fantan. Mary Cassatt went to Paris to learn more about painting; Harriet Beecher Stowe stayed home and wrote *Uncle Tom's Cabin;* Carrie Nation was appointed by God to destroy the saloon with her hatchet. (There were also some strong men: Mr. Lincoln, for instance.)

And through it all, American womanhood stayed mainly in the kitchen, the church and the bedroom, blandly grateful for this appointed lot. Examples were held up constantly, to dispel any evil vapors of revolt such as affected a tiny and powerful scattering of females like Susan B. Anthony and Lucy Stone. Sermons taught, in discreet terms, all the beauties of a good wife—and what better example was there than Victoria Regina, whose home life was always described as "a marvel of domestic felicity" and who always found time to supervise her own staff of kitchen servants at Windsor Castle?

The kitchen, humble or rich, was a prime target of this decorous insistence upon the duties of a good woman. It was, indeed, a favorite subject of the popular art of the time, as is amply demonstrated in the panoramic show, "The Painters' America, Rural and Urban Life, 1810–1910," which opens Wednesday at the Whitney Museum. Throughout the century, management of the kitchen was considered worthy of dedicated study on both sides of the Atlantic.

Her Majesty's French?—Italian? English? chef, Charles Edmé Francatelli, wrote *The Modern Cook* in 1846, and it sold almost as well in America as in England. Few kitchens here could follow all its directions for the light Gallic dainties Francatelli introduced to counteract the basic heaviness of royal dining habits, but gradually his style of making two courses of a meal, with a predominance of sweet dishes in the second, was adapted by our housekeepers to shape the way we now eat lunch and dinner.

In the Queen's menus, there were often three soups, three fishes, a kind of savory (for instance, marrow patties with a *fines-herbes* sauce), four meat dishes and eight entrees in the first course, all served at once. In the second there were three roasts and poultry and game, three sweet desserts, two more side desserts of pastry, and twelve *entremets*, including vegetables, aspics and fruit tartlets.

At Windsor Castle Francatelli, and then the royal chefs who followed him during Victoria's long reign, had at least two Yeomen of the Kitchen and twenty-four assistant chefs to prepare these meals, and then, of course, all kinds of servers and lackeys were involved in washing, table-setting, serving and clearing away. Nonetheless, American housewives as far west as Iowa and then beyond, helped by one or two immigrant servants, read *The Modern Cook* and its lesser imitators and gradually changed the accustomed pattern of one long hodge-podge of dishes served together, even in a plain Family Meal, to two courses, with sweets alone finally constituting the second course. This might consist of two kinds of pies or tarts, a cool pudding, a jelly and a tall layered cake, but at least these did not appear side by side with roast pigeons, asparagus soup and a haunch of venison flanked by boiled vegetables.

Mrs. Isabella Beeton, perhaps the epitome of all intelligent, loving, child-bearing Victorian housewives, published her *Book of Household Management* in England in 1861, and for the first time Anglo-Saxon females were addressed as peers of that peerless lady. They were told how much meals would and should cost, as well as how to train an illiterate kitchen maid or treat a sickly child. Immediately American women took to their hearts Mrs. Beeton's personal example as well as her recipes for "Mashed Turnips" and "Marmalade and Vermicelli Pudding." Similar books by Yankee writers like Marion Harland and Miss Parloa sold as well in Kansas City as they did in Philadelphia.

Mrs. Beeton favored the fairly newfangled "Russian" style of serving three or four separate courses, even at Family Meals, but in this country the fashion of two main presentations of dishes favored by the kitchens at Windsor Castle was followed loyally, no matter whose recipes were being consulted nor how simplified the menu. What was good enough for the Queen was good enough (even one hundred years later!) for her politically estranged and far-flung daughters. By now we may eat a soup or salad, but always an entree and then a dessert in the most simple as well as formal meal: a decorous compromise with Mrs. Beeton and Mrs. Harland, and a firm pledge of allegiance to Victoria herself.

In spite of the millions of immigrants who arrived in this Promised Land during the nineteenth century, their own culinary habits had small effect, for many decades, on the firmly based "English" customs of the earlier settlers. It is only in this century that we have begun to exercise our gastronomical tolerance, so that people in Cleveland know the cuisines brought to the Far West by the Chinese and the Spaniards, and in Oregon and Vermont they know the peculiar combination of German and Mexican cooking called Tex-Mex in the Southwest. Gradually, Italian, French, Swiss and Scandinavian cooking patterns have become a part of our whole kitchen, supplementing the good old Anglican scheme of meat, potatoes, gravy and apple pie. Who now winces at the term *hors d'oeuvre* or looks blank about hibachi dinners or plett-pans? But my grandmother would have been lost in this new lingo, just as she would have been helpless without an unlimited supply of household domestics and a guiding glance each morning, after the Bible, at her trusted receipt books.

Of course, I had three other middle-class grandparents, all of them descended from several American-born generations, but for me my grandmother's childhood flight from County Tyrone to Pittsburgh lent a special romantic aura to her most Puritanical acts. She was a little different from her hundreds of thousands of fellow refugees in that she was literate. In spite of the fact that her father fled Ireland with a price on his head for composing broadsides against the Queen, she persisted to her last days in emulating Victoria in all the touted virtues of that lady.

My grandmother now seems an archetype of her century in America, gastronomically and in almost every other way. First, she was an immigrant. For most of the Civil War she was caught below the Mason-Dixon Line, where she worked as governess to the children on a rich plantation and knew what near starvation meant. Several of her bright younger brothers became tycoons in Pittsburgh with the booming railroads and industries of the postwar period, but she and her husband fled the "crowded" East for the prairies in a wagon loaded with books. It is said in our family that the young wife forded the Missouri River with a crock of yeast-starter between her knees, which would traditionally qualify her as a pioneer.

She did not like foreigners, which meant people of creed and color different from her own; throughout her life she preferred to deal indirectly with the Indians through her church missionary circles (in which she was nobly energetic), no matter how closely she was surrounded by her beneficiaries. She, of course, did not see Blondin as he teetered over Niagara Falls in 1859, and she probably skipped with a frown the reports of these "foreign antics" in *Blackwood's Magazine,* which was delivered by Pony Express to her outpost in Iowa, more or less on time, depending on the mood of the Indians. It is not known if she ever heard of Mary Cassatt, but of course she read *Uncle Tom's Cabin,* mostly because of the eminently Christian and genteel background of the writer. And naturally she knew about Mr. Lincoln, who during the Civil War had employed the man who later became her betrothed as a surveyor, in territories comfortably distant from battle.

In her home, Grandmother was the same admirable middle-class queen as Victoria at Windsor. As far as is known, adverse words about her husband never passed her lips, and while she was not subjected to as early a widowhood as her model, she spent it regally in a kind of self-immolation, bereft but Christian, noted and respected by all beholders. Both women bore nine children, although the rigors of court life seemed more merciful than those of the Western prairies, and Grandmother saw only five live to maturity.

Victoria did not approve of loose talk, especially when induced by alcohol, and neither did my grandmother. Both women frowned on spirits in the home. It was culturally and politically necessary to serve them at Windsor, with comparative stinginess and only a perfunctory lingering of the port, but at the Iowa table wines never showed their faces, and the known fact that Grandmother's revered husband kept a generously full decanter in his sanctum sanctorum was a lasting grievance to her teetotaler's spirit, little though she let it show in her ladylike stoicism. He was a gentleman, and all ladies know that gentlemen have physical needs that must be satisfied.

So here was this true product of her time, and the effects of her culinary discipline still affect my own manners at the stove and table or rather they still shape my revolt against my grandmother's gastronomical rules.

Apparently Victoria believed that "household management" was based on the stern curbing of all low animal instincts, so that kindly guidance away from them was both indicated and desirable. Francatelli and his successors managed to supply the Queen's courtiers with sufficiently spiced and indigestible dishes, but any ordinary kitchen manual of that period, whether published in London or Chicago, will accentuate little seasoning, long cooking and an almost parsimonious hand with the butter. Good Victorian ladies saw to it that their immigrant kitchen help skimped on salt as well as fat, served clean gravies instead of fancy "Frenchified" sauces and simple steamed puddings instead of soufflés. A forthright style of cooking, based somewhat indirectly on revolt from the Old World extravagances and from the elaborate dicta of famous male chefs, emerged gradually in the American Middle West. It was ample, with no frills.

As a newcomer to the state of Iowa, my grandmother learned to make Indian corn a staple part of her diet, and I remember that she talked nostalgically of how much better it was when she first learned to parch it for winter cooking. It had to be so dry that it would need two days of soaking before it could be boiled for hours into a kind of stew. Later in her life somebody sent her a little sack of corn from the state she had left for California, and it was prepared according to strict directions—and even she admitted that it was a gritty mess, not worth the bother.

I doubt that my grandmother knew much about the starved, scurvy-weakened Pilgrims who founded New England. Or that they took what was probably the first step in this country's gastronomical history when they learned from benevolent Indians the trick of planting grains of corn, four to a hill, with a dead fish alongside for fertilizer. It is said that, in honor of their Indian guests at the first Thanksgiving dinner, they served succotash (m'sickquatash), a thick porridge of fresh corn cut from the cob, kidney beans, bear grease and probably nuggets of dog meat, a recipe that the settlers had gladly followed.

By the time my grandmother was including the dish in her menus, it had been bowdlerized by the Victorians, as neatly as were many other masterpieces, into a lengthily cooked stew. Marion Harland's recipe is probably the most appetizing to be found in the standard cookbooks of that period and is still one that my taste buds tell me was served in about 1920 as well as in the 1870s. It called for slightly more cut kernels than lima or string beans, all simmered together—in enough water to cover—for half an hour "or until tender." Then the pottage was drained, milk was added, and it was stirred for another hour or so. Butter, flour stirred in more milk, and salt and pepper were added. When the mixture had thickened, the cook was told: "Boil up once, and put into a deep vegetable dish."

It seems odd that I can remember this flabby mess with something of nostalgia. Perhaps it is because I knew even so long ago that it was completely American, and that it *could* be delicious, prepared somewhat differently. The one recipe for succotash I have turned up that duplicates in any way the original with the dog-meat ingredient is from Martha's Vineyard; it substitutes a piece of salt pork and calls for butter. The pork is simmered in water before the beans and finally the cut corn are added; then it is discarded before serving, which seems a merciful precaution. I prefer my own emasculated version of all this, eliminating the Victorian hours of simmering and stirring. Here it is, with a respectful salute to both Chief Massasoit of what was to be called Plymouth, and to the shades of many well-fed ladies like my grandmother.

Twentieth-Century Succotash

2 cups fresh small lima beans
1 scant cup water
2 cups young green corn cut from cob
½ cup rich cream
3–4 tablespoons sweet butter
salt
freshly ground pepper

Boil beans, covered, in water until barely tender. Add green corn, cover, and shake well at high heat for perhaps five minutes. Add cream, shake, then butter. Shake, add seasoning, and serve.

This should be almost crisp, and rich but not soupy. Frozen baby limas and canned baby corn can be substituted, but with much less interesting results. However, they are edible.

Hail, Chief Massasoit! Hail, regal Grandmother! Hail, all other Yanks!

[*The New York Times Magazine*, 1974]

SHELF LIFE

MY KITCHEN LIBRARY must of necessity fill not more than twenty-four inches on one shelf. For a long time I resented this. The new books were so handsome, in their giddy jackets. The French collections were so quaint, and the old blue and gold copies of such things as *The Compleat Household and Unedited Ladies' Companion* looked so funny and so nice there on my shelf, that for a long time I refused to admit their uselessness.

I piled them sideways to gain space, and even put the tallest ones in a sneak-row at the back. It was untidy, and very inconvenient, and I finally had to admit that the books I was keeping for sentiment or past amusement were not only hindering my use of the more important ones, but were never opened.

I made a rule, then, which I have kept in spite of occasional regret: I move to another part of the room any book which I find I am not opening at least occasionally, for actual use.

At first it was hard. I hesitated a long time before I gave up the old dirty copybook my mother had found once in a midwestern kitchen. Then I made myself admit that its fine Spencerian writing was almost as faded as the blue space-lines, and much less practical. I put it from me. And then I took away from that special Shelf an 1890 edition of Marion Harland kept for its amazing pictures of dinner rolls tied with rosebuds and ribbons, *and* the 1813 edition of John Simpson ("Roast meat if not well salted would eat insipid," he observed solemnly), *and The Closet of Sir Kenelm Digby, Knight* ("My Lady Middlesex makes sillabubs for little glasses with spouts..."), *and*...

My Shelf was tidier, and much easier to use. With some stern self-discipline I've kept it that way, even after birthdays and such.

Sometimes the books I've put out have been new ones. Sometimes, to my surprise, I find that one of the old standbys has been pushed gradually down to the wrong end of the Shelf. And since I always put the last book I read at the right end, it is damning proof of uselessness if even an old favorite stays very long at the left. Out it goes.

In every family there is this one Shelf, where a certain cookbook stays there as long as the woman of the house goes near a kitchen, whether to cook or merely to snoop around a bit on the cook's day out. In my own case it was for a long time *Mrs. Simon Kander's Settlement Cook Book: "The Way to a Man's Heart,"* not only because I thought it was good but because my mother started housekeeping with it and gave a copy automatically to every bride she knew.

I used it for many years and although I added more spice than it advised, and substituted butter for its goose grease, and read about "Aufleuf" and "Dimpes Dampes" without ever making them, I felt that it was an excellent basic book for American kitchens, and I still do. Other people feel the same way about any of a dozen well-known classics, like Fanny Farmer's, or Mrs. Rorer's, or those of other regional literary goddesses.

Of course for a long time Mrs. William Vaughn Moody's *Cook Book* seemed essential to me. When I first got it I thought it would be one of those charming, faintly precious books which are pleasant to read but useless. I still think that some of its recipes are decidedly la-di-da, like the one which says peremptorily, "Reduce the quart of cream to a pint...." But Mrs. Moody is still well worth the space she once occupied on my special Shelf, as when she writes, "And what about the hen, notably of Bourg? Is it her diet that makes her so surpass all other hens? So handsome! So seductive! I knew a man once, and an army officer at that, who fed the hens for his own table on ice cream...." In other words, her recipes are, in spite of their somewhat literary costliness, among the best I have ever used.

Mrs. Moody has old-fashioned ones like "Ammonia Cookies," and extravagant ones like "Sweetbreads de Conier," and downright exotic ones like her rule for *bortsch*, which Russians both high and low have told me is the finest they have ever eaten.

Another book which was for many years always near the right end of my Shelf was my small, dark green, spotted copy of the 1873 edition of Marion Harland's *Common Sense in the Household: A Manual of Practical Housewifery.* It is now in a big section called Americana in the bookcase at the other end of the kitchen. My grandmother's brother gave it to her, newly married, and wrote solemnly on the flyleaf that is by now almost a saffron color, "Improve each shining hour."

And when this book by Mrs. Harland, then a leading novelist in America, first came out, a reviewer said of it, "The very best, the most sensible, the most practical, the most honest book on this matter of getting up good dinners, and living in a decent Christian way, that has yet found its way in our household." Such wide praise is rather startling, today when Christianity is not necessarily considered a part of household gastronomy, until you read the book. Then its chapters, from the first one, "Familiar Talk with my Fellow-Housekeeper and Reader," to the last, "Sundries," which begins, "Boil a double handful of hay or grass in a new iron pot," show themselves truly filled with wisdom, charity, and wit. It is, besides, a most entertaining book to read. The counsels about overeating and desirable daintiness in manners are quite blandly followed by such things as "Company" instructions, in which Mrs. Harland says, "Soup should be sent up accompanied only by bread, and by such sauce as may be fashionable or suitable.... It is not customary to offer a second plateful. When the table is cleared, the fish should come in, with potatoes: no other vegetables, unless it be a salad or stewed tomatoes. Fish is usually attended by pickles and sauces. After a thorough change of plates, etc., *come the substantials.* (The italics are mine.) Game and other meats are often set on together, unless the dinner is a very formal one. Various vegetables are passed.... Pastry is the first relay of dessert, and puddings may be served from the other end of the table. Next appear creams, jellies, charlotte russes, cakes, and the like; then fruit and nuts; lastly coffee, often accompanied with crackers and cheese. Wine," Mrs. Harland adds reluctantly, since she professed to believe that alcoholic drinks were good only to cure such things as scurvy, "wine, of course, goes around during the dessert, *if it flows at all.*" (These italics are mine too, needless to say.)

Such passages have long since made me careful not to open *Common Sense* when in a hurry, since it is so hard to close it again. In spite of its strange antiquated air, though, it is full of good sensible recipes, some of them starred to show approval...and one, written in the back, in my grandmother's beautiful hand, which starts out, "Knox Ginger Cakes... not fit to eat!!!"

By now, I myself honestly think that my personal kitchen bible is *The Joy of Cooking* by Irma Rombauer and her daughter! This violent change happened as abruptly as my third marriage, at exactly the same time, and is one of the most important results of that brief interlude. In fact, the two girls who were the other results are obviously quite willing to share honors with this book, and are as proud as I am to acknowledge their debt to Donald Friede, their father and my husband and a well-known wolf, who made me promise even before our marriage that I would not admit to any authority but his and Mrs. Rombauer's culinary as well as any other way. In fact, by now each of the two daughters has her own well-worn copy of my household bible, and we three women are proud to bow to both Donald and Irma.

Another book that for a long time stayed well to the right end of the Shelf was Henry Low's *Cook at Home in Chinese*. It is now out on the front porch, with many other minor masterpieces of Oriental cookery. It still seems practical as well as exotic, and for the most part all the rules are easy to follow, given a small supply of such commonplace ingredients as gourmet powder and soy sauce. "Sy Wu Yu" and "Hor Lan Dow Gai" turn out to be sea bass with vegetables and chicken with peas, but as delicious as you have ever dreamed of. Of course recipes for dried squid and "Sweet and Pungent Snails" might not be universally appreciated, but who could resist the surrealist tone to the direction: "Hack chicken gizzards (not through) crisscross, then cut in half. This will make them look like flowers"?

And there are always pamphlets. One, for instance, used to be, and probably still is, about wines: the hows, the whys, and whens. The first one I remember was from the Wine Institute in San Francisco. It had excellent simple rules for things like *zabaglione* and fish chowder and such. And there is usually a solid little booklet sent from the South or even California to advertise rice. Another may be put out by a baking powder company, and there is always another good one from some such unlikely source as an artificial piecrust factory, or the supplier of a ghastly powdered cake mix or pudding company. And then there is a calendar given to faithful subscribers by a gas company in Lausanne in

Switzerland, and one sent free from Boston with a set of baking dishes. In each of these there is at least one honest-to-god reason for its being there on the Shelf. And like almost every cookbook written, there is one jewel shining there alone in its toadlike head. The only problem is to find it, cut it out, and discard the rest. And meanwhile, they do pile up.

In the old days I kept two copies of Brillat-Savarin's *The Physiology of Taste* on the Shelf.

It seems silly, or even affected, ever to have kept two of them. I doubt if I looked at either more than once a month. But I liked to have them where I could see them and reach out for them: like everyone who has read *The Physiology*, I feel that it is the perfect antidote for gastronomical fatigue. It is a book about eating which never becomes gross. It is fresh, witty, and all the required rare virtues of good living are a part of it. (And I can say this as blandly today as when I first read B-S, although by now I've written my own translation of him, and for a time longer can consider it the best, *so far. . . .*)

One of my copies, bound in black calf and rich marbled boards, was printed in Paris in 1870. At the back are two long poems, "Las Gastronomie" by Berchoux, and Colnet's "L'Art de Diner en Ville." They are pompous, windy, and delightful, especially when they are read in the ringing accents of an aged member of the Comedie Francaise, which I am, now and then, alone in my kitchen, with the doors shut.

The other copy is the one I would keep if I had to choose. It is smaller, printed in Paris in 1838, and very ugly, maroon, blue, and blotched inside like an old man's cheek. But it has a good smell, a good feel, and whenever I find myself bored or cross or stuffy, I read a little from it and am well. And of course, both these copies have long since been taken from the Shelf and put at the far end of the room, alongside several other editions of this little masterpiece, including my own! The Shelf must be practical and therefore kept within its prescribed two-foot length.

And then, of course, at least three of those twenty-four inches are taken up by the card index, made of sturdy tin and sent for one dollar by a "home magazine" many years ago. It holds the lees, the rare sediment of all my small kitchen learning. It holds newspaper clippings, letters written by haughty Austrians about *Bischopsbrot*, the world's finest rule for cheese *soufflé* scrawled in purple ink by a French confectioner, my own discoveries set down hastily on paper towels and the edges of old vegetable bags.

It is one of those things that I swear I'll keep more tidily and never get around to doing. But even now in spite of its terrible confusion, I know exactly where to put my hand on "Edith's Gingerbread" (which one day will be correctly under *Cakes* but is now, for some strange reason, at the back of *Soups* and in front of *Pickles*). And if I reach now for it and it is not there, I know that some other fool has tried to put order in my own private chaos.

The books I have taken off this short Shelf continue to be a source of amusement and fun, but always now at the other end of the room ... the other end of any room at all, either actual or spiritual. And the better I know this and admit it, the easier it is for me to keep within the two feet allotted to the essential bibles of my home kitchen. In fact, there are only a few books I really read now. I have two volumes of Julia Child's *Mastering the Art of French Cookery*, which seem to be nearer the left end of the row as time passes. Actually, I use only one small section of Volume II, under "Z": I can never remember how to make correctly a "Zucchini Tian," and unless I look up the true way in Mrs. Child's masterpiece, mine is gooey, or gummy, or watery, and always a bit messier than it should be. "Do as Julia says," I *always* say, "and you cannot go wrong." (I could add an ominous "otherwise" to this dictum!)

I must admit that even Volume I of this modern kitchen bible is often found drifting a bit to the left. The truth is that I am surer if Julia is to hand. What she says is infallible. My grandmother used to say, "When in doubt, consult the dictionary." And when I'm not sure about timing or amounts or methods, I can always consult Mrs. Child as long as she's there on the Shelf.

Probably *The Joy of Cooking* is the one most often at the far right. And somewhere near it and Mrs. Child are two books of my own, mostly because they have many family tried-and-trues in them, so that instead of fumbling through the messy card index, I simply turn to page so-and-so in *Serve It Forth* or *With Bold Knife and Fork*, if my own memory fails me.

Then there are two or three books from *Sunset* magazine for things like "Fiesta Bread" and good straight Italian as well as Mexican and Hawaiian recipes. There is the usual clutter of absolutely essential pamphlets seldom consulted and eminently discardable in general, and then there is a big thing at the very end that I know I should look at. I have known this for at least thirty years. It takes up at least two and a half inches of the valuable space. It contains the essence of a lifetime of wonderful food lived by one of my sisters, who never enjoyed eating herself, but kept us all beautifully fed, and I keep looking at it and putting off doing anything more, although I know that there are at least two shatteringly good books in it that I myself could and should write...that I could and should have written thirty years ago, or even last week. And there it sits, probably unknown forever except that I admit that it acts like a continual thorn under my saddle blanket...a kind of pleasant, horrible, itching little goad.

I know that no matter how short my Shelf may grow as I lean less upon the advice of others, this ugly old manila folder will stay there at the left end of it. And no matter how the right end of the Shelf fattens and/or withers with the advent of new kitchen bibles of temporary importance, the dirty old metal card file and then the manila folder are forever essential. This probably proves that absolutely no book or culinary instruction is essential to us as long as we can nourish ourselves.

[*San Francisco Review of Books,* 1989]

FOOD, WINE, AND OTHER POTABLES

THROUGH A GLASS DARKLY

WINE, like most other products of the land, has gone to war: into the making of tartrates for munitions, ethyl alcohol for smokeless powder and synthetic rubber, vital chemicals for rayon and for medicines. Hundreds of tank cars have been released voluntarily for government use. Distilleries have been converted to the production of nondrinkable liquids. There has been a drop of about 40 percent in crushed grapes in the past three years. And men whose fathers once spoke French, Bohemian, Hungarian—every wine-mellowed tongue—have left their vines for battle.

Because of these things, most of the vintners of any repute are rationing themselves. They may be producing as much as before, because of good "years," but they are holding on to as much as 60 percent of their stocks, except for minimum deliveries to keep their names alive, and are paying more attention to the intricacies of developing and aging their fine wines.

This policy, farsighted and probably good, reduces most merchants to a state of helpless exasperation: they turn away hundreds of customers with the somewhat comfortless assurance that at least they can satisfy ten or fifteen. And for every fifteen, several dozen more, no matter how thirsty, remember from the skillful national advertising on the air and in the magazines that this or that wine, such and such a sherry or brandy, is *the* one to ask for when the war is over.

There are several reasons why what wine we are now able to buy costs so much more than it should, so much more than it must if it is ever to become a part of our national diet and normal living instead of something saved for weddings and wakes. Many of these reasons can, according to the style of the times, be blamed in one way or another on the OPA.

There seems to be a state of mutual confusion between the Administration and the growers, in spite of numerous conferences. The one bald fact to emerge is that, although a 1943 ceiling for retail wines was based on the price of $30 a ton for crushing grapes in 1942, the average price in 1942 was really higher, and in 1943 was $87. And when it is known that the finer wine grapes, which constitute less than 10 percent of the total wine grape acreage in California, fetched anywhere from $100 to $125 a ton last year, it can be seen why prices have risen in spite of (if not because of) government restrictions. This is especially unfortunate when the truth is that decent wine should cost no more than milk, which now sells for under 20 cents a quart!

Artful dodges thrive in such a situation, of course. One of the most natural is to stop selling bulk wine. Selling in bulk in California, Wisconsin, and Louisiana can only be done from the keg, even in peacetime, but until lately gallon jugs of bad to middling table wines have been procurable almost everywhere. What stocks still exist are almost surely prewar, and often fit only for poor vinegar. A wineman can make more money if a gallon is split into five parts instead of four, so most reputable wines are now marketed only in fifths or tenths—a sad blow to the average purse. And to escape labeling restrictions and more ceilings, many vineyards are now issuing "signature" or "reserve" bottles, which for the most part are all right but cost more than they should.

One of the most exciting things about the California wine industry is its size: over 90 percent of the American vineyards are in this state. Unfortunately, and unlike the smaller Eastern vineyards, a safe 90 percent of this acreage is planted with quick-producing, cheap, easily cultivated, and undistinguished stock. (Haraszthy alone brought more than 1,400 varieties here in 1862, some of which were of necessity inferior.)

Furthermore this acreage is owned and cared for, very often, by people whose only idea of viticulture is how quickly they can market what they grow. This is largely the fault of prohibition, during which many despondent, ignorant, or impatient farmers plowed under their fine, slower vines—and then as quickly planted their land to mediocre stock when the tide turned. Probably a large percentage of the winegrowers even today are men without either idealism or knowledge of their grapes.

Now that a growing appreciation of table wines and a rapid decrease in the supplies of hard liquors have thinned the shelves of every merchant, the shrewder farmers are not only forcing their vines: they are stretching their wines unmercifully. This is true of even a few of the good vineyards as well as the bad—vineyards which for years have struggled to maintain a certain standard of quality and which now, because of natural cupidity or a change of ownership, are buying indiscriminately from their less prosperous neighbors in order to turn out a larger number of bottles each year.

This, I think, is the main reason why wines from California are so often disappointing. A case bought in December will be good. Three or six months later the same product, ordered from the same vintner and cared for in the same way, will be flat, flabby, ignoble. This is more than disconcerting, especially to a person who not only likes to serve good wine but has a certain adopted, if not native, pride.

It is reassuring to know that there are still a few vineyards whose wines, when procurable, are steadfast. My great regret is that their products are too expensive for the average American to serve as they should be served: as a complement to the daily fare of our tables. They are for the most part produced in small vineyards, so that the quantity is limited. They are made with skillful care, from vines that need much attention —a method which of course raises the price. Most of them come from Northern California, and until lately have been almost unknown outside the state, except by a few connoisseurs and wine stewards.

If I wanted to buy them (which I do!) I'd do it by the case if possible, and from the best merchant near me. If I wanted only one good bottle, to share with a friend in time of travail or of joy, I'd go either to an upper-class dealer or to a large hotel, and I'd ask for a full fine Grey Riesling, a Sauvignon, or a delicate Ugni Blanc from Livermore, or best of all a Pinot Chardonnay; a Cabernet, a Gamay, a native Zinfandel; a Pinot Noir from Napa or Sonoma County or even from Santa Cruz or Santa Clara. If it was an inexpensive honest red wine I looked for, not too high in tannic acid for Gargantuan consumption, I'd buy some of that still blended and bottled in straw-wrapped flasks near Asti.

I'd be safe—safe from the cupidity, the lack of standardization, the tumultuous confusion of the California wine industry. I'd be drinking well, and storing as patiently as possible the knowledge that there is gradually emerging, through all the turmoil, a quality of production that cannot be harmed by war or prejudice or even man's dishonesty. The winegrowers with increasing skill are bottling three or four types of wine instead of an indiscriminate twenty or a horrible something called Maiden's Breath or Old Saint Murgatroyd, and thanks to some sixty-five years of research by the state oenologists, are at this moment increasing the production of finer wines from a possible 10 percent to a probable 25 percent or 30 percent.

The Wine Institute, Delphic source of all such cheering prophecies, says that the trade secret that prices are soon to plunge downward (with the resumption of distilling) can now be whispered encouragingly by all wine lovers, such as I, who feel at times that they see through a glass very darkly indeed. Distribution, too, will make it possible to buy a decent Zinfandel in Keokuk and Kalamazoo. War has at last brought financial stability and a resulting professional zeal, the Institute says happily; things are *much* better than they were three years or even three months ago.

And meantime, there is good wine to be found for the looking, an earnest for the future, and it still "comforteth the harte and causeth a body to be mery"—fair enough in these days.

[*Atlantic Monthly,* 1944]

COFFEE

COMPARISONS are odious, of course. They are also difficult, especially when they are concerned with such a complex question as the worst coffee of my life.

When I think of the coffee I drank one night in the railway station at Valence, while I waited for the Paris express to stop for me and three Spahis in their long, scarlet-lined capes, I am sure it was the worst. Over the greasy steamed window of the café the rain dripped interminably down, and I thought of how cool and clean it must taste. I was cold and tired and shy. The pale, stinking brew I swallowed offered me a kind of sensory comfort, upon which my throat muscles closed like the coat of an outraged snake. The Spahis spat out their first mouthful and matter-of-factly filled the nasty thick-grimed glasses with rum, and I watched them, wishing I could be as easy in my white skin as they seemed in their shining dark ones.

Coffee almost as hideous was brewed every few hours in a big hotel in Cornwall. Perhaps the fact that it happened more than once was the most unpleasant thing about it.

I would smell it, slithering and sneaking up the elevator shaft like the gray-brown ghost of a long-dead, forgotten scrubwoman. I would know that after the interminable dinner with its pink fish sauce and its limp savory, after the last tipple of digestive or purgative tonics, the other solemn souls and I would sit in the drawing room, politely vying for places near the tiny fire and waiting impatiently for the waiter to come with his tray of small cups. "Black or white, Madam?" he would ask, bending over the sweetened grayish brew. "Black," I would say stubbornly, hating the implications of his description, and wondering each time if I could swallow what I chose.

It had a burned taste to it: that was what I smelled always a few hours before its appearance. And there was a disgusting fatness about it, like ancient boiled mutton. I thought perhaps the dripping-pans were charred and then rinsed out, to color it. But as in Valence, in the station café, it was hot—and I was very cold.

It is surprising that in a country as standardized as ours we still manage to make our coffee in almost as many ways as there are people to make it. It comes in uniform jars, which we buy loyally according to which radio program hires the best writers, so that whether the label is green or scarlet the contents are safely alike, safely middling. Once in the pot, however, its individuality becomes evident, a watery monster full of venom or sweet promise, as the case may be. Coffee in a roadside waffle joint may outdo nectar, and some made most carefully, measured and boiled just so and with the pot heated and swabbed and such according to directions, may be a loathsome brew in my best friend's kitchen.

There are vintners who believe that certain human beings have a chemical (or spiritual?) aura about them which will make wine turn over and mope in the bottles. Perhaps it is as true that some people breed trouble in the fragile oils of roasted coffee beans. I have at least three familiars who could no more make a potable cup of coffee than they could walk upon the waters. They have tried, too—and even wept at their defeat.

Methods can be amusing or merely finicky—elaborate or as simple as spilling some grounds into boiling water and letting them settle, unmeasured, unhindered by directions. And what people want is even plainer. First of all, coffee must be hot, they say—all except a stern old man I once knew who frowned on "stimulants" but drank quarts of cold black coffee every day, instead of water. And then coffee must be fresh, made shortly before its drinking and made only once. (In Cornwall, water was boiled twice or more over the same sad grounds, in defiance of counsel I found in an old cookery book: "Dried coffee, once used, is best employed as filling for pin-cushions, and will not pack down nor rust the needles.")

And some people like a light delicate brew and others, equally firm about the freshness of the grinding and the rest, will settle for strength or nothing. Their coffee, like tea for the Irish lady, must be strong enough to trot a mouse upon.

I like to lead strangers and intimates, in that order, to tell me the only right way to do a thing, their way. Scrambled eggs, reducing, surrealism, are all good gambits, but coffee making is the best.

One woman who lived for years in Guatemala will grow soft-eyed and gentle in the telling, over and over, of the way coffee smells in the air down there, dark and sweet with the sugar which is stirred into the pan of green beans in the oven. It turns black finally, in a kind of glaze, and when the beans are ground they have a fine richness about them.

A tall man, usually preoccupied with such things as laparotomies and the tightrope balance between death and life in the "closed closed" wards, will discuss with voluptuous candor how to blend and boil true Turkish brew. It is an elaborate ritual, like part of a ballet, and he the *premier danseur*.

A woman now more remote from the present than the past will tell me, and her voice becomes younger in the telling, of the coffee at Aunt Annie's, in the days of Sam Ward and Diamond Jim and all the gilt-edged gluttons.

It came every week from Park and Tilford, freshly roasted, and cost fifteen cents a pound. It was from Maracaibo! It was ground in the kitchen by a big hand-mill, two pounds at a time, and mixed into a paste with four beaten eggs. Then, spread thinly on a pan, it dried out in a slow oven until it could be broken up into a powdery mess again, while the whole of the great house was perfumed by its tantalizing fresh, strong smell. And it was used like any other coffee: a heaping tablespoonful for each cup of water, and one-plus for the pot. But I can never tire of hearing, and believing, that it was the best ever made. Maracaibo—the word is magic, as that weary woman says it, as I listen.

Of course I have my formula, less charmed but more misquoted. At least ten philosophers from half that many countries have claimed it as their own, so why not me? Coffee, I say, should be

Fresh as the springtime,
Black as death,
Strong as a long-gone lover's arms,
And hot as hell.

Then, whether it be shipped, a bag of green beans, from some foreign port, or, true-test roasted, be poured from a vacuum-sealed, dealer-dated jar, it will be good. It will, being good at all, be perfect.

[*Atlantic Monthly,* 1945]

SPOON BREAD AND MOONLIGHT

IN 1880, when Mark Twain wrote nostalgically from Italy of the American food he missed so sorely, the list of dishes to be waiting for him in New York when his ship docked included at least nine that were Southern. So was he, of course. But it is probable that almost any of us would have chosen much as he did, so strong is the influence of Southern cooking on our national gastronomy.

Whether the influence is justified has often been questioned, bitterly, dyspeptically, by natives of every state in the Union, but our romantic minds still curtsey to the mumbo-jumbo of "ante-bellum days" and "the old South," even in the face of such a present monstrosity as the average restaurant's Southern Fried Chicken. Moonlight-and-magnolias cover a multitude of dietetic sins, thanks to our innate sentimentality, and we gladly pay triple to have fobbed off on us a mediocre plum cake baked by the delicate hands of a decayed Kentucky gentlewoman whose shrewd publicity describes her as unwillingly sacrificing her family's most treasured recipe, in order to save the old plantation from seizure by the damyankees.

Expensive tearooms, whether in Louisville or Los Angeles, serve incredible masterpieces of pecan nuts, gelatin, and whipped cream with impunity and the promise that they are "adapted" from another secret Confederate recipe; and cookery books "translated from Southern lore" sell like hot cakes (or should I say canebrake biscuits?) in stores frequented by large soft ladies with inherited or acquired drawls.

"My old mammy told me this," they say gently, cutting into a Dixie Sunshine or a Prince of Wales. "It never was written, to keep it secret of course. But if you take thirteen eggs instead of eleven, honey—"

And the cake is delicious, and rich, and the fact that it has moved gradually from the plantation to the bridge club cannot dim its delicate splendor—as long as some people still have dozens of eggs and quarts of thick cream and, preferably, the strong, unquestioning black arm of a slave woman to beat them all together. The recipes are whispered, even on paper, and no bilious cynic from Detroit or Sioux City can deny that they deserve to survive as long as anyone can make them.

It is the commoner foods, the breads, the daily belly-fillers, that are mistreated from one end of America to the other because of the hypnosis of the adjective "Southern." That is wrong, because food that can be made by poor and rich, old and young, should always be worth the swallowing. And good corn pone, for instance, is indeed just that. Mark Twain was right when he put it, and hoecake too, on that list of dishes that made him long for home.

One thing that makes good corn bread difficult to get is regional prejudice: a man from Arkansas blanches, for example, at the thought of putting molasses on his dodger like a Missourian, and instead wants it buttered, or plain with a dish of black-eyed peas and sowbelly. And he wants it made of white meal, never yellow.

Another difficulty is that recipes for corn bread are seldom written, not because they must be kept as hallowed family secrets, like Aunt Chloe's Teacake or Belle of New Orleans Pie, but because they are made as automatically as breathing, and as often—a handful of meal, a pinch of salt, a couple of eggs, some sweet milk, and there you are!

Or rather, there you are if you have been doing it all your life. If not, you probably buy something in a box and try to convince yourself that it is just as good.

I tried, a long time ago, to learn how our cook Bea made biscuits. She could not write or read, and smiled mockingly when I confessed that I had to copy down a recipe in order to remember it, but she let me stand beside her many times in the kitchen while her slender blue-black hands tossed together the biscuit mix. She always did it at the last minute, when several other things for the meal had reached their climaxes of preparation, so that it was hard for me to separate them from the bowl I was watching. Every time, the ingredients were the same but in maddeningly different proportions; and every time, the biscuits were the same too: light, flaky but not crumbly, moist in the middle—as a cloud is moist, not a sponge.

I never learned, and Bea told my mother that I was not as bright as I looked to be.

Now I have a friend from Arkansas, and she makes corn bread the same way. It is truly impossible for her to tell me how, and one reason I am sorry is that she makes the most delicious dressing in the world, and it takes corn bread to do it. I watch her, and she tries hard to tell me, and every time, as with Bea and the biscuits, the ingredients are every which way and the bread is exactly the same delicious thing.

If you can make corn bread that is respectable, though, whether it be with white or yellow meal, here is how to make the dressing, to serve with chicken or turkey ("But you haven't eaten turkey," my friend says, "so long as you haven't eaten wild-turkey steaks, cut thick from the raw breasts and fried in butter." I agree sadly, and think with amazement that the great wild birds Brillat-Savarin wrote about so tenderly are still flying over the pinewoods. "Very good! exceedingly good! oh! dear sir, what a glorious bit!" his guests cried out as they ate the last morsel of his game, more than a hundred years ago—and I would do the same today, could I but taste a sliver from the breast. Meanwhile I comfort myself with this recipe, so much better than any I have ever found in a book):

Take fresh corn bread, about what would be in an 8-inch square pan, and crumble it lightly with 4 or 5 leftover biscuits or slices of stale white bread. Add 6 eggs, and finely chopped celery and onions to taste. Season simply: salt, pepper, perhaps a little sage. Baste the roasting bird generously and often, and put all the drippings from it into the bowl of dressing, which must be moist but not sodden. Add good rich stock if it seems dry. When the bird is a scant hour from being done, stuff it lightly with the dressing, and put what is left under and around it in the pan.

(Some people like fresh peanuts or pecans chopped coarsely into this dressing, but not my friend—and therefore not I.)

The same impossibility of getting a good corn bread or biscuit recipe holds for spoon bread. Bea used to make that, literally, with one hand. I tried reading recipes to her, and although she pretended to find all of them ridiculous, the following one produces the nearest copy of her infinitely better dish:

> *2 cups milk*
> *1 scant cup sifted corn meal*
> *1 tablespoon brown sugar*
> *½ teaspoon salt*
> *1 cup butter, melted or in tiny pieces*
> *6 egg yolks, beaten*
> *6 egg whites, beaten*

Heat milk to scalding point, then very slowly stir in the corn meal, sugar, and salt. Add the butter gradually, stirring the mixture up from the bottom of the pan. Cool, and add the beaten yolks slowly, stirring hard the while. Fold in the stiffly beaten whites. Turn into a well-buttered casserole or soufflé dish and bake about twenty-five minutes in a 425° oven (hot), until the bread is set in the middle and lightly crusted. Serve very hot, always from a large spoon.

Most places specializing in "real Southern cooking" serve spoon bread with chicken or ham. Usually, even in the South, it is a hot fuzzy mush, neither pudding nor porridge but possessing most of the disagreeable attributes of both.

"But," said my mother reasonably when we talked of such things, "that's the way it is, down there. I never knew restaurants, of course, but I went to school there for several years, and spent all my vacations with friends on what was left of their plantations—that was in the nineties. They were still fighting the War Between the States, and I don't yet see why they were so kind to a Yankee girl—and it seems to me that we lived on hot-breads and cakes and pies and fried chicken."

"That sounds good," I said greedily.

"It was—but only because I was young and ravenous," Mother said. "We ate four or five kinds of soggy rich hot-breads every day for breakfast, besides corncakes and beaten biscuits always. And big bowls of jam, as if it were fresh fruit. We all had headaches all the time, and took pills. And," she lowered her voice politely, "everyone was constipated."

She looked slightly embarrassed at her unaccustomed boldness, and then went on energetically to camouflage it, "Fry, *fry*, FRY! Everything was fried. I do believe those cooks could dip old corncobs in batter and serve them up as crisp hot fritters."

"That sounds good too," I said, being even hungrier by now.

"It gets tiresome after five years or so," my mother said. "It's why Southern belles are so languorous, probably—they all have indigestion, although usually it's called love in one form or another." Mother snorted. "And I don't want to see another Southern fried chicken as long as I live!"

A great many people feel the same way, although not because of "love in one form or another." "Southern Fried Chicken" is advertised with callous regularity as the specialty of most of the eating houses in the United States, no matter how far they are from the Mason-Dixon line or what clientele they serve, but I have yet to hear of any that is notably good. The obvious fact that a great many people order it and eat it is perhaps one more proof of the dangerous magic of calling a thing "Southern": it *must* be good, we reason unconsciously, evoking all we have been taught about ante-bellum delicacy and richness and crispness, and knowing very well that we will be presented with one more mistreated, steam-heated carcass, parboiled before it was fried, to ensure a kind of tenderness, no matter what its age and antecedents.

The worst I ever ate, I am almost sure, was in a lakeside tavern in northern Minnesota. People whose gastronomical judgment I respected, largely because they had tipped me off to the local caviar, assured me that no drive was too long if at the end of it there waited a platter of superlative Southern fried chicken prepared by the tavern's master cook.

I telephoned ahead, as they told me to, and mentioned their names, and then drove a very long drive indeed through spicy woods that made me hungry in an almost violent way. And the platter that was set before me was reward enough, heaped with crisp sizzling half-fryers, piled extravagantly high, sending off a visible perfume of brown, savory delight. Southern fried chicken, I told myself—at last I would taste it as it should be, as it never was.

The outer skin, dripping with rancid grease that soon overpowered the first fine aroma, was a thick half-done batter which slipped off in a horrid way, entire, and was inwardly pale and pasty. The flesh was grayish, boiled to death and dead to look at. Worst of all was the way it cut, like putty or suet, and then the fact that a half-inch from the surface it was cold—cold from the icebox where it had lain cooked for days before it was dipped quickly into a ready-mix batter and then into ancient fat, for my arrival.

It was a bad thing to meet, in northern Minnesota or southern California or in the Deep South itself—and the sad part of the story is that the same thing will happen again, in any of those places, to anyone fool enough to ask for it.

Me, I am cured—except spiritually of course. And I think this recipe, the nearest I can come to my dream of what Southern fried chicken should be, helps soothe my good American sentimentality about Confederate gastronomy, and may even lay Mark Twain's outraged ghost as it hovers over the pier in New York, waiting for the Southern fried chicken that he so hungered for in Italy in 1880:

> Cut up a young chicken and soak the pieces in sweet cream overnight. Drain them, saving the cream for the gravy. Pat each piece partly dry with a cloth, and salt and pepper amply. Dredge in a mixture of half bread flour and half corn meal. Mix one part butter with two parts lard, and have just hot enough to hiss when a crust is dropped in. Fit the chicken carefully into the skillet, and cover closely for about fifteen minutes. Then turn frequently to make the chicken brown and crisp, taking care not to let the fat become too hot.
>
> For the gravy, pour off most of the fat from the skillet, add the chopped giblets and a little flour, brown, and then add seasoning and lastly the cream.

[*Atlantic Monthly,* 1947]

THE TASTE FOR BORTSCH

THE TASTE for bortsch and the prejudices thereof can involve as many personal quirks as a recipe for hangovers, as many racial, social, and political eyebrow liftings as an ambassadorial visit. I have ceased to take them very seriously, after years of listening worshipfully to one famous comedian swear that he would eat bortsch at only one restaurant in the whole world, where it was prepared magnificently and as it *should* be. When I went to that restaurant and ordered that bortsch, I found it a pale, watery, and indeed completely dishonest shadow of what I myself, un-famous, un-comedian, think good bortsch should be.

I believe that it is one of the best soups in the world. It can be hot, cold, thick, thin, rich, meager, and still be good. It can be easy or intricate to make.

Some people like it hot with boiled beef in it, or quarters of cabbage (the variations on cabbage alone are almost infinite: chopped, minced, quartered, whole, on and on).

Some people like it cold with chilled sour cream poured over a steaming hot boiled potato in the middle of the plate.

Some people like grated fresh beets in it, and some like nothing at all, just the clear red consommé—and, of course, the cream.

Some people like little poached forcemeat balls in it.

Some people, apparently, like my famous comedian friend, like it *bad*.

And then again, there is the aspect of its sourness. Should it be fermented beets that give it its own peculiar sharpness, or fresh, sliced beets in honest vinegar? Is it a heinous gastronomical sin not to use salts-of-lemon from the corner drug store instead of the handier fresh lemon juice or vinegar? Should you spit it out and stalk from the table if it has no sour taste at all, but rather the bland smoothness of a Little Bortsch that can only be Polish if you are Russian, or Russian if you are Finnish, and so on and so thus intrinsically prejudiced.

Well, I like it two ways best, and these are they—one cold and easy to make; the other hot and comparatively complicated, as you can see from the ingredients:

Hot Winter Bortsch

16 young beets
2½ cups good vinegar
3 tablespoons butter or chicken fat
2 sweet onions
4 young carrots
2 bay leaves
handful of parsley sprigs
salt, pepper
3 tablespoons flour
3 quarts good rich beef stock

Scrape and wash the beets, and put 12 of them through the coarse meat grinder. Cover with vinegar for several hours. Melt the fat, add the onions and carrots which have been coarsely ground, the chopped parsley, and the bay leaves and seasoning. Stir until golden, add one-half the flour, brown all well, then stir in the rest of the flour. Drain the ground beets thoroughly, saving one-half to a cup of the vinegar, and add them to the braised vegetables. Add the stock. Let simmer a half hour or until the vegetables are tender. Grate on a cheese grater the four remaining beets, mix them with the vinegar, and add to the soup five minutes before serving.

Little sausage balls poached in boiling water can be added and, of course, an accompanying bowl of thick, sour cream is a necessary addition to the tureen of deep red soup.

Cold Summer Bortsch

1 quart vegetable juice
1 pint strong stock (canned consommé is all right)
1 can sliced beets with juice
½ to ¾ cup good vinegar
1 thinly sliced onion
salt, pepper, and so on

I say "and so on" because some people like a touch of clove or küm-mel. The vegetable juice can be tinned or what is left over from pressure-cooking.

Pour the liquids into a casserole containing the canned sliced beets, their juice, the sliced onion, and the seasoning. Chill for 12 hours or more. Strain off the liquids, and serve very cold with sour cream—and hot potatoes, if desired.

[*House Beautiful*, 1949]

A HYMN TO LEFT-OVERS

I GRADUATED (years ago and *summa cum laude*) from the What's-Left-Over School, and am at this very moment earning my postgraduate degree, a Doctorate of Gastronomical Subterfuge.

I love everything about it, including my professors. Since classes in this completely nonexclusive college can last anywhere from five minutes to five decades, my teachers have been legion, from a large Englishwoman born in a jungle hammock in New Guinea to an equally ample American born in a dirt-floored shack in Tennessee. And they and my own active taste buds have convinced me that left-overs are often much better than freshly cooked foods, for a dozen good reasons including their demand for more ingenuity.

The hardest thing to cope with, I have learned, is Prejudice.

My father, for instance, leers downward and to the left of his long nose whenever we serve anything baked in a casserole.

Casseroles, praise be, are generally considered a part of modern living. They can, and often do, contain appetizing mixtures of good food which can be prepared in advance by busy housekeepers and heated at will.

But to my father, raised in an age of simplicity as well as plenty, they are an insult. A casserole, even if I have used a whole young chicken and a pound of fresh mushrooms and a pint of good broth and some priceless saffron and a package of wild rice, is to him simply an excuse to thrust upon him a "foreign" mishmosh of *old scraps*, and not a *risotto à la milanaise et mode de moi-meme*...

He firmly believes that left-overs should be treated candidly as such, preferably when he has to go to a Chamber of Commerce banquet. If by chance he must be at home, a hash can be made, and the whole put upon hot biscuits, and downed with an uncomplaining but blatant resignation which inspires in me, if not all other women, an almost homicidal exasperation.

There is, happily for us graduates, a technique involving a few bald-faced tricks, called in my current vocabulary Fooling Father (or George, or Uncle Wilbert). It demands at least a working knowledge of both the kitchen and the victim, and when the two are well blended the results can be superb.

A certain amount of quiet indoctrination is needed. To Father, all cold chicken is what couldn't be eaten while the bird was hot. It has apparently never occurred to him that a fowl can be roasted, allowed to cool, and then served, proud and entire, for a summer feast. Therefore I do exactly that: I take care to baste well with a mixture of half butter and half olive oil, to make a fine glaze; I let the bird cool but not become chilled, which would dull both its looks and its flavor and make it less succulent.

Most important of all, I present it with discreet fanfare, instead of slipping it almost covertly upon the table in creamed tattered pieces, or else picked from the bones into a salad, as Pappy has always thought "left-over chicken" would, indeed *must*, be served.

He is baffled . . . and I am happy, for nothing is more devoutly to be wished for in family gastronomy than the strong element of bewilderment.

As a direct result of this treatment of both my father and the chicken, the next time we have something good made from beef, for instance, he does not eat it in resigned recognition of last Sunday's roast. He titillates his weary old taste buds with the possibility that perhaps I, in a wild, extravagant moment, actually bought a cut of meat and grilled it, just for this one dish! Decades of conditioning fall comfortably from him, and he tucks into the delicacy without a single thought of the bad word "left-over."

There are a few basic rules in such a course. I usually let at least thirty-six hours go by before I use the same food for the second time. I change it radically: green beans tossed with sweet butter and salt and pepper the first time, and simmered with more butter and sliced mush-rooms and perhaps fresh tomatoes the next. I use plenty of fresh chopped herbs and seasonings the second time: parsley, marjoram and basil, scallions, dill. I cook more than enough for the first, but so lightly that I can increase the potency of flavor the second time without exhausting it.

It all comes down to a feeling of *interest*, I suppose. The Ho-Hum attitude can spread so quickly from diner to cook and back again, that it is more than merely amusing to put it into a kind of reverse, and as cook plan new camouflages and then as diner be baffled (as well as satisfied) by where the dish came from!

Here, for instance, are some recipes for (let us whisper the word) *leftovers:*

For hashes, generally speaking, it's best to cut up or chop, but never grind, the well-done, cold meat. Discard most of the fat. Mix well with the herbs, seasonings and moisture, and then *let stand* for a few hours before the final gentle browning or baking.

Chicken Hash

> *2 cups cut-up chicken*
> *1 cup mixed parsley and green onions, finely chopped*
> *salt, pepper, optional pinch nutmeg*
> *½ cup dry white wine or broth*
> *fresh cream*
> *butter, or chicken fat*

Mix chicken, herbs and seasoning lightly together. Add enough liquids to bind all without making the mixture mushy. Let stand, and taste for seasoning just before using. Use good shortening, in gently heated skillet. Stir well and then let alone if a crisp crust is desired, when the whole should be folded once like an omelet. Or sherry can be added at the last, and the mixture served on crisp toast.

Cubed lamb is very good cooked into a kind of American hash with onions, green pepper, olive oil and cream, and then baked for a few minutes on thick rounds of grilled eggplant... with rice or a pilaf, of course.

As for beef, a good hash of it is unbeatable, but the following recipe or a modification of it is always more "impressive":

Boeuf Moreno

½ cup thinly sliced pepper or pimiento
½ cup minced parsley and onion
½ cup button mushrooms or pitted ripe olives
½ cup butter
1 pound left-over steak or roast beef, cut in thin strips (preferably
    about ½ inch by 2 by 3 inches)
2 cups good basic brown sauce (flour, butter, beef stock,
    seasoning)
½ cup sour thick cream
3 tablespoons brandy or whisky

Simmer the pepper, parsley, onion and mushrooms in the butter in a shallow casserole until just tender. Add the strips of
meat and heat through. Add the cream slowly to the sauce.
Add brandy. Pour sauce into the casserole and serve at once,
with rice, toast or buttered noodles.

Meat pies are fine in this category too—with rich crusts green with
chopped watercress, with diced cold pork tossed with chopped apple
and sliced almonds.

And then ham and pork and even beef are wonderful as the Chinese
treat them, scrambled with eggs and then rice (yes, left-over rice!). . . .

As for curries, here is the basic recipe that haunted my childhood,
which can be very good indeed:

Hurry-up Curry

1 large onion, sliced thin
½ cup bacon fat
2 tablespoons hot curry powder
¼ cup vinegar
¼ cup water
1 small can tomato sauce
about 2 cups chopped cooked meat
any gravy left over

Fry onion golden in fat. Mix curry well with vinegar and water. Add to onion and fry well. Add tomato sauce. Cook five minutes. Add meat and possible gravy, then let simmer for a few minutes. Serve with rice. (This really sounds shockingly bad, but I loved it when I was somewhat younger and less devoted to curries which take three days to make.)

To tell the whole truth in gastronomical humility: I like left-overs so much that I usually manage to *hide* a few scraps. I feel, like any artist, that they would be wasted in the shared pot. I tuck them behind a pile of butter cubes or a bowl of prunes in the icebox. Then I wait until everyone is away . . .

And perhaps my subtlest masterpieces are eaten in proud solitude simply because I could never *explain* them. Recipes for such dishes are almost impossible to set down, depending as they do on accident and mood. Who can ever foresee, in an ordinary pantry, when there will be exactly one slice of grilled liver, three shallots, a small jelly-glass of mushrooms-in-sour-cream, the bottom of a bottle of Tio Pepe sherry, and one hungry woman with A Plan?

One of my latest triumphs was an ugly thing composed of a small tin of chopped olives simmered lightly in their own and a little more good oil, and then tossed with about two cups of last night's green beans and a small handful of minced parsley and scallions. (As I retaste this on my mind's palate I think a little tin of sliced pimento would have added valuably to the flavor and the color.) At the last, when it was sending up a fine fume, I put in a pat of butter and a couple of douses of soy sauce. Delicious!

It is possible that some night I'll be alone and have a cup of truffled broth, a cold squab, and a small bottle of correctly cold champagne.

I do hope not! As a graduate of the What's-Left-Over School, I'd rather look by myself in the icebox, find for myself a jar of yesterday noon's potato soup, and a couple of withered chicken wings, and the rapidly flattening remains of a bottle of stout . . . *left-overs.*

[*Pageant*, 1950]

THE BEST WAY TO ENTERTAIN

To ME an evening of happy dining and conversation can take the place of bridge, the theater, or any other form of entertainment.

I was propelled somewhat precociously, perhaps, into such theorizing, by what my family always referred to as Grandmother's Nervous Stomach, an ultimately fortunate condition which forced all of us to eat bland things like boiled rice or soda crackers steamed in milk.

Now and then Grandmother's conscience drove her to attend religious conventions in distant places, and then we indulged in a voluptuous riot of things like mayonnaise, thin pastry under the Tuesday hash, rare roast beef on Sunday instead of boiled hen. Mother ate all she wanted of cream of fresh mushroom soup, and with the steak Father served a local wine which we called red ink. We ate grilled sweetbreads and skewered kidneys with a daring dash of sherry on them. Best of all, we talked-laughed-sang-kissed and in general exposed ourselves to sensations forbidden when the matriarchal stomach rumbled amongst us. And my thoughts on how gastronomy should influence the pattern of any happy person's life became more and more firm.

Later I met another family, which from its start—that is, as soon as their two sons and daughter began to sprout—had flourished on just such ideas as my long-held theory. The father was a business executive turned winegrower. The mother was a gracious creature. They all worked like slaves to restore a vineyard abandoned during Prohibition. They raised most of their own food and cured their own meats in the chimney; the kids worked before breakfast, rode their ponies over the tawny hills to school, then rode home for more chores. They lived a fine life.

The parents insisted that their children learn to try every edible part of everything that walked, flew, swam or grew. Once each child formed his own opinions, it was up to him to repeat the tastings—or not. My two children, raised on the same dictum, are additional proofs of its soundness.

Eating any meal with this family was fun. They were all good cooks. Breakfast during the grape harvest was as lusty as a Brueghel painting, with brown, black, yellow and white men and women speaking all their languages in the light of the sun rising over Mission San Jose. The boss—the father—turned out, on the enormous old iron stove, little hot cakes as delicate as dove feathers; the younger boy sizzled sausages he and his sister had made from the piglet they had raised together from the first oink to final seasoning; the older brother poured coffee from a big Mexican urn—coffee he had roasted and ground and brewed himself. The mother was everywhere, quiet as a diamond cutter, watching the cups, the piles of freshly baked bread, the pots of honey...listening with a half-secret smile to all the animated voices.

Dinner there was fine too. It might be very simple, with two or three dishes on a buffet, and some good wine...or it could be elaborate like the annual game dinner served on one occasion for three college presidents, a guru priest, a shipowner from the Islands and two movie belles. With it were five fine wines for the five slow, impressive courses, and the featured five kinds of game—of course including jack rabbit in a mammoth pie. The children were always there, as cooks, deft helpers, gay friends.

"That's how I learned how to listen and how to talk," one of them—now grown up—told me one night recently. "I already knew how to eat. But those breakfasts, those suppers and game dinners—and all those people gathered there. What wonderful times and what *talk!*"

Today this young man is a basso with an opera company, a fine, big fellow who does indeed know how to eat, to drink properly, how to listen and how to talk. He is another comforting proof of my theory.

On that night I watched him sitting at a wobbly card table in my new apartment amidst a mess caused by the arrival of most everything I own from Aix-en-Provence, where I had stayed a year. He had tuned an old ukulele which somehow floated to the top of the five-room pile, and his version of "St. James Infirmary" was good and very blue. My girls gaped blissfully at him, as at a blazing Christmas tree in August. A few other people listened and then talked, over and around his strumming and singing.

We drank a thinnish rosé from Napa Valley and ate a meal which I managed to produce despite the confusion, and the boy who had won a prize for a heifer, and several medals in the South Pacific...the one who at eleven invented a new kind of *pâté de foie* for his parents' *canapés*... who had made his own dry-vermouth formula while he studied oenology at Davis—put aside the ukulele. He sat there easily, merrily, talking and talking, eating and drinking, even listening—which is perhaps rarest.

He savored every bite of the simple meal (salmon steaks baked with mushrooms, rice, oak-leaf-lettuce salad, mild Jack cheese, coffee...) and he asked questions of the cook—me—which is always fun for any cook. With warmth in his voice he told of the days it was touch and go for the family vineyard. Then he bolted for the opera house to be made up for *Andrea Chénier*.

And I sat back with the feeling of a smug ghost—Franklin's or maybe Einstein's: my theory was right.

People do start early to appreciate good food and good eating companions, if they are allowed to, as a very special sort of entertainment—one, in fact, for which I have never discovered a substitute. And this truth has become increasingly important as more and more of us find pleasure and relaxation in cooking.

When it first became clear that life in midcentury America could not include swarms of domestics, people put a too-brave face on it. They wore cute aprons and even chef's bonnets and leaned heavily on herbs in their over-intricate stews and sauces, and invested in too many copper pots and casseroles. It was what might be called gastronomical growing pains.

By now, thankfully, we have settled into a period of enjoying what was, for a while, a basically frightening chore: cooking and serving good meals to people who gather to savor them—along with companionship.

Men, instead of mastering one dish for a stag dinner before a poker game, and another for a mixed group, followed swiftly by bridge or the theater, now read a wide variety of cookbooks. They neglect the financial page in favor of learning ways to freeze Escoffier's five basic sauces, and even take an afternoon off from golf to try a recipe in a new pressure cooker or blender.

Women have outgrown putting marshmallows in their salads and, further, have not served a candied cherry outside a fruitcake for years. Press agents beam when they can spread the news that a duchess (real) or a queen (movie) is actually able to buy, cook and serve a commendable dinner: their battle to woo public approval is half won.

One is fortunate to come by this interest in cooking early in life, but it can be acquired any time. At this moment I know seven newly married couples who are, with varying degrees of timidity, starting to become good hosts and hostesses; they have devised ways to serve simple interesting meals to guests numbering from four to twenty without too much strain.

Five of my seven young couples work in offices. The two remaining females are pregnant, and one has three tots from her husband's first marriage—all of which complicates entertaining. These people wisely depend on one or two dishes planned for three kinds of simplicity: easy to prepare and store for reheating; easy to serve; easy to eat in the various positions dictated by modern rooms—squatting, crouching, half-lying, or best of all, sitting at an honest-to-goodness table.

Next big-game night one of my young couples plans to serve fish Muchi *and* deviled drumsticks, instead of just fish Muchi, her trusted standby. It involves borrowing a second chafing dish, and that's also fun—watching the two of them flicker along importantly.

Muchi may or may not be Japanese. I sometimes suspect, when it is clumsily assembled, that its name stems from the same root as *mish-mosh*. It is as changeable as a seasick remedy and as dependable as the host who serves it.

It can be made with most any canned or frozen fish, but of course it is best when all ingredients are fresh, crisp and firm. It can be assembled several hours before the party, preferably in two parts—the sauce and the solids—and then mixed, heated, and served from a chafing dish on a table or sideboard or even from a fine big old-fashioned double boiler in the kitchen, where people always gravitate. It is best with rice, but perhaps easier to serve on hot toast squares.

A Muchi for six or eight people calls for about two quarts of good cream sauce (a Béchamel but without the veal); it can even be made with equal parts clam juice and milk if the main ingredients are shellfish; and about two quarts of cooked (and shelled) shrimps, prawns, crab legs, lobster, scallops—according to time, place and luck. From there on, it is chef's delight: a cup or so of thinly sliced black olives, or pimientos red or green, or mushrooms, or slivered almonds, or, or, or . . . For a mad touch of elegance, the various fishes can be tossed lightly in hot butter and then "flamed" with a small glass of good brandy or even dry gin. In this case, skip the conventional fillip of dry sherry just before serving.

The progression from one culinary guest-catcher to two or more, as in the case of the fifth bride, who plans to serve deviled drumsticks alongside as a daring effort, is very promising gastronomically. Two to four drumsticks should be allowed for each guest, since they are delicious by themselves and even more irresistible served alongside a good Muchi.

They should be rubbed with a little sweet butter and put in a covered casserole and baked at low heat (325°) for about forty minutes or until tender to a fork. Then, according to a recipe which I have used a long time and which can be found in Helen Evans Brown's *Chafing Dish Book* with her own merry directions, they should be slashed crosswise to the bone two or three times, to make for better flavor and easier eating, and then rolled in flour which has been seasoned highly with salt, cayenne pepper, and dry mustard, and a little mace if desired.

Next they should be browned in a mixture half butter and half olive oil—an inch or so deep—and stacked loosely on layers of absorbent paper in a gentle oven. Helen Brown keeps them in the casserole and pours rich chicken stock over them, with a dash of Worcestershire in it. But there are few chafing dishes big enough for eight drumsticks, and I have found that it is all right to keep them warm and then dunk them at the last, hot and juicy, in a pint of broth simmering in the "blazer," basting and turning a few times before serving. This involves a certain amount of attention, which in itself is quite impressive when carried off with nonchalance. It also involves practice.

For a supper like this, rice can go along with both chafing dishes, kept hot and light, if possible, in one of the wooden vessels the Chinese and Japanese use. Good substitutes are tender noodles or hot buttered toast. There should be a big bowl of chilled greens, say: Bibb and oak-leaf lettuce hearts, curly endive, chicory—dressed or naked. Another bowl should be filled with cold fruits, fresh, or artfully chosen tinned ones, marinated four to six hours in anything from lemon-juice-and-honey to brown rum. Coffee later…and a wine described as "decent but unimpressive, domestic or imported," in cool bottles or carafes, and/or cool beer…and depending on the company, of course, there should be whatever liquor or liqueur your group is known to prefer.

Dinners become slower, smaller, quieter, and infinitely more savorable as social pressures grow less demanding, and the amorous and financial pursuits less of a hunger. In other words, hunger itself can be admitted to the sensory circle.

If my seven brides, for instance, were several years older, they would find themselves less breathless and more firmly in command. It used to be essential in the raw United States to deny one's setting. Now, if we live in San Francisco we can serve *cioppino* instead of striving for a *bouillabaisse*, especially if we had an Italian grandmother; in the Minnesota lake country we can find fresh, unsalted caviar, crude but delicious; anywhere near the Mexican border we can adapt red-hot chilies to a hundred milder *Yanqui* recipes; hogcheek and greens, if a relative came from Tennessee and betrayed the secret formula, can be as good to eat as anything. The trick, I suppose, is to carry on *old* table tricks.

One thing we often heard mentioned but seldom ate, when I was little, was an Irish boiled dinner. From what I remember of my grandmother's predilection for annihilating all semblance of taste in her cookery, it is perhaps fortunate that my experience was mostly conversational. The Irish dinner involved a boiled hen, a boiled ham, some boiled potatoes which, when my grandmother left Donaghmore, were even rarer than the meats, and of course some boiled turnips and cabbage to make it diplomatically Anglican. I have always meant to make one, a gesture toward my granddam's flagging gastronomical honor.

One thing we never failed to eat when Grandmother was away was an ostentatious filet of grilled rare beef, served on an ample Crown Derby platter and ringed with watercress which we had sneaked that afternoon from the fruity stream running through a friend's dairy. Needless to say, the cress was loaded with all kinds of bacilli unknown to modern packaged greens, but it tasted fine and we continued to feel fine, too, not at all typhoidic.

The best part, though, was the blotters, which Father put carefully alongside the filet to catch every drop of juice as he carved. Each person was asked in turn if he wanted one of these soggy slices of fresh home-made bread, and with a yes, Father put one, brown and dripping, on a hot plate and then laid a slice of the filet on it or beside it according to requests. And then everyone helped himself to a big airy dollop of mashed potatoes on which Father impressed a dimple filled with meat juice. Altogether, this was one of those rituals of good family life which people never forget.

It can be duplicated, more or less, and there is no better investment for a small quiet party than the best available whole filet of beef. (This presupposes sitting properly at a solid table, since it is not lap food.) It should be prepared and served as simply as my parents did it.

As much depends on the butcher as on sentimental treatment of the filet, of course; it must be well hung, and not too assiduously trimmed and prettied. It should be left in a warm room for at least six hours before cooking time, painted with a pure soy sauce. Then put it on a rack in a very hot oven, up to 525° or 550°, for about ten minutes to the pound or until the outside is thoroughly seared and the inside gives a thermometer reading of about 120°. If the rack is not high off the pan, one cautious turning will be enough, taking care not to pierce the surface. Slice rare and thick into its own juices (or proudly paper thin, as my father did), and keep warm for serving. For the blotters, use the best bread you can buy.

Buttery baked potatoes are good with such a monumental slab of beef, and a tossed green salad or a simple casserole of cauliflower and cheese for instance; and ale is fine, or a full-bodied but velvety red wine—a Pinot Noir from California or France. Two or three cheeses—a mild, a nippy, and a blue—and more of the top-quality bread could follow, and a bowl of firm apples, and then, with coffee, some Scotch or a fine sour-mash whisky or a noggin of cognac, the evening will slide painlessly into its last phase of lazy companionship...perhaps some music, hot or cool...perhaps some fancy *talking*, but never too much of one or the other with such a bolstering of the adrenals as rare roast beef and congeniality can give.

Another way to insure such ease is more often the privilege of the older than the young gastronomers, probably because it takes time both to prepare and to have learned to savor it. It hinges on the preparation of either one somewhat fabulous course (a nine-boy curry, for instance...)

as the highlight of an otherwise simple meal, or on an arbitrary but skillful following of a classic pattern.

The latter is the rarer trick these days. Few of us can command the time or the domestic assistance to serve forth what Doctor Saintsbury would have noted as routine in his *Cellar Book:* shellfish, soup, fish, meat, fowl, sweet and savory, with four wines and "without champagne." I can number on one hand the people I know who could offer such an obsolete if charming show, and all five of them are very rich and one is a general with a good staff and the others are fanatics, or perhaps just gastronomical maniacs.

For the rest of us, the people who plan and prepare and serve their own meals, with perhaps some paid assistance at the last minute, the pattern of how to have a good time in all the stages of giving a dinner party becomes clearer with practice.

Plainly, few of us with jobs and crowded apartments and children have adequate silver, plates, glasses, room and so on, for a lot of people at once. We cut down and reassemble our lists, unconsciously agreeing with Edith Wharton who asserted, successfully too, that no self-respecting host would attempt to entertain more than eight at a time. Depending on the people themselves, and their degrees of intimacy, six can be even more pleasant.

We lean unhesitatingly on some blatant tricks, usually dictated by circumstance. For instance—I have an ugly white-and-gold soup tureen left over somehow from my great-grandmother's wedding set, and I have found that most people, even those who profess to loathe soup, are pleased to be able to serve themselves at will from this early-Irish terror. They consider it an adventure. It makes them feel deliciously free and easy to stroll to the great tureen (I keep it filled from ample hot pots in the kitchen) and serve themselves from the steamy mysterious depths.

What comes before such a "meal in itself," as Mary Frost Mabon called it, is dictated by the soup itself. A *garbure* or a respectable *minestrone* should be preceded by rather hefty *canapés* like small grilled sausages, shrimps or oysters, to dip into something clean-cut like a mixture of horseradish and sour cream, or a variation on the theme of an *anchoiade*.

An *anchoiade* is really spread right onto the bread, as the savor is built into a *pizza*, but it also can be a sauce to dip things into. Smash with a wooden spoon, or grind in a mortar, two small tins of flat anchovy filets, one finely minced garlic clove, some freshly ground pepper and olive oil—about half a cup. Finally, when it is rather thin and not at all pretty, work in the juice of a small lemon or the equivalent of some strong wine vinegar. You can toy with this sauce; a handful of chopped parsley turns it a strange, delicious color; another trick is to work in a small tin of sweet red peppers.

In other words, what precedes a "meal in itself" depends on what's in the early-Irish terror. If it is a rich oyster stew, then a tray of all kinds of raw, crisp cold vegetables is indicated, depending upon the locality and the season. If the tureen contains a chilled *gaspacho* on a summer night, tangy nibbles reminiscent of Spain or Mexico are fun: bowls of smoked or marinated abalone meat, oysters, mussels; little pickled green and red peppers, not too hot; a chafing dish of slowly roasted spiced pork cubes. Here in San Francisco it is easy to lean with several culinary influences—Chinese, Mexican, Far West, French. Every one of them is fun, and all can be bolstered by some such familial prop as Aunt Bessie's pan dowdie or the old Jockey Club *café diable* or even great-grandmother's tureen.

When I came back from a year in Provence, I brought another tureen horror, this time from Marseille. It is saffron yellow and bright pink, with slashes of turquoise on the bellies of some of the fish painted on its sides, and strands of bile-green kelp. Its feet are made of vicious little fish called *rascasse* along the *bouillabaisse* coast (from Martigues past Toulon), and the handle for the top is a big lobster with black, leering eyes. There are a dozen each of deep soup plates and dinner plates, each with a Mediterranean rockfish glowering from it—the *loup,* the *roucaou,* the *baudroie,* and nine others. Although the whole astonishing affair is meant definitely for *bouillabaisse,* I, and perhaps generations after me, will use it for many another soup, many another delightful supper in the glow of its impossible ugliness.

It is easy to assemble an almost authentic *bouillabaisse* right here under Nob Hill, thanks to the Monterey fishermen who are not disdainful of netting the little rockfish along the cliffs. And there is the local unsaffroned version called *cioppino.* But for christening the Marseille monster and its two dozen plates, I plan to serve a *soupe de poissons* made like this!

I will buy about three pounds of small fresh sea creatures in North Beach, including a few little rock crabs, some so-called bait, a couple of baby squid, a small eel cut in pieces (if I'm lucky); and six freshly cooked, lightly cracked crabs at Fisherman's Wharf.

In a scant cup of olive oil I'll sauté until golden two or three chopped leeks and two onions, all in a large pot. Then, with a long wooden spoon, I'll stir in three chopped, unpeeled tomatoes, two smashed garlic cloves, two or three bay leaves and the quarter of an orange peel. When all this is thoroughly stirred and bubbling, I'll add four or five quarts of water and, when boiling, all the seafood except the cracked crab. Salt and pepper and let boil rapidly for fifteen minutes. Next, strain all the bouillon into another pot.

In the fish-soup country around Marseille, quantities of vermicelli are then added to the reheated broth, and it is generously flavored with saffron. But for this first and unorthodox soup on far shores, I shall leave out vermicelli and saffron, and even rice, which I could substitute, and serve the hot broth with piles of sourdough bread—very crusty—for dunking.

Now I put the best bits of the cracked crabs, shell and all, into a quick steamer to heat them through, and then lay them, lumpy and challenging, in the top section of my tureen, which is a kind of pottery sieve, with a couple more painted rock monsters cavorting around it. Then—final step—I'll pour the fish bouillon over the crab into the hot tureen beneath, and serve it forth.

Everything—the ceramic nightmare from Provence and what is in it, the warm simple bread, the company—is good. The crab season is open again. The wine-boy basso is back from the Los Angeles opera season and hungry. His soprano wife, off-stage for another baby, is back from the hospital and hungry. An ancient but chipper adventurer and his young wife are back from two years in Sardinia, hungrier than ever. There is the man who drives a cab to put himself through veterinarian school so that he can raise rare birds: he's bound to be hungry. There are a couple of psychiatrists who can go home and analyze their reactions to the soup after they have stayed their hunger with it. And so on. And me? I plan to enjoy myself with all this fine company.

I'll serve cold vodka or dry chilled vermouth with the several bowls of Provencal hors d'oeuvres (frozen olive oil with herbs, roasted slivers of green pepper and eggplant, chopped olives and anchovies in a paste, and...) and then a dry still champagne, the nearest thing I can get to the *blanc de blanc* which is made back-country from Toulon. It is a heady wine, perfect to abet the assault on a soup such as this one.

Afterward come peeled slices of a late melon with a touch of lemon juice and nutmeg, chilled; coffee on the sideboard with rum to add as wished; and a cognac and a Scotch and a pitcher of cool water; and as the wine boy said, what talk, what *Talk*. I'll lean back in a shadow, to hide my smugness over my theory, soup tureens, and even children large and small, keep proving that I was right, when I decided at the age of nine that one of the best ways to grow up is to eat and talk quietly with good people.

[*Holiday*, 1956]

PASTA: ITALIAN-BORN, AMERICAN-MADE

PROBABLY one of the best things Italy ever did for the world was to invent spaghetti and all the little curls and twists and strings of pasta, the same flour-and-water paste that is called lovely names like "little reeds" *(cannelli)* and *"very* little reeds" *(cannellini)* and *amorini* (little loves) and even some morsels named *tirabaci* (kiss catchers)....

There are infinite variations on this theme, of course, all in the macaroni family, with the dough spread out very thin and rolled into sheets which are then cut and twisted and otherwise played with, to make all the silly, delightful varieties of pasta we buy, cook, eat.

It would never have occurred to my mother to serve any of these pastas at home: she was from Iowa, and her mother, who lived in California with us—or we with her—was from Ireland, and in either country there was no such frivolous thing as little twisted-up pieces of boiled dough called "tiny faithful ones" *(fidelini)*!

But...that wonderful *but* in American lives, full of racial and other contradictions...*but* my mother agreed with my father (also from Iowa) that any civilized person should know at least one good Italian restaurant. We did. We knew the best.

I can still smell the fine whiff of herbs and simmered tomato and oil and of freshly scraped cheese that met us when we went into our restaurant, all of us feeling happy and escaped in our own ways. It was a long time ago.

There were not many Italians in Southern California then, but most of them went to that place to eat, for a birthday or a saint's day or even a wedding, and it was always gay there, the way a good Sunday should be gay, with God prayed to and various sins accounted for and all the family together.

"Well, what do you say?" my father would ask solemnly, a routine bit of buffooning protocol.

"Oh, yes," we'd answer happily. "Everything."

That meant ordering the monumental "Sunday dinner," but the thing we concentrated on was the course of fresh, steaming, odorous pasta, after the generous platters of thin ham and crisp raw vegetables, the bowls of *minestrone* . . . before the "real dinner" . . . One time it would be little crinkled things, and another it would be shells. The next time it was fine silky "angels' hairs." Once it would be served with plain sweet butter and grated, bitey cheese . . . the next, a sauce of field mushrooms and beefstock and herbs . . . then fresh rosemary and bits of lean ham with tomatoes . . . on and on.

Afterward, threeish or fourish, we went out into the echoing streets and homeward, through the yellow meadows in the spring, through the calm dust in other seasons.

Then we'd be home, and my sister and I would trot off to our room and wait for the next time we could eat "big reeds" or "little reeds" or *"very* little reeds" with all the gay people, including our own. . . .

Now that I am several hundred years older, living in a little wine valley, this same fine feeling of ease and amusement sweeps through me when I go down the road to see my neighbors, the Dinato family. A man and his wife and some children and grandchildren and so on, they have pushed three of the big old redwood casks that have been used for a long time in California for ordinary table wine into a kind of house in front of their small winery. They really *live* there, and the smells that come from the kitchen, which is a coop added on at the back of the casks, send such delicious messages out through the low round rooms that I often stop there without any excuse to see what they may say to me.

"What are you making today?" I always feel shy and young when I ask this, for Mrs. Dinato, perhaps only a few years or weeks older than I, answers me with patience and knowingness, so that I seem a child. She smiles remotely. She shrugs.

"Today, as always," she says, "I am cooking some *pasta* or other."

"What kind of *pasta?*" I ask.

"Oh," she says softly, "today, I have some little what-you-call-thems, baby butterflies...*farfallini*, I think. You know, pinched in the middle. Very nice, if fresh."

"Yes, but what are you going to do with them?" I ask, for the perfume, the smell, the tantalizing scent of the sauce is almost intoxicating.

She looks patiently at me. "Today with the *farfallini* I thought some black olives would be good. And about four ripe tomatoes because in this weather my garden is pushing so fast. Canned would do. And a little basil...tomatoes like basil.

"Then I put the herbs into the olive oil while it's plenty hot, the garlic simmering too, of course. Then...what did I do next? I think I added the tomatoes and the black olives together. Then I put the top on and I let it get married, if you know what I mean. It can simmer along without too much heat or attention." She looks fleetingly at me. "Like people. It smells all right, eh?"

I keep on breathing as deeply and unobtrusively as possible, not to betray too callously the way I am actually nourishing myself.

Another day the wonderful smell is oregano, with some thin slices of good smoked pork sausage simmering in the juices. Juices of what? It is, perhaps, freshly grated soft Gruyère, with a little pan of sweet butter, melting and ready? And what will the pasta be this time? Long, short, thick or thin, flat, hollow, twisted?

I cannot care. I sniff happily. I am young and hungry again, and unabashed.

"You like it today?" Mrs. Donato is interested, not malicious.

I nod and ask, "What did you do this time?"

She shrugs. "Well, there was a little lamb left from last night. I chopped it and tossed it in some of its fat and a little olive oil of course, and then I took it off the fire and added about a glass of dry white wine and some anchovy filets and a handful of raisins. Now they are all puffed out and ready, so you will excuse me? Oh...we are eating it with those 'little hats'...You know, *cappelletti*."

My friend smiles at me. "I must go now to stir the sauce. I can hear ...they've turned off the conveyor belt in the winery. Wait...I'll get you a couple things from the garden, eh?"

She helps me put the stuff in the back of the car: jugs of vermouth, bottles of *vin rosé* and the wine vinegar, a bottle of Moscato for my youngest girl's next birthday ... the beautiful vegetables.

So I come home from there, and from the wine casks, and tonight for dinner we'll eat something odd and tantalizing.

Tonight we'll have a big hot bowl of pasta shells, the medium-size ones. They all come in packages now. I'll grill some tomatoes, whole. I'll make a green sauce to pour over the little shells and fill them, so that they are best eaten with a good fat soup spoon: two handfuls of fresh parsley, a small onion, a good grab of watercress, all finely chopped or half-puréed in the electric mixer and then heated with about ½ cup of olive oil and a cup of sweet butter, to bubbling but no further. This sauce usually needs no salt, but a shaker and a pepper mill will be to hand and so will a bowl of grated cheese ... and some wine in a pitcher, wine from Joe Dinato's, red and plain.

The house will smell good ... perhaps not as good as a couple of old wine casks, but not everybody can live in those!

[*McCall's*, 1956]

MARTINI-ZHEEN, ANYONE?

ACROSS the Bay in the City, which is the way you talk about San Francisco if you live just outside it, people drink whatever has the quickest answer. The bleak, stylish bars off Montgomery Street are straightfaced about Gibsons, a more or less western and much ginnier version of the dry Martini, which is to say that a Gibson has almost nothing in it but cold gin, with an onion instead of an olive for the fussy oldsters. One barman ostentatiously puts a single drop of vermouth from an ophthalmologist's instrument into his concoction at the last minute; another, with half an eye on the publicity department, uses a perfume atomizer to spray a first and at the same time final whiff of the fortified wine over the glass of icy liquor.

Across the land in Boston, too, the proportions of gin to vermouth have risen, even since Robert Benchely's dictum that there should be just enough of the latter to take away "that ghastly *watery* look." Now even the best clubs serve Martinis which are almost colorless.

As one travels towards Europe, the dryness of a dry Martini depends on the type and nationality of the transportation.

Most of the airlines have now come to the same conclusion that I did in 1929 on a ship: that there is nothing much better to combat a general feeling of queasiness than a judicious application of gin and vermouth, except of course champagne *sec*, which I could not afford. Numerous bored or frightened air passengers have found relief and courage in the little noggins of ready-mixed cocktail put into their hands as the safety belts tightened around them near La Guardia. And in the same way, the people who still think there is nothing quite as exciting as the sea approach to a new continent reach for a dry Martini in the ship's bar and feel better for it in spite of the increased volume of vermouth as they approach Plymouth, Antwerp, Hamburg, or Cannes.

The same rule applies by air and by sea: subtly and irrevocably the cocktail becomes more wine and less liquor the nearer one gets to Europe. And this isn't for reasons of economy, since gin costs ten times as much as vermouth, but because European bartenders believe firmly and stubbornly and even passionately that anyone who asks for a Martini wants a drink made mostly of Martini—and Martini is the name of a vermouth, is it not so?

By the time the plane lands at Orly or the boat train pulls into the Paris station, strong men and resolute women who, in San Francisco or Boston, would turn gray or even green at the idea of swallowing a Martini that is less than perfect, feel what probably amounts to resignation about the European version of the silvery cocktail. They know that if they make themselves very loud, and scowling or pouty depending on their age, sex, and general tendencies, they may possibly get something reminiscent of what Dad used to shake up during Prohibition. It will be made of a local version of English gin, unless they are knowing enough to demand *English* gin. It will be made of sweetened vermouth unless the American tourist is knowing enough to demand dry white vermouth, and it will be made without ice unless he demands ice. And if he is foresighted enough to demand ice, it will be served in a lump in the glass, which will often be a tall lemonade glass with the "cocktail" down in the bottom. The cocktail will be made, if the American is very fortunate, in the proportions of half and half—and if he is less so, in The City's proportions but in reverse, so that a flick of gin has been gently and cautiously passed over the ruddy, sweet, herby, and strangely bolstering potion.

This dispassionate description of a European Martini springs, I must point out, from what I have observed here in Aix-en-Provence on behalf of a Visiting American. As a footnote to the footnote, I shall add that there are bars, in most great cities of France, which can and often do serve Martinis as dry and as impeccable as those of the United States. But in Aix ("Ancient city of fountains, culture, music, almond cakes and carnival; population some 32,000; 747 kilometers south of Paris and 29 kilometers north of Marseille"), people who drink before meals are comparatively few. Those who do, usually outsiders from Paris or Lyons or even Marseille, are, according to the Aixois, nervous or overtired or just plain crazy.

I have often found myself in this category, and very pleasurably so, but have seldom felt it enough to insist on a dry Martini. To most people in Provence (including me, except in states of dire and fortunately rare duress), a glass of the cool pink wine I plan to drink with the meal is also very good indeed beforehand—and much simpler!

But this is not the case with my Visiting American, a good sensitive creature who had flown thousands of miles to spend a few crowded days here with me. Perhaps I have a lingering feeling of guilt because I exposed my friend to the local vagaries of *"le cocktail."* Certainly this visit and its accompanying alcoholic research would not have happened if I, and therefore my guest, had been in Casablanca or Caracas. No wonder I find myself worrying and even having predawn nightmares about dry Martinis, my inadequacy in procuring them, and their ultimate unattainablity in the south of France.

To get the whole thing into a fairly practicable formula which can be used by other people faced with the same problem when they are somewhat off the beaten path (that is, not in Cannes or Nice or even St. Tropez), let it be understood that there is no use asking for a dry Martini. Even more so, one must not try to Gallicize the name and ask for a Martini dry: this means a dry white vermouth made, if one is lucky, in Martini, Italy—and in the back room of the bar, if one is not. This is sometimes served chilled as it is supposed to be and occasionally one finds in it a little piece of tired lemon peel. To get a dry Martini, one must unhesitatingly ask for a *Martini-gin*, pronounced *zheen*. In hamlets, gin is usually unheard of anyway; in villages, there may possibly be one half-empty faded bottle left from the Liberation in '44, and in towns of 10,000 and over, one may actually find real gin.

Furthermore, one must say first, firmly and loudly, *"gin francais"* (if the pocketbook is thin), or *"gin anglais,"* if the visiting American is picking up the chit. Then say "very little vermouth," and finally "with ice." The latter is the most important part.

I myself have never cared much about ice. I like chilled things or even frozen things, but I feel that too much chilling or freezing often kills the flavors I want to taste. Some of my best friends, however, like, love,

crave ice to the point of ruthless addiction. My Visiting American managed to ask for and get ice by what amounted to a desperate artistry.

There is probably a permanent frost burn across the face of
Provence after our memorable ten-day pursuit of the dry Martini. I suspect that ice buckets still stand, half full of melted cubes rushed in from
butcher shops of astonished neighbors, in a dozen little places like Le
Relai Bleu in La Palatte (population 214) and Aux Cigales in Luynes
(population 382), where nobody had ever asked for ice before and quite
possibly never will again. And although nothing has been said, I feel
fairly sure that the amiable and discreet Visiting American still nurses
an aftertaste of vermouth. And I, like Provence, may be faintly but forever scarred.

This enforced bit of research, sociological as well as alcoholic, made
me wonder about the connotations of the words "dry Martini," or,
more precisely, of the word "cocktail" in what is loosely called The
French Mind. And I decided that in spite of general familiarity with Yankee movies and who-dunits and other efforts at foreign culture, to the
French, cocktail means about what it did before World War I, or even
before then—say, in the Edwardian heyday. In the midst of my semantic
musings, I happened, by coincidence, to receive from Paris a fat book
called The Drinker's Breviary, and, to my very real astonishment, I found
that in spite of its oddly old-fashioned-sounding contents it had been
published only a few years ago and not in the nineteenth century.

The book states the usual good rules for drinking in this Western
World: the reasons for drinking red wines and white wines as we do, the
care of wines, and their general significance in our culture. It also
includes ways to transfigure or pollute these viny miracles, according to
one's proclivities. There are, for instance, some appalling punch recipes,
most of them dating from long before Edward and many of them long
unused. Some, though, are still being concocted—and even drunk—at
hunt breakfasts in Lanarkshire and rectors' teas in Brookline.

The introduction in the Breviary to the subject "Les Cocktails" starts
out, "There is no firm rule about the preparation of cocktails, and as a
matter of fact fantasy and imagination are often the only guides. However, in order to compose a drink maintaining a modicum of flavor, it is
almost always essential to remember the rule that there should be, in

spite of everything and above all, a mixture of one or two strong liquors and one or two syrups."

Having briefed the gay dog of a cocktail mixer thus firmly ("in spite of everything and above all"), the *Breviary* adds in a terse sentence before its list of recipes, "Thus, for beginners, we present a few formulae which are, in a manner of speaking, *classic*."

To make a Scotch Cocktail, the *Breviary* instructs, use Scotch, sugar syrup, orange juice, lemon juice and (heaven help us!) raspberry syrup. Martini Flip calls for a lethal-sounding combination of Scotch, vermouth, eggs, powdered sugar and a pinch of nutmeg. The Vermouth Cocktail, I think, must have been intended to do in unwelcome droppers-in at cocktailtime. It is a mixture of Scotch, sweet red vermouth, powdered sugar, orange juice, lemon juice and grapefruit juice. There are also recipes for drinks called Normandy Cocktail and Cocktail Brandy. If the word "cocktail" comes first, the drink is old-fashioned. For instance, the Normandy Cocktail dates from after World War II, whereas Grandpa may have imbibed a Cocktail Brandy in London in 1911.

Probably my favorite in the French *Breviary* is the recipe for a cocktail called *Le Pink*, pronounced *pangk* or *peenk*, depending on one's social and educational level in Aix. The recipe for this drink reminded me that when I was young my father made something for parties that was fuzzy, potent, and of course pink, from applejack, eggs and grenadine. It could not possibly have been as heavenly as I remember it—nor as awful as it sounds now. *Le Pink* is composed of sweet vermouth, currant juice, cherry brandy, and the ubiquitous raspberry syrup, apparently as necessary to the old-time bar as it is to the American drugstore today. These disparate ingredients were put into a shaker, and then some ("some" seems the best way to translate *"une certaine quantité"*) shaved ice was added, the drink shaken and then served over a currant and a raspberry.

How pretty it must have looked! But I wonder what the Visiting American would have thought of it—aside from the essential "certain quantity" of ice, of course!

[*Gourmet*, 1957]

THE PLEASURES OF PICNICS

Picnicky is a tickling word, like *persnickety* or *peakedy*, and the Oxford Pocket Dictionary says that it may be used to express the desire we have, especially in good weather, to "indulge in a pleasure excursion including an outdoor meal." I agree. I feel picnicky at the very sound of it. Italian and French dictionaries stipulate a few more conditions about picnicking (the Petit Larousse, for instance, says that a *pique-nique* is a meal which everyone helps pay for), but there is one firm mutual requirement: any picnic must be eaten outdoors, *al fresco, en plein air*. I agree with this, as a serious disciple of the art of eating and drinking under trees, on rocks and on logs, beside brooks, in and on dunes of both beach and desert, and even in caves. There is a subtle yet blunt difference, though, between a true picnic and a meal eaten, no matter how delightfully, in the fresh air. A true picnic must be carried away from human dwellings, and it must be kept simple. It can consist of a piece of bread and an apple, eaten anywhere in the outdoors that will make it taste good, but it is not, strictly speaking, a *picnic* if it is on a terrace, or in a patio, or under the linden tree in the backyard. There must be some separation between man's work and God's, between the hewn tree of fine house walls and fences and the living tree whose sap runs under the bark along our backs as we lean against it. And even so, with the tree still rooted in the mountain meadow, a picnic can be no more than a beautiful outdoor meal if there are too many people assembled there for reasons other than feeling picnicky, too many measures taken to insure their bland, comfortable acceptance. A true picnic must have a certain amount of hazard about it: rough ground, stones, ants—It must be eaten, too, in the company of at least one intimate or a good number, ten or so including dogs, of fairly close people. A loaf of bread and a jug of wine are fine beneath the bough, but they do not make a picnic without the "thou." They are nourishment for the soul, as well as the more immediate body, but they cannot make themselves into a feast unless they are savored by one other hungry body, one other acquiescent soul. And a real picnic is always a feast, no matter how plain. There is some sort of allure about it, pagan perhaps, exotic and exciting. It carries a feeling of adventure, of dash and derring-do, even to take two hard-boiled eggs and a couple of ripe tomatoes out into the poison-ivy patch in April, and sit listening to birds and beetles and the soft sound of a loved voice.

There are other requisites, of course; the weather should be good, the food should be the best procurable (or none at all!), and perhaps most important the people should like picnicking. People who do not should, *must* indeed, be dismissed immediately, for want of space on this page as well as for want of space—spiritual and otherwise—beneath the bough, or on the salty sand, or beside the small singing waters of a secret stream.

The weather can play tricks, and is not thus easily disposed of. It is best, picnickily, if I may jump one syllable ahead of the Pocket Oxford, during the late spring, coolish parts of summer, and early autumn. It should be dependably clear, with only light showers in the offing. There should also be as little thunder as possible, unless the feast is reserved for two lovers who may welcome such tumult and rejoice in an emergency of self-protection. And it is always best without oppressive hot humidity, a succulent invitation to mosquitoes and wasps and suchlike party crashers. A weather-wise picnic should not be given in the middle of the day, except when there is either the green freshness of April and May in the air, or the crisp tang of October; but rather, in midsummer say, it should be held toward twilight, when the light is blue across the little valleys and along the beaches, and the sounds of brooks and waves seem more intense, more truly understandable.

As for the fare, besides being the best, it must be fitted to the season, the weather, and the people who will eat it, preferably with their fingers. It can be the classic bread and wine, with a piece of cheese alongside, but the bread must be fresh and crisp on the edges and above all honest, the kind to break open at the last minute to catch its little breath of the oven; the wine will be simple, and cool if white and air-warm if red, and right for the simple cheese. The cheese? For this kind of feast, it is silly to bother with knives and plates and anything else that can complicate life, and a good chunk of Gruyère or Cheddar will be admirable, to be pared off with a pocketknife in bites the right size for the pieces of bread and the swallows of good wine.

My girls, when they were about eight and eleven, used to go out every fair day with the shepherd into the meadows near Aix-en-Provence, and eat probably their lives' most Elysian of such feasts, at least until they were old enough to choose one other person, the "thou."

The old man would sit down, in the middle of the day, in a way which meant to the children and the three dogs, "Now we shall rest ourselves and eat," and they watched him pull from the inside pockets of his big cape a handful of garlic cloves, a half-loaf of sour, grayish bread with a good crust on it, and a liter of harsh, purplish wine drawn that morning from the cask. He would slowly cut off hunks of bread for all of them, and with his big folding knife peel the garlic cloves and slice them onto the flat surfaces of the humans' bread. Then he would wipe the knife on his baggy trousers, which the children knew must unbutton in a certain way so that shepherds in the cruel wintertime need not expose too much of themselves to the wind and the rain: the knife would be needed later to take a stone out of an ewe's hoof, or mend a shoe, or kill an adder. Then he would uncork the bottle with his black scarce teeth, and without much talk the six of them would sit under the pine tree and drink and eat their feast, with turns about at the bottle for the two-legged ones. At sundown they would come home to the slow flood of sound from the many sheep-bells, and they reeked of garlic and bad wine, and I knew they had lived beyond one dream of perfection in the rest of us. They had found it without knowing or looking.

At the other end of the scale is the kind of *jête champêtre* I once went to in Utah. It could as easily have happened in Spain or England or even Russia. The scenery would change, but the measured elegance, requisite for such a ballet of protocol and decorum, would have been the same anywhere. It was without the jollity of Mr. Pickwick's wonderful picnic after a military show, complete with an open barouche, comic rustics, fair ladies giggling picnickily, and "cold fowls, tongues, and bottles of wine." But all the Pickwickian essentials except perhaps Mr. Pickwick himself were there: the fine air, the hampers, even the rustics. There were perhaps too many people, but they were all very important and they seemed to accept one another—at least as such.

They sat with casual caution on logs which they knew had been brushed off discreetly before our arrival in a cavalcade of imported sports cars, and since they were either born Westerners or people who had fun pretending to be, they knew the several servants as Hank and Shorty and Quong-Ho and suchlike, and were as unamazed at drinking from crystal goblets in a mountain meadow as if they had been in Ridgeway or Stockholm or Salt Lake City. It was not astonishing to them to spoon fat gray caviar from a great chunk of ice trucked forty miles over the desert and up the grades that day. The vodka and the Moët Chandon were cold and commendable too, and the high singsong of Quong-Ho, talking with his grandson over the trout leaping in hot sweet butter at the edge of the clearing, sounded no stranger than it would have in a *parc privé* near Versailles or the grounds of a Bavarian hunting lodge.

There were little cold ducklings, each with a truffle and a kumquat in its belly. There were peas flown from a copper-baron's hothouse near Denver. There were wild strawberries banked around a vanilla mousse as high and impeccable as a bishop's miter. And when we sat drinking coffee made by a black dwarf one of the guests had brought from Algeria because he could always make such coffee, three men who had served the wines all evening sang to us, soft love songs from Mexico and wild border ballads. The moon was full over the Rockies, and the forest all around was black and sighing. I sucked at the thin sweet air, and thought of other ways of being picnicky.

Al fresco—en plein air—that's the secret of course. But now that more and more of us know the pleasures of eating in patios and on terraces, we may forget the mysterious excitement and allure of eating far from houses, tables, barns, chairs—"beneath the bough" of any tree at all that will shade us from the hot sun, shelter us, and the birds too, from the sudden shower. We forget that it is worth every step, once there, to have walked away from paved courtyards and paths in the deep meadow-weeds and the mosses. The heavy basket of bundles and bottles is not as convenient as the artful pantry-slides most houses now have between kitchen and patio, no matter whether in a twenty-room cottage near Sewickley or a five-room, G-1 mansion near Los Angeles, but once the sandwiches have been passed around and the beer cans are bubbling, picnickery takes over and we wonder why we don't bother oftener to do it this way, since we must eat to live. The air smells different, up on the hill. There is no sound from the superhighway half a mile below. It will be too soon, when we must leave.

Of course there can be a picnic without sandwiches, and it can be a true one. But nothing is easier to eat than this ubiquitous concoction of slices of bread with something between them, supposedly invented by a hungry earl (unless of course it is the hard-boiled egg, which in its own turn can remain its simple self or be doctored delightfully with everything from mayonnaise to minced lobster).

The best sandwich I have ever made, not to mention eaten countless times, is known in our family as a "Railroad." I think this is because I got its beginning idea from the ham sandwiches served in French railroad stations, from little carts that are pushed alongside the trains: a crisp roll slit lengthwise and buttered, with a slice of boiled ham hanging out all around. I went on from there, over many years, and by now the family Railroad is quite impressive, mainly because I insist that it be sat upon. This rite delights any picnickers under eighty-seven years of age, of course, and it is solemnly admitted by anyone who has ever eaten a Railroad that the sitting does something mysterious and essential to its special flavor. Choosing the sitter can become something of a rite too, and it is agreed that with a good fresh loaf of sourdough he or she can weigh between 100 and 160 pounds, but that anyone heavier is liable to flatten things *too* much.

Here is the procedure (since it requires one human being, a less cannibalistic word than *recipe* is needed in this case): Split a fresh long or round loaf of French bread, preferably the sour type, and remove every possible crumb of its middle. Spread both hollowed halves generously with sweet butter. Lay thinly sliced boiled ham on the bottom half, four or five slices thick. Put the loaf together, wrap firmly in a large clean cloth, and then fifteen minutes before it is to be eaten, have someone sit quietly upon it. It will be squashed quite flat and pressed firmly into a loaf that can be cut into generous slices (or wedges if a round loaf) and eaten even by people who are sometimes daunted, dentally at least, by tackling a thick crusty piece of bread and ham.

Railroads are fine with beer, of course, but my family prefers a light cold wine like a Riesling, or a rosé.

A good variation on this theme, which does not need to be sat upon, is to hollow a long crusty loaf and spread it thickly with slices of ripe avocado, heavily sprinkled with coarse salt and freshly ground pepper. This should be eaten within the hour, and is delicious with very cold tomato or vegetable juice (with or without a picnicky spike of gin or vodka in it) on a hot day in July.

A wide basket of the ripest fruits, dripping coolly from ice cubes put over them the last minute at home, is the best possible end to a simple feast like this: easy to carry, beautiful to savor, with no need for plates and spoons and all the things that can make the end of even the finest picnic seem cluttered and boring to reassemble and tote down the hills and over the hummocks to the station wagon.

Another good formula, especially in late autumn, leans upon a big pot of baked beans, with small warmed casseroles to eat them from and to feel good on cold hands. There should be plenty of rather crude, crisp things to eat with them—like sticks of cabbage heart, cauliflower, celery, white radish—buttered rounds of brown bread, plenty of beer or hot toddies, and coffee smoking into the nippy air.

Here is the best recipe I know for baked beans:

1 quart navy beans
¾ pound salt pork
2 onions, finely chopped
1 tablespoon salt
2 teaspoons hot mustard
4 tablespoons molasses
5 tablespoons dark brown sugar
½ cup dark rum
2 cups boiling water from beans
2 tablespoons bacon drippings

Soak beans overnight in cold water. Drain, cover again with water, and let simmer at low heat until the skins burst when blown upon. Drain again, saving about two cups of the liquid. Put in large casserole, preferably of pottery. Now scald the salt pork, and scald it quickly. Drain, and with a sharp knife cut slashes in the rind about half an inch apart. Bury the pork in the beans so that the rind just shows. Mix onion, salt, mustard, molasses, and sugar with bean water, and bring to a boil. Add rum, and pour this mixture over the beans. Add more boiling water if necessary: the beans must be covered. Put on a good tight lid, and bake the beans at about 300° to 325° for *eight hours*. About an hour before serving, remove the lid and dribble the melted bacon fat over the top. Add more boiling water gently if the beans are drying too fast, after about four hours of cooking.

This recipe owes its goodness to the last-hour flavor of the bacon drippings and to the very slow cooking, according to the man who gave it to me. Myself, I think the rum does its bit, too.

For something a bit more elegant, what could be more than a bit more so than little cold roasted squabs or pullets? They should be juicy but not fat, cool but not chilled, and never stuffed with anything that will fall out when as is inevitable at any *true* picnic, they are picked up to be savored to the full.

A fairly fine light red wine or a rosé, or a dry champagne, should accompany the little fellows, preferably with piles of thin sandwiches stuffed to the danger-point with watercress and held together with sweet butter, with an iced bowl of the tiny pear-shaped tomatoes called San Marzanos, or their even smaller cousins the round ones—unpeeled of course, and to be eaten with fingers and unadorned with sauces.

A little mousse, chilled on its platter and resting temporarily upon a convenient log or gatepost in the meadow clearing, is something nobody will pass by. It can be delicious and still simple, although admittedly it turns a picnic into something almost rococo. Here is a good recipe for one:

> 2 cans (2 cups) white tuna
> 1 cup very thick cream
> 1 cup dry white wine
> ¼ cup lemon juice
> 1 package plain gelatin
> pinch of cayenne pepper

Either blend fish and cream thoroughly in an electric mixer or beat together the thoroughly mashed tuna and the cream which has been whipped. Heat the wine but do not boil, and add to it the lemon juice into which the gelatin has been mixed. Season with the cayenne. Mix quickly with the fish and cream and pour into a mold. Chill several hours. Serve with wedges of cucumber and thin dry toast.

In the same way as this simple mousse, a dessert which can be eaten from little pots or cups is fun on any *al fresco* feast that still qualifies as a true picnic. The cups are easy to hold, as well as to carry to the brook's side and home again, and in the sweet air the subtly strong flavor of a chocolate or lemon cream is very good indeed. There is probably one such tried-and-true recipe for every family in our land, and here for good measure is one of ours:

> *1 package (1½ cups) semisweet chocolate "bits"*
> *1 square bitter chocolate*
> *7 or 8 egg yolks*
> *salt*
> *2 tablespoons dark rum, or*
> *1 teaspoon vanilla, and ½ teaspoon essence of mint*
> *7 or 8 egg whites*

Melt the chocolate gently, beat the yolks, and mix together with the rum or vanilla/mint and the salt. Fold in the beaten whites. Pour the whole into little pots or cups, and chill well in the coldest part of the refrigerator overnight or for at least twelve hours, to stiffen. Serve with thin dry wafers and plenty of very black coffee. This basic recipe can be toyed with: sprinkled with shaved nuts, tinkered with kirsch instead of rum, and so on.

I myself do not like to cope with open-air hearths and spitting casseroles and frying pans on a picnic. They are for patio dining. I like to clamber and puff my way toward a place where I can settle almost immediately into the proper position to appreciate what one unsung Englishman called "pretty peeps and noble vistas," and stay there as long as the light lasts and the digestive pleasures of my body and my soul sustain me.

If it be indicated, by various pressures, that I serve a more or less Lucullan feast, I still like to keep it as plain and easy as possible, with the best of every food and wine that is compatible with its surroundings. I select the weather carefully, and above all I choose the people who are most likely to be ready to go away from their familiar walls, into the woods or out upon the cool dunes. They must not be afraid of the love-calls of frogs, sea gulls, gnats—nor affronted by them. They must be able to accept the salty attack of pressed caviar and a cold roasted bird, or a plate of hot baked beans, with champagne or a can of beer as the case may be.

They must, in other words, feel picnicky.

[*Harper's Bazaar,* 1957]

APÉRITIFS: THE CIVILIZING INFLUENCE

SINCE THE earliest days of banqueting, the best parties have started off with a little something to whet the appetite for things to come. It may begin the evening with a bang—a shot of the vodka or aquavit which seems to flow almost limitlessly down Nordic throats. Or it may be the civilized whisper of an apéritif, doing its work as quietly as a witch. Apéritif—the very word speaks of sidewalk cafés under the bright shadows of the plane trees, of marble-topped tables and the hum of foreign conversation. It goes by a dozen tantalizing names—Vermouth Cassis, Americano, Byrrh. But what is it? Actually nothing more than a drink of between fifteen to twenty degrees of alcoholic content; a wine fortified with herbs, seeds, and varied medicaments and excitants which will serve to open (or *apertire*) the appetite to an agreeable sensation, whether it is toasted cheese on rye or breast of pheasant *sous cloche*. It can also be one of the blended and/or fortified wines like port and sherry. And, since this is America, where everything is sooner or later revved up to a brighter color, a larger size or a stronger flavor, it can include— by extension—a form of cocktail, made by adding vodka, gin, etc., to the original apéritif wine.

Vermouths, the prime example of a blended apéritif wine, are increasingly fashionable today, even without the addition of something stronger. For one thing, they are relatively noncaloric—compared ounce for ounce with gin, for instance, or Scotch, they are good dietary drinks—provided you don't take enough of them to get the same alcoholic bounce as from hard liquor. They are also a boon to those who want something less explosive than the solid gin Martini. (And by the

way, what ever happened to the classic four-to-one formula for this illus-
trious cocktail, in which the vermouth subtly tempered a flavored gin?)

The nationality of a vermouth can be told by its taste and color. Italian vermouth is a clear amber, tinged with a savory sweetness; while the
French variety is pale gold and dry. The home of Italian vermouth is
Torino, where the house of Francesco Cinzano & Cia. has flourished
since 1835. French vermouth, on the other hand, comes from paler varieties of white grapes in the Hérault section of France. Both are made by
a time-honored process which involves the steeping of as many as thirty macerated, pounded, crumbled herbs and spices—and even flower
pods—in good white wine. After the addition of 20 percent in bulk of
the essential *vin de liqueur*, which is a kind of brandified young wine with
plenty of grape sugar, the mixture is aged a couple of years, decanted,
filtered, clarified, pasteurized and refrigerated. These last are the only
new tricks in the whole process. Originally undertaken to ensure good
keeping in the tropics, pasteurization and refrigeration turned out also
to mature the wine to the equivalent of four or five years in the wood.

Imported vermouths vary greatly. Some of the cheaper ones are
poorly corked, and have an unpredictable overload of anise. It is safe to
say that no cheap vermouth is a bargain. It will either be raw or nox-
iously colored with caramel, and it will give off a potent, tricky fume
which promises nothing but trouble. But there are a number of commendable vermouths, domestic as well as foreign, to be found at reputable wine shops everywhere—Italian Cinzano (superior to the
Cinzano made in Argentina and Chile), and the French Noilly Prat and
Lillet are all reliable names. Once a pleasing one has been found, a good
store of it should be laid in—for drinking straight, involved in cocktails,
and as an excellent substitute for white wine in basting and marinating.
Jug vermouth of good quality is fine, too, and holds up well if decanted
into clean, clear bottles.

There are several schools of thought about the serving of vermouth.
Purists, who include most Frenchmen, usually drink it straight and at
room temperature. Another group insists, rightly we think, that mild
chilling brings out the flavor of the aromatics, which are at least as
important as the taste of the wine itself. Still other people quite frankly
pour it over ice. This is all right, provided you remember never, never to

shake up any iced wine drink. It produces a cloudy, dubious look that is distinctly unappetizing. When "rocks" are involved, stir gently.

Byrrh is as red as Dubonnet, its sibling if not its twin, and an infallible butt for jokes about Anglo-Saxons who order it on French trains, and are served a glass of beer instead. Like all other aromatized wines, Byrrh and Dubonnet are secret blends of fortified wine with herbs, flowers, spices, and in the case of Byrrh, a few medicaments such as quinine, held stable with added sugar. They can be drunk straight, or as cooling highballs in summer—the Dubonnet with a sliver of lemon, the Byrrh with a fat twist of grapefruit peel to add to its delicately harsh bitterness. A pleasant variation of the latter is what we call a "Byrrh Chaser": two jiggers of Byrrh and the juice of half a lime, gently blended in a highball glass with soda and ice.

A glass of any apéritif wine is turned into a cocktail by mixing half or more of its content with another apéritif, or with something stronger like gin or vodka or even brandy. There can be a certain snobbism attached to this behavior, depending on the political as well as the professional weather: a Dubonnet-and-gin carries more weight in certain clubs, for instance, than a blunt double-Gibson—balderdash is always fun, given the right surroundings. There can be an element of nostalgia, too—the merest whiff of a Negroni or an Americano is enough to bring the Via Veneto sharply to the senses. Both depend on Campari, those distinctively Italianate bitters, for their peculiar savor. For a Negroni, mix one-third Campari with one-third gin and one-third Cinzano; stir over ice, and strain into a cocktail glass. The mysteriously named Americano (most Americans discover it in Italy) is simply an iced highball made of two jiggers of sweet vermouth, plus one of Campari, with soda added. Switzerland's contribution to apéritif-based drinks, the Swiss, can be medium strong or potent depending on how many parts of kirsch (anything from one to five) you add to one part of Dubonnet. The Merry Widow consists of a jigger of dry vermouth and a jigger of Dubonnet plus a twist of lemon (and, optionally, a dash of orange bitters).

When cassis, which is the French name for black currant cordial, is added to either vermouth or white wine, the result is an apéritif salubrious enough to deserve more knowing in this country. Two jiggers of dry vermouth plus two-thirds of a jigger of *crème de cassis* make a Vermouth Cassis, which is usually served with ice and soda as a highball.

Some people remember drinking white wine with cassis long ago in Dijon (the home of cassis) where the mixture has, since the liberation, acquired the name of "Kir"—after the doughty little priest who was mayor while the town pulled itself together again. It is a comparatively harmless and inexpensive drink, and a pretty sight when served: a stemmed glass of chilled dry white wine with a dash of cassis in it can lead gracefully to all kinds of skullduggery, gastronomical or otherwise.

The fortified wine called sherry or sack or Jerez has been drunk with pleasure for at least four hundred years, in almost every color and degree of sweetness. Of the three basic types—Fino, Amontillado and Oloroso—most Americans lean to the pale, dry Finos, or the slightly darker and medium-dry Amontillados. It is curious that this general taste for lightness and dryness has not led more people to discovering the deliciously ozonic Manzanilla—the Fino of Finos and the absolute favorite of the Spaniards themselves. Though it is by no means as universally stocked as sherry, a bottle of it can usually be located at any good wine seller's. As for our domestic sherries, produced in Eastern or California vineyards, some of them are excellent cousins to the original wines of Jerez, though none of them quite compare with, say, a Gonzalez Byass Fino, or a Duff Gordon Amontillado.

Sherry is a subtle potion, but it needn't be taken too solemnly. A good glass of it will work wonders before any kind of food, and it is a decent wine to drink at those other hours of the day when a nice, unfuddling stimulant is called for. A tot of it at eleven in the morning has saved many a man from the dustbin, and many a contract from the wastebasket. Before meals Fino or Manzanilla seem to suit the palate best, and they should be served chilled. But toward five o'clock when the shades are drawn and somebody bids five no trump, let it be a browner, sweeter sherry—a rich Oloroso—served at room temperature.

One of the best apéritifs in the world, according to a certain knowledgeable counselor-at-law, is "a glass of sherry, having first been chilled, poured over four to eight drops of Worcestershire sauce." This may sound a curious drink, but we agree with the lawyer that it opens all the windows of the palate, whether for a bowl of soup and baked apple or a Lucullan feast.

Rich mixed drinks made with sherry—cobblers, flips, eggnogs and such—have gone out of fashion, in most cases deservedly. But there *are*

a few simple cocktails involving sherry which have a fresh yet not outlandish accent. The Adonis (one part Italian vermouth, two parts sherry, dash of bitters) and the Bamboo (one jigger dry sherry, one jigger
vermouth, dash of bitters) are urbane substitutes for, respectively, the
sweet and the dry Manhattan. And the Valencia—one part sherry and
four or five parts gin—is a powerful variant of the Martini.

Famous and delicious in cookery, Madeira is every bit as good as an
apéritif wine. Tasting like a relative to sherry (which it isn't), it was the
American apéritif par excellence in Colonial times, and is still served as
such in the South. It might well be revived elsewhere. Taken in the
eighteenth-century manner with the accompaniment of a dry biscuit, a
glass of light, aromatic Madeira is a formidable competitor to sherry or
port as a preprandial drink, and can go along nicely with the soup. Two
of the lightest and best are the famous Rainwater, made by Welsh Brothers,
and Leacock and Company's Gloria Mundi—it may take a little effort,
north of the Mason-Dixon line, to find them.

A glass of port before meals may be considered horrendous by some
schools of gastronomical thought, but extended research by several
highly qualified trenchermen has established that a glass drunk a good
half hour before dinner can make an admirable apéritif, and is indeed
widely taken as such in France. In America, it is regrettably in disrepute—
as a favorite tipple of skid row, and because so much of the cheap stuff
sold as port in this country is a sickly travesty of the real thing. It is high
time to rescue this delicious and noble wine from neglect.

Port, which comes from vineyards on the cruel slopes of Duoro in
Portugal is, in its standard form, a contrived blend of wines, each
matured in its own cask and at its own speed—"port from the wood" to
the trade. Vintage port, the noblest of the breed, is chosen from the
wines of a superlative year, and never blended. Most of its aging takes
place in the bottle, and it can live as long as eighty or ninety years without losing its savor, whereas a standard port may reach maturity in a
decade. Assuming no fakery is involved, you can tell the age of a given
port by its color—ink-dark in its first youth, changing to ruby in its
prime, and finally to tawny which is the beautiful color of its old age. The
older it is, the less will be the actual sensation of sweetness on the palate.

What is called "white port" is the French favorite. It is made in the
same meticulous and time-consuming way as red ports, and is a

thoroughly pleasing salute to what the cooks and the gods may plan to follow it. White port, too, can have nostalgic overtones. There was a time in France when a glass of it cost four francs—a princely sum in 1929 or so when many a young expatriate discovered it. Even today, it seems to suggest soft rain on the Quai Voltaire and hot chestnuts to buy.

One of the most sturdily distinguished ports procurable is made by the Ficklin family of Madeira in our own California. For Portuguese ports, Sandeman, Cockburn, Harvey's and Robertson's are all reputable labels. Extremely fine vintage port, however, is hard to come by—you have to depend on the honesty and discernment of your wine seller.

One good thing about serving apéritifs is that there seems to be little temptation to nibble alongside. The classic dry biscuit of English novels, or a few salty wafers or almonds, will be more to home with an *apéro* than a doodad fancified with a flute of creamed cheese, one caper and six beads of caviar. Even better are matzoth wafers, or their Armenian variants—so neutral in their basic flavor that they are often used by professional wine tasters to keep their palates fresh. They should be brushed well with soft, sweet butter, and then sprinkled generously with curry powder, paprika, cayenne, garlic salt, well-macerated *oregano* or whatever flavor seems fun to try—not mixed, of course, but one or two wafers of each. Then give them a slow heating in the oven until they start to turn gold and they are done, for today or later. (They can be kept for several weeks, and warmed up as needed.) A variation of the same heinous but delightful procedure is matzoth well buttered and sprinkled with coarse white or brown sugar and cinnamon or nutmeg, at will. They should be toasted well, and then broken into pieces and served in a little basket. These sweet or heavily seasoned frivolities are a nice change from the omnipresent salted almonds and things that go dunk in the night.

Thus served, the apéritif becomes the benign stimulus it ought to be—neither filling nor fuddling. Whether we take it at room temperature or chilled, with ice, with soda water or bitters added, with a dash of this or that according to our whim, we will be starting the evening under a civilizing influence.

[*Harper's Bazaar*, 1958]

ODE TO THE OLIVE

I ATE MY first olive when I was about five, and it was a dreadful experience. I was a newcomer to Southern California, when an older girl named Ruby shook down a ripe olive onto the sidewalk and said gently (snake in tree), "Just put it in your mouth and chew it up, the way we do. You'll love it." Then she watched while I munched the almost impossibly bitter pulp as directed, and swallowed it and the pointy seed with no more than a few tears in my eyes. She laughed loudly, and for a long time, and I did not like her ever again.

I did, however, acquire a taste for it at once and did decide, in spite of what happened that early day (waves of revulsion form the painful bitterness, some nausea, and a sense of potential danger from the seed heading for my innards), that olives would be one of my favorite things in life. I did not yet know about their oil. In fact, I did not know it existed until about four years later, when a new baby appeared in the family and a two-ounce bottle of pure olive oil was put in the family medicine closet with our panaceas like Mentholatum, Phenolax and Baume Bengué. It was to rub on my little sister's mysterious navel and her petal skin. The bottle had a delicious smell, and so did she.

As for the olives themselves, cured green or black, nobody in the household knew what to do with them, except now and then to nibble or discard the impossible large, hard things served along with celery stalks as an "appetizer" in expensive restaurants. But I am convinced that I knew before I ever bit into one that olives and all their products would give me pleasure for the rest of my days.

Cultivated olive trees have been growing for more than 5,000 years of recorded history. Their cured fruit was probably first used as a food in

Asia Minor, and then turned up in Egypt. The Greeks took olive trees on to Spain and Italy, France, Portugal.

In Spain the berries are dry and bitter, and in Provence they are somewhat fatter, and their oil is a little more unctuous. In Italy there is more water from the mountain streams, and the quality of both berry and oil is sweeter, more generous, milder. But everywhere there is a rigid grading: in Greece and Spain, with their arid, sterile hillsides, olives can be small, with mean large seeds and hardly enough flesh to pickle; in France they will be nutty and crisp, and perhaps worth somewhat more in the oil vat than on the table, but with equal demand; in Italy the oil is most valuable to the growers, and table olives are often brought in from neighboring countries for the requisite fillip, the subtle texture, in great cooking.

Picking and pressing these godsent fruits that spring from barren, windswept hillsides follow a fairly stern pattern. For eating, green olives are pulled off the willowy twigs by hand, carefully, and are then put through a process of soaking in an alkaline solution and then in a brine, often spiced in various regional ways, to make them edible. Ripe black or purple olives are treated even more gently, since they bruise more easily, and some are put aside for eating, and treated in hot brine, then dried, and often pickled in pure oil, although many are sold in brine. The oil itself, though, is made from ripe dark olives, and the first pressing of these beautiful fruits, which have never fallen from the tree, is sweet, full-bodied and gastronomically irresistible. It is labeled as "pure," "virgin," and when it can be bought, it should be. A virgin pressing stays fresh the longest, and in its purest state cannot spoil.

A second grade of oil is made after this first production, from the first pulp and from poorer grades of fruit. It is extracted in the same way, by pressure, but under heat, to pull it out. It can grow rancid with time, and milky or cloudy until filtered. It was used 3,000 years ago by Egyptian ladies for their hair and skin, as it still is today, in shampoos and soaps. It is also used widely in cooking, being less expensive than the "virgin," but with a ranker yet still subtle flavor.

A third grade of oil, extracted from almost any ripe fruit left on or under the trees, is usually treated with a solvent and is employed widely in industry as a lubricant and adulterant. Until a few centuries ago, without chemicals of course, olive oil was used in lamps or stoves.

Naturally a regional style of eating is shaped by what grows best the most cheaply, and ever since the Greeks brought olives to the Mediterranean they have been part of the culture there. Olives of every size, shape, color, grade, flavor are sold routinely in open-air markets in Mediterranean towns and villages, and are as much a part of the cuisine as broth or flour, wine or eggs. They are brought to the stalls on market days in big tubs, in their brine, which is sometimes nothing but salty water and sometimes spiced with local herbs or floating with everything from sweet peppers to bitter oranges. The merchant holds a long wooden scoop (olive wood, of course) with a deep, round bowl pierced with small holes, and will dip into any of his tubs for a taste of this color, that flavor, depending on what one plans to eat that day: a chicken fried in pure oil, then simmered with onions, tomato, garlic, wine, with small black pitted olives added for the last few minutes; a three-part plate of black, purple, green olives, all with a different flavor and texture, as hors d'oeuvres with fresh crusty bread and sweet butter, perhaps.

I know a thousand ways I like to eat and use olives and their oil, and I continue to indulge myself in them, albeit with some small difficulties in California. I feel almost traitorous, or at least apologetic, when I admit that I do not like the olives I can buy here, and that when I must serve them whole I first heat them gently in a little good oil (olive, of course) with a clove or two of garlic, and then let them cool. At their appetizing best, I like them salty and unadorned, in a little crude, flat dish like the one in a Modigliani painting I remember fondly, and they can be as small as peas and as green as grass. Now and then some fine dish of cracked Dungeness crab, potato salad or cold salmon cries out for mayonnaise, and now and then I listen and agree, and make one from a light but pungent oil.

There are many cooks who mix half olive oil and half unsalted or rendered butter for easy and good frying. There are many cooks, too, who mix one part of olive oil with one of vegetable oil for what they feel is good mayonnaise. I have tried these methods and can approve of them, but I do not really understand them gastronomically, and prefer to stay with the best olive oil I can buy, light for this, heavier for that. A good honest one is expensive (about $15 a gallon) and seems to get more so all the time. It should be, just as good wine should be, when one thinks of how they both are produced, with labor and love.

Given the best procurable oil, I would sauté and marinate and blend and coat and soak with it, and given honest native berries that have been respected enough to keep their intrinsic tastes and textures, I would add them to dishes of fowl, beef, pork. For me, olives and their oil are more essential than many other things I may want, like a vintage Rolls-Royce (not really), or an aluminum ladder so that I can mend my roof myself.

Pan Bagnat

A *pan bagnat* is a flat, round roll, sliced crosswise, with the cut side bathed in olive oil and covered with available delicacies like thinly sliced onions, tomatoes, pitted black olives, anchovy filets, sliced hard-boiled eggs or almost anything at hand.

According to many devotees, the top is put back on, but it is not the way my source, an old fisherman's wife from Cros-de-Cagnes in the south of France, did them, served warm on thick brown pottery plates Renoir had made and signed for her on the backs.

She sliced the rolls in half, bathed them properly in good oil from her farm, and covered them to about twice their thickness with two or three things that might be handy, but never a great mishmash. One day it would be chopped green peppers, pitted olives and sliced hard-boiled eggs. Another time it would be sliced tomatoes, chopped artichoke hearts and anchovies. Always, though, she topped the pretty thing with a mixture of finely minced garlic and whatever green herb she had gathered—parsley, thyme, rosemary, sage—and made into a loose paste with more olive oil. She put this generously on each round, and pressed it down firmly into the oiled bread with a fork or the back of a spoon. She never put the second half of the roll on top, so that each looked more like a rough pizza than a sandwich.

About a half hour before I was to be there, she put them into the oven that was still warm from her day's baking. By the time I arrived, Renoir's plates and her thick goblets were on the kitchen table, with a pitcher of coarse, cool rosé from another relative's vineyard, and the thick rounds of bread were crisp on the bottoms, brimming with a heady, warm mixture that had wilted deliciously together and yet still was fresh—completely Provencale.

[*Travel and Leisure,* 1976]

THE MIDNIGHT EGG AND OTHER REVIVERS

"A cold potato at midnight..." and at about the turn of our century, a Midwestern writer put this haunting phrase in one of her forgotten essays, although I can find no reference to it. I remember it clearly from when I first heard it in about 1940. She was lonely. She felt comforted, or perhaps merely revived, when she could sneak down to the silent family kitchen and pull out a boiled potato from a bowl of them in the icebox. As I see it now, she ate it standing up in the shadows, without salt, but voluptuously, like a cat taking one mouseling from a nest and leaving the rest to fatten for another night.

In general, there is a clear difference between revivers and comforters, of course aside from their equal importance in our survival.

Most of us have a few private revivers, which we administer knowingly to ourselves, usually in the company of one or more companions. Comforters we eat or drink alone. Revivers demand a certain amount of public ceremony and can be cold or hot, no matter how plain, but comforters are a private ritual and almost always warm.

One dependable reviver is The Midnight Egg, or at least I found it so for several years when I danced late at night. My partner and I would make it in two small flat casseroles on top of the electric stove and eat it standing up. As I look far back on it, there is a cooked resemblance in this prescription to the prairie oysters that have revived many a wan drinker in the morning hours, but then it seemed merely restorative, delicious, digestible.

The recipe, as in all these concoctions, is simple-unto-idiocy: butter melted very gently in little pans, about one tablespoonful of cream and one of Worcestershire sauce laid in for each one, an egg or two broken in, lid put on. The minute the egg white has set and the juices are bubbling, it is time to eat and go to bed.

Another familiar reviver is Boeuf Tartare, at least in my own past uses and needs. For a healthy person who can enjoy finely chopped raw beef, this loosely ruled concoction is perhaps the most easily digested of all "energy" boosters. The teased, mushy, expensive patties turned out by headwaiters in fancy restaurants, often with a killer of cognac added on top of all the herbs and pickles and egg yolks and dribdrabs in the basically innocent dab of meat, are not what I mean. By a Boeuf Tartare I mean, as a dependable reviver for those who can cope with its surprising powers, a quarter pound of finely chopped beef of the leanest and best quality, mixed lightly with some minced fresh herbs and probably an egg yolk to bind it, a little olive oil, and pepper and salt to taste. It can grow more sophisticated with a dollop of oyster sauce or Worcestershire, but if the demand is urgent, such extras are merely that: *extra*. The reaction is immediate and healthy, if the full prescription has been followed: pinker cheeks, brighter eyes and a general look of benign revival.

Of course plain sugar, the plainer the better, is a natural helper. Again the system must be functioning well. Once I drove slowly across the southern part of this country from California to Florida, and for a lot of the trip, my partner and I treated ourselves to a midafternoon praline, a fresh brown patty of melted (butter? cream?) sugar spread over some pecans, that we had bought yesterday or today at a roadside stand. They were simple and revivifying, and made us feel sure that we would arrive sometime at the next night-stop and ask the bellhop to bring us a sample of the local White Mule.

Perhaps the most innocent of all the revivers were the large "kitchen bowls" of cornflakes that I dished out in my late teens. My mother had learned, early on, that young people need food at all hours when she left two neighbor girls alone in the house and they desperately ate all the chocolate laxative in the medicine cupboards. Since then, she had bowls and pitchers put in the kitchen at night to foil prowlers and to placate latecomers, and my younger sister and I benefited happily from her self-protective thoughtfulness.

It was during Prohibition. Our dates had to drive many miles to fetch and carry us to the available jazz stands in Southern California. Then they had to bring us back to the ranch. And before they started out again to Pasadena or Oceanside or someplace, they needed stoking, though we had stopped at a currently stylish chili hut along the way.

And there was the cornflake bowl on the kitchen table! Big pitcher of cool milk—glasses for drinking it—brown sugar, big spoons, soup dishes. We *pounced* on it. My sister and I did not drink bootleg booze, always wondering if anyone would date us prudies, but some young men did, because we liked jazz music and we had an invisible but generous mother who bought cornflakes lavishly.

Those delicious light unobtrusive morsels invented by Mr. Kellogg can act as a comforter as well as a reviver. I know a man who depends on them. He is popularly considered to be a party fellow, always either entertaining or having a wild fling. Probably much of this contrived, if cynically dismal, smoke screen is true, but behind it lives somebody who leaves the scene at times to go to bed at about sundown with a large bowl of cornflakes and milk. What else he does, I do not know. But the next day he always arises bright and snappy—no more social doldrums—ready to take on the British Embassy or the Queen of Kassabah.

Potatoes seem to have some of this magical comforting quality, too. I have known one woman, perhaps decadent enough to belong to Aubrey Beardsley's drawings rather than current depictions of raddled witches of early age. She lived longer than she cared to, but often comforted herself secretly by baking a potato. She baked only *one*. It was carefully chosen and kept for this spiritual emergency. It was an Idaho Russet, as I remember, in perfect condition, like a bull ready for the *corrida*.

Of course I never shared these secret potatoes, but I know about them. The woman withdrew from the world while she waited for one to be ready. She dismissed her servant, took the telephone off the hook, prepared herself in sloppy old loose clothes and slippers, and waited sensuously for the moment when the spud would be baked through and she could sit alone at the kitchen table and cut it open and watch the butter (forbidden) and salt (tut, tut!) and pepper (oh!) soak into it. Then she ate it, skin and all. She felt *comforted*, when she went alone to bed.

And oysters are comforting too. (Of course, one must like them to begin with. . . .) Where I live, they can be bought, freshly shucked, in little cold jars, and they are delicious, and a bowl of creamy stew made from them can warm any such soul and body as mine. But perhaps this is not a general taste. . . .

Another remedy, for of course, all these revivers-comforters can qualify as folk medicine, I feel very sure, is one used by friends of mine when they are "feeling somewhat better" or simply lonely or peckish. It is called Hungarian Caraway Soup, and the recipe is from Sylvia Vaughn Thompson's small classic, *Economy Gastronomy:*

> *½ stick butter or margarine*
> *2 tablespoon flour*
> *1 tablespoon caraway seeds*
> *2 cups hot water*
> *salt if wished*
> *rye toast or croutons, buttered*

Melt butter, stir in flour and seeds, and brown slowly until seeds pop. Add hot water carefully, bring to boil, simmer a few minutes, and serve, poured over a slice of hot buttered rye toast or with croutons on the top.

And then there is plain old Milk Toast! It has been a source of re-assurance and moral and physical strength for hundreds of years, I am sure, and like many such friends, it perhaps does its best work when eaten in solitude. It seems to soothe nerves and muscles and mind all together. The easiest place to eat it is, of course, at the kitchen table instead of, for instance, alone in a dining room. (It is excellent in bed, too, if somewhat precarious. . . .)

Once I watched enviously in a famous elegant restaurant while my companion ate peacefully through two or three large bowls of it and left me to cope with a small truffled quail in aspic. The headwaiter gave his full attention to concocting the Milk Toast at the table, and the sommelier spilled a little of my vintage bottle while he watched the ballet. It was all because my escort, who was diagnosed as a near genius in molecular physics, had well-advanced ulcers at the age of twenty-five and had been advised by a peerless doctor to ask for the nursery pap whenever he was in doubt. It was memorably impressive.

Milk Toast does not need silver chafing dishes and deft swooping waiters, of course. Basically it needs the wish to eat it and nothing else, which that young man had. Then there must be good ingredients. It would be a sorry dish, made of blue-thin milk and squeezy puffy packaged "bread" served in a cold bowl. (Moral, perhaps: Choose either a gastronomical palace or the kitchen table for its full savoring!)

To make a restful, nourishing, delicious Milk Toast, on a cold night or any time at all when solitude seems indicated, warm a generous bowl while making two slices of toast. The bread should be firm and hearty, but not strongly flavored as is rye or pumpernickel. Warm two cups of creamy milk, just to the simmer point. Butter the toast generously and cut into cubes. Season the milk with salt, pepper and paprika if desired. Put the bits of buttery toasted bread in the warm bowl, pour the seasoned milk over them, and walk gently to wherever you have decided to feel right in your skin.

When I was very young, my sister and I sometimes ate Sunday Night Supper with our Aunt Gwen, and it was multiplied bliss when she would give us bowls of hot milk toast made with *cocoa!* By now the prospect is untenable to me, but then it meant much more than the soft brown color and smell, the taste and feel of the exotic blend of hot sweet chocolate, rich milk, homemade bread toasted and buttered.

When I think of such simple comfort, I feel almost but not quite convinced that Milk Toast is the best of all possible remedies, at no matter what age and in no matter what situations. But for decades, I have been dedicated, almost, to a cure-all, a surefire palliative, that I should perhaps never confess to. It involves a brand of "cream of tomato" soup so well known that it fortunately need not be named, and an equal amount of the best possible plain milk I can buy, and some cinnamon.

I have tried other brands of soup. I have even made a superb version of my own. The Secret Ingredient in the ubiquitous can gives my comforter exactly what it needs. So, I heat equal parts of the soup and milk and put a generous dollop of powdered cinnamon into the bottom of the little fat pitcher I drink from, and go to bed with it and a book.

Perhaps this should be a footnote, but it must be made clear that what one eats or drinks from can often become ritualistic, with true comforters. I don't know about plates for baked potatoes. Probably regular addicts of cornflakes and milk have their preferred bowls. With

Milk Toast people, though, the dish can become almost foolishly impor-tant, and once when I was doing some kitchen aid for a friend with a broken ankle and got out a chipped old brown bowl to crack some eggs into, she almost snapped at me, "No, not that one!" Then she said, as if in explanation, which indeed it was, "That's the Milk Toast Bowl."

I feel that same way about my Tomato Soup Pitcher. It is blue and white, with a wide lip, and is called a *boccalino* in Italian Switzerland where I got it. It is really meant for wine, and one drinks from the side, since the pinched spout dribbles clumsily. I keep it at the back of my cup-board so that nobody will use it for something unimportant like cream or flowers. It is for Tomato Soup.

The right time comes. I feel tired or merely *ready*, and I shake some cinnamon into my fat little pitcher, open the ridiculous can into a saucepan and put in the milk, and stir until there is steam. Then I pour the sweetish bland pink smerch onto the spice and head for what I am almost sure will be a pleasurable time of sipping and reading and feeling myself grow warm and sleepy. It is a placebo—a nipple, maybe. And it is phony and vulgar. I love it, because it is my comforter . . . better, for me anyway, than a cold potato at midnight.

[*Bon Appétit,* 1978]

SIMPLE THINGS

A FRIEND who was talking about beach picnics with young children said, "It's strange how one's tastes can diminish with age." We were speaking about people under eleven who like and even need to roast marshmallows on long forks or sticks. The brown caramelized perfumes rise up over the wet sand and the cold kelpy breeze, and the ceremonial delicate brown candy-skin is offered to the older people around the embers. It is a ritual, and as age takes over the celebrants, it becomes almost arduous to accept the innocent offering. The grandparent who talked no matter how lovingly about such ceremonies said, "I turn pale. I need a secret store of edibles...bread and cheese, or a mussel or oyster."

Of course there are more than beach picnics to try the gastric endurance of people who have grown beyond such childhood pleasures. There is, for instance, day-to-day living with friends still in their first two decades of The Eating Game, who need peanut butter, tuna fish, bananas, fudge brownies.

I suspect that many children say they want these staples because their elders assume that, as youngsters, they must do so. I cannot understand why this is the case. I never did, for one: nobody ever told me I was suppose to like this or that. But of course when I was growing up, I never tasted peanut butter because it was a "store product," and canned tuna was not recognized in our kitchen, although salmon was. (Sardines were unknown.) As for bananas, they were almost equally strange to us: the cut-glass fruit bowl on the dining room sideboard held oranges and apples and avocados in season.

Fudge was made for treats, and I felt almost adult when I turned out my first batch for the serious appraisal of the family when I was about nine. As for fudge brownies, they were introduced to our cuisine when I was twelve, by a voluptuous aunt from the "East" (Michigan), and they were indeed delicious and insidious small squares of rich moist darkness, with a slight crackle on top. Gradually they grew soggier and lumpier and generally less appealing, as Time and our succession of kitchen slaveys rolled on, until finally I forwent them forever as I watched a familiar to our croquet suppers drop one into a sunken wicket from a copy of the *Youth's Companion*, which he held with careful nonchalance to hide his deed. Our relief was mutual, even if it was unacknowledged.

He was perhaps in preadolescent agony with shyness, but I knew as I saw this little act that he was extremely courteous. The fudge brownie was indeed inedible, and he wished to spare himself and all of us the flat admission. He was a nice boy. (He is now a retired minister, and I have never served anyone another fudge brownie, although I know from the first heady introduction that they can be very good.)

As for fudge itself, I cannot envisage eating it at this point in my life. I know it too can be good, although I wonder how many little people make it anymore. I see shops on city streets where it lies in sworls on long pans in the windows and customers throng for it. They look elderly and forlorn.

Bananas are good. By now, in the apparent diminishment that aging brings, I seldom eat them, and when I do, I like them in compotes or lightly sautéed or baked: a decadence in the flavors! I keep them on hand for people who seem to eat them more innocently as a kind of pick-me-up, monkey-style with the peel laid back.

Tuna is a puzzler to me, since I never ate it when I was at the tuna stage. I have known young mothers who insist that all their children ask for is tuna, and older ones who profess to retch at the thought of the tons of it they have been forced to serve their children, but lately a grandmother left two young visitors and six cans of fish for a lunch with a friend, and the little people never touched the supplies. (They did not even mention peanut butter!)

By now, peanut butter is a part of prepuberty life and onward, we are told by the media, and there are connoisseurs of nine years of age. It is a serious subject, because sometimes a lack of the unguent can menace actual survival! (I feel removed from this syndrome, since it did not exist in my upbringing. I am sure that I would remember it if I had been hooked and then dried out. . . .) Once I prepared for a young friend's visit by putting in or laying down, as the wine buffs might say, some reputable brands of the stuff. But "smooth" was out. "Chunky" was in and vice versa. All of it was savored on equally well-dictated graham crackers in the afternoon, old pieces of toast midmorning, white soda crackers for a snack in private after the "good-nights" had been accomplished. It was to the young palate what Mentholatum or even a small gin-and-French might be to older bones and bodies.

Peanut butter varies with the jars it is put in, and I think the best that can be bought may be found in so-called health food stores. This is as true of many other nut butters, and if I had to eat any of them I would probably settle for cashew, although few young people really like it better than the more familiar stronger peanut stuff.

Perhaps it is wiser for people past the age of thirty to forget all this lost sensuality and think about remembered pleasures that might possibly taste good to them, as taste itself diminishes and it actually becomes more fun to talk about fudge and tuna and bananas than to eat any of them. So . . . how about catsup? Or applesauce?

I once had a fairly secret craving for catsup, which was among the "bought" things we did not serve when I was little. Since Grandmother, who was our gastric arbiter, did not approve of tomatoes, a "boughty" dish, we never even ate sauces made from them. (Now and then we were served a little side dish of a pinkish watery concoction made mostly of soaked bread. It was revolting, and proved Grandmother's point that tomatoes were not fit to eat.) So catsup was a forbidden fruit, which may explain its immortality for me.

I still love it. I like a little spoonful of it now and then or a lick from the bottle top after I have poured out some of it. I like to make versions of it from recipes by Marian Harland and Mrs. Beeton. I like one or two of the available brands on the store shelves. A splash of it is good in a cup of hot broth.

But my early dreams of eating a big puddle of it in a deep bowl of mashed potatoes no longer seem worth trying to realize. What a crazy idea! Who in these days would ever bother to make enough beautiful fresh whipped beaten rich potatoes, to begin with? Would it be worth the game, to build this monument and then sit down doggedly to it and pretend that it was good?

As for applesauce and even baked apples, they are still a worthy gamble. The apples are not as dependable as they once were, so that I never know whether they'll turn into sludge or be photogenic and impenetrable beauties in a decorative bowl, and I try to cope with this basic puzzlement by "doctoring" as I go along. I like to dig out the cores, sniff the flavors, and then stuff them with raw sugar or leftover jam or mincemeat, according to their messages. I add cinnamon or nutmeg. I usually put a good dollop of sweet butter on top of each and cover them closely in a slow oven for a couple of hours (this would be at 325°). At the last, I give them a quick sprinkle of sugar and a turn under the broiler.

Sometimes modern baking apples, no matter how well treated, turn into a leathery mush. Then one must fall back on the stuffing, or even a little help from the brandy bottle and the butter bowl. Or they may remain like bullets, in which case it is best to taste a few spoonfuls of their juice and then throw them into the nearest pit.

On considering this chancy problem about finding friendly apples, I am inclined to skip them as one of the undiminished foods! Perhaps they should all be made into applesauce, which can be one of man's best table-helps. Of course applesauce stands being gussied with spices and enrichments, to be served either with meats in the Germanic style or as a hot dessert. It can be from a jar, even store-bought. But a bowl of fresh homemade applesauce, cool and with a big spoonful of cottage cheese staring up from its middle, is a fine greeting for a new day, whether one is innocent or old. And for dessert, as I remember from the first twenty ravenous years of my life, chilled applesauce and squares of a hot thick slab of gingerbread can make life blissful. What is more, I think it might be like that, anytime... tonight... *now*.

I suppose that the actual diminishment my friend spoke of, in saying how, when she was plied as an elder with crusty brown marshmallow skins on the dark cold beach by the fire, all she really wanted was a piece of bread and three fresh mussels, I suppose this really implies a lack of interest in preparing the dainties. I myself have no desire at all, when I reflect seriously, to bake a pan of Edith's Gingerbread (an infallible recipe!) and open a jar of fresh applesauce that has been brought to me by a reliable friend, and sit and eat it.

What has waned, then, may perhaps be appetite rather than interest. I like to think about all these diminishments, but I know that I am simply not as hungry as I used to be. I certainly don't want a tuna sandwich right now, nor a brownie. But I might settle, for breakfast tomorrow, for some *Apfelmus mit Schmierkäse*, with perhaps a slice of hot buttered toast— homemade, all of it, of course. (Actually, I doubt it.)

Or how about potato chips? I discovered them rather late. They were not known at all to the hinterlands of Southern California when I grew up, and I was perhaps about twenty when I first ate one. Life has been different since then, torn between searching for the good ones and spurning, often with gastric frustration, the obviously bad.

Potato chips are mainly dreadful, but I still like them, and almost never let them cross my doorstep for fear I'll eat them *anyway*. When they have been correctly made, correctly served, correctly savored, they are ineffable. (That is a word seldom used by me, but I mean it now, and on this subject.)

The best I ever ate were in Germany in about 1932, but the ones I had the most fun with were at the old Lausanne Palace in Switzerland, where one day they tasted delicately like fish and the next like mush- rooms and then perhaps like lamb chops, depending upon what the fry cook had in his kettle. But they were always fresh and subtly reminiscent of what had already gone on, a kind of promissory note, too.

My friend on the beach was right: decent bread and a few mussels or oysters. Still it is nice to *think* of other less possible comforts, like gin- gerbread and catsup... and for me, potato chips.

And I know a man well toward one hundred who still loves bananas in any style but preferably straight from the skin. He loves tuna, prefer- ably in sandwiches. He loves fudge, and especially fudge brownies, preferably topped with peanut butter. But all this may diminish as he grows older.

[*Bon Appétit*, 1979]

EATING CATSUP FROM A BOTTLE

PROBABLY one of the best things about the current trend or vogue, or fad, or whatever you would call our sudden interest in regional foods in America, is that we are in a kind of revolt against what transportation has done to our eating habits.

Suddenly, we are saying that just because there are strawberries from Mexico and pineapples from Hawaii and Alaskan salmon almost any time of year, we do not really need them. We are less impressed than we have ever been by transported delicacies. It is *very* stylish, we find, to eat peas from down the road when they are in season, rather than having them grown in hothouses and kept in cold storage and brought 1,000 miles. And corn: now the "nicest" people eat corn when it grows at its sweetest and milkiest from a neighbor's backyard, and talk knowingly of ways to cook it, the same hour or even the day it was picked, whereas only a few years ago, we felt that corn itself was a poor thing at best, suited to cows and farm boys.

The whole trend is heartening. But it may be a pain to the self-styled greengrocers who for so long have counted on "ripening rooms" and colored lights to sell their half-ripe produce. What can a man do with his green papayas and white-bottomed strawberries, and his wax-covered cucumbers, when all his old customers are growing their own produce or buying their neighbors'? It's a puzzlement!

Of course, the best answer so far, and one of the most exciting, is that local farmers' markets are "in"! They used to be called "produce farms," or "stands," or something equally drab. Now, even a ten-lug-box plant table is called, at least by the loyal admirers, a Farmers' Market.

(Perhaps if there's only one man to run the stand, it is called *The Farmer's Market.*)

In general, though, we usually think of any such venture as a kind of cooperative, organized by people who never held a hoe, who get a number of local people to agree to bring in any extra produce they may have for as long as they have any to bring. This then is sold at current market prices, and the profits (or losses) are divided equally among the many contributors to the supplies. It's a cold-blooded system, but of true local benefit.

Usually, things are tough for the first year. The second year, some of the local merchants who were openly hostile have come to realize that most people who have extra corn or beans or blackberries are not at all interested in hurting the sales of a merchant nearby who sells T-shirts, prescription drugs, or even old feather boas. By the third year, any so-called Farmers' Market that has from the first been correctly organized is going strong. And what is best of all, the feeling about it is *good.*

I've watched this happen several times lately. It is always true: one bad year, with slander and insults eddying about; a second better year, and then everything is just dandy, and we can breathe in peace and sit back with our bellies full of fresh corn and squash and dark red strawberries....

And the finest part is that many people who never knew or even cared much about anything except frozen convenience foods eaten on the run now feel almost neglected if they cannot have good canned things all winter, picked and bought at their cheapest in the summer and then "put up" by moms of every sex and color who until a little while ago did not know the difference between a Mason jar and a microwave dish!

When I was little, I longed desperately to eat catsup from a bottle. It was, of course, strictly forbidden because the sauce was not made in our own kitchen (and anyway bottles were vulgar, especially on the table). I still think I may never really get enough catsup. I like to keep two jars on hand, in the face of the cold fact that I almost never even think of using them. I don't really like catsup much. But my mother's firm idea that "bought" things were no good still dominates my general ideas of how and what to feed my families over the years.

I know that fresh tomatoes are better than ones cooked down to a bottle-able liquid. Perhaps even a salsa...something fresh and hot and wonderful? Or, at worst, I might try to make a kind of paste myself...

but only if there are too many wonderfully pungent cheap fruits going to waste. And of course, they would be from all my friends' gardens, plus from two or three other nearby produce markets. If possible, I would use some tomatillos, which are now available anyplace here in the West where Mexicans live. And there would be green peppers chopped up, mostly the sweet kind, but of course one or two jalapenos, strictly for the heat. And there would be handfuls of parsley and basil and cilantro and whatever else my own balcony boxes and the lusher better gardens of the countryside around me could offer. In other words, if I ever bottled any catsup, it would be better than store-bought, and I'd drink it to the memory of my mother, and to all prejudiced people, including myself.

Dependence on Farmers' Markets rather than on nearby defunct railway systems and the somewhat faltering airplane schedules of today is indeed prejudiced. It is almost as bad as the old idea of feeling that only the rails and the airways could keep us nourished. But prejudice or not, I refuse to believe ever again we will have to depend on gasses and waxes and airtight plastic skins, not to mention infrared and other death-ray treatments, to be able to *eat*. I pray that as long as there are children in the world they will be able to live on fresh, good food from local produce markets, whether the farmers wear overalls or white lab coats... or even gray flannel suits. I really do pray, and sincerely, that it will never happen again that anything from a foreign land, even picked green and shipped fast, is thought to be better than local produce.

[*True Food: Wholefoods for Modern Times,* 1988]

TRAVEL NOTES: CAFÉ OLIVES

THE AIR OF Provence is almost as nourishing as the food it breathes from and with and over and around... wild aromatic herbs, garlic and tomatoes and melons, and olive trees on all the gray flinty hillsides.

When I think of the things I have eaten and picked and bought and caught and cooked there, I feel full and happy, and never surfeited, and it is fine to look back on.

One thing I like to remember now about a taste of Provence, perhaps top in my thoughts for some reason as inexplicable to me as flavors themselves... It is the little shallow dish of black or green olives that always comes with a drink in a decent open watering hole.

The olives are tiny, and have sharp seeds that God forbid you swallow. In middle- or upper-class cafés they are called Niçoises, but in small plain places where you can sit and watch men playing boules and drink a thick sweet *vin cuit*, the olives put alongside your glass on the tabletop are obviously a hit-or-miss batch of culls from that ageless tree of Uncle Oscar's down the lane. They are equal in potent subdued black *zing* to anything from Nice, and they make whatever is in your glass taste even better than it should, and feel warmer as it goes down.

(If you know Uncle Oscar and especially his new girlfriend, you compliment the café owner on a subtle suspicion of thyme or perhaps rosemary that you have sniffed as you nibble the little withered things, and if you ask for another drink he will take off the saucer filled with its carefully sucked pointy pits and bring you a fresh supply, along with your new tipple. You'll raise your glass to Oscar with due thanks, for usually one dish of olives is considered generous enough for any drinker, and rightly.)

My fellow Californians, though, who in Provence would munch happily at Niçoises or their country cousins, on an elegant terrasse just off the Promenade des Anglais in Nice or at a village pub near Nyons, seem both baffled and annoyed to be given an unpitted olive in New York/Cleveland/Los Angeles. I have tried many times to serve them here to people who obviously know of them as one of Nature's most delicious preprandial nibbles, and uniformly they ignore them, or take one politely and then look around with what seems exaggerated dismay for someplace, anyplace, to put the horrid little pit. This annoys the hell out of me, and often I simply let them suffer. Put it back in its saucer, I snarl to myself. Or hide it in a pocket until you get home...! Or secretly push it under the couch cushion while I watch you, you stupid oaf!

For a while I thought local friends were being especially generous when they brought me fancy glass jars filled with tiny gleaming Niçoises. Then I realized that other friends had brought them to *them*, a reminder of their last blissful trip to Provence, and that they did not know what to do with them, once at home. By now I never even bother to open the jars, for anyone but myself and exactly two other people: my sister, Norah, and one of my two girls (and only a few thousand miles keep the other girl away...). Singly or together we manage to empty every jar available through gift or purchase, and need more, with never a thought about where to put the pits.

Actually, where do olive pits go? On a café terrace I usually put them into my little saucer. Perhaps this is because each drink comes with its own supply, so that there is no need for any social embarrassment about letting your well-sucked olive pit contaminate your neighbor's olives (?) But at home I always give each guest his own tiny bowl, just as I have often seen him served in Provence, and yet here he does not find the delightful ceremony anything but crude, revolting, peculiarly *furrin*.

Too bad... and it means more pungent tiny morsels for us few American refugees from the Deux Garcons in Aix in its golden days... from the Relais Bleu behind the stations in Paris or Marseilles or Nimes....

So "come onna my house"... and I'll give you about a dozen of the tiniest olives you ever saw, in your own shallow little dish! (And, no, don't bring me that fancy jar you got at Christmas, delicious though I know the *"petites Niçoises noires à l'huile épicée"* will be. I have some superb mottled tinies from the last crop down near Fresno, cured by trusted friends . . . and I think that olive pickers need to be trusted almost as wholly as mushroom gatherers, although possibly for less potentially lethal reasons. I remember that when I was small, we never ate home-cured olives in California, because my grandmother damned them with the strange word *botulism* . . . How sad!)

And along with the little saucer of gutty tidbits we may . . . yes (This is a special day like July 14 or Mary Magdalene's birthday or even yours!) . . . yes, why not break out my last bottle of Pernod? Of course it never tastes as good here as it does in Provence (What does?), but it is definitely "indicated," as our good doctor in Aix used to say, for everything from an aspirin to Extreme Unction . . . and *celebrations*.

And if you suddenly wonder what to do with the tiny neat pit, just put it on the tip of your tongue and see if you can spit it over the edge of my balcony, the way we used to do, very rarely of course, when we were on the Cours Mirabeau waiting for all the church bells to ring twelve times so that we could go like discreetly raving wolves to eat, eat, eat in the bright odorous air. . . . (We almost never hit even a passing dog, but it added a completely unnecessary fillip to Life. . . .)

[*Architectural Digest*, 1989]

PLACES AND PEOPLE

SAN JUAN CAPISTRANO

ONE OF THE most exciting and beautiful rides in the world is from Elsinore westward over the Ortega Highway to San Juan Capistrano. It soars into air thin and cold. It hangs incredibly above the flat lake waters straight below. It swoops like music down and down from the mountains, through rolling rich pasturage, into the peaceful little mission valley. It is wonderful.

But it is not the way I most delight to go there. The right way for me is to travel the easy curves of the old Camino Real, which follow sweetly the low sloping lands along the coast, and then turn inland between two widespread headlands to the village, and on north toward San Gabriel.

That is the way I went there long ago, the first of countless times, when the sad ruins of the mission lay quietly under the hot sun, and the swallows nested unsung on the sagging walls. Now there is a fiesta for their mysterious coming, on March 19, St. Joseph's day, of every year: radio and moviemakers scurry through the crowds, little choir-boys sing enthusiastically in Latin, bells ring, and the birds swoop in a dark cloud over the patio. They drive out the white-throated swifts who have lived in their nests. The air is full of noise and awe. And there they are, symbols of faith or love or what you will, until on October 23, St. John's Day, they are irrevocably pulled away again. It has been thus for long years.

It was thus when I was a child, and used to wander unguided through the tragic tumble of the mission, and sit on the warm fallen stones bedazzled by more flowers than I had ever seen, more bees and butterflies and happy doves. It was about then, 1920 or so, that Father

O'Sullivan, tireless savior of the buildings from complete decay, began
his work.

The adobe chapel, long used for a warehouse and worse, was cleaned
out and strengthened and purified. Now it is the proudest old building
in all California, the only one where Junipero Serra actually conducted
services. It is a long, dark, cool place, and at the end glimmers deeply the
pure gold leaf of a great carved altar from Spain, set with myriad angels'
faces, golden too. There are holy bones under the tiled floor, rightly....

Outside the gleaming dimness of the chapel the light always shocks
at first, even under the arches of the adobe walks that connect all the
buildings. They are swept neatly, and benches along them invite calm
repose, and it is hard to tell, unless you remember the place as I do when
it lay mostly on the ground, where the old walls end and the artfully
constructed new ones begin. Even the Parochial School, which Father
O'Sullivan built in 1928 on the north side of the old patio, seems as much
a part of the architectural pattern of the mission as if it had been there
for many generations of little Indians and Yankees instead of a very few.

At first, from 1776 when the first mass was said under an arbor, until
1812 when a great earthquake wrecked the beautiful stone church and
started the slow disintegration of "the jewel of the missions," the patio
at San Juan was a great uneven square, where the life of the whole prosperous contented settlement was lived. Weavers under the direction of
artisans from Monterey made rugs, blankets, coarse cloth to sell and
trade with foreign ships that stopped in the peaceful cove a mile or so
away. Stonecutters carved skillfully at the decorations for the nobly elaborate church, and always the brick-makers labored to supply enthusiastic builders, both priests and neophytes. Warehouses and storerooms
bulged with richness from the grain lands of the valley, watered by the
San Juan and Trabuco streams, and ships like the one Dana wrote about
in *Two Years Before the Mast* waited offshore for fine hides.

Outside the mission, good adobe houses made the natives different
from any other California Indians, most of who lived happily enough in
huts of mud and tule weed. Some of these graceful galleried buildings
still stand along the quiet curving street of the little town, with their
backs to the shallow riverbeds where watercress grows knee-high near
the willows, and small succulent crayfish hide in the shadows from

people like me who prefer them tossed in hot butter with paprika and lemon juice. . . .

It is good that the grim days are over for San Juan, the days when Governor Pio Pico sold it to a relative for $710, when Abraham Lincoln returned it to the Church but it still lay rotting in the rains, when the Landmarks Club fought futilely to save its lovely arches . . . the fabulous seven-domed roof of the stone church may never rise again, but the sanctuary still stands, safe now, its beautiful carvings well guarded from the vandalism of man and weather. Ivy climbs strongly on the walls, and the flowers and bees and doves seem to thrive there in the peaceful courtyards as in no other place I know. It was that way many years ago, as it was with the faithfully returning swallows, reassurance in a changing world. . . .

[*See Your West Program,* 1945]

BONANZA BANQUETS

THERE ARE degrees of elegance, as of pain and passion, and the appearance of stylish richness in this menu for a banquet given in San Francisco in 1864 is increasingly revelatory as it is savored and investigated.

At first glance it seems the height of Victorian fashion, listing some sixty-five dishes in twelve divisions which, as the evening progresses and the waiters grow tired and the diners replete, overlap and impinge one upon another in a gastronomical chaos. It is elegant.

Then...we see the West, new and awkward and uncowed. And we wonder about "Oysters on half shell, with Hock Wine." The briny succulent little monsters were reserved in Victoria's England for pubs and upper chambers, where strengths different from the merely politic were needed. True, the Queen's chef used them, but only when pounded to a sad pulp for occasional sauces. As for the Hock, its name fashionably Anglicized from *Hochheimer*, was it the only wine served to the Knights? Did it flow like water, with and then past the oysters, or was it a stylish bit of flotsam washed down on a tide of other unmentioned frontier liquors: red-eye, rot-gut, gulley p'ison and the rest?

And the dishes: at first glance, again, they seem correctly Victorian and elegant...and suddenly they are almost poignantly native and naive. It is true that there are five "Cold Ornamented Dishes," all partly named in bastard kitchen French; but the lobster, let us face it, was *local*; the "Bush of Quail à la Périgueax" came up on mule-back from the dry valleys to the south; the stylish "Bruxelles Sprouts" were grown by a couple of pigtailed China-boys on a vacant lot....

The Game, perhaps, serves as the neatest cue to the extreme naiveté of the seemingly suave repast: quail again, really not modish but plentiful in the hills roundabout; three kinds of duck, including the unfashionable but delicious widgeon, ofttimes more elegantly dubbed teal; stewed terrapin, American as all get out. . . .

And the Ornaments! What a throwback to the Middle Ages from which those Nineteenth-Century Templars sprang! How beautiful they must have been, chastely untouched in the midst of the silver half-emptied platters, the discarded bones! They were the "subtleties" of Richard's lion-bellied court: a fair Knight of sugar and gilt, rampant upon an only slightly melting field of chocolate; the Temple of Liberty and the Emblem of Purity, two ambiguous but impressive monuments of baked meringue and inedible glitter: the Magic Fountain spouting, now and then, a cautious jet of mysterious liquid into its sugar-crystal basin, propelled by a pastry boy crouched under the sideboard; and best of all, the Pyramid and the Beehive, unmelting timelessly, lighted from within by candles that never seemed to die.

Yes, that was medieval splendor. That was elegance.

And by then the charlotte russe had grown soggy and mussed. The custard pie had vanished. And I cannot but believe that something besides water or tired Hock still sang in the fogged glasses. The Knights had met, and without knowing it had perpetuated a finer combination of Middle Ages and Wild West than Victoria's chefs could ever dream of.

[*The Book Club of California*, 1950]

AN EPICURE REVIEWS
WEST COAST WINE AWARDS

MOST LOVERS, admirers and just plain citizens of the state of California admit that it is divided by a clear if intangible Mason-Dixon line into two parts. Whether the Line crosses north or south of Santa Barbara matters a great deal to residents of that city, of course, but to the rest of the Californians it is enough that the Line exists, in everything from "climate" to "culture."

Among the plainest examples of its subtle power are the two state fairs, one generously financed by the County of Los Angeles and lodged in a small town called Pomona, and the other held with a bow to tradition in the capitol, like most other such annual American fiestas.

Each fair has its own official wine jury, to add to the split-personality problems faced by all good Californians, and only the fact that the powerful wine industry accepts both their verdicts makes any sense in the resulting confusion of doubled awards and medals, injured pride and outraged loyalties.

The juries are as disparate as their judgings: "up North," according to benevolent critics, they are a group of honored scientists, solemnly comparing tartrates and tannic acids; "down South" they are a bunch of locally prominent amateurs, tasting for fun with the idea that most people drink for the same reason. Somewhere and somehow, between the oenologists and the comparatively untutored enthusiasts, a lot of intelligent firm judging emerges, and the medals are passed out with only a mild stir of amazement and headshaking.

1953 was no different, in this respect, from any other year: Pomona and Sacramento simply proved once more, and resoundingly, that California wines can hold their own with the finest anywhere, and that quality in the cask and bottle, as in anything else, increases with the increasing demand for it.

The tried-and-true boys, the Old Reliables like Louis Martini and Beaulieu and Inglenook, held their noble own, or better. The youngsters, like the two Mondavi brothers, who in a few years have brought the Charles Krug label back to its rightful place among the great ones, piled honor upon honor, and properly. The infants, in size if not in age, submitted modest amounts of astonishingly fine wines from their little mountain vineyards. And perhaps most significant of all, the new vogue for "signature" wines had a real chance to prove itself, which it did very proudly.

There have been signed bottles for centuries, of course. Any good wine man is glad to write his name on something he has given a good part of his life to produce. In California such minor and diverse deities in the industry as Georges de la Tour and Angelo Petri have over the years launched many a good bottle with their penmanship preserved in printer's ink upon it, and by now the obvious value of this custom has reached imposing commercial proportions.

On the one hand J. F. M. Taylor of the Mayacamas Vineyards near Napa offers to autograph Christmas bottles, but only two to a customer, of his fine Chardonnay 1951. On the other hand, three world-famous authorities on wine, one in Boston and one in Chicago and one, naturally enough, in San Francisco, offer the fruit of their annual judging under a "signature" label marked "Tasters' Selections." Each effort, the small and independent vintner's and the big well-financed and well-backed promotional scheme, is a good one which in such hands should do no harm to the California wine industry, and perhaps much good. Mr. Taylor offers a kind of gastronomical curiosity of real worth; the three epicures, who taste some 200 carefully screened wines each year, are equally sure of making available fourteen or fifteen of them for general consumption, each type sound and clean and good to drink.

In between these extremes in a revived vogue for signatures, there remain the solid stalwarts who go on year after year making good wines and distributing them as widely as interstate laws and international trade agreements will permit. They are people like Herman Wente, of

Wente Brothers in Livermore (two Gold Medals this year, for his Sauvignon Blanc and Sweet Semillon); the Mondavi family, whose Charles Krug Winery a little north of St. Helena in Napa County walked off with a formidable total of some forty awards at the two fairs; Joseph Concannon Jr., whose family vineyard in Livermore won Gold Medals for its Zinfandel and Haut Sauternes, and the usual Silvers and Bronzes and so on; Louis Martini in St. Helena, John Daniel of Inglenook, Peter Jurgens of the Almaden vineyards down the Peninsula in Los Gatos— these men and many more like them face the oenological whims of a comparative handful of judges each year in Sacramento and Pomona, and emerge quietly confident that their devotion to the art of wine making will go right on producing fine bottles, this year and next year and the next and the next.

Judges are as unpredictable as the invisible line which divides Northern from Southern California, and while the "red table wines" jury in Pomona decided last autumn that the Charles Krug Cabernet was by far the noblest wine submitted to either fair, the Northerners said otherwise, in spite of the fact that the Krug entry, a 1947 of which 352 gallons were submitted fairly at both judgings, easily took a Gold Medal both times.

This would seem to mean that the Cabernet possesses unusual merit, and that it is a wine (as it is) which any man would be proud to serve as well as own, but some of the Sacramento judges were convinced, and perhaps rightly, that the king of all the wines submitted this past year was once more a Pinot Noir sent in by Beaulieu.

The odd things about this entry is that, although it was a 1946 which had been submitted in both '51 and '52 with Gold Medals each time, it got only a Bronze in Sacramento in '53 and did not even place in Pomona. Louis Martini's placed first in Pomona and not at all up North, and Pinot Noir entries from both Inglenook and Paul Masson placed well at both fairs, ahead of this Beaulieu wine which one former judge has called "perhaps the greatest red (table wine) which has ever been submitted... since the repeal of Prohibition." He goes on to say of it "...great by every standard: it has the true Pinot aroma, a bouquet of exceptional degree, breed, fine acid content, charm... in a word, it is distinguished."

What this passionate advocate of the Beaulieu offering of 1,700 gallons of "Beaumont"-labeled Pinot Noir at the past three fairs has probably forgotten is that other judges believe just as passionately in the virtues of a dozen others of the wines judged, and that a majority of the hundreds so judged were "good and satisfying, and wines to drink copiously."

Some were too good to stay hidden in this agreeable medley, and stood out like bugle calls. More often than not, they got just about the medals they deserved, from both North and South, and close behind them came a symphony of fine varietals, the Gamays and Rieslings, Pinots red and white, Cabernets, Sauvignons. Then, an honorable harmony indeed, came the wines labeled Burgundy, Claret, Sauternes, Chablis, all bottled simply but never carelessly by the good wine men: wines to drink every day, they are fastidious blends of this grape and that, and make honest table wines to drink with honest food.

Red and white, Burgundy and Sauternes, they remain what more and more of us can feel free to serve, thanks to the infinite attentions of the men who produce them. And thanks to such juries as serve in Sacramento and Pomona each autumn, these vintners as well as their admirers know that for the special zest, the exciting companion in everything from a crab leg to a chop, the combined awards of the California fairs can be trusted to supply a fine firm list of exceptional wines.

Lists of all the awards in all classes can be got from the Wine Institute in San Francisco, or from the Fair Associations of Los Angeles County and/or the State of California. They can be seen in several trade journals such as *Wines and Vines* (September 1953), and reputable liquor stores which handle wines are able to produce one or another of these lists, if you ask for them.

Perhaps the best thing to do about procuring the wines themselves, outside of California and because of the complex interstate regulations, is to write directly to the vineyards and ask for their nearest distributors. And of course the vineyard addresses, thanks to a neat trick of Fate, are most easily gleaned from the labels on their bottles, preferably empty on the dining table—*your* dining table!

There is a champagne in California now selling for something over a hundred dollars a case when it can be bought at all. It is possibly the best yet produced there, because of the way it is grown and made and bottled by its meticulous owner, Martin Ray of Saratoga. There is also a champagne selling for very much less, very much less *indeed:* it won a Gold and Silver this year and a couple of Honorable Mentions, and wears the Sutter Home Winery Label in Brut, Pink and Sparkling (or Rouge) on good shelves in almost every part of the country.

This same contrast shows throughout the enormous industry: two signed and costly bottles of the Mayacamas Chardonnay for those who hurry and write to the vineyard...innumerable cases with the "signature" label, widely distributed and comparatively inexpensive...both excellent buys, both helping in their own way to spread the word that California wines are good wines.

If the state split itself ten ways instead of two, with ten juries even more disparate than the two existing ones, the wines would simply win ten gold medals, or ten silver or ten bronze...!

[*House Beautiful,* 1954]

A BUNCH OF WINE BUFFS
WERE RAPPING IT UP, WHEN . . .

CLOSE RELATIVES of a thriving, handsome, intelligent child can be obnoxiously bland and boastful about him, and it is impossible for me, personally, to mention the Napa Valley Wine Library without beaming proudly: I was in on its birth, in 1961!

Since that year, the library has grown past any of our original hopes, and is now an integral part of the culture of Napa Valley, of Northern California, and indeed of many distant centers of wine interest. During the first year we managed to gather what seemed a fine nucleus of almost 100 books, some of them of real value. By now we have about 1,000, expertly catalogued, as well as rare collections of bottle labels, brochures, house organs, and periodicals devoted in one way or another to enology, lodged in the St. Helena Public Library until larger quarters can be found.

Members of the Napa Valley Wine Library Association, which our small enterprise became legally in 1963, feel proud as punch to have got the baby off to such a fine start, and are delighted to see the public circulation of our books increase in direct ratio of the membership list and the bank account.

It all started over the generous dinner tables of the valley, where talk had centered ineffectually for a long time on the sad truth that countless valuable documents and books about local wine history were mouldering in attic trunks, or being thrown out by tidy housewives, or going up in smoke of one origin or another. The pioneers of the industry were disappearing, in spite of the basic fact that wine people are mysteriously inclined to outlive ordinary mortals. And there was no information available to local people who wanted to study more facets of their own life-work. . . .

Francis Lewis Gould, an almost legendary authority on wine judging and tasting, has probably sat at more good tables and shared more fine bottles than most men alive, and he grew so impressed with the truth of what he heard, and so impatient with the lack of anything but dining room chit-chat about the problem, that he plunged characteristically into action.

He bullied, coaxed, wheedled, and otherwise awed St. Helenans into handing him something over $700, and then pulled together seven enthusiastic "trustees," and the Napa Valley Wine Library was born. Its first cries were loud and healthy, and within less than two years became so well heard and understood that the association was formed, with the first little band of officers enlarged by yearly elections and called an executive committee.

Of course, the original and continuing purpose of the library, to make it one of the important printed collections of the wine world, was amplified and made firmer by skilled legal counsel. It states that the association shall be maintained by and for "persons interested in books and other documents relating to wine, and to the history of wine; to acquire funds for the Napa Valley Wine Library; to encourage and solicit books, manuscripts, and other documents pertaining to wine, particularly those relating to Napa Valley viticulture, enology, and wine lore; to encourage cooperation from the St. Helena Public Library . . ."

And so it was and is, thanks to the determination of Francis Gould (fondly and widely known as Paco). We have some money in the bank from membership dues and gifts. We have a library of increasing value and reputation, available to anyone with a public library card that can be served by the inter-library loan system. We have devoted helpers, both professional and volunteer. At the regular board meetings there is an annually changing collection of lawyers, teachers, bankers, vintners, retired tycoons. In other words, the baby is now a fine sturdy kid, with great promise!

One thing that got it/us on our feet was the annual tasting for the members. At first we had to scramble to make things look festive for a handful of dogged supporters. Within five years or so we had to limit the attendance sternly to 2,000! The first tastings were held in everything from a condemned lumberyard to an empty automobile salesroom, and then moved to the gracious but limited lawns of old Spottswoode, one of St. Helena's Victorian prides. By now, the increasingly well-organized parties have been held at various valley landmarks: Beaulieu, Krug, the nobly restored Niebaum House. They are pretty things to go to, on the wide green lawns in the August twilights, and members who can get in are gently hypnotized by them. So, fortunately, are the vintners who provide their best table wines: Rieslings one year, rosés another, then white or red Pinots, Zinfandel...There is no need for music at these celebrations: local ladies drift about in stylish summer cottons, with apparently inexhaustible trays of nibbles; there is a brave supply of Rouge et Noir cheeses; the most famous vintners in the state stand proudly behind their tables, pouring tirelessly. There are even special wine glasses available for a slight fee (the association is strictly nonprofit), valuable for nostalgic reasons and for their imprint of the fine library insigne designed by Mallette Dean.

In other words, it's quite a party! And it costs $5 (or one annual membership), and it brings in money to buy as many books as we can, which is what it's all about.

An acquisitions committee directs new purchases, subscriptions, and donations of manuscripts and various other artifacts. (We love old bills of lading and photographs and deeds....) Gradually, as we come to be taken seriously by "the outside world," we are accumulating an impressive if still somewhat modest collection.

Most of it is on the open shelves of the St. Helena Library for public circulation, and only the rarest of the books are kept behind glass, to be used in the reading rooms with permission. A careful shelf list is brought up to date and reissued every two or three years, with current additions every few months in insertable sheets, and all this is available to association members and anyone who will write to the wine librarian, St. Helena Public Library, St. Helena, Calif. 94574.

This lady is, hopefully forever, Mrs. Elizabeth Reed, who manages with unflappable skill to handle both the public library and our own wine shelves. She is helped by several trained librarians, apprentices in librarianship, and volunteers. All of them answer questions happily, pull files for research, check out books both trivial and technical for home enjoyment. Our small collection of rarities, like the 1862 edition of

Haraszthy's *Grape Culture*, for instance, is locked up but available to qualified readers . . . and meanwhile we have invested in two excellent photocopies of this vital book on California viticulture, which circulate steadily.

Several other valuable documents and volumes have been photocopied, and many more, like a complete run of the St. Helena *Star*, can be viewed through the weird machine in the main reading room. Tapes of wine pioneers are being made constantly, and one large volume of their transcripts is already available for in-library use. Also, transcripts of the interviews done by the Bancroft Library in Berkeley are gradually being added to our collection, for in-library use. There are a few recordings which can be borrowed with special permission—i.e., Alexis Lichine's *The Joy of Wine*, and we have reprints or photocopies of many California classics like Waite's *Wines and Vines*.

The list of our open-shelf books starts off inevitably with the highly reputable name of Leon Adams, and ends with the 1968 edition of *The Wines of Burgundy*, by H. W. Yoxall. In between are hundreds of treasures to be read (bottles to be quaffed . . .), from the weightiest technical treatises to lighthearted studies of Bacchanalian revels in old London. There are books in German, French, Italian, Spanish, even Latin, dating from several centuries to the present.

The list of periodicals is based on California grape growing and wine drinking, but includes subscriptions to magazines and pamphlets from several other countries. Our increasingly valuable files of house organs, labels, and brochures relating to the wine industry, both American and worldwide, are constantly being updated by paid assistants. All this can be discussed with the wine librarian, of course, for use in the reading rooms or for regular circulation.

The monthly withdrawal list of wine library books, which has been greatly helped by the inter-library loan system, has grown most pleasingly, and is heaviest during the weekends when wine appreciation courses are given, and students can prowl the shelves.

These courses, directed by James E. Beard, master printer and one of the founders of the library in 1961, were started in 1966, and are counted as something of a phenomenon. They followed two seasons of the highly technical but successful extension course given by the University of

California and sponsored by the Napa Valley Wine Library in St. Helena. They are much more informal, naturally, but in their own way are equally valuable to people eager to know more about wine growing, wine making, wine drinking. So far, almost 2,000 exhausted but happy "graduates" have received their diplomas (of course designed and printed by Jim Beard himself). A firm and successful effort has been made to keep the courses limited in both size and number, but Beard could easily fill every weekend of the year, if he and his faculty were not merely human.

As it is, the courses are hard work for all concerned, thoroughly delightful as well as of real value, and do a great deal to help the image of the association as an important and serious part of Napa Valley life. The instructors are well-known enologists and vintners; the pace they set is heavy but exciting, through vineyards and cellars and classrooms and delicious lunches (and many a good bottle!), and "alumni" hold nostalgic annual meetings in far-off wine enclaves like Redondo Beach in Southern California and Cleveland, Ohio.

Anyone who takes the appreciation course is automatically a member of the association, and information can be obtained from James E. Beard, Post Office Box 16, St. Helena, Calif. 94574. The fee remains ridiculously low. It does not include lodging, or breakfasts and dinners, but there are several good answers to these problems, throughout the valley.

It is strange by now to look back on our first clumsy efforts to get started, even with Paco Gould's lovely nest egg to goad us. Once we gave a showing (to raise more money, of course) of the apparently deathless old flick, *They Knew What They Wanted*, made in the valley and starring Carole Lombard and Charles Laughton, and found at the last minute that we could not serve wine during the intermission because we were in the grammar school. Needless to add, the affair was something of a fiasco. From then on, we carefully avoided such zonings, and while our lawn parties have always been pleasantly well mannered, we have been able to serve and drink local wines as we have seen fit. Only once did we have a rough moment, when gate crashers who had been turned away invaded an annual tasting through the back vineyards: a good record for some fifteen years of public enjoyment of a fermented product!

Meanwhile the bibliography grows longer every year and month.

The files of labels, old photographs, local maps and manuscripts are becoming fatter. The bank account looks plump. Our baby, like the public library, has plainly outgrown its present housing... But the Napa Valley Wine Library Association remains so healthy and handsome that there is no doubt about its fine future, nor about the unflagging enthusiasm of everyone who works for it. It is indeed offering vintage quality to us all, even so young in the bottle.

[*Golden Gate North*, 1975]

NAPA AND SONOMA:
THE BEST OF BOTH WORLDS

IT IS PROBABLY debatable that a conviction can be unfounded, but in spite of patent contradictions I still believe that any small town is better off if it has a *plaza* to grow around, than any small town that does not. That is why I almost settled in Sonoma, California, with my two little girls, when in 1950 or so I found myself footloose and free to choose where we would spend the next years.

Sonoma was and is a lovely little place. It is the southern door to Jack London's Valley of the Moon, and a two-lane highway heads north from it through about twenty miles of bucolic countryside, to Santa Rosa, the Big Town of the county.

The Plaza has the Court House in it, with four identical facades, so that nobody in any direction can feel offended, and there are a rose garden and a duck pond and a small amphitheater, and public toilets, and good places to picnic under the handsome trees. (By now there are overhead night-lights to discourage satyrs in the bushes.) And around the leafy, lovely little square there are old hotels and historical monuments and stores, and even some "scarlet dens of sin and iniquity," just as there should be.

I did not settle there, in spite of my conviction about plazas, but instead went one valley eastward, toward Napa. My girls and I lived for the next twenty years or so in St. Helena, which has a two-block Main Street and no square at all. (There is a nice little park, though, with an honest-to-God bandstand in it, just north of the business rialto.) And now I live near Sonoma, almost full circle, but my heart is mostly in what the Napans call "Up-Valley," and perhaps it is because of the sweetness of the air there....

The minute you turn off Route 101, going north from San Francisco toward Vallejo, you know that you are heading for the Napa Valley, away from soft coastal fogs and into air that has a special fragrant snap to it. The hills are tender green for a few short weeks in spring, but mostly keep the tawny color of a healthy lioness, with her same tense voluptuous curves. There are live oaks in the hollows, or patchy groves of eucalyptus, but increasingly the slow slopes of the hill ranges are covered with vineyards, and by the time Route 29 bypasses the town of Napa, the valley floor is an almost unspoiled carpet of grapevines, half buried in blazing golden mustard in early spring, brilliant as a Turkish rug when the leaves turn in October, and rising in priceless clearings high into the hills on both sides.

Once the flat valley floor, made of volcanic ash when Mt. St. Helena blew off its top some six million years ago, was covered with oak trees and wild grasses as tall as the Wappo Indians who lived there. Then white men cut down everything both rooted and two-legged, and planted wheat, while some of them, from Italy and Germany and France, put in vines on the high slopes, as they had always done in their former homelands. By now the wheat too has yielded to quick-growing vineyards, easier to cultivate than the first plantings. The mountain vines, cannily grown in weather pockets to be safe from sudden killing frosts, still make the rarer bottles, but even down on the valley floor the grapes produce better wines than almost anywhere in America, thanks to an old volcano and the perseverance of the immigrants' progeny.

I knew, the first time I ever smelled the pure sweet air as I drove from Napa to St. Helena, that I would live there. That was during the Second World War, when I was given a "tour of the wine country" by some friends in San Francisco. We stopped in Napa at a dark old bar that out-of-towners have always found quaint, and then, warmed by unaccustomed morning tipples, headed due north, up a true valley that gradually tapered to its end at the base of the great topless mountain, and I knew I would be back. And several years and a marriage and a divorce and two little girls later, I was. We were.

We stayed in St. Helena for more than twenty years. The air was always sweet, except rarely when some of the winegrowers had to light their smudge pots against a late freeze. My children grew up and moved away, and finally I did too.

Perhaps the people in St. Helena are so fine because of the air they breathe. I shall never know. But some of them became my close friends for the rest of our lives, and many of them who for one reason or another did not turn into anything but cordial allies in our daily survival will stay always in my mind and heart. I knew while I lived there a butcher who hated his job but performed it with elegance, and a plumber who possessed the same remote delicacy as he flushed out my clogged sewage pipes. They had been born in the town and they died there, and they made me feel as if they liked me because I recognized them as artists. There were many more of their breed....

Most of the people I knew while I lived Up-Valley were teachers, retired or active, and winemakers and growers. They were and are hard-working people, with a fine capacity for other serious activities like eating and drinking and talking. When they meet, which takes some arranging because of term papers and harvesting and all that, the convocations are almost *sub-rosa*, a kind of secret life steaming along quietly, under the fine testimonial banquets and festive barbecues that any small town must indulge in.

These people lend themselves to Good Works, and build libraries and fight against bootleg subdividing and dubious contracts for dams and so on. They serve time on school boards, and even run for office. But underneath all this natural concern with what happens to their lands and their children, there is the stratum of plain conviviality that makes an occasional "evening" essential. They meet, anywhere from three to twenty of them, and eat good simple food (mostly Italianate), and open a surprising number of their pet bottles, and talk a lot.

There are many more levels of social living in Napa Valley, of course, and they are in a state of great change now that it is a kind of haven for affluent refugees from city life. There will always be what natives call without mockery the Château Set, owners of established vineyards and wineries who do not, any longer, work their own lands actively, but visit them from time to time. They live gracefully, in good old houses they may have been born in and that now belong to multi-corporations that make incongruous things like hairnets and gasohol and powdered chocolate. The Château Set can entertain well but seldom does so, with a certain formality that is not spurned but still not emulated by the other natives who got their vineyard holdings from their peasant grandfathers, or who chose to live Up-Valley because of the sweet air, as I did.

There are a lot of "new people," of course. I was one of them, and when I bought a house one block off Main Street in St. Helena and put my girls into school there and joined the PTA, and even became a Brownie Mother and a member of the Chamber of Commerce, I was told that it would take me exactly forty-two years to be "accepted" as a native. The *new* newcomers are being much more constructive than I was, and whether they live firmly in the town itself, or in the lush and costly hills around it, or in Oakville or Calistoga, I know that their lives there can be full and good. Many of the new people are investing in vineyards and wineries, even if they do not work in them, and they and their friends rent châteaus or their guesthouses and play backgammon feverishly whenever they can get away from the city. And they are breathing that magical air. . . .

Some ten years ago I decided to move one mountain range to the west, into Sonoma Valley. I did this partly because my house in St. Helena was too big to manage, once my girls had left it and I no longer commanded their slave labor. And by that time I had no legitimate reason to be a Brownie Mother. . . I needed a small place where I could work (which means *write*, happily), and now and then eat and drink and talk with old and new companions. I built a cottage on a friend's ranch, at the edge of his vineyard, in the Valley of the Moon, just six miles north of the town plaza. I look westward across meadows and hills to Jack London's mountains, a great stretch of unattainable peaks that turn sensuously rose-gold at dawn, and as blue-black as onyx in stormy weather.

This Sonoma country does not seem like a real valley to me, after Napa, because it opens out, to the north instead of tapering into the base of a volcano. But it is beautiful. Vineyards are increasingly respected here, and their wines can be very good, although one of the vintners says sadly that they and their wineries are about a half-century behind Napa Valley. Perhaps this is partly because of the soil, which is not as densely volcanic. Perhaps it is because Sonoma and its valley have always been a more political, less rural entity.

The first agrarians, led by the mission fathers and then by General Mariano Vallejo, used the gently rolling terrain for raising cattle and wheat, and most of the early vineyards were planted some time after the

Yankee flag had been raised over Sonoma, around 1850. There are good vineyards in this valley, getting better all the time, and their grapes go into clean small wineries instead of dirty kegs under the family kitchens.

So...the Sonoma Valley does not really seem to be one, and I do not live here as an active citizen, but I see and respect much more than the beautiful things that lie all around. There is not the same discreet understanding that once existed between a butcher and a plumber and me in St. Helena. But people are fine here too: architects and grocers and vintners and politicians, and even a banker and a retired ventriloquist....

How can anyone lose the game, given lives in these two valleys? The wines and the air in one are a shade better than in the other. But on the Sonoma Plaza is one of the best bread shops in the Western world, with two good little cheese factories close by...and near Petaluma, to the west, there is the home of Rouge et Noir, whose Camembert and Brie outdo much that is now shipped from Normandy to Paris and Provence, not to mention dispatched from Charles de Gaulle Airport to New York and Seattle.

A Jug of (honest) Wine, a Loaf of (sourdough) Bread (and some superb cheeses)...Paradise Enow!

[*Food and Wine*, 1979]

THE ART OF EATING, CALIFORNIA STYLE

PEOPLE FROM everywhere ask why the food of California is different from any other in this enormous country. Some reasons seem self-evident. But still we try to tell why it is so, and what makes it so, and why everything tastes *different*. I never much thought about all this until I was asked point-blank. I was, after all, an almost-native.

I have lived in California for most of my life, or at least since I was going on three, and all I really know from the experience is that the California way is the best, gastronomically, except perhaps for small places in southern France. But I have talked about California style with other people who know a lot more than I do, and they all agree that the eating, the foods, the dishes and the styles of cooking are for some reason better here than anywhere else in the United States.

Why? I repeat. They reply: it's the freshness, the easiness, the availability. Or is it the ethnic influences? Or perhaps the climate?

For lack of anything firmer, I have tentatively concluded that all of those factors are involved.

First, I must make clear that I was raised in Southern California when smog and the general pollutants of subdivisions and untrammeled tourism were not yet recognizable. We had a neighbor who kept chickens and sent us at least a dozen of the night's crop of eggs each morning before breakfast. Another friend ran a small dairy, and six quarts of her milk ("Fit for Whittier's Best Babies") were on our front step every day. All around town more friends grew fruits and vegetables from seeds and slips they had brought from their homelands—corn and rhubarb and spinach and lettuce, and saucer-peaches and Sickel pears. And we always had some sort of kitchen helper who did exactly as Mother and

Grandmother told her to do with whatever we were to eat, no matter if Grandmother preferred Irish boiled dressing to a vinaigrette, and Mother liked Iowa-style chocolate cornstarch pudding better than fresh ripe strawberries. We ate well then and, in my case, forever after.

The last half of my life has been spent in Northern California, and I know only by hearsay of the present gastronomical scene "down there." When I was growing up, there was always good Mexican and Chinese and Japanese and Filipino cooking available, and Italian and French. By now there are a dozen new ethnic influences in the Southern California markets and restaurants. Friends tell me that it is exciting.

Of course all this change and influx happened in San Francisco too, in a less obvious way, along with other culinary revolutions. For instance, the ex-flower children and hippies, with their wishful attempts at macrobiotic and Zen and lacto-veg regimes, have had a valid and basically commendable influence on many of our marketing and eating habits.

Food here in California, both south and north, is somehow fresher than it smells and feels and tastes in Dubuque or El Paso. A Venetian once told me that the reason the vegetables sold on a famous bridge in his city were so delectable was that they were all picked from window boxes fed with night soil along the canals, and brought in and eaten before the sun set. There is no doubt that a lot of our own fresh produce has been fertilized artificially (if somewhat less primitively) and it comes by fast transit rather than gondola, but it is usually picked and sold in its prime and seems to have more flavor than produce does in any other place (except perhaps Venice).

Another difference in the food Out Here (a Californianism that we all fall heir to after a few months) is a result of the increasing trend toward simplicity. Many people who could well afford to have a cook and/or other servants (if there were any to be had) do most of the kitchen work themselves. Food is presented in an informal, fresh way, when it is at its procurable best. Fortunately for us, this seems to be easier to do in California than almost anywhere else, at least in this country. The weather is mostly good-to-superb, and the noons and twilights of each season are ever changing and beautiful. Local wines are inexpensive, as potables go, and even bottled water tastes better Out Here. And the produce is almost always succulent, even when one goes on a dark winter day to the market, expecting to cope only with apples, oranges or bananas. Suddenly (often at stiff prices), there are mangoes, papayas, kiwis, strawberries, and then the more ordinary exotica like ripe pineapples and all kinds of artichokes and honest tomatoes, not the kind that can be bounced across the room. Of course these can also be found in New York, and probably Phoenix, but Out Here they come to the table in a special way.

This "special way" means easygoing—simple and straightforward. Our way of cooking and presenting food is based mostly, I think, on the immediate use of what is available each day, even each hour. This quick, light approach with the freshest foods is perforce a stepchild, and a happy one, of California's Chinese and Japanese settlers.

There are also things about our cooking that depend as much on climate and lifestyle as on the supplies. For instance, there are a lot of people who backpack on weekends, or jog, or sit in the lotus position and meditate. Most of them breathe good air and, perhaps in the same ratio, most of them eat well, if sparingly, of whole grains and fresh pasta and organically grown vegetables. (Though organically grown produce is runty and unattractive if one is accustomed to the pretty stuff offered under pink mirrored lights in supermarkets, it is often deep in flavor. A neighbor Out Here grows several kinds of melons, all organically; they are small and ugly, and the best I ever ate. The same is true of tomatoes.) And there are herbs, all kinds, everywhere.

One reason our cooking is different is because of our regular use of fresh citrus fruits. We eat a lot of salads, both plain and complex, and many of their dressings use lemon juice instead of vinegar. (Good wine vinegars are also much used here, often obtained from friends who turn up a dubious batch of zinfandel or chardonnay and make it honest and sour.) All California citrus fruits are a daily joy, prepared in countless ways, but almost never cooked. They are served in generous lengthwise wedges with everything fishy, from Dungeness crabs to steamed petrale sole to broiled shark to marinated squid (elegantly called *calamari* for the squeamish). Their zest is seldom wasted, and their peel is often added to cook lightly in soups and stews.

Besides the abundance of all kinds of fruits and salad greens, we have delicious avocados almost the year round. I happen to love a good avocado almost as much as I used to love good Russian caviar. There are several kinds here (like caviar), some of them better than others and a few to be ignored. The best way to attack a ripe perfect one is head-on. Slit it lengthwise, tip out the exquisitely molded seed and fill its cavity with fresh lemon or lime juice. Then all one needs is a spoon, and perhaps some crisp thin toast or tortillas, a little salt and fresh-ground pepper maybe, and surely a glass of cold white jug wine, for all the forthright flavor.

When I migrated to Northern California, I fortunately already knew something about fresh, honest food. But I did not know about sourdough bread, which I think can be, as it is here in Sonoma Valley and in San Francisco, the best bread in our country. It seems to be unique to this area, although its fermented yeast "starter" has been carried around for centuries by miners and sheepherders and suchlike, in many lands. By now some has been commercialized, of course, but the base will probably exist as long as life grows, and we must hope that there will forever be a few bakers who use it wisely. One of the breed is in Sonoma, my nearest town, and except for a few weeks a year when he lets his ovens sleep and takes relatives back to his Basque country, I buy his bread. When I know he is going off, I fill the freezer with what will last best: white dinner rolls and small whole wheat loaves, all of sourdough.

The bread, even though it is spread across the nation now, is, I think, strictly Northern California. When French people come here and gobble our bread voraciously, as only the French can, I ask them innocently if they have ever tasted the local sourdough. They are appalled at the thought and return to Marseille or Lyon or even Paris, wondering why the California bread is almost as good as their own. They don't admit, of course, that what they have been eating in San Francisco and Sonoma *is* sourdough, and much better than a lot they now buy in France.

The current cultural fever about what is called California Cooking, or even "the new California cuisine," is being described and copied by writers from New York to Seattle. And all around the Bay Area—and beyond—restaurants are serving it, often with great success: light sauces and fresh local produce. It is an approach that seemed revolutionary in France a few years ago.

The premise, hardly revolutionary but very pleasant, is that local and seasonal foods be used, and that ethnic methods (in California, going back past the Mexicans to the first Indians) be followed whenever possible.

California restaurateurs and their chefs now travel countless miles to buy a certain breed of lamb to be roasted over mesquite charcoal, and serve Pacific caviar in three different sauces with poached salmon caught yesterday. As one of my scouts reported, "Slices of orange twisted as though about to take wing are all over the place," and kumquats and guavas and the ubiquitous kiwis stud everything from soups to *boeuf tartare.*

And why not? This passing vogue is a mild hysteria, perhaps, but it can leave only good behind it. The freshness of fruits and vegetables and herbs, and the good bread, and the many good wines will always be a remembrance of the California way that is so much a part of the extraordinary gastronomic life Out Here.

[*Signature,* 1981]

ONLY IN SPOTS HAVE
WE TAMED THE CALIFORNIA COAST

THE CALIFORNIA coast stretches, for some thirteen hundred miles, from the Oregon border to Mexico. I have spent many of the good moments of my life along it, from the time I was three years old until now, and I would ask no better than to end my days with the smell and sound of its wild surf wrapped around me.

There are some twenty million human beings teeming and seething and otherwise being human in this Western state, mostly along its coastline. But when one looks at that savage and majestic and occasionally placid presence, from an offshore sailboat or freighter, or from a plane, people seem relatively unimportant.

On land it is a different story, and the intricate freeways and highways that lace the Coast pose a problem that can affray almost all citizens... at least when they want to get in and out of the cities. Once in the country, the main roads make it easy for motorists to cover a lot of ground fast, and even to see many good things. When the giant routes find it swifter to move into the coastal valleys, there are good secondary roads right along the ocean: from Morro Bay north to Carmel and Monterey, for instance, or from San Francisco on up as far as Rockport, through Bodega Bay and Jenner, and Point Arena, and Mendocino and Fort Bragg. At Rockport, the engineers bowed to Nature, and on up to Eureka the road is, to be succinct, wild. On the AAA map it is indicated by a very thin line, with the equally succinct advice, "Inquire locally." This means that mountains are high and cliffs are steep, and that fogs are fast moving as they sweep in to bathe the awesome redwood forests. In some areas where logging is active, trucks whirl around curves with incredible loads, and they are nothing to argue with on a narrow mountain road with visibility down to a few feet. Yes, one should inquire locally.

Crescent City is the farthest town to the north, a small, tight place filled with people involved in fishing and timber. Life is simple and hard, and it is difficult to find good fresh fish to eat: perhaps it is well prepared at home, as is true in most fisherman's ports, but travelers are not pampered gastronomically. The wind blows, rain falls and fogs roll in and lose themselves among the giant forests, and there is the almost atavistic mystery and comfort of the St. George Reef Station north of town, one of the first lighthouses along the California Coast.

A few miles back into the redwoods Route 101 heads north, and Route 199 branches from it eastward, toward Grant's Pass and other beauties not yet known to me. South, though, there is the majestic adventure called the Redwood Highway, one of the most exciting rides in the world. It sticks bravely to the coastline as far as Eureka and then must admit geographical defeat and go farther inland clear to San Francisco: the terrain is plainly too wild for men to assault with puny explosives and bulldozers and the astounded brains of engineers. In other words, from Eureka south, a coast-motorist drives through the usual gusts and fogs on a good but two-way road dedicated to loggers and other trucking demons, and it is wise to be clearheaded when heading from Westport south to Gualala, say.

Eureka is probably a dozen times as big as Crescent City; it is also a county seat, and it is also a fishing and timber community, founded about the same time, in the mid-nineteenth century. Fort Humboldt is on the western edge of the town, built to shelter the white invaders from the Indians, who finally faded away about 1865, as they were doing everywhere in California, discouraged by such white inventions as bullets, prejudice and the common cold.

Hardy travelers, which I am not unless well bolstered by superlative drivers and a general sense of well-being, will leave Highway 101 at Fernbridge, about fifteen miles south of Eureka, and go stand for a minute at the westernmost spot in the continental United States, Point Mendocino. There is something intrinsically thrilling about this, I like to imagine, although I have not yet done it. It is the great "landfall" of the days in the sixteenth century and later when Spanish galleons loaded with treasure sailed as straight as possible toward it from the Philippines and then turned south toward Panama, always hoping to outsail foxy English pirates like Sir Francis Drake, who prowled the Coast in hopes of catching them.

Those ships lost 50 percent of their men, mostly from scurvy and despair, and always carried a priest along to administer the last rites. The priests could write, and in their journals a hideous and wonderful report of man's basic lust and courage can be read. The poor seamen never went ashore: the Indians were at first friendly but then unreceptive in those bleak wild northern parts, and there were no safe ways to land. I know one man who has made the Coast Run at least forty times on a lumber boat of decent size, and he has yet to see Point Mendocino, through the raging wind and fog.

I am assured that there is a pretty good road southward from the Point, given the usual hazards of driving rains, heavy drifting fogs, wind, and the eternal dripping from trees so huge that humans feel almost psychotically puny *anyway*. The trail has had to move back from the Coast, just like 101! It goes through places called Petrolia and Honeydew. Increasingly there are bad-to-wonderful motels with cabins, even on the small roads, and over and beyond the weeping of the trees one hears the intermittent roar of the loggers gunning toward mills and depots. What does one eat in such stupendous surroundings? I cannot imagine, but I shall always want to find out for myself.

At Rockport there is a juncture, with a well-paved, cunningly graded secondary route along the cliffs, which takes one on down to San Francisco itself. There are a few parts of it I prefer not to think about, especially if they must be driven on a Sunday afternoon, when large cars leaving the stylish restaurants along the otherwise bleak coast careen around corners. I met one once, as I descended the abrupt curves of the highway into the mouth of the Russian River and little Jenner, and I was on the outside, looking down the elephant-bare cliffs perhaps five hundred feet, and the station wagon was full of Pink Old Ladies full of Martinis or perhaps even old Pink Ladies, and I felt the brush of the Angel's wing. This long stretch of good road is beautiful, except in fog which is frequent and scary.

Southward, the terrain changes fast, and the redwoods drop inland, so that high, rolling lands, bare except for scrubby bushes, stand up from the sea. Occasionally there is a dip for a little stream or river and its tiny port. In the spring the hills are green and lovely, and then they turn a salty gold, and then elephant gray, even more beautiful to me. Many wild native plants grow in the wind-beaten hollows, and idiots like me go for blackberries into some of the known folds of the hills, to make jam in the early autumn. Things mature slowly there, for the air is usually cool and misty. Fogs still roll over or lie firmly against the land, pressing down toward the sea always, along the many little rivers.

At Fort Bragg, about thirty miles south of Rockport where the road gets better, there is another lighthouse, on Point Cabrillo. It is, of course, named for Juan Rodriguez Cabrillo, a Portuguese hired to the Spaniards, who discovered California in 1542. He was a mild-tempered man, as conquistadores went, and after some twenty-five years of adventure, during which he sailed the Coast without once suspecting that behind the Golden Gate lay a great bay, he died in 1543 from lassitude attributed to a minor infection. His lighthouse holds, as all of them do on any coast in the whole world, an almost primeval allure.

And with it, a part of it, is Fort Bragg. It is a small place, and its citizens are fishermen, lumbermen and farmers of the bleak but rich coastal meadows. It was founded in 1850, like the other northern towns, and in 1857 the Americans, suspicious in a time of change, built a fort there, and named it for their commander Braxton Bragg, whose parents must in turn have had a fine time naming him: he could have been a general, or he could have been a popular novelist, or even a Shakespearean actor.

I like Fort Bragg, quite aside from the carefully restored remnants of our past dubious glory in the fortress against Indians, Spaniards and occasional renegade Anglo-Saxons. The lighthouse seems to hold the place firmly onto Point Cabrillo. It rouses my wonder about living there for a few months or a year, to feel the storms and the changes. Surely there must be a small tight cabin for rent, or perhaps a room with the widow of a sea captain or fisherman? This latent curiosity about such a caper is something I have had to guard against since I first set foot in Cornwall and decided, not far from Mousehole, that surely there must be...So far I have successfully resisted most direct action, involving a deserted lighthouse and a winter in Tierra del Fuego, and my only rescue may be that the clock keeps ticking. But I *like* Fort Bragg.

On down the coast, always close to the glitter or soft invisibility of the ocean, there are fine places to stop. Just north of Mendocino City, which has become a stepchild of the old-old Carmel, with earnest and real and ersatz artists living in it, there is a beautiful piece of land where an eccentric donor has given the cliffs and little beaches and roads, and even decent toilet facilities, to The People. It is fine for picnics, as are many other such patches along the great coast. Mendocino City is already "quaint," and like all such enclaves it will survive on a quiet substratum of serious workers, while the tourists gasp and thrill to quick, bright art posters, guitars played on street corners by bearded refugees from the Haight-Ashbury district, and pseudoespresso served in small smudged cups on foggy street-side *terrasses*.

There are some fine places nearby. One is the Little River Inn, where there is perhaps the handsomest wooden bar I have ever seen. The bar is long and solid and plain, and across it one looks out at an illimitable stretch of water, usually dancing or roaring. There are also eucalyptus trees, and many pines twisted by the winds.

Further south is Elk, one of several abandoned lumber camps along that part of the coast. For a time, the Company House for important customers was run as an inn, and it was good. The paneling of the walls was of fine, rubbed redwood, like that of the bar in the Clift Hotel in San Francisco, and the whole big house had a special perfume, underneath that of good cooking, of salt and sap.

Still farther along this heady road, which rides high most of the way but swoops down where streams have worn through to the sea, is Point Arena with its lighthouse. There is a little sheltered port there, and when in season a deep-sea boat comes in, there are stone-cold fresh albacores to be bought. They are a handsome, gleaming fish, even when dead for a few hours, and are almost unprocurable because they are so profitable for canning as top-quality tuna. To be eaten fresh, they must be hung, like game, to drain off their rich blood from the spinal region and to prepare them for their delicate fate. Fresh albacore is a special thing, and addicts drive to such places as Point Arena or more prosaically to Bodega Bay, from San Francisco, to catch the fish as it is tossed onto the wharf from the doughty tubs the fishermen spend most of their lives on. I like Point Arena too, and often think passively of a small, tight cabin that might be *there* for an eccentric quiet observer.

There are of course some roads going inland through the forests to meet somehow, the main highway, but many of them who turn back on themselves and the few human beings along them do not seem to have any answers to a lost motorist's questions; they usually point, and usually it is westward. It is best, if one is driving (and that, except for shank's mare, is the only way to go down the coast), to stay right on the tricky two-lane road, at least as far as Jenner, at the mouth of the Russian River.

About twelve miles before Jenner there is Fort Ross. It is partly in replica, but fun. The Russians built the original early in the 1800s, along with several houses around its stockade, and from it they not only decimated the otters for fur but sent scientists into the back country to gather specimens of California plants which no longer exist, and which are now a closely guarded Soviet possession, carefully dried and mounted. Those roving botanists even named Mt. St. Helena, under which I live. And on the windswept, fog-drenched cliffs at Fort Ross they made as merry as they could: one homesick, giddy wife of a commander even had a piano sent from Moscow, on which the handsomest young officers of the garrison used to play to their own singing. It is a strange little oasis of invasion, and the sea otters probably suffered the most...and the seals...and perhaps some of the whales.

The Russians lived as far south as Jenner, which later under the Americans became a logging depot. It is usually a flat, soft gray inlet, tidal of course, with the occasional thunder of the surf in stormy weather, but mostly with a quiet that is peculiar to such places. My sister Norah bought the abandoned logging hospital, a strange house with mysteriously placed windowless rooms (operating theaters?) and long alcoved corridors (wards for broken legs?) It is high above the curve of road, and there is a serene view of the inlet, which when the Russian River is rushing can be very exciting. There are a couple of motels and a general store down below the house, but so far I have felt no urge to look for that cabin. Behind the old house and across the inlet from it, gently rounded high hills lead on to the north and south, and inland a few miles the redwoods start again.

It is a good idea to cross the bridge a little inland from Jenner, and go on down south. There are things to see along the Sonoma Coast and into Marin County. There is Bodega Bay, for instance. And then one comes to Point Reyes, a strange broken-off chip of the continent, with Tomales Bay holding it to the mainland and, at its westernmost tip, the Point Reyes Light Station, lonely and compelling. There is a little town called Inverness, which was once very stylish, and old-guard San Francisco society still hangs onto its summer places there. And botanists both amateur and professional come from everywhere to look at the plants of the almost-island, because they are more purely pre-historical than any others left on the mainland. They grow differently, and they look different, and in time the people around Inverness take on a look apart, I feel, because of the leaves and roots there. (This may be wishful thinking.)

There is a nice little port at Bodega, and good fish can be bought if a boat happens to be unloading. It is fine if there is a run of the crabs that have made San Francisco famous; they are best from a boat. They are a pest too, and will crawl desperately around the back of a car, and even gasp their way out of an amateur's crab pot, but still they are one of the sweetest tastes from the ocean's deeps. (In SF they are served as "cracked crab," to be eaten with fingers and a little help from the crab pick, accompanied by sourdough bread and fresh mayonnaise made with olive oil, and plenty of fat wedges of lemon. There is always ample light dry wine with this, preferably a Grey Riesling. Or they are served chilled in salads. Or their juicy delicate claw meat is masked in sauces and served hot in concoctions always called "specialty of the house.")

All along this fantastic coastline, facing as it does the vast Pacific, and given the state of the world in general, there are countless government projects underway that cannot directly mean much to us as ordinary inhabitants. There are little white bubbles along the coastal ranges, on their peaks, which have something to do with satellites or guided missiles or something. There are vast installations with buildings and diggings which may or may not involve nuclear or electronic reactions and which would or would not kill all the fish and perhaps all the human tadpoles skinny-bathing in July. There are peculiar-looking jetties being built, supposedly to provide recreational areas and marinas and bathing beaches for us, but they look surprisingly like coastal bases for submarines.

At Stinson Beach, still heading south, it is fun on a good day to turn inland and drive through the Muir Woods. On this northern half of the coastal range, the redwood trees have returned almost to the edge of the Pacific again, and in this beautiful little monument to a great California naturalist, they can be seen in true majesty.

And then one is at Sausalito! Hoho! This cliffside village that holds a current reputation as the last stand for alcoholics and homosexuals is a good place, and if I should live so long I would state it many years from now. It has had a fine life.

A certain amount of aesthetic compassion is needed to condone some Sausalito antics. I feel that the little Portuguese fishing village will survive, just as I feel that the coastal currents will survive the submarine bases called "recreational areas." I have known some of the retired British Navy people who settled in Sausalito because it reminded them of parts of Italy or Cornwall. And I have known widows of American admirals who settled there for much the same reason, plus the fact that there were a lot of English and that made it *so nice*. I have known a fire chief who was usually as drunk as many people are in that hilly town, but was able to put out any fire at any time. There are clouds of sexual butterflies. And there is of course a famous ex-madame who runs a restaurant.

And across the water to the south, blazing and twinkling at night and serene in all the changing lights of day, is San Francisco.

Its court jester has named it Baghdad-on-the-Bay. This evocative title will do until a better one happens, but the City is literally indescribable, in less than too many words. I have yet to leave San Francisco willingly. I always want more of it, and when I am there for a weekend I invent excuses for staying another day or two. My only comfort is that I am confident I'll return, in one way or another, even as a ghost. And since that is my intention, I like to think of myself as approaching it from the southern part of California, just as I always like to think of coming down to it from the north. It is the focal point of the whole beautiful coastline.

Therefore, with one reckless jump I am down at the southern end of California on the Mexican border, and heading due north to, of all places, San Francisco. And instead of the wild headlands and crags that push back the freeways between Rockport and Eureka, and keep all but secondary roads from following the shores, down here is Route 5, which seeps up the coast as far as Oxnard, where it veers inland a little to Ventura, becoming 101. There is steady traffic, and there seem to be too many towns, or really one large, sprawling, settled area, from San Diego right up past Los Angeles to Santa Barbara.

Perhaps the best view of this basically beautiful coastline of southern California is still from the sea, or from a light plane that can follow the contours of the gently rolling hills and the crumbling cliffs and little rockbound beaches. I have often sailed up and down it in passenger freighters, and flown over it, and always I am reassured by its familiarity, past all spoiling by my fellows. In a sea view, at night, the coast twinkles like music, now loud, now soft, and always with a row of moving lights along the highway; from a plane the spreading subdivisions and suburbs and "developments" look like a kind of mildew which can easily be brushed off.

There are few tourists who do not know that Tijuana is right over the Mexican line from San Diego. As border towns go, it is probably no sadder than the rest, and I had fun there in my younger days. It flourished during Prohibition, of course, and in about 1931 or so it was an adventure to drive down to the romantic hotel casino called Agua Caliente and eat lunch by the swimming pool, with wine on the table and a marimba band wandering. But on the way back there were the slums of Tijuana to skirt, and even wine did not make them prettier, nor does it yet.

San Diego is an impressive high-rise city now, and its magnificent bay is an important military base and port of entry, with about twenty square miles of navigable water. It is beautiful, stretching down ten miles or so, almost to the Mexican border, and shut off from the ocean by the narrow Silver Strand, which goes south from Coronado. The best way to explore its varied shores, wild and overbuilt with an almost Hollywood lavishness, is to spend a few hours or a full day on a small boat.

I am told that the big town is a swinger, thanks to plenty of young military personnel and generally affluent locals whose huge inland ranches produce cattle-fruit-dairy stuff. There is good music and theater, and a bar for every taste. All I know about this high life is that in 1923 I saw Jane Cowl and Rollo Peters play *Romeo and Juliet* there, while I was on a wild spree from boarding school in La Jolla. And a few years later I felt in my bones that the ballroom floor of the Hotel Del Coronado was the best thing I had ever felt under my feet, at least with shoes on. The hotel is still there, an impossible wooden palace with its own boathouse. And it is still fun, perhaps less decorous than when I swooped languorously through "Three O'Clock in the Morning" with very junior naval officers. In those days, most of the permanent guests were widows of admirals, who dressed and behaved according to their rank and setting, which meant in late Victorian rigidity. Things have changed, and for the better.

La Jolla, where I spent a few years learning how to prepare myself for a hopefully fruitful Episcopalian life, remains a strong fortress of well-to-do respectability. It is still a pretty town, built along high cliffs and back onto the rolling hills, and the kind of people who used to pass their winters comfortably there in flight from Evanston, Illinois, now live there all year. There are good hotels, schools, teashops. There are ample chances to play golf and bridge. There is Culture.

A few miles northward, Del Mar and the inland Rancho Santa Fe keep up this respectable tradition, in beautiful wooded hills which have held out with surprising success against the uglier aspects of current "land developments," sometimes called rapid subdividing. Then things grow more lax, architecturally, and the highway runs along what seems almost a suburb of San Diego perhaps, or of Long Beach to the north. Traffic is heavy, but the occasional glimpses of the coastline are fine, and there are good places to stop for almost any kind of food and drink. There is a big military installation, Camp Pendelton, between Oceanside and San Clemente, and somewhere nearby is where *my* country begins, stretching as far north as Newport and perhaps seven miles inland at its widest point.

I have walked, and ridden my summertime horse, and climbed, and held onto a Model-T Ford, over most of the dry, rolling hills of that country, and up the cliffs and down into the rocky coves. It is a fine thing to have in my past, now that the hills and cliffs are thick with houses, and the beaches with people. In 1913, there was no real road south from Laguna, where we settled for several months. A kind of cow path staggered down past Serra, now called Dana Point, to San Juan Capistrano, but there was nothing north of our village as far as Balboa and Newport. We reached Laguna through the canyon, on a narrow paved road which branched westward from the El Toro railroad station and the bean fields at Irvine. Now all that country is solid with high-rise shopping centers and an airport and a university and a leisure world and *people.*

Whittier, where we lived, was exactly forty-two miles from Isch's General Store and Post Office in the middle of Laguna, and we always counted on taking a good two hours to cover it, unless we had a flat or some other breakdown common then to Fords and even Maxwells. We would stop in the canyon for jugs of fresh water; our trickle of water at the beach was sulphurous and generally noisome. That night or the next morning we would buy whatever vegetables the local rancher had on hand, and then get bread and such from Mr. Isch.

Today, coming fast up Highway 5 from the south, one can pass San Clemente and the summer White House, and turn inland at the mouth of a small, marshy river, to stop at the lovely mission in San Juan Capistrano. Then, back to the beach some three miles, one is on the coast road again, now called 1. To the left, on the ocean side, lies Dana Point, where young Charles during his two years before the mast helped haul hides from the mission and lower them to the dinghies far below the cliffs of the headland. Now, from the same place, one can see from a neat glass observation room the new look of the once-lovely little bay lying frighteningly far down. What the government paternally calls "a refuge-harbor and marina" has been built, purportedly for the thousands of small craft that now crowd the more natural ports of San Diego, Newport, Santa Barbara and San Francisco. This masterpiece of jetty building, hill cutting and bulldozing is one of three new marinas being "given" to the people of Southern California, and there are others in the works.

Both San Clemente, which was a wildcat real estate dream hit by the 1929 crash, and Capistrano Beach are rambling collections of largely impressive villas, some of them occupied by retired Midwestern businessmen and retired naval officers who must stay within the smell of the sea.

Up past Dana Point the road rides slickly over hills which used to make me and/or my pony pant to climb, and the pressure of building is constant. At night, from a good cliff or better yet a boat, one can see the far, haughty twinkling of the new communities being built on the old Irvine Ranch, where small, exclusive villages cluster around discreetly designed drugstores and supermarkets. The highway is a long ribbon of light, and there are few dark patches on it, up past Long Beach, Los Angeles, even Santa Barbara. For many years now that road has speeded travelers past the new, affluent sprawl of Laguna Beach to Balboa-Newport, basically unrecognizable to old-timers like me. It is an important spot for both Sunday sailors and serious boat people, and almost ten thousand small craft manage somehow to cram their way toward its docks. Peaceful, brackish inlets thread the back country, and will eventually be deepened to take some of the pressure off the bay waters. Meanwhile the atmosphere in the little towns, once remote silent villages, is young and excited, often wild.

I have always liked San Pedro, which many people consider to be the port of Los Angeles. It has a good feeling about it, and I used to drive down there from Whittier when I was a moony adolescent, to watch the dingy freighters dock, and hurry primly past the cafés where the restless sailors got their land legs readied. Near it is Marineland, a watery Disneyland from what I hear. One reason I would almost agree to go back to San Pedro is not the mysterious pull of a great aquarium but the fact that near it, on the western tip of the headland, is the Point Vincente Light Station, which was the first one I ever saw, and therefore special to me.

Off the coast of San Pedro lies Catalina, a magic place. The first time I rode the Catalina boat it was a luxury liner to me, because I was eleven and a virgin traveler. The last time was perhaps ten years ago, and I shuddered quietly until we reached the little port of Avalon and then bolstered myself for the return voyage with a glass crutch: I was by then the protector of two small daughters, and my jaded eyes had seen and my nose had smelled sure signs of rot. But the dolphins, the whales in November, the flying fish and the occasional seals, the sea birds: all still frolicked in the channel between Santa Catalina and the never-changing outline of the tawny California hills.

North of San Pedro and the Vicente light, a motorist is pulled helplessly toward the magnet of Los Angeles, whether on the coast highway or any of the inland routes. In plain fact, it is almost impossible to slow down, and one can only guess, from a map, that towns are flashing past which are important to the people along the slow curve, for instance, that bends into the shore from Vincente to Malibu.

It is said that Santa Monica was once thought to be the "port of tomorrow" for Southern California. This seems wishful and even Utopian thinking on the part of the land developers, for in spite of many breakwaters that have been built, the open roadstead is ridiculous for commercial anchorage, and precarious even for skilled yachtsmen.

Inland from the abortive port, ribbons of light lead to Los Angeles proper, through places like Beverly Hills that were once hamlets separated from the city by waving fields of mustard. Los Angeles is an exciting place to visit. One must pray for a fortunate hole in the curtain of smog, but there are many things to do and see, and the hotels are plentiful, and a car is essential. If this were my first visit, I would want to see the downtown area and go to Olvera Street and the Mission, and visit a movie studio, and eat at three or four good restaurants, and see Bel-Air as a modern phenomenon because, at least in part, of the UCLA campus next to its lush "exclusiveness" ... and the Art Center and several other museums and Sunset Strip on a Saturday midnight if I were of *that* bent. There is wonderful Griffith Park, bigger but not less contained than Golden Gate to the north.

On northward the country along the coast highway grows wilder, and if one could slow down, the spaciousness would be clearer. There are seafood places and motels, but behind the road rise the hills. If ever I am overwhelmed by the impingement of the human beast upon nature, I take a plane on a small airline from San Francisco south, and more than half the time we fly over the coast south to Ventura and the hills, and I feel better. Animals can still live there; there is still air.

Between Ventura and the mother town of Santa Barbara the land is gentle, with lemon groves and fine stands of odorous eucalyptus trees where the subdivisions still spare them. Santa Barbara itself is basically a beautiful place, with estates spread like an elegant shawl around its three sides of available land, and a tidy yacht basin. It has, a friend has said to me, somewhat the mysterious attraction of a charming lady without obvious means of support. No big industries, no important military installations, but it still exists gracefully for its wealthy retired tax-payers, after an occasionally shady past under Spanish, Mexican, Californian and, finally American flags. There is a beautiful mission, with a small tranquil burying ground. There are good restaurants and bars, for the inner man is tenderly cared for in the town and its purlieus. There are lots of parties in Santa Barbara.

On up the coast about thirty-five miles on 101, there is a branch-off at Las Cruces which leads to two lighthouses, dramatic mainly because they are so close together. This automatically means danger: currents, winds, reefs, general wildness. They are the Point Conception and the Point Arguello lights, and they are thrilling to observe from any distance. They are remote and seldom visited, and I think it is a good idea to wave, in case some crotchety old hermit still watches intruders with his spyglass . . . or a lonely young Coast Guarder counts the hours until his leave for Oscaloosa, Iowa.

There are three types of road on up to Santa Maria, and all of them avoid the increasingly wild coast. Around Santa Maria the land is biblical, with figs and prunes and great sweeps of blossoms grown for their seeds. And finally, after such dry fertility, the highway swerves westward again, along beaches and through little towns and toward the San Luis Obispo light station. It beats a quick retreat inland; what wild country there.

The next town, and one to go to on my own calendar of special events, is Morro Bay. It changes with the times, of course, and where there was once a single motel there are now perhaps three score. But abalone is still caught and canned there, and the fishing is not only good but exciting, even from the pier. And always there is the looming Rock— a kind of semidetached Gibraltar which once made me burst into tears of happiness, when I sighted it from a reformed Liberty ship flying the wrong flag, seventy days out of Genoa instead of thirty-two. That beautiful great lump! Behind it twinkled the little town, which carries always with it the detachment of a fishermen's port.

From there most drivers head north along the scenic highway, which is a good road if one likes cliff-edge curves and noble vistas. There is San Simeon itself, a synthesis of bad taste and beauty. It is as necessary to sightsee as Disneyland, and there is always the comforting thought that farther north there will be Nepenthe and the Big Sur Hot Springs and then Carmel, a bigger Del Mar but with a stronger heritage of past creative glory. The streets still wander about among the cypresses, mostly with invisible name signs, but artists like Lincoln Steffens and Robinson Jeffers are gone. There are almost fabulous hostelries and restaurants, and even clinics where intricate operations are performed upon the inner ear. There are shops where one can buy everything from pâté de foie gras to corn plasters, and boutique-style scarves from Paris, and handwoven tweeds. It is a nice place to retire to, and fun to visit . . . and for me there is no snug cabin to rent.

Next comes Monterey. The Seventeen Mile Drive is an essential to any self-respecting motorist. It will give him a fine idea of how public property can be used intelligently for the good of everybody. Monterey has been touristized but it is still fine. Men still stake their lives on a day's catch of deep-sea fish. Some canneries still work a week or two a year. There are a lot of enlistees from the nearby military bases, and absorbed-looking officers from the nearby language school, and a general air of relax-men-relax. There are beautiful adobe buildings, well restored, and the place prickles with early-California history. It is hard to leave, or at least I have always found it so.

It is easy to follow the coast road around the gentle sweep of Monterey Bay as far as Santa Cruz, but it is a shame to miss the artichoke fields on the road that heads inland toward Salinas; they are beautiful any time of the year, like controlled ferns growing in rows, in the cool, moist air that nourishes them. Roadside stands sell them, cheap if one buys the culls, which are the best. This is a gastronomical frustration for someone in a rented car, heading back to Detroit tomorrow, but for many Californians it is an ever-present prospect of delight.

Santa Cruz, at the north end of Monterey Bay, is an interesting little town. I say this in the face of many people who deplore its jaunty but perhaps obsolescent waterfront "midway." In the winter months when the roller coasters and Ferris wheels and loudspeakers go into hibernation, wrapped in fog, the locals have Santa Cruz to themselves. In the summer, they can withdraw to their late-Victorian caves and let children and soldiers and their girls swarm into town again.

The coast road north from Santa Cruz, old 1 once more, is both good and beautiful, like an occasional woman. The shore itself is rugged, as it has been in varying degrees since Santa Barbara, and the quick rise of the coastal range from the ocean bed is cut only occasionally by little valleys. Some of them are still carpeted with the peculiar silver-green of small artichoke farms, but the suburbs of San Francisco are spreading fast, and it grows harder to know whether one is driving through Granada or Pacifica. Half Moon Bay is still recognizable, and of course there is a lighthouse on Point Montara ... and then, almost too fast, one is in the orderly swooping outskirts of the City, with its rows of white houses, parkways and high-rise apartment buildings and shopping centers.

It quickens the pulse, for anyone who has been in San Francisco before, to be nearing her again, and there is something especially romantic about approaching from the western side, rather than on swift 101 along the bay, or even across the beautiful, soaring bridges, Bay and Golden Gate ... a different air, a less-harried effort.

The City, as its lovers smugly call it, rises pearly on its many hills, and all roads, at least in California, seem to lead to it. People feel lighter there, in their myriad ways, and there are clip joints and penthouses of utmost squalor or elegance to satisfy them, as they breathe the wonderful washed air and walk with unaccustomed vigor along the tipping streets. It is a fine place to be, the glowing jewel of the California coastline, in the planet's crown of such mysterious happenings.

[*Holiday*, 1985]

A MISTAKE

OF COURSE it was too good to be true, that we could have a year in the dream city of San Francisco after a fine full fat year in Aix-en-Provence! But it was the mid-'50s and I grabbed greedily at the chance, and before we knew it, I had signed a lease for a year in a beautiful high sunny old apartment just a block off Van Ness. It was next to a noble church of a reputable American sect, which held a famous organ, and I had convinced my children that life would be so full of pleasant sounds from there that they would never need a television. That was the second great mistake.

The first was that I parked the new car under an unfamiliar tow-away zone sign on our arrival in the City, so that for three days we had to stay in a motel without our clothes. It was the beginning of the end, of course, although I stubbornly kept my original pattern for at least a week after we finally moved in to the apartment.

We soon learned to ignore Wednesday night prayer meetings and all-day Sunday services when our apartment shook from the roar of the mighty organ next door. Life there was good in the main, though, if we were content to become full-fledged couch potatoes permanently. The girls lay on their beds reading comic books, unaccustomed to having any free time left over from their French schooling, and without any friends of any ages at all, because they were the only so-called white people in the school with 97 percent children of angry Japanese returnees from concentration camps, with one taxi-load per day of black crippled children from Hunter's Point to prove that the school was fully integrated. What is more, they were not permitted to cross Van Ness Street alone, in spite of my assurances to the PTA that they were well used to dodging French traffic, and all parks were out of bounds being reportedly full of satyrs behind every bush. And we could never find any time when all of us could go together to any of the free shows that had seemed so plentiful when I myself had been a yearning teenager. San Francisco had been my rosy escape hatch from the monotony of ordinary life in boarding schools in Southern California.

One time I went out to a high protocol dinner party given at Quarters One on Treasure Island, followed by a dutiful drink or two at Barnaby Conrad's Spanish pub, but the strain of finding proper babysitters was too much and I stayed home the rest of the time, until Christmas Eve, when we closed our apartment at noon and took all our presents and decorations as far as the Opera House. We went to see the *Nutcracker Suite* on our way to Christmas vacation in Berkeley with my sister Norah and her family. During the performance, though, the basement parking lot was flooded and we got home to our empty dead apartment with everything soaked past repair and spent the next four days drying out ourselves and everything we owned.

That was the bleak end of the year's experiment for me and we were installed for the duration in St. Helena in time for the second semester of schoolwork. In other words, San Francisco had collapsed in three months into pure hell, and the dull little town seemed like heaven and we knew the City was not for us to live in, but would be forever the family escape hatch, as it really always had been.

[1989]

MUSIC ON SUNDAY

THE BEST DAYS in Dijon were Sundays. Then Papazi, an apron over his pinstriped trousers and his skullcap set somewhat more jauntily than usual on his smooth pink head, made a tart for the grandchildren.

On feast days, on the innumerable birthdays, he worked alone in the kitchen. He created now a *diplomate au kirsch*, now a *bombe Nesselrode* or a dozen *coupes Dame Blanche*. He worked in a controlled frenzy, if such there be: his moustache, when we peeked silently at him through the one dim window into the courtyard, vibrated like a small, pale crescent moon above his tight mouth, and his little fat hands flicked aspishly, with delicate dead reckoning, from the bowls to the bottles to the jars and back again.

It would have been impudence raised to the celestial degree to interrupt him then. He was inviolate, a Jehovah *en cuisine*.

Sundays were different. They were really more fun. We could approach him, always with respect, but on that holy day with a kind of affectionate curiosity. He opened the heavenly doors and for a short time after church allowed us to watch while he threw together something completely simple, he insisted—something we were perhaps capable of understanding and one day even copying.

Papazi had been a Lutheran for fifty years in Alsace, not so much from conviction as from a melodramatic hope that he might have to fight for his "faith," or perhaps even be stoned. Now, in Dijon, he stalked through the Sunday streets with an exalted glare on his round old face, praying, I am sure, for a little Catholic persecution.

He never got anything but most respectful nods, of course, from all the other retired pastry and candy makers and their wives, but by the time he returned home and tied the Sunday apron over his pinstripes he was in a state of quasi-religious elation.

"Hah," he would mutter above the sound of the symphony coming from Berlin on the radio. "Hah! We Protestants are a small sect here. That I admit. Small but strong! We can fight when provoked! Separate burial grounds! Hah!"

And Plume and Doudouce and I, and the eldest brother Dédé and his roommates down from St.-Cyr now and then, would huddle in awe in the dark corners of the room, watching Papazi grit his strong teeth (teeth that had lived for almost eighty years in a constant sweet syrup of his own concoctions!) while he tossed together the Sunday Tart.

It was almost always a tart. Occasionally, if the symphonies were too good to be listened to without both his ears, he would wait until about an hour before supper and make some kind of fritters. They were of apples or cherries or cheese, and he piled them like small, dark clouds on the big platter in the center of the supper table, and we ate perhaps a hundred of them and slept deeply and sweetly through the night.

We always liked it a little better, though, when he started to work as soon as Radio Berlin or Prague came on. That would be in the middle of the afternoon. The music would swell and thunder through the stuffy dining room into the miserable cramped, dark kitchen, and Papazi's nose under his skullcap would shine cheeringly in the glare from the one dangling lightbulb, and his little hands would dart into the making of the Tart.

It was always the same kind. It always looked exactly like the last one. It always tasted like what it was: the most delicious tart in a whole land famous for them.

Papazi made the pastry first, with a nonchalance I've only seen in one other cook, a colored woman named Bea, who threw flour and shortening into a bowl at least three times a week and pulled out the lightest, tenderest soda biscuits ever to be baked and eaten. There was the same airy, almost unconscious concentration about both people, the old, fat *confiseur* in Dijon and the young, smooth, laughing woman in California.

[*Atlantic Monthly,* 1944]

TRUFFLES FOR WEARINESS

ANY MAN who has pondered on his occasional and inescapable exhaustion can give some sort of prescription for it: Brillat-Savarin counseled the measured drinking of a strong soup based on the flesh of an old cock-rooster, while present-day doctors, amateur and professional, depend more on benzedrine. I am as innocent of the old French lawyer's nostrum as I am of the Hollywood writer's, but I do know that one time the invisible aura of *truffles* pulled me honorably through the most tiring ordeal of my gastronomical life.

There was a village high on a crag in southern France, where truffles were commoner than potatoes, and where an ancient and much-honored chef drew out his last days happily as owner-cook of the sole café, expending the black mysterious nuggets as he had never dared to do in Paris.

Gold became dross for me, the day I ate with him, and I who had never thought to have enough of the flavor, the savor, of a truffle wished fleetingly that I might never see another: they were in great slices and chunks in every one of the five or six courses of the noonday meal. I reeled where I sat, but I knew the old man watched me from the kitchen as each dish appeared.

He served forth a broth with grated truffles, which tasted Chinese. There was an omelet, like a cloud with truffle blackbirds winging through it. There was a kind of sole with a kind of sauce, but all I can remember is the heady overlay of truffles. There was a rich, deep brown ragout, of wild boar I think, with more truffles than meat in it. There was a salad, and it was of Belgian endive, brought with what difficulty to this high outpost of Lucullus, and over it lay delicate slivers and rounds and crumbs of truffle.

The meal ended, as unmistakably as any overpowering if well-constructed fugue. I sat back. I did it politely, although what I dreamed of was to slide gently onto the good stone floor. I was, literally, finished.

The aged chef came in, spry as a cricket and looking as pleased as any surgeon after a well-done hysterectomy. "Madame feels somewhat tired?" His voice was sympathetic, and I hoped I was mistaken in the note of expectation I heard in it. He held up his hand before I could speak. "Madam is, shall I say, truly at the end of her gastronomical forces?"

I nodded.

"Ah," he said happily, and trotted away.

I sat in as near a stupor as I have ever known. Outside the café, I could hear the wind, and my driver playing *boule* with a one-legged man whose crutch tapped like a goat's hoof over the flags. Inside the café a fancy coffee machine hissed on the bar counter. Inside me . . . surfeit, despair, and a kind of drugged, sensual delight. . . .

The chef stood by my table holding a flat crusty thing in a pan. It looked a little like what is called a Washington pie. He set it down gently before me, himself sat down across from me, and divided the dish into halves.

"This is an unimportant biscuit of my own invention," he said in a pleasant, chatty way, as if I were not semiconscious there before him. "It is, to be blunt, of great digestive powers."

He lifted half the biscuit onto a plate, put it in front of me, and served himself with the same formidable generosity.

"But digestive? That is a ponderous word, truly. So I make it less so by calling my little invention the *Gâteau des Moineaux de Sainte Anne.*" He held up his fork, and there was a kind of excitement and delight about him, and suddenly I felt much older than he would ever be. I felt tipsy, too, not from the heady flavors of the wines that I had drunk, but from the countless, endless, indescribable truffles. "The title means, candidly, absolutely nothing," he said. He nodded, and in a kind way, as if I were the child and not he, he said, "Try it."

I was helpless before his shiny ancient face. I took a bite of the crisp light cake. Then I ate my whole big portion of it. At the end I felt as crisp and light and fresh as it. It was miraculous.

The chef polished his plate too, and sat back smiling at me. Without speaking, he got up and brought glasses of a thick greeny liqueur, made by a brotherhood near the village. We drank slowly, surfeit forgotten.

Finally he remarked, in a detached way, "Madame is curious, no doubt. Who would not be? With this particular biscuit it is, of course, a question of freshness...the eggs, the cream, even the flour. But that is nothing extraordinary. Then the filling to put in the split, at the last minute, must be lightly seasoned with pounded tangerine peel and this local elixir made by the Brothers. And," he smiled like a restrained but keen old satyr across our emptied plates, "the person who concocts the whole must be as I am—as I have indeed spent my whole life, becoming— imbued with, saturated by, odorous of, impregnated by, the strange, potent, restorative powers, Madam, of *truffles!*"

He leaned back in his chair, laughing with a triumphant and faintly mocking amusement. I thought that I had never seen such an old man look so young.

"Truffles not only stimulate pleasure," he said. "That, incidentally and as one who long ago tested the old wives' tale, is true...to those who must call upon such comfort. Truffles, Madame, cure satiety! That is something that has not yet been mentioned, even by Brillat-Savarin himself!" He smiled consolingly at me. "As a true gastronomer, the Professor perhaps never knew that evil. But for us lesser souls, there are at least a few cooks in the world like me!"

He sniffed speculatively at his fingers, as if they were a kind of invisibly betruffled pomander ball. "My biscuit was delicious, was it not?"

I nodded, for I'd have eaten more...

[*Vogue*, 1948]

ALL THE FOOD AND WINES WERE THERE

WHEN I last visited Dijon in 1954, it looked pretty much as it did when I first saw it in 1929. It was still the ancient proud capital of old Burgundy in France (now the Department Côte-d'Or) and, according to its citizens it was still the world capital of gastronomy. And when I make my next visit there, I hope its status is unchanged.

The people of Lyon, about a hundred and twenty miles to the south, smile cynically at this claim, and with some justification, since *Guide Michelin* usually credits Lyon with five or so two-star restaurants, ten one-stars, and in the outskirts one three-star, (not counting the fabulous Pyramide, sixteen miles down the Rhone Valley at Vienne), a two-star and a one-star; while up at Dijon, admittedly a smaller city but no less haughty for it, there are only two restaurants with one-star rating: *Le Trois Faisans* and *Le Chapeau Rouge*.

The Dijonnais explain this contradiction by saying blandly that the general level of cooking in the Burgundy region is so high that average Dijon restaurants would blaze with three stars in a less privileged area. This is nonsense, of course, and to the Lyonnais it would also be blasphemy if they did not detect a tinge of desperation which makes Dijon merely pathetic to them.

"Take away the Burgundian wines, whose capital as a matter of truth is Beaune—not Dijon—and what is left?" the Lyonnais ask teasingly. "Monuments and gingerbread and mustard! Take away the gingerbread and mustard and—*phhttt!—fini!*"

"And the *Foire Gastronomique?*" the Dijonnais ask in return, with the equable unconcern of people who know there is no reasonable reply. For Dijon has, indeed, the Gastronomic Fair, and if pressure and politics and even a bit of bloodshed count in this world, it will always have it. Lyon wants it. Lyon is big and powerful; but, Dijon has it.

This *Foire Gastronomique* has been flourishing there each November since the early '20s, except for a few years during the recent German tenancy. By 1954 it had moved into "permanent quarters" which seemed very fancy to me after 1929, but which all the officials assured me were but a shoddy shadow of the dream buildings still on paper.

As I listened, I thought with real regret of the first rowdy days in the old tent, when the fair was a healthy infant and I was an untried student of French (and gastronomy) at the university nearby.

In 1929 the fair was still being held in a long narrow canvas shelter which billowed along the Cours du Parc for what seemed a good mile or so from the Place Wilson. Music from carousels blared at either end, and inside the tent the wine stands sold foaming white Burgundy *mousseux* for about a dime a glass, and by the time you got from the entrance to the exit you felt high and happy.

Vintners and nougat makers and vendors of elastic supporters crowded side by side down the grubby aisles. It was noisy and inexpert and fun.

It was fun on my last visit, too, in a tidier way, although it was still noisy with piped phonograph records and paid commercials for Dijon newspapers and electric appliance dealers. It was above all more *expert*, except for the unchanging crowds.

There were busses running every fifteen minutes from the railroad station to the new fairgrounds, and as they neared its gates they passed rows of grim booths full of imitation Oriental rugs and oak (pine) bedroom furniture, the first indication of how neat the new fair was. There were some carousels and shooting galleries, too, severely separate. Progress, I said each time I passed them, remembering the razzle-dazzle of the old days, when the music made such a whoop and hiccup at the gates and all along the tent sides; that's what you call progress.

That November, the bright pennants of the *Foire Gastronomique* hung on all the lamp posts, wearing the insigne of Burgundy—red, blue and gold—looped by the green-and-gold terrestrial globe with a gold fork piercing France, and holding a Lucullan tray of wines, fish, pheasants and snails.

On each side of the entrances were great painted globes with silver dinner forks several yards long stabbing the center of France where Dijon is, "proving" it to be the world's capital of gastronomy. Banners whipped bravely, people pushed and the loudspeakers boomed, "Have your correct change ready." Every day I headed firmly through the crowd of handsome old rogues trying to convince me that I needed still another copy of the fair program toward the main entry hall, where I would stand gaping like everybody else at the Table of Lucullus.

It was a round table perhaps twenty feet across, which daily was decorated by a different crew of professional cooks, with the help of merchants of glassware and silver and linen, florists, cake bakers, candy makers. It was heaped with the flower of *la cuisine classique francaise*. Some forty-eight prizes are given each year for its various aspects, but even without them the culinary competition would be high, there in Dijon. The table had changed since I first saw it in '29 of course. By 1954 it was electrified and revolved majestically, if with an occasional overloaded shudder; it was Gargantuan in the best sense of the word.

Imagine the Table of Lucullus being dressed. First came the designs, then the consultations among cooks and storekeepers; the agonizing decisions as to what would be the main course, which apprentice should peel the shrimps, which tube for icing the Griottes Dijonnaises, those morsels of glazed almond paste surrounding the heady brandied cherry considered almost tonic after a typical Burgundian meal.... Would the day's table be cleared off in time after the doors closed at 9 PM? Would the violets flown up from Nice in huge coffins of woven reeds wilt before noon next day if they were arranged before midnight? Would the jelly around the stars of truffled pâté melt if the weather changed and the crowd was as big and as overheated as the previous Sunday's?

The day I liked best the great revolving table was covered with pale gold linen and artfully divided into sections for the various exhibits on a background of myriad violets and deep pink roses. I took care to keep my eyes upon it, wildly vulgar and beautiful, and also to save my quasi-official visit to the Alsatian (or Rhone or Provence or Arbois or Bordeaux, or, or, or...) wine stands until after I had thoroughly inspected it, for one careless look away from its slow revolutions, or one glass of Sylvaner, would have sent me reeling.

The head chef that day was from the *Buffet de la Gare*, which in spite of bombings, strikes, and various temporary quarters, has remained one of the best in France for years. Its chef and his staff had submitted the following menu:

Truffled pâté de foie gras in jelly, and cold ham, and another pâté of tiny larks, black with its own rich decadence and baked in a crust as tall as a master chef's bonnet; then a *bar au Cliquot* at least four feet long, swimming in its own sea of wine jelly with a cloud of delicate pink shrimps to keep it company; a *Baron d'Agneau Bouquetière*, decorated so that it had real dignity and even nobility about it. Finally there were elaborate spun-sugar baskets filled with tiny tidbits, half cake and half bonbon, called *Délices,* and sprinkled everywhere with crystallized strawberries and violets. There was a large sugar replica (or was it in pastry?) of the fountains in the public gardens across from the Hotel de la Cloche...oh, there were models of pink lobsters which, if the dinner had been prepared to be eaten instead of merely stared at, probably would have been made of frozen custards and mousses and ices, at which the Dijonnaise excel.

All this magic revolved slowly on the Table of Lucullus in the grand entry hall from nine in the morning until late that night, impeccably unwilted, glowing with black, purple and pink grapes, black truffles, and the deep rose of wild strawberries on the pale gold cloth, the pink of ham and brook shrimps and the gold of aspics and glazes.

By the time I had absorbed the Table of Lucullus that day, I found myself looking up at my favorite of the enormous photo montages which decorated the entrance to the three alleys of the fair building.

It was a tall block of scarlet, chartreuse and turquoise, lettered in bold black and skillfully covered with blow-ups of fine photographs. At the top a sign said, *"Sic Transit Gloria Mundi."* There, mixed with pictures of the tomb of Philippe le Hardi, the spire of St. Bénigne and a prophet from Sluter's fifteenth-century Well of Moses, were the most naked close-ups I have ever seen of a small dead hare, a pheasant still in its plumage but plainly long hung, and a young cock which had nothing left of its dignity but its beak.

Fortified by this far-from-subtle reminder to my spirit if not my liver, I would head down one of the three alleys, sniffing my way toward what smelled the best. The alley to the right usually won me, sooner or later—the one called *Vins et Alimentations.*

The one to the left, *Arts Ménagers,* was interesting, but after strolling past refrigerators, electric mixers and carrot-peelers, I felt as if I were in almost any fair in the Western world, and I headed past the stands in the middle, the *Alle d'Honneur*, and on to my favorite right-hand alley, even more French-Burgundian-Dijonnais—*Vins et Alimentations*.

The *Allée d'Honneur* featured foreign products: Dutch beers and cheeses, English teas, vermouths and Chiantis and sparkling Astis from Italy, wines and cheeses and chocolates from Switzerland, and gay costumes everywhere to woo you. There were fat chefs demonstrating how, with certain products, you could make perfect mayonnaise in twenty seconds. Fine Brazilian and African coffee smoked in little cups; packaged soups steamed much more appetizingly than they ever would in private kitchens; a man made beautiful thin crêpes, and his pretty helper doused them with a liqueur for advertising purposes and rolled them into a highly edible twist for fifty francs; nougat makers from Montélimar and lesser candy capitals boasted of the colors, flavors and nuttiness of their wares and begged the public to decide, *decide*. Algerians, Tunisians, Moroccans sold spices and powdery slabs of *loukoum* and bowls of hot, hearty *couscous*, served at little tables by swarthy, sad-eyed boys. At one stand bakers made delicate brioches and croissants behind thick glass to keep the constant crowd of gapers from burning themselves on the ovens. Chickens turned on electric spits, ostensibly to advertise the spits but really to hypnotize the people with the smells of sweet butter and olive oil and condiments and above all *chicken*. Mustard and gingerbread sent up their own peculiar fumes from a dozen stands, naturally and rightfully in their hometown.

Snails sizzled on little dimpled platters if you felt an immediate hunger, or lay greenly cool and lovely to take home: 200 francs a dozen for the *escargots super-extra gros*, which I swear were as big as apples; 180 for the *extra gros*, and even these were bigger than any I had ever tackled; 140 for the *choisis*, which began to be recognizable, and 90 francs for the *moyens*, the size of giant walnuts.

And the oysters! They were waiting on beds of seaweed brought that morning from the tidal basins near Arcachon in the Gironde, and you could stand at a long counter and eat them with brown bread and tarragon vinegar. The people who served them seemed to enjoy each gulp along with you, and if the crowd was not too thick would join you in a glass of whatever wine you brought from the vintners' stands.

Those stands were certainly better mounted and much more efficient than they were in 1929, but for some reason, a little of the old good-natured jostle seemed missing, and the accent was more on placing large orders with the businesslike young men in tweeds who sat at desks behind the counters than on buying a glass or two of wine, for *fun*, from the pretty girls who served you.

Even so, it was pleasant to stop at some of the wine stands and talk with the people in them. They soon recognized my eager innocence, and seemed to enjoy telling me of their favorite bottles with the enthusiasm and indeed the passion of men and women who live night and day with the vines they nurture. Then I would sample the red or rosé or white, light or full-bodied, full of tender promise or already at its peak— in other words, one of the beautiful "table wines" of France.

Among my favorite stands were the ones festooned like Christmas trees with garlands of all kinds of regional smoked foods, and piled with great cheeses and mounds of split crisp rolls and sweet butter in pats as big as drums, to be slapped together into that appetizing gastronomical pattern called, in almost every country, a sandwich.

Fat, motherly women stood smiling beneath the garlands and among the cheeses, dressed in their crisp village costumes. Their men held out thin sample slices on the points of wickedly long knives. One taste and you were lost: such weird black, pink, yellow, polished, moldy or wrinkled masterpieces of seasonings and such sweet hams, such unctuous pâtés, such crusty rolls and pale fine butter and such fiery, taunting mustard. . . .

Aside from the valiant reminder of the thousands of official banners on the lampposts of Dijon, local merchants seemed to have lost their 1929 enthusiasm for the fair, and my friend the secretary general admitted, after my gentle needling, that the thing already had grown so big that visitors would come into their shops whether they had amusing windows or not.

Together we clicked glasses—tired both of us, for it was the third and last weekend—and talked of the early days of the fair, when the Dijonnais butchers and bakers and mustard makers went into a happy frenzy of decorating their windows with five-foot replicas of the church of St. Michael in carved white lard, with bacon pigeons . . . gingerbread wine bottles bigger than barrels, with their famous labels made of white nougat and almond paste, lettered in chocolate...huge mustard pots and snail shells shaped in marzipan....Ice for the chocolate buckets of pastry *mousseux* was made of crystal rock candy. Streamers of sugar confetti went looping everywhere. Ah, it was gay and silly. In the windows of haberdashers' shops were dummies dressed like vintage-happy visitors, diving into great pots of Dijon mustard, or lying a little tiddly on loaves of gingerbread as big as beds.

Every morning ambassadors and princes and other dignitaries were trotted around the fairgrounds, shown the special fishing exhibits, fed oysters and *mousseux*, and then presented with the scheduled banquet, complete with speeches, which usually lasted until four or so in the afternoon.

Every evening the ambassadors and suchlike were expected to lift glasses of white wine and cassis in honor of something or other, and then go on to another somewhat less formal banquet, like the ones held weekly during the fair for the Chevaliers du Tastevin, which would last until four or so in the morning.

Time in the chilly fine old city got well dislocated, so that dawn and dusk were very much alike, and the miracle was that neither came out of joint because of indigestion or what is succinctly called *une gueule de bois* in French drinking circles. The meals were so well prepared of the freshest, purest edibles, and so deftly served; the wines that flowed gently through each course were so rightly proud; perhaps above all everything was savored at such a perfect pace that even ambassadors could not complain...and as for princes and other dignitaries, they became almost themselves!

What was perhaps most important, at least to the Dijonnais, was that scouts sent up from Lyon, armed with political pincers as well as gastronomical gauges, crept home again well-dined, well-wined, and full of doubt that they ever could win the *Foire* away from its hometown. And on my next visit—I hope not far in the future—I am confident that I shall be delighted to find the situation unchanged.

[*Holiday*, 1957]

HOW TO CATCH A SEA MONSTER

THE FIRST TIME I saw the tureen in Aix-en-Provence I was hurrying for the plumber, or rather the chimney man, not the one in a tall silk hat and a heavy frockcoat of soot, but the somewhat more modern one who installed little porcelain stoves every October in the seventeenth-century rooms of the quarter.

My stove, lit the day before in the first cold snap, oozed a black bitter smoke at first, and then started to spit a kind of ink from all the loose seams of its battered pipe, like a perpendicular squid. The walls, floor, bed and desk in my room in the old Grignan townhouse, where Madame de Sévigné had eaten and squabbled, but never *slept*, were spotted, reeking and above all icy.

I turned two corners on the double toward the ancient shop marked Zinguerie, and there in the dim windows on the second corner, the dustiest store windows I ever knew, was the tureen. I stared. I faltered. It was self-preservation, or perhaps only common sense, that pushed me on to the chimney man's with one thought in my dazzled mind, to return to the Petit Bonheur as soon as possible.

Ten minutes later I did, for the boss at the Zinguerie shop knew not only Madam de Sévigné's descendant niece in the Gringan monument, but every whim and quirk of its network of obsolete pipes, draft doors, pulleys, levers and peepholes needed to keep the occupants half alive through an average winter in Aix.

He smiled, I smiled, and then I was off at the triple this time, to peer through the dust at my tureen.

Mine it was. I stared at it happily, and went into the Petit Bonheur somewhat as a bride walks up the aisle. I left all the money I had with the tiny pointy woman who later became a sympathetic accomplice. I had about half the price. She put my bills right into the tureen, and when I told her that it might be six months before I could pay the rest, she said, "Good, good. Then I shan't have to dust the window. And the money won't spoil there, either." We cackled excitedly together, and I reeled off, drunk with possessing.

The next day I started educating my two girls to the knowledge that the tureen was in some ways part of the family—that they must share my love. I was canny. I did not actually tell them I had *bought* it, or half-bought it, for several weeks. I started by slowing down in front of the Petit Bonheur as we walked home from their school or the ballet class. We looked, purportedly with Christmas in mind, at the incredible dusty clutter of bent aluminum egg poachers, shoddy skillets left over from the Occupation, beautiful olive-green pitchers and bowls of Provençal glazed clay, ash trays with sunsets painted on them and marked *Souvenir d'Aix-en-Provence*.

When I finally said, "And take a look at that fantastic soup tureen," and held my breath, both tired, cold, perhaps homesick, little girls let out a gasp of half-phony dismay, or horror, or amazement.

"Murder," one said, and then added her newest phrase, not taught her by the Dominicans, *"et punaises en bôite!"*

The other said simply, but with a significant leer upward to me, "Oh, no!"

I stood firm, remarking more and more baldly as the afternoon walks grew darker and colder and the tureen gleamed more beautifully through the lighted dusty gloom, that I found something strangely appealing about it. I'm a sly one, I am, and by about December 12 or 15 both girls stopped by themselves to stare and wonder.

Finally we took a less bedimmed look at it from within the shop, I managing to slip the tiny ancient lady a signal to keep mum, while the children were choosing a green glazed water-whistle with a locust on it and an eggcup for Christmas presents.

"Look at this beautiful monster," I said in a feverishly detached way. And they did, hypnotized.

It stands about eighteen inches high, on a generous platter (for bones, later) painted with bile-green kelp on the pungent mustard background. It has four feet made in the shape of mean, twisty, proud little bright lobster-pink fish, the prickly kind called *rascasse* in the Bouillabaisse Belt around Marseilles. (The *rascasse* is considered essential to a true bouilla-baisse, but mainly by the Marseillais. It is usually served whole, dour as hell to look at except for its color, alive or boiled or steamed or even immortalized as legs for our tureen.)

The top, and all this one unbelievable mustard-color edged with rich brown and decked now and then with sprays of seaweed, has a big lusty rearing *langouste* for a handle, his own most violent pink with his own most clawless outrage.

Underneath the top is a kind of porcelain sieve, about four inches deep, which lifts out and into which the fish of the bouillabaisse, the meats and vegetables and other solid ingredients of any worthy soup are poured, to drip into the big pot below.

On one side of the strainer section and of the tureen itself are painted twins of angry red fish, very prickly but longer than the four *rascasses*, and on the other side are two electric-blue sleek ones, disdainful. They are all called Provençal names like *fielas, bandroie, loup, roucoau,* and are consid-ered essential by the Marseillais to a real bouillabaisse (mistakenly).

The handles to the strainer and the tureen proper are, with innate good taste, vaguely like scallop shells, and in the same wild mustard color as the general whole.

"Wow," one of my girls said.

"*Mon Dieu,*" the other murmured respectfully.

My game was won, but I did not know how thoroughly until the tiny old lady beckoned to me soon after, and told me that the children had come into the Petit Bonheur to see if they could buy the tureen for me for Christmas.

"I betrayed absolutely nothing," she grinned at me, "but those poor innocents! What can we do? I hadn't the heart to tell them the price, all hand-painted and signed as it is. So I simply told them that it was sold already, to a rich American."

She peeked at me from her pointy little eyes, and we cackled pleasurably. She went on, "One of them asked me why it was still in the window, if it was sold. She's a bright girl. I replied discreetly that the rich American was temporarily out of funds..." and off we went again, giggling among the tottering piles of dusty ashtrays, rattling the cobwebs on the blackened skillets.

That night I told my nice girls who it was who owned the tureen; *we* did, or almost.

They rolled and roared on the paper-thin but authentic Aubusson in the converted boudoir where Madame de Sévigné had never actually slept. They were like little bears, too amused by the double plot to stay upright and calm.

"It's ghastly, absolutely ghastly," one moaned with obvious pleasure.

"*Horripilant,*" the other said and cried out happily, "It's just impossible, that's all! It's so hideous and so beautiful!"

And suddenly it was Christmas, and my sister Anne, who by some genetical freak also manages to be one of my best friends, came to Aix, and on the iron-cold sidewalk we stood peering into the Petit Bonheur's window on another rush call to the chimney man, and she said, "My God! That is the most impossible thing I ever saw! Those colors. Those pop-eyed fish. They shouldn't happen."

I must have sent out some sort of whiff of warning, because my girls dashed down to the corner and into the pastry shop, and my sister Anne turned toward me.

"If you buy that nightmare, I'll never speak to you again, so help me," she said.

"Don't worry, don't worry a bit," I said, and we went on to the pastry shop and brought back the children and then went as fast as we could over the ringing-cold cobbles to the Cours Mirabeau and the warm shabby glow of the Deux Garçons where we drank gin-and-It or hot chocolate according to our ages, all the time my girls not quite looking at me, and simmering with mischief.

About a month after Anne got back to San Francisco, she wrote, "...and don't think you fooled me, the day I discovered that fantastic soup-tureen-thing. I could actually *feel* you deciding that you might buy it!

You're crazy. Think what it might do to your unborn grandchildren. *Think*. Even your daughters ran and hid from it...."

The daughters rolled and roared again on the Grignan carpets, for by now it was a Grand Plot.

"Oh, I can hardly wait," one sighed. "Will the customs officer open it right on the dock, where people will stare? Will Ti-Anne be there? Oh, murder!"

The other said, with voluptuous anticipation, *"Eh bien, et mince alors!"*

By the time a friend wrote to us that the tureen had been graphically described in San Francisco as perhaps the most ghoulish highlight of my sister's Christmas flight to Provence, the children and I had decided to go the whole way: we bought twelve deep soup plates and twelve shallow soup plates, all painted on their wild kelp and mustard backgrounds with brilliantly blue or angrily red rock fish, all signed by the bold artist of the whole amazing set, all called things like *baudroie* and *rascasse*, and mistakenly considered essential, in Marseille, that is, to a bouillabaisse.

Now we are at home, and so is the tureen with its plates. It will be a part of the family as long as we have the strength to tote it around (and my sister Anne continues to dip into it), and the means to fill it with anything from a good old beef stew or stewed hen with all their juices down below in the pot, to a locally reasonable facsimile of

Bouillabaise
or
Fish Soup
or
Cioppino
or

[*House Beautiful*, 1957]

IN NICE, SNACKING

IN THE FLOWER MARKET

SOCCA IS a thin, flat bread, served hot by street vendors at the flower market and other open-air markets in Nice. It's also available in the caves, those below-ground restaurants where working people eat. It's mostly a specialty of Nice, but I've also eaten it in Marseilles. It seems to be made only in the morning—at least I've never seen any sold past lunchtime. It's made of chickpea flour, water, olive oil and salt. You don't need butter. It has that good taste of the olive oil.

In the caves of Nice, socca is made in something like a pizza oven. The men who sell it on the street make it at home—they probably have to dash back to their wood-ash ovens several times during the morning to replenish their supply—and keep it hot over charcoal in their carts.

That socca is made of chickpeas is significant, because chickpeas are traditionally associated with Mary Magdalene, who is a leading citizen of Provence, especially Marseilles. The legend is that when the Magdalene and her cohorts, Les Saintes Maries, were kicked out of Jerusalem, they came to Provence and were kept alive by a miraculously endless pot of cooked chickpeas.

When I make socca at home, I take equal parts of water and chickpea flour (about one cup each), two tablespoons of olive oil and one tablespoon of salt. Then I beat it hard—you've got to beat the hell out of it, really—and, since there are always a few lumps, I pour it through a sieve onto an oiled one-inch-deep cookie sheet. I put it in the middle of a really hot oven, preheated to 500°, then I turn on the broiler. It goes very fast, only a few minutes, but you have to keep your eye on it and use a long fork to prick the big bubbles as they form. It should go right from oven to table. It's wonderful food, and I've never had bad luck with it, no matter what changes I make in the recipe—except once when I didn't use chickpea flour.

[*The New York Times Magazine,* 1986]

SOME OTHER PICNICS

ONE TIME in about 1953, when my young girls Anne and Mary and I were living above the empty stables of the château at Le Tholonet, a few miles outside of Aix-en-Provence, we gave what seemed to us a very formal "picnic" on a fine June Sunday.

We asked the cook at Thomé, the inn nearby, to roast a lot of little chickens, and make an enormous flat yellow cake, which we covered with wild strawberries. The caretaker of the sadly abused old château, which soon was turned into a spanking "Ag" school by the government, helped us rustle enough canvas chairs of many shapes and a long trestle table, which we set out under the two great linden trees by our stables. We had a lot of good local wines cooling in the brook between us and the shepherd's house, and of course there was plenty of bread brought in that morning from Palette.

By noon almost twenty people were there, lying back in the chairs or sitting on the long June grasses under the tall trees, and until the sun went low that day we ate and talked and wandered and drank. Of course a few wasps came in, to try to scare away the timid from any meat on any bones, but almost everyone there accepted them with the disarming nonchalance of people who for centuries have chosen to eat together in the dappled southern sunlight. Warm laughter and wasps...good food and drink...a picnic under the tall trees in Provence....

The shepherd's wife brought a big bowl of clabbered ewe's milk for the strawberries. My girls and Sa-Sa Tailleux from a nearby *mas* made hot coffee later, and tottered out with a pot of it from our kitchen above the hollow dim vault of the stables. There were a few small children and dogs, I remember, and the enormous château cat sat placidly watching

from a high branch. We all talked, and were silent, and then talked softly again, until little frogs began to sing from the two long ponds in front
of the château.

It was a fine picnic, but not real, in the way most of them were in the
several years we lived in Provence. That was because we felt as if the
château stables were "home." Most of the time we lived in other people's
houses, as lodgers, or the girls were in school and I seemed to be alive
only on Thursdays and Sundays, when I could be with them instead of in
some nicenicenice (or dreadful) boardinghouse. Or we lived in a hotel
near their school, and had no kitchen, no place to eat by ourselves.

It was in those strange times, though, that we had our best picnics. And
often other people came along. Or we went along with them. We would
meet at a bus stop at a given time, weather on our side of course. We wore
backpacks or carried canvas bags, and unlike Girl Scouts and 4-H potluck
suppers in California there never seemed to be too much or too little of
anything...no plethora of Jell-O salads and fudge brownies...! We all had
good go-down-easy wine, and plenty of water, and there were big crusty
loaves of bread, and slices of cheese or meat, and there was always fruit,
plenty of fruit of every season, fruit that was ripe that week, that day.

Now and then we'd take another little bus, but usually we'd walk to
a planned *wherever*. Once there, we'd eat and drink, always talking and
looking. It was very simple.

The best times were more private, of course...a special place, a special person. Once when my girls and I were house-sitting at Château
Noir while the owner-friends were sketching in Italy, Eda came down to
Provence from London. We were abashed by her generosity, and knew
without any puzzling that our best way to thank her would be to take
her to Bibémus for a picnic.

It was a little involved, of course, as all such celebrations must be,
because of their immortal importance. Anne and Mary discussed some
of the logistics with M. Lov', who had a car. They also bought a few special supplies in town after the Lycée let out, because Eda was a reformed
drunkard and needed a lot of fruit sodas that we were not used to.

She also smoked steadily, to compensate for the other lost pleasure,
so the children talked with their friend the pharmacist and bought some
nicotine gum, because of course nobody would think of smoking at
Bibémus, high in the pine woods.

And they bought four fresh madeleines, which we left home (Home? Home was where Cézanne used to be, but it was ours for a while), and four little meat pies and four beautiful early peaches.

The picnic was to be a surprise, so when M. Lov' trundled up to our *mas* in midmorning, we pretended not to have our duffel bags packed, and he and Anne and Mary hurried into the back of his old Renault before I led Eda slowly down past the pigeons pecking along the path, and into the car and on to the Route due Tholonet. I knew she knew that it was a plot, a surprise. And she played it perfectly, as always, and murmured and clucked as we moved off with unaccustomed grandeur, at least on a plain old weekday, in an ancient car with an ancient chauffeur, and for no apparent reason.

My girls were blazing with love and amusement. Eda and I sat back and purred and now and then said things like *"Well"* and *"What on earth!?"* Finally one of the girls asked in a very false voice, "Oh, M. Lov', where are you taking us?" and he answered on cue, as we wound up and up through thick pine woods and rocky canyons, "Whoooo knooooows????"

And by the time he had to stop at the end of the little road, he and Anne and Mary were laughing, and I was trying not to, and we unloaded the car fast and he was gone, calling back that he'd see us at five sharp.

Eda kept on pretending that this was what happened every day. But when she pulled out another cigarette, one of the children produced the newfangled chewing gum, and told her firmly it was that or nothing, because we were at Bibémus. She scared us with her courteous resignation, until she laughed in her quiet mocking way and we all started walking up toward a special place where we knew without doubt that we should go. We would feel very close to one another there, as we looked far from the Roman quarries with their strange straight cuts into the stone, and across the rolling land to the great cruel enigmatic face of the Mont St.-Victoire. We knew, because we went there often.

And the children knew the Mont, because they had gone up two of its sides with other young pilgrims, to burn fires at the top. Once it was on Bastille Day, and another time, on an August 25, to celebrate the feast day of Saint Louis, who had stopped there on his victorious way to or from one of his holy crusades or perhaps less holy wars against the Infidels, in about 1270. According to Anne and Mary, who were absorbing local religious legends like thirsty young blotters, to climb the Mont St.-Victoire safely, there were no two ways about it: You either believed in Saint Louis and the True Cross he won in the Holy Land and planted again in Provence, or you did not *climb*, there or any other place.

Eda and I, older and less concerned with spiritual demands, still felt the aloof power of the holy mountain that bright day, and the four of us hardly spoke as we sat with our backs against a sun-warmed slab of crude marble in the old Roman quarries. Young fervor and jaded acceptance of pure beauty were probably part of our good appetites, and we ate and drank well... happy animals, with words few and soft. And only one wasp came, to try a meat pie and then spurn it and us!

Gradually the bottles emptied, and the four little meat pies and all the bread and then the first peaches of the summer disappeared. The great flat stones grew cold. Across the valley the Mont looked farther away, and harsher. Almost silently we tidied our resting place and left it, with some crumbs on a ledge for the ants and four peach pits in a straight line, for possible puzzlement of the next wanderers to sit there and feel the strange spell of Saint Louis' mountain.

M. Lov' was down at the end of the little road. None of us had much to say. But once back at Château Noir we drank hot tea, in honor of the four fresh madeleines, and our tongues loosened and we decided that today's picnic was the most magical one we would ever have. I thought perhaps it was Eda's being there and our lifelong loving respect, but she and my girls said a firm flat no to that. It was partly the stars and planets, they said, and mostly Mont St.-Victoire, so far-near and so mysterious and powerful.

Then we all began to laugh and chatter: the food, the *food!* The flaky little meat pies. The unaccustomed soda pop! Those heavenly peaches, the first of dozens-hundreds-thousands more. "And that amazing gum to chew," Eda said solemnly. "*Lou shwang-goom*, as we say in Provence!" And we agreed that we were all of us high, one way or another, on nicotine and love and good food and generally victorious feeling. We raised our teacups to old Saint Louis, and then "Bibémus!" we said, and laid plans for another picnic that we all knew would never happen, at least for a few hundred more years.

[*Architectural Digest*, 1989]

THE FLANNERS

I FEEL I must renege on my first bland agreement to write a review of Brenda Wineapple's new book. I really feel that it would be basically tasteless of me to try to write a firm, dispassionate appraisal of a book that has been written about women I knew well, by a third woman whom I hope to know better but whom I already like.

I met Brenda Wineapple after we had corresponded politely for some time about a biography she planned to write about Janet Flanner, when she was connected with Union College in New York. I admired her style of writing as well as her academic approach. I thought that she was a somewhat dried-up faculty member, and her correspondence did nothing to change this first too easy view. But she suddenly appeared on a visit to this part of the country and I felt genuinely abashed to find that the dried-up, elderly, eastern academic was in truth young, attractive, and vital. She came out to this part of the world to talk with me about the two Flanner women.

I first met Janet Flanner on one of her visits to her sister Hildegarde, who lived near Calistoga in the Napa Valley. Janet was already a celebrity and I felt pleased to be included in the casual meetings at Hildegarde's house. I had admired Janet's writing for a long time. It was one of the main reasons I read *The New Yorker* steadily, and I think I read every one of her Paris Letters. I still remember some of them clearly. There was one about the opening night of the Paris opera season, and I felt as if I had been there.

Janet was impersonal but kindly, and she was plainly playing the part of the visiting sister. She was a small woman, always very smartly dressed, and I was in awe of her. I was interested in the obvious relationship between the two sisters more than the fact that each was well known in her own right. Though Hildegarde was already famous as a poet, she was always secondary to Janet, who was much more of a vivid character.

Hildegarde was by then married to Frederic Monhoff, and their son lived on the ranch below their hill house. I often saw the Monhoffs and was very much drawn to them, but it took them many years to realize that they were as important to me as Janet herself. I was always aware that Hildegarde was deeply jealous of Janet, and I felt an innate hatred in her for the way she had been left to take care of their mother, when Janet simply divorced the family and moved first to New York and then to Europe. She was the ruthless one of the two, and there was always a certain tension when they were together. She was very generous to Hildegarde and showered her with presents, including a beautiful car.

Her relationship with Frederic was interesting too, and I was always aware of his attitude toward her, which was a strange mixture of affectionate condescension and very firm condemnation of her sexual freedom. He treated her with great respect always but seemed doubly affectionate and loving to Hildegarde when Janet stayed with them. Hildegarde on the other hand was almost servile, or so it seemed to me, and she would blush like a schoolgirl at the fulsome compliments Janet paid to her for the way she tied a scarf around her neck, or served a special meal to the few people who were always entertained, especially when Janet was in town.

The Monhoffs' house was a peculiar one, up a steep road in the foothills between St. Helena and Calistoga. It had been designed especially for Hildegarde by Frederic, who was a skilled architect. And its gardens were oddly patterned of rare bamboo trees, which led to the house itself, an improbable structure that went down into the earth two storeys, with a kind of atrium around which the house was built. I never went to the bottom of the atrium, but just peered down into it from the top floors. As I remember there was a window placed so that the moon shone through it only once a year, and for only a few minutes, onto the head of the bed where Hildegarde would lie, rather like the small window in the dome of the Cathedral of Milano, which was designed so that the light from one star would shine directly on a certain place every hundred years or so. It was very mysterious. I have often wondered about what Frederic saw when the light fell just where it was supposed to be, on the face of the woman he loved so much. I was glad that he could build it as a kind of reward for the years they had spent taking care of her mother who was a most demanding woman.

Then in 1966 I went to Paris to do the writing for a book that was a kind of tri-cake for a series put out by Time-Life to be called something like *The Foods of the World*. At first I balked at the idea. I had never done a real job like that and I knew nothing about expense accounts and so on, and I said firmly I could easily write the text they needed right there in St. Helena. All of this was true, except that I was eager to return to France once more, and I did not have the money to do it. My French friends were much older than I and I wanted to see them once more before they died and I too was old and unable to travel. So I agreed to take the queer-sounding job, and I went to Paris.

I had never been in Paris alone and I felt very frightened, so I insisted that I stay at the Hotel Continental in a two-room apartment in the grenier that Timmy and I had planned to use as a pied-à-terre, a kind of escape hatch from our life in Vevey. We'd really thought we could swing it financially, since it was very cheap and not at all stylish. We had looked forward to it, but as all such plans it was too idyllic, and the war came along and then we went home and Timmy died. And I thought that when I went back alone all the ghosts would be there to give me strength to live alone. As it turned out, I had no need for any ghosts at all: I was too busy.

At first, though, I was somewhat peeved to find that half of the apartment we had planned to rent so many years before was now occupied by Janet Flanner. Her room would have been mine in the original plan and the door between the two rooms was of course locked, and it stayed that way. But Janet's room became almost as familiar to me as if I'd lived there.

They were both long and narrow with small balconies looking far down upon the Rue de Rivoli and then across the Louvre to the Left Bank. To my left as I looked out were the long grey buildings of the Louvre, and just below the window was a gate that went down in the Tuileries Gardens, where once my father had lifted his cane and cried out in a loud voice, "God, do I feel good!" The sounds that arose from the streets at night were familiar to me: the predawn clopping of the feet of the big farm horses carrying their loads of vegetables into Les Halles, and the rare noise of the wheels of a fiacre bringing some tourists home. They all mounted to the attic windows for one last summer, which I spent mostly with Janet Flanner, to my real astonishment.

We recognized each other at once, like old friends, although our meetings in St. Helena had been few and on my part very shy. She was much older than I, of course, and used me mercilessly, so that I was often exhausted by her welcome demands. I acted as a kind of errand girl as well as a companion and willing stooge. It was a fine experience in every way, and I felt very pleased indeed that she seemed to enjoy my company during what would have been a rather dull assignment other-wise. I spent more time in Paris than I meant to and went unwillingly down to the house of Julia Child, with whom I was collaborating on the job along with Michael Field and Guy Kaufmann, near Cannes.

The summer was a long one fortunately, and I finally came home to finish the job knowing that I had made a true friend in Janet. And per-haps because of this unexpected lagniappe several other good people had fallen into my circle, and although some of them have since died their memories have made me much richer. Perhaps it is foolish of me to think that knowing Janet made the other friendships become more important, but certainly they did change my life, and for the better, and I still bask in their warmth.

About ten years later in Paris I saw Janet again when she had moved into the Ritz Hotel, and I often saw her whenever she came to Califor-nia, which was oftener as she grew older. She finally moved permanent-ly to New York during the last years of her life and I never saw her again, as traveling became more difficult for her. She lived with Natalia, the last of her dear friends, and I would hear reports of her from Hildegarde. They grew sadder and it was plain that Janet was not long for this world. The last picture I have of her is a haunting one: she was not allowed to go out much and spent most of her time in the company of a series of worshipful young writers from The House, as she referred to *The New Yorker* magazine. They were chosen for their discretion and their ability to sing along with her endlessly all the old hymns that could be recol-lected by any of them. They sang day and night without any accompa-niment, with all the words falling in place neatly: "The Old Rugged Cross," and "Rock of Ages," and then all the Pentecostal songs.

And suddenly I realize how futile any attempts to write about Janet Flanner and Hildegarde are, in the face of a series of embroidered pictures shown me once by Hildegarde many years ago. She produced them shyly with many excuses for their bleak and often inept embroidery and explained to me in an embarrassed way that they were a kind of diary she kept of her year of escape from her mother, with Frederic, very early in their life together on a long trip they took to Mexico.

They told in her neat stitchery the story of her escape from the family tyranny, and of her hatred and love for her sister and her mother, and of the terrible power of Janet's personality, in a triumphant way that is indescribable. They were more like Janet's clear fine prose and less like Hildegarde's tortured and finely carved ornate poetry and the prim nature of Hildegarde herself. They were free and violent and beautiful.

I think now of these embroideries with awe and I am sure that they would put any possible words to shame if they were ever to appear again. I remember being so impressed by them that I asked Hildegarde to see them soon after she first showed them to me, and I realized at once, by her evasive manner, that she regretted having bared herself to me. Over the years I mentioned them again, and she became increasingly evasive, and said that she had given them to her daughter-in-law, and that they were in a drawer someplace being kept for her grandchildren.

I don't remember ever talking about them with Janet, nor with Frederic, and I never knew her son well enough to inquire about something that was obviously a family secret. But I know that if they still exist, they are stronger than anything that can ever be written about either of the two Flanner women. And they would make anything seem unimportant, even such good books as the current one by Brenda Wineapple, and certainly anything written by people like me.

[*San Francisco Review of Books,* 1990]

THE GEORGIAN SUGAR SHAKER

In our family Mother knew more than any of us about the niceties of Belleek teacups and Baluchistan rugs and hallmarks on good English silver. Gradually my younger sister Anne took over some of this occasionally dramatic role, and one summer in about 1931, in London, it was a heyday for Anne, because Mother bent her knee the wrong way the first night there, and was largely kept from prowling the antiquity trails that she had told us Californians about for years.

I followed Anne in bland but admiring silence then, through all the fashionable mews, and up and down the Burlington Arcade and into the open flea markets of the majestic city, snooping for tiny treasures. I could afford to be generous and patient: I was the elder, and I was married, and Anne was still nonchalantly available. We had a fine time, while our poor dam read piles of new and old novels in her hotel sitting room with her knee on a pillow.

Toward the end of this strange "season," Anne and I decided that what our father, sweating away at his editor's desk back in California, needed more than anything in the world was a Georgian silver sugar shaker.

We talked with Mother about this. She agreed that it would be fun to look for, although not really needed. She suggested that perhaps we should learn more than we now thought we did about what we wanted, and drop in at the Victoria and Albert to look at some pictures... and then she went back to Trollope and we went forth.

Of course, we ignored her gently mocking instructions and headed for a mews shop, very small and packed with old minutiae like ivory *netsukes* as big as nuts and small silver caskets to hold a pinch or two of saint's ashes. We liked the willowy, flute-voiced young owner because whenever we paid him for our small finds, whether with a fairly large bill or a few coins, he always fluttered into a curtained recess for the change, whimpering "Oh, crumbs! Oh, *crumbs!*" It was as if we had hurt him more than any man could tolerate. We were fascinated and touched by his passionate and yet routine squeaks.

When we told him we wanted to find a Georgian sugar shaker, though...a really good piece, properly identifiable...he looked at us hard and asked flatly, "Why?"

Anne and I said that when we were children, every time we had cut-up fruit for dessert Father would politely ask for sugar, and Mother would say from her end of the table in a cold way, "It has already been thoroughly sweetened, Rex," and Father would say, "Yes, but I like to feel the *crunch!*" Mother would ring her little bell, and the sugar bowl would be brought to Father, and while we all sat politely waiting he would sensuously, voluptuously sprinkle a tiny snow over his peaches or berries. None of us dared ask for some too. Mother was imposingly aloof about this seasonal bit of conjugal teasing, and....

The antiquarian interrupted us. He looked almost radiant. "Oh, yes, of *course.* Oh God how *divine!* I know it *all! Yes!*

And he sent us post haste to talk with a friend of his in the Burlington Arcade, who would understand exactly why we had come because Mr. Crumbs would telephone him while we were in the cab. He literally shoved us out of the shop, his eyes shining.

We knew his friend's place, but only through its windows, because it was plainly too expensive for our summer squanderings. This time we went right in. A suave, plump little man, not willowy but with a vague likeness to our dealer, made us feel at once that unlike most of his summer visitors (rich, ignorant American tourists, he meant), we seemed to know exactly what we were looking for. Furthermore, he added coyly, he'd heard somewhere....

Anne, of course, reacted to all this overt wooing like a thirsty young pony to copious fresh cool water, and I stood back with the newfound docility of a married older sister while she and the Englishman practiced their neatest one-upmanship about flutings, molds, silversmiths in general and the Georgians in particular, and, of course, HALLMARKS. I was genuinely impressed.

The dealer brought out a few silver shakers that I thought beautiful, but both he and Anne frowned and shrugged until finally he pulled out one that both of them could smile at. They looked at me politely for tacit approval, and I said, "It is really lovely," and it was.

It was about six or seven inches tall, with a fat little belly above a graceful base. The belly was six-sided, I believe, and rose into a rounded throat and then a top with a dainty finial. The top had little star-shaped holes in it, and unscrewed neatly for refilling. And there were hallmarks on the bright hollowed bottom of the base, and some up along the bottom of one of the six sides, as I remember.

While Anne, proud and busy, checked the symbols in books that the man pulled down from his desktop, I wondered vaguely if Father would learn not to tip the thing up and shake it wildly as he always did with his saltcellar spoon, so that the grains flew everywhere. Mother would be more remotely disapproving than ever. . . .

Anne said, with the complacency of all siblings who are close enough to read each other's thoughts, "Of course, our Father will have to learn to tip this sideways, and not shake sugar all over the table." The man said, "He'll learn fast enough, loves, with this little beauty!"

And indeed Rex did. He used it with grace and enjoyment for more than twenty years. It stood at his place whenever he ate cut-up fruits, which was often in California. Now and then he would pass it gravely to us, if we asked as gravely. And now and then he would tell people, "Those girls knew what they were doing in London! Probably picked this up for pennies, in some flea market."

We never told him, nor did Mother, that it had cost us more than we had between us that summer day in the Burlington Arcade. We left what money we had with the dealer, and telephoned to Mr. Crumbs about our little pickle. He assured us and the dealer that his own honor was at stake, and that between them they would arrange as fair a price as was possible for what was obviously a most rare and even extraordinary find . . . indubitably a bargain, by God!

Back at our hotel we tried to describe to Mother what we needed to borrow money for, and she and Anne mulled over papers about hallmarks and sources and finials, and she loaned us enough to get back to the Arcade before it closed.

The shaker met with her approval, although she said that we were extravagant fools, since Father would settle anytime for a spoonful of sugar from the family bowl. We asked her if she would not like to see this lovely thing at the other end of the table, and even smile a little when Rex played his teasing game of sprinkling sugar on his already sugared fruits . . . Of *course*, she agreed.

We ordered extra seedcake for our tea beside her couch, and set the lovely gleaming shaker on the tray near some dark grapes we had brought from a street cart. And that night Mother went very slowly to the theater, with us at either elbow. Summer had turned sweet at last, like extra sugar on ripe cut-up peaches.

[*Art and Antiques,* 1985]

A VIEW OF THE DELTA QUEEN

TRYING TO WRITE about New Orleans is trouble. People think you
have to sound like Tennessee Williams or the Underground Gourmet or
maybe Mark Twain. I think I am different from any of those characters
because I spent two fine times in and even on the town in 1941. That was
before World War II, which some people blame for the decline of places
like Antoine's: lines of hungry GIs and all that, waiting for their crêpes
Suzette. I doubt this. But I was happy, well fed, smiled upon . . . in other
words, receptive. I decided that it would be a good idea to rent an apartment for exactly one month in the French Quarter, preferably near Jackson Square and if possible in May.

Then in about 1964 I spent most of a year in Mississippi, teaching and
learning, and I decided that I could never go to New Orleans again, not
even for one month, one *day:* I would be too aware of cultural biases,
ethnic balances and imbalances.

And then in 1971, a magazine proposed that I go to New Orleans, and
right off I said I would. I wanted to see if I could lay a few ghosts to rest
and after thirty years still find the place good enough to return to in the
sweet distant future.

Behind its soft drawl there is the machine-gun rattle of what may be
the smartest Public Relations Bureau in modern times. Behind the languorous smell of magnolias and rum and the salty sexy whiff of cool
oysters on the half shell there is the reek, no matter how discreetly
siphoned off by omnipresent air-conditioning, of Diesel engines, oil,
sweat, tidal sewage, electric furious *Big Business* . . . commercial success
everywhere, around all of the edges of the hundred square blocks of
building Bienville drew in the sand in 1718.

Most people go there and leave there and never pick up the artful folders spread everywhere, in bars and boardinghouses and myriad motor hotels, taxis, busses, visitors' free entrances, group benefits. They don't know, lulled as they are by the wet blanket of heat outside their temporary cover, and the medicine of icy drinks and then pepper and garlic in the sauces everywhere, that they are in perhaps the most air-conditioned city in the world. They have not read about the percentage of shipping, of mineral products, of air flights in and out from dozens of South American and Stateside ports, of—most of all—people just like themselves, sweating and smiling and hopefully digesting. They don't know, and mostly they don't care, that the local tourist bureaus are the canniest going. The sound on Bourbon Street, of people and cars and trumpets and drums and tinkling ice, drowns out that of other wheels sucking money from their pockets. Why read a folder about Bienville and all that?

I feel the same way. New Orleans is a magical place. Why litter it with folders and suchlike? Anybody who wants to can tell you that it was founded in 1718 by the Frenchman who scratched out its formal shape; that in 1750 a moat was built around it on what are now Rampart and Canal Streets and Esplanade Avenue; that great battles were fought there, by the French, the Spanish, the Americans. When the Yanks moved in after the Louisiana Purchase in 1803 and then the Civil War, they found the life in Bienville's Vieux Carre much too lax and lovely for their puritanical blood, and moved across Canal Street to what was to remain "their" country, *un-Creole,* an Anglo-Saxon city surrounding the French Quarter on three sides. Andrew Jackson helped win one of the battles, and so there is Jackson Square, with a French cathedral and a Spanish town hall, the Cabildo, and a lot of other beauties of several nations and races in and around.... And all of this is free information, for anybody wanting it, and there is plenty more, even up to the number of kilowatts of electricity used by the air-conditioning each hour of the day. And then there is a discreet handling in the brochures, if less so in the best-selling paperbacks, about the riverboat gamblers and their madams and brothels and all that pagan side....

But most of the people from out of town don't have much time for study...of anything, that is, but the peculiar witchlike bitchlike magnetism of the Vieux Carre, almost embraced by the mighty crescent of

The River, tight in a square of precisely one hundred blocks of court-yards and their fountains and the heady streets linking them: Conti, Decatur, Iberville, the saints Anne and Dumaine. The names sound right, and the streets feel right too, well rooted in more than history. The architecture is beautiful-bastard, a wonderful melding of French and Spanish and the necessary touch of God-knows-what that makes it Cre-ole. Nothing towers over you as you walk along the musky sidewalks.

Outside the Vieux Carre lie many other quarters the Americans fled to from the evil lazy Creoles. The best known to tourists is the Garden District. It is beautiful too, very proper, with fabulous gardens, haunted by O'Haras, heavy voluptuous balconies hanging like yearning breasts, signs discreetly hidden in the Azalea patch by the mailbox: Rooms for Rent. The rockers on the front verandas match the new paint around the front veranda steps, and silent people sit in them.

The Streetcar Named Desire has its own elegant fence around it, visited daily by an increasing number of people who never heard of Tennessee Williams but who are drawn to its dreamlike name as he was. Meanwhile the good old electric car rockets back and forth on St. Charles Avenue, and is one of the few public commodities not yet air-conditioned. Elbows and even faces hang out open windows; tired black ones heading for another day of housecleaning for white ladies, and even white ones heading for their genteel flowery nests, looking relaxed and almost eager. The mansions roll past them, the moving air feels cooler than it possibly can be, and the lawns are the greenest anywhere from that St. Charles car. For thirty cents you can have one of the longest and prettiest round-trips in the world, with no withdrawal symptoms except anticipation for the next one.

The people of every color in New Orleans have always liked to cele-brate. They know how to. Mardi Gras! Books could be written, and fat armfuls have been, about the intricate protocol that dictates this whole fantastic rite. People who are invited by any of the sixty-five recognized "Carnival organizations" to their balls and parades know that they are blessed by the gods. People, who stand on the sidewalks and listen to the music everywhere, and eat and drink whatever comes to hand, know that they are indeed watching "the greatest free show on earth." You have to be in top physical health, with a head for noise and liquor, to survive even the Day itself, and Mardi Gras lasts officially for two full weeks before

Shrove Tuesday, with countless balls prancing along from Twelfth Night, January 6! New Orleanians understand all this, and consider it simply the main party of the whole yearly caper. They *thrive* on parties.

The French Quarter, the Vieux Carre, is one of the most exciting cities-within-a-city in the world, and thanks to the local and current lust for money and prestige it grows better with time. When I saw it in 1941 it was littered, dingy, with a smell of open gutters and closed drains like that of the Old Port in Marseilles before 1944, but not as ancient. Court-yards seen from the sidewalks were overgrown with dank weeds and vines, and cluttered with abandoned garden furniture. Balconies hung tipsily from the walls, which were faded, stained, peeling.

By 1971, the Quarter was one of the most pleasing of all tourist teasers in the Western world. Mostly it smelled good, not "sanitized for your protection" but still not verging on the raunchy reekiness of before. It looked dazzlingly pretty, and even downright beautiful in many spots, with discreet restorations everywhere of the old walls, the laciness of the balconies, the air leafy loveliness of the courtyards. The sidewalks were as rough as ever, deliberately quaint: cobbles, brick, asphalt, marble. But they were *clean,* except of course late Saturday nights or where a bedazzled tourist spilled his portable rum drink or even himself now and then.

It took strength, physical fortitude, *eupepsia* to go to two or more restaurants a day, and at least that many bars, and not fall down or see dark spots or just plain hurt. This was because most of the food was not good, and most of the drinks were mediocre to dreadful, and most of the wines were second or third rate. Of course there were some brilliant glittering gems in the pattern, and the gastric moments brightened fast.

Except for New York City, New Orleans is perhaps the biggest tourist attraction in the United States. And New York cannot really count, for it is a phenomenon, and New Orleans is small enough to seem *real.* It is beautiful. It is alive. It is romantic, and if you can ignore or forget for a while the tensions of all its subcultures, it is the place to BE: be human, be romantic, be alive and even happy.

[1971]

THE FABLED DAYS OF DIAMOND JIM

IN 1856, James Buchannan Brady was born, and for several years after was nurtured in the saloon below his birthplace, in New York's lowest and farthest west of the low West Side. His father, Daniel, believed passionately in the Irish patriot cause, and Jim grew up to the sound of high discussion and the sights and smells of a public house. He learned to believe in laughter and the "free lunch" and to shun hard liquor and tobacco for the rest of his days.

Jim was tall and strong, and when he was eleven he said he was fifteen and got a job in the St. James Hotel, on Broadway at Twenty-sixth, where he dreamed of trotting as a bellboy for untold years among the potted palms and the awesome marble columns. But he was made bar-help instead, ironically: back again to the cigar stubs and fumes and spillings.

He reconciled himself as best he could by promising not to drink (the right to do so was a valuable privilege of any bar boy in those days) but instead only to nibble at the lunch counter. At first the arrangement seemed good, and certainly the child was a fine worker...but before many days were past his carte blanche was withdrawn: never in the hotel's history had the free lunch disappeared so quickly. It was incredible that one human could do away hourly with as many lobster claws, hard-boiled eggs, cheese sandwiches, hot potatoes, and slabs of roast beef as Dan Brady's boy.

He kept on working and growing, feeding himself in devious and apparently satisfactory ways. Every off-day he would go alone to Catherine Slip to eat eel pies in the little fish shops there. When he had absorbed enough of this questionable delicacy, he would walk resolutely to South Street and stand for the rest of the day among the oystermen, swallowing their catch and clams for a penny each.

Only once in his life, when he was still a young man, did Jim actually steal, and then he did it to reimburse his company for funds he had somehow lost. The remainder of what he took, however, he spent on a good dinner in one of the gaudy restaurants he always loved.

Before he was very old, he was "on the road," playing cards for diamonds, as all his fellow salesmen did. He bought one for $90 to flash at hotel clerks, and from then on the service was so good that he resolved to wear the biggest stones he could buy. He used to carry them in his wallet and roll them out on the desk while he talked railroad supplies with Midwestern tycoons. When they blinked and doubted, he wrote his name dramatically across their windows with his best stone.

It is hardly surprising that Jim soon became the world's first supersalesman, and with his success he was given an unlimited entertainment budget. As his biographer Parker Morell says, "Between Mr. Brady and the Expense Account it was a case of love at first sight." Jim made up for all the puny entertainments of beer and sandwiches he had endured for several careful years by embarking on a fabulous life of *real* parties. "Hell! I'm rich," he said with some astonishment. "It's time I had some fun!" Fifteen-course dinners with at least six wines were now the order of his evenings, and he demanded the most ravishing "feminine cooperation," as Morell puts it, that each particular town could offer. He had a three-carat stone inlaid in the head of his cane and became famous for his eccentricities—but never infamous.

Records of Jim's early life are somewhat shrouded, not through his own discretion but because most of his companions of those days were led cheerfully and inexorably to an early grave by the rich food and late hours Diamond Jim prescribed for them. He survived, strong as an Irish bull.

His visits to New York were sparkling benders. He led a crowd of theatrical people, "society," and sycophants from one famous restaurant to another, bought the best bottles for everyone he knew in every place, and himself drank only pure orange juice—two gallons or more at a meal.

He liked men, and Stanford White, the architect, together with many another blood of the times, counted him as an intimate. But beautiful women were as necessary to Jim as air, and he moved in a permanent crowd of exquisitely lovely ladies, most of them sporting and all of them hungry and thirsty. His after-theater entrance into Rector's elegant, mirrored rooms or into Jack Dunstan's rowdier place on Sixth Avenue was like the fantastic Sultan's Parade in a Barnum show.

Diamond Jim's table was always in the center of any restaurant. His midnight suppers at such prominent tables were the envy of lesser gastronomes, who flocked like overstuffed sheep into the plush of Rector's or Tony Pastor's for this fifth meal of the day.

It was at Pastor's that Jim first saw Lillian Russell, and the look of amazed admiration he threw her over his snack of oysters, planked steak, vanilla mousse, bonbons, and orange juice was destined to reappear on his face often until he died. He adored Lillian for many things but perhaps mainly because she was honest with him and loved to eat. When she was wowing them in 1893 at the Columbian Exposition in Chicago, Jim wooed her by finding restaurants that served corn as she liked it, and, although he brought her presents from every trip he took (Lillian was not one to look a gift horse in the mouth, notes Morell, especially when it had diamond teeth), she liked best to hear of new recipes. She and Jim grew fat together and loved it.

(Lillian passed her last days in a state of surprising respectability, long after her lonely friend had offered her a million dollars in cash to spend them with him more dyspeptically. But the rides Lillian took with Jim on her diamond-studded bicycle—rides punctuated by tall, cold drinks and finished off by five-hour feasts up on Riverside Drive—must always have seemed more real to her than her somewhat tardy entry into the bourgeoisie.)

Jim had his own periods of wanting to be socially acceptable and occasionally resented the fact that his high-toned friends were more than glad to dine with him but never asked him to their own proper, stuffy, antiques-addled homes. He was as forgiving as he was shrewd, though, and compromised by installing his mistress Edna McCauley in a house on Eighty-sixth Street that had, judging from photographs of it, the brownstone front to end all brownstone fronts. Edna was sweet and intelligent, and Jim grew proud and happy to see her entertain with every bit as much tact as any Mrs. Fish.

The Eighty-sixth Street house was a tangled mass of Jim's enthusi-asms and the best of 1890s taste. Bronze nudes and Gobelin tapestries fought it out valiantly in almost all of the many salons, and the main guest room seems to have consisted entirely of leopards, tigers, and lions, all with bared fangs. Jim's favored company—well-filled with one of his light midnight suppers of lobster, rarebits, ices, rich puddings, and Champagne drunk alternately with Scotch whisky—must have been hardy indeed to sleep amid that ghastly luxury.

Jim's dining room was either a somber masterpiece of biliousness-inducing over indulgence or the dream of a typical epicure of those rich, ripe days. It was dark and populated by bronze figurines on pedestals. It had concealed lights to show up the modeling of countless stags, bison, grouse, and other metallic wildlife. There were tapestries. The massive chairs and table were carved to order in San Domingan mahogany; the floor was lush with the Orient's finest rugs. And behind the best tapes-try of them all was a most Roman gesture—a perfectly appointed bath-room (in the tub of which a little tired man once curled up, as only Charlie Chaplin could, and slept peacefully amidst the din of one of Jim's gargantuan entertainments).

There was something Roman about Jim's kitchen, too, and some-thing noble. It also had a bath and showers, where the servants were required to bathe once daily. The walls and ceiling of the kitchen itself were covered in green and white marble. Every afternoon, all the furni-ture was taken out into the lovely garden that opened from the big airy room, and the whole place was hosed down like a Thoroughbred. Flow-ers grew against the windows, and on the fine modern stoves the cooks turned out pâtisserie, roasts, and various hors d'oeuvres like *mousselines*, palmettes, and croustades that would have pleased an even sterner judge than Diamond Jim.

He was stern, indeed. His proportions and his appetites may have seemed crass, but his instincts were true. He ate prodigiously and made no bones about it, yet he knew the nuances of the classic sauces as well as any Parisian chef. The fact that he ate five portions of quail *financière* and topped them off, after the rest of the meal, with a pound or two of bonbons did not mean so much that he was gluttonous but rather that he was simply on a different scale from the rest of us. (In fact, his stomach was later found to be some six times larger than normal.) He was like Gulliver, who astonished the Lilliputians by eating twenty wagonloads of their meat and drinking a full ton of wine: it was all a question of relativity.

Jim's day started, either in New York or at the seashore, with a breakfast of steak, chops, half-a-dozen eggs smothered with bacon, a tall stack of pancakes, fried potatoes in a large casserole, hominy floating in butter, and corn bread with jam.

He usually came up from the beach—or dropped into the "square bar" at the Waldorf-Astoria if he were in town—for a midmorning snack of a few dozen oysters.

For lunch he ate more oysters, with lobster to follow, as well as roast beef, a hearty salad, a fruit pie, and the inevitable candy, all of which he washed down with orange juice.

For dinner at about seven thirty, he started again with oysters, extra-large lynn havens sent especially for him from Maryland. The healthy little crabs that crawled out of the oysters would wander about the table until Jim speared them with his fork, making all the lovely ladies squeal. Then, if he were at Rector's, which was more often than not the case, he would ask George himself to come to the table and fix him a decent *homard à l'américaine*—with two lobsters instead of one. Next, after a dozen or so crabs, would come thick red meat ("Brady liked his oysters sprinkled with clams and his steaks smothered in veal cutlets," observed Wilson Mizner, one of Lillian's admirers, with a certain tart envy) and five or six vegetables, most of them doused with the incredibly complex sauces of the period.

After the rest of the typical dinner, of which Diamond Jim ate several portions of everything he liked (which was apparently everything), he called for his enormous box of chocolate candies and had his tall pitcher of fresh orange juice filled for the last time. Despite such gorging, Jim only weighed about 250 pounds.

After the theater (he went to every new show on the first night and claimed that bonbons were appropriate with Shaw and glacéed fruits with Ibsen), Jim started his extraordinary midnight supper, surrounded as always by his well-paid bevy of even better-fed beauties. His diamonds flashed—a new and dazzling array of tie clips, watch chains, shirt studs, and so on for every day of the month—and Champagne popped at his expense.

Jim believed with philosophical calm that money is to be spent and that most men are not exactly bad but more often just frightened and lonely. He entertained them all with a kind of devotion; it was, in fact, a vocation. The more money he made, the more he spent and the more he gave away. One evening, after watching a succession of men and women appeal successfully to Jim for money as he ate his dinner at Rector's, George spoke up and told the multimillionaire that he thought he was being taken advantage of. "As long as I live," recalled George, "I'll never forget the way he looked at me, closed one eye in a wink, and said, 'George, I know they're pullin' my leg, but did you ever stop to think that it's fun to be a sucker—if you can afford it?'"

Eventually Jim began to send weekly presents to some three hundred people. Usually they got a regular routine of candy, fruit, candy, flowers, which would then start all over again, but there were many of them who were shipped, with thoughtful delicacy, produce from his New Jersey farm. Zinc hampers—which he invented to keep food cold—arrived, filled with his lavish country stuff, at various greenrooms, roundhouses, and depressed brokers' Wall Street offices. There would be roast fowls and big fat pats of fresh butter; crisp celery, carrots, and lettuces; and asparagus and peas. There would be Port for those who needed it, zinc cans of fresh milk and cream, or nourishing Dublin stout. "What the hell," Jim would say, "We got so much food down there that I had to do somethin' with it! It's a case of feedin' it to the pigs or sendin' it to my friends—and the pigs got too much to eat as it is."

As he grew older, he horrified himself by having unpleasant bellyaches, and before he knew it he was in and out of Johns Hopkins, leaving a trail of bediamonded, well-fed nurses and interns and a fabulous sum of money for research. Broadway, ready to weep at his demise, looked upon him as a gastronomical Lazarus and whispered that he had paid for the stomach of a horse to be grafted onto his own. It was medicine rather than miracles, though, that brought Jim back for a few more years to the brash, extravagant life he loved so well. The parties he gave after his sojourn among the surgeons were, if possible, more fantastic than the ones before.

Jim and his incredible sets of diamonds were as well known in the hinterlands as Niagara and the Flatiron Building, and when hayseeds came to town they steered straight for the places Diamond Jim might frequent. Not all of them could pay Rector's stiff *couvert;* instead, they gathered at Corey's on Sixth for a "beefsteak." They dressed in ample aprons, ate dripping meat with their fingers, and cheered Jim to the rafters when he stopped there between acts or on his way to a tonier joint. Occasionally they plucked—with some success—at his dollar-size cuff links or his locomotive scarfpin paved with gems, so that, to his shame, he began to wear paste to some of the four or five parties he threw each night. He never blamed the awed souls—only himself for their chagrin next morning at the pawnbrokers'.

Once, at one of the few events he was ever invited to at a swell country house, Jim ate twenty-five ears of exquisitely tender corn, perhaps with a silent toast to his adorable Lillian, and then led a party of more or less sober socialites out into the corn patch to pick some twenty more for him to nibble on. Naturally, the evening's events were recounted with disdainful relish many times over in the salons of upper Fifth Avenue.

Today, Jim's hunger seems either revolting or abysmally unhealthy, but in the frantic golden days of the 1890s, such behavior was considered not so much awful as admirable. The more men spent, the more they mattered.

In such an age, Diamond Jim knew very well what he was doing. His small, close-set eyes remained sharp and clear, no matter how suffused his bulldog face became from the purplish, brown, red, green, and orange sauces New York's chefs simmered for him. His mouth had a quick, merry smile that in an instant dispelled its basic hardness. And he knew what was good.

When Jim discovered sole Marguéry on his jaunt to Europe with Edna McCauley and an imposing retinue, he hurried home to tell old man Rector. Within the hour, young George was hauled from his third year of law at Cornell and sent into the Marguéry kitchens in Paris. When he finally came home and cooked a kind of examination dinner for Jim and a group of other *bons vivants*, the former called him into the twinkling, mirrored dining room around midnight and said: "George, that sole was marvelous. I've had nine helpings—and even right now, if you poured some of the sauce over a Turkish towel, I believe I could eat all of it."

Much as this grossness may repel us, Rector himself, who said that Jim was the best twenty-five customers his place ever had, claimed (with what should be considered a somewhat biased judgment) that Mr. Brady was "the greatest gourmet of his time." Certainly he was an amazing embodiment of his own amazing gaudy period. Or was that time of eighteen-hour oyster suppers and orchid-plastered ballrooms an off-shoot of Jim's immense gusto?

When Jim died in 1917—after a last few years of whirling and twirling in his elephantine way about the new dancing palaces of New York with a Dolly Sister or a less imposing beauty in his arms—he was laid out solemnly in his favorite set of sparklers. All Broadway looked upon him in his twinkling coffin, soon to be so dark, and found its appetite had left it for a few hours.

The vulgarity, the crass lustiness of all young growing, pushing America lay with Diamond Jim in his narrow bed. Never again would a Yankee eat as much, as publicly. Never again would a man love life to the tune of such a large brass band.

[*Gourmet*, 1992]

SEASONS AND CELEBRATIONS

ON CELEBRATING A
GLORIOUS FOURTH IN A FREE LAND

ONE SUMMER DAY, in 1765, near Athens, the Reverend Doctor Chandler and his party sat themselves down to what he called in his book, *Travels in Asia Minor and Greece,* "A Pic-Nic on Mount Hymettos."

While two of his servants went in search of wild honey, others hacked down pine boughs with their sabers and built a great fire, and then they "embowelled the carcass of a sheep fed on the fragrant herbage of Hymettos, and fixed it whole and warm on a wooden spit, which was turned by one of them sitting on the ground." Green pine boughs served as both tablecloth and plates, and they "fell to with knives or fingers, and a Greek, kneeling, circulated wine, pouring it into a shell...."

The "Pic-Nic" is long gone, with all its fragrance of resin and roasting meat, and sun on the wild thyme and the thirty bees. Now Mount Hymettos lies under a dark cloud—a real reason, it might seem, for us here in the light to celebrate our Independence Day with a picnic as nourishing to our spirits as to our bodies. It won't feed any small wan Greeks, of course, but it may give us strength to help fight for them, having spent one more golden day lying close to the earth, with people we like.

Picnics should always be for two people, usually in love, or for a great many, of all ages and natures. One way of telling whether an old man is a nice old man is to see how he acts on a picnic. And the same is true of a middle-aged woman and a young child. Either they frankly loathe such giddy gluttonous affairs and have the good sense to stay away from them, or they come and add to the sum total of enjoyment.

The chances are that if things are kept simple and unclattered, and you choose a place that boasts neither ant hills nor high chill winds, and you regulate the proportions of youth and age judiciously, confirmed picnic-haters will soon send out their delicate feelers of appreciation like sea anemones in a fresh tide. Or, to make things even simpler, you might work the same miracle, and with small damage to the children's high hopes of scratched knees and bee stings, by setting tables and chairs under the apple trees near the house or on a terrace. Then cooking can be done indoors, and when it is brought out it will have almost as good a smell, almost as celestial a flavor, as if it had been done over a pit in the earth. Indeed, to the still somewhat timid skeptics, it will be immeasurably sweeter.

Here is a meal that is easy to carry to a hill above the lake, or to make less arduously in a proper kitchen and then serve out of doors. It uses things that grow in gardens and orchards in the fine hot month of July, or that come from shops without too painful a blow to the ration book. And if it seems not to cost very much, for such a jolly meal, the leftover pennies might find their way to the Child Feeding Station in Athens, via the Near East Foundation.

GASPACHO

CHEESE PUFFS

BARBECUED SPARERIBS

FRENCH FRIED POTATOES

STUFFED MELON

ALE   COFFEE

The *Gaspacho* is a chilled soup from Spain, via Paul Reboux and a few other people, and it is one of the freshest and most stimulating things ever to be served on a hot day. It is simple, like a peasant dish, but tantalizing enough for any sophisticate.

Gaspacho

1 *big handful mixed fresh herbs—parsley, chives, basil,*
 marjoram, savory, etc.
1 *large clove garlic*
1 *sweet pepper, red or green*

> *3 peeled and seeded tomatoes*
> *½ cup olive oil*
> *juice of 1 lemon*
> *1 quart clear stock, or water*
> *1 mild onion, sliced very thin*
> *1 cup diced cucumber*
> *salt*
> *½ cup fine toasted crumbs*

Chop the herbs and mash them thoroughly with the garlic, pepper, and tomatoes, adding the oil and lemon juice very slowly until the mixture is a pastelike consistency. Stir in the stock or water gradually. Add the cucumber, onion, and salt, sprinkle with the bread crumbs, and ice for four hours in the same bowl, before serving.

This strange delicious soup stands alone with dignity, but it is fun to offset its cold tang with some such little hot mouthfuls as:

Cheese Puffs

> *1 package cream cheese*
> *¼ cup Cheddar, Parmesan, or whatever, well grated*
> *½ cup shortening*
> *1 cup flour*
> *celery salt (or powdered oregano, thyme, etc.)*

Cream the cheese and shortening, work in the flour and seasoning, and make into a thin roll. Chill overnight in the icebox, slice thinly as needed, and bake until done in a 425° oven.

These little hot wafers are good made with celery seeds, too, for salads or to serve with cocktails. They are very convenient, because they will keep for many days and can be produced practically with a twist of the wrist for unexpected and awestruck guests.

The next course, plain barbecued spareribs, can be done at home perhaps even more simply than over a low steady fire out of doors, and the only trouble with such common sense is that not so many people can smell it, nor help splash on the basting sauce. (The sauce, please note, is probably the simplest liquid ever dignified with the name, and to my jaded mind a sweet relief from all the intricate recipes for such things.)

Barbecued Spareribs

1 pound (at least) spareribs per person
equal parts (about ¼ cup) butter, catsup,
steak sauce and boiling water

Be sure the ribs are fresh and have the center bones cracked. Broil slowly about ½ hour. Keep the sauce hot, for frequent basting.

Myself, I like crisp French-fried potatoes with this meal—the kind called Long Branch, with plenty of coarse salt sprinkled on them. Spareribs simply have to be eaten with the fingers, like Doctor Chandler's roasted sheep on the slopes of Mount Hymettos—and as long as everybody is happily covered with barbecue sauce, anyway, why not enjoy such laissez-faire to the limit? Pick up hot crisp lengths of potato from a great bowl of them, or from your plate, the way you used to eat the chips part of fish-and-chips in Plymouth.

The stuffed melon, once you've located a large fine one or several babies, is something that is up to you and the fruits now growing near you. Pineapple helps, if you can spare a tin of it, but such prewar staples as bananas are easily foregone. The trick is to let the mixture of lightly blended fruits sit for several hours inside the hollowed melon, chilling (instead of stewing) in their own juices. It is fun, and may even add something to the flavor, to use a plug of nasturtium leaves to stop the hole, or some fresh mint.

Stuffed Melon

Make a hole of a convenient size in a very ripe melon and carefully scoop out the fruit and put it in a large bowl. Then add whole strawberries, pitted cherries, halved or quartered apricots, ripe plums, peaches, fresh currants, raspberries—any fruits that are firm but ripe. Grate the peel of a lemon over them. And sugar according to taste, and then for one large melon for six people add a half cup of good kirsch or any preferred liquor, or one cup of dry white wine. Put the fruits and juice carefully into the shell, plug it, wrap it in a dry cloth, and let it chill thoroughly for about six hours. Serve on a bed of leaves and ice.

As for the drinks for this simple orgy, this delightful nine-to-ninety debauch, they depend upon who comes under nine-to-ninety. Since I myself am middling, I'll settle for good whisky highballs before, and plenty of a local ale or beer during the meal, rather than Doctor Chandler's wine poured into a shell. And if there is kirsch in the fruits, why not a little glass of clear pungent kirsch later with the coffee? After all, I'm a free woman, celebrating that fact on one summer's day in my own free land! I shall drink to others, silent and waiting for their day to come.

[*House Beautiful*, 1944]

HEARTS AND FLOWERS

HE THAT IS of a merry heart hath a continual feast, the Old Testament says. Perhaps that is what all the saints named Valentine taught, too. But it is certain that no matter how continual a feast the merry heart may enjoy, a little extra celebration will do nothing to sadden it!

And February, the month of hearts and flowers and pink lovers' knots, is one that can always bear to be a little happier. It comes at a time of the year when winter seems to have lasted too long, and when spring sounds more like something from a prophecy than from a calendar.

A little luncheon, giddy and silly as a sweetheart's valentine, is better than anything I know to make the season brighter, the heart merrier. It should be pretty and light, and just a little cockeyed in a thoroughly safe way. It should be, for instance, the one below.

Hearts and Flowers at Noon-time

FILETS OF ANCHOVY AND HERRING

LITTLE SANDWICHES IN A BOAT

EGGS VALENTINE WITH MUSHROOMS

ENDIVES WITH VIOLETS

CREAM HEART

STRAWBERRY PRESERVES

TOAST

BACCHUS COCKTAILS

VIN ROSÉ

COFFEE

The Bacchus cocktail, which properly sets the theme with its evocative name, is delicate, appetizing, and of a rosy color that sings out loud.

It is best served at noon without any accompaniment of canapés or salt-ed nuts, because otherwise the light gaiety of the luncheon will be cut into. It is made of one part Dubonnet and one part either very dry ver-mouth or dry white wine. The wine, of course, makes the drink less alco-holic, if anything so mild can truly be called that, and, although it is also somewhat less piquant, it is infinitely preferable to a sweetish vermouth. The two should be poured over ice and stirred until very cold, as for a Martini, and then served with a twist of lemon in champagne glasses.

The *vins rosés* in this country grow better every year. The one for this lunch should be as near like a Tavel as possible and chilled—but not too much. A Grignolino or a Grenache, for instance, can be very good, win-ter or summer, at such a merry-hearted meal.

The meal itself must be one of sharp astonishing contrasts, to tease people who expect a "ladies' lunch." After the somewhat dainty flavor at the Bacchuses, when the guests with their lightening hearts will be expecting something conventionally harmless to follow and to match, serve at the table a fine large platter of filets of anchovy and pickled her-ring, arranged as you will but unadorned by anything but quarters of lemon. To accompany them hollow one or two long French loaves, and fill them with small thin bread and butter sandwiches, cut in heart shapes—if you are so inclined. The high, almost crude flavor of the fish will scare off any lurking inanity of the cocktail, and should flaunt itself alone, except for the tender, sparsely buttered sandwiches.

The next course, which seems intricate, is really simple to prepare. First, the rose-wine should be chilled, ready to serve in ample goblets always half full. The pancakes can be made some time before, cut into their prop-er shape, and kept warm in a gentle oven. The mushrooms in cream can be made beforehand, too, except for the last dash of sherry. The endives can be prepared and put in the refrigerator for at least an hour with the dressing in a bowl beside them. And that leaves nothing to do at the end but scramble the eggs, and assemble the whole, a trick that should best be done while your slightly astounded guests are nibbling with much less slight enthusiasm at the tantalizing filets of the little fishes.

The Eggs Valentine and the salad should be served from a large round platter and a large bowl, with only one plate for each guest, since you will probably have gone fairly crazy on the decoration of the table, with little room left for such niceties as salad plates. There need be no bread with this course.

And, of course, there should be some precautions taken to have hot second helpings at hand. The luncheon is simple, and it will be so good that the stiffest dowager will unbend enough to take more. (Shades of Mrs. Fish and Mrs. Astor and the gawdy days of Newport, when "ladies" toyed with a procession of truffled grouse and soufflés at noontime from gold plates, sent them back untouched, and then gnawed ham sandwiches in the comparative privacy of their boudoirs!)

The endive salad is one that must be made with the blanched kind, called French or Belgian in the markets, or whitloof by people who can say it without giggling. It is best with a simple lemon-juice dressing, because of the slight pleasant bitterness, but because of the rose-wine a light wine-vinegar should be used this time, mixed in gently just before serving, among the inch-long pieces—and as a final ridiculous and faintly decadent touch, a handful of half-opened violets or little pansies tossed upon it. At the end of the last century the insinuating odor of full-blown Parma violets was recommended for such a salad, but at that I must draw the line: the flowers here are nothing but fantasy, like the melon blossoms on a Chinese roasted duck.

The dessert, another shock to guests expecting at the least some elaborate mousse, is a flat pat, half "cottage" cheese and half cream cheese put through a sieve with enough cream to moisten, and then molded in a wicker heart or cut into heart shape when it is well drained on a napkin, with rich gleaming strawberry preserves in a hole in the center. It is served, not with the little cakes so correctly expected, but with crisp, lightly toasted slices of sourdough bread. And coffee. And that is the meal that will add another feast to the merry hearts.

Eggs Valentine

24 thin pancakes
melted butter
soft scrambled eggs, well seasoned

2 pounds fresh mushrooms, coarsely chopped
butter
lemon juice
salt, cayenne pepper
4 cups Béchamel or cream sauce
sherry (dry)

Cut pancakes into uniform rounds or hearts four inches across. Keep warm. Toss chopped mushrooms in hot butter until tender, not more than about ten minutes. Add lemon juice and seasoning, shake, and mix at once with heated sauce. Thin at the last with dry sherry if too thick. Scramble eggs very gently just before serving. Put spoonful of egg on each pancake, fold in center, and lay side by side (or fold against fold to make hearts if heart shaped, like valentines), around edge of platter. Brush with butter and put in hot oven for almost one minute. Fill center of platter with creamed mushrooms, and serve at once.

Pancakes

2 cups sifted all-purpose flour
4 teaspoons baking powder
6 tablespoons granulated sugar
1½ teaspoons salt
2 eggs, beaten
1½ cups milk
6 tablespoons melted shortening

Sift together flour, baking powder, sugar, and salt. Combine eggs, milk, and melted fat, and add to dry ingredients all at once, beating with a spoon, or an egg beater, until smooth. (It should be a thin batter, so add more milk if too thick.) Drop batter from tablespoon on to hot griddle. You can make all cakes the same size if they are baked in a small heavy frying pan. Cook on one side until they are puffed, but don't wait for the bubbles to break. Turn and cook on the other side.

[*House Beautiful,* 1945]

IN HONOR OF SPRING

A Dinner in Honor of Spring

EASTER SOUP

STUFFED OYSTERS

ROAST SADDLE (OR LEG) OF LAMB

NEW POTATOES WITH MARJORAM   ASPARAGUS

RHUBARB TARTS

CHABLIS   CLARET

COFFEE

"AYPRILL, AYPRILL...Lahf thy guhlish lahftuh...then the moment ahftuh, weeeeeep thy guhlish te-uhs." So I sang in the late 1920s, when I took "vocal lessons" at prep school and held my hands in front of my almost nonexistent bosom exactly the way my goddess Madame Matzenauer did in her publicity releases.

Now that I have reached an age of greater discretion, I can safely say that for me April need not weep at all. I am not interested in tears, girlish or matronly. I am interested in holding body and soul together with the greatest possible enjoyment to both. If April, that capricious time of year, can bring us any liaison between the upholstered structure of the body and the skeleton of the mind, so full of thoughts of Easter's religious pain and forbearance, then it is a good month indeed, and worthy of celebration. Flowers blossom, hens lay, lambs jump in the meadows, rabbits raise other smaller rabbits. There are apple blossoms on the boughs, most beautiful and mysterious of blossoming things; and in human hearts there are needs that spring, too—for love, for song, for food.

The last one can be coped with, certainly with more ease than the others and perhaps with less lasting results. It should be done simply, the way a kiss follows a kiss, or another yawn a yawn. But it should be ceremonial—*Le Sacre du Printemps*. It should have a solemnity in it, leaving no room for tears.

It is plain to see that this meal is made up of things newly sprung from the warming earth, newly born. The first course is made by simmering ten whole new tender green onions, cut into pieces in a little butter, with two cups of fresh green peas. Then one quart of chicken consommé is poured in. The whole is covered and allowed to simmer for half an hour, and then put through a fine sieve. It is served in cups, with a tablespoonful of thick or whipped cream and an artful dash of cayenne on top. And it is a very charming soup, simple and yet sly. Dry sherry can carry on from the apéritif.

The second course, with which a good Chablis or Grey Riesling from California should be served, is a salute to the last oyster before a long period of R-less months. It is a fine recipe, allegedly from New Orleans (which means that good canned oysters can be substituted for the somewhat flabby mollusks gathered in that city's warmish waters).

Stuffed Oysters

> 2 tablespoons butter
> 2 tablespoons flour
> 2 small cloves garlic, minced
> 2 tablespoons minced parsley
> 2 tablespoons green onions
> 2½ dozen large oysters, finely cut
> 1 cup canned mushrooms, coarsely chopped
> ½ cup good dry sherry
> fine cracker crumbs
> butter
> cayenne pepper
> lemons

Cook butter and flour until nicely brown, and add minced herbs. Add prepared oysters and mushrooms, and simmer gently for fifteen minutes. Stir in the sherry, and put into shells or small ramekins. Sprinkle with the crumbs, dot with butter, and brown in a hot oven. Serve with a dash of cayenne pepper and a slice of lemon.

As for the lamb, the best thing to do is read a few books about it— Sheila Hibben's *Kitchen Manual*, Escoffier, Louis Diat. Such books are exciting; they tell a great deal and well and clearly, and they keep the mind alive to flavors of words as well as of roasts and cutlets. The special Easter meat, as they will all agree, should be simple. It should be roasted in a slow oven from the start, since, if it is real lamb, it will not have any juices to be seared in as with an older cut. It should be basted with butter or its own fat. Its gravy should be made from its juices.

And when it is fifteen minutes from being done, counting twenty-four minutes to the pound if rare lamb is disliked, a paste of bread crumbs and pounded garlic and minced parsley with butter might be put over its top to make a fresh new flavor.

The little potatoes, so nutlike, should be boiled in their skins and then tossed in melted butter and chopped marjoram just before serving. The asparagus tips, cooked in chicken stock (to be used later for a delicious cream soup, thickened with egg yolk), should be tossed in their turn in some of the juices from the roast and put about it on the platter. They should be tender, but still almost crisp, and seasoned at the last minute with a little salt and freshly ground pepper.

For the tarts, which will not be good with the rather young and lively claret-type wine served with the roast, but will make a nice clean taste for later bibbings, small shells of rich pastry should be baked and then filled just before serving with a marmalade of fresh pink rhubarb, well sweetened, and put in a hot oven for about one minute, or just long enough to intensify the flavor of the crust.

And all that should prove, I think, that spring is here. April weeps no girlish tears, but she seems to know very well indeed what to do with herself—at least at the table!

[*House Beautiful*, 1945]

FOR SUPPER...ON A SULTRY NIGHT

AN OLD NURSERY RHYME, ticking off the months for little minds, says, "Hot July brings cooling showers, apricocks and gillyflowers." Perhaps it does, but the first word is the truest: hot, hot July! By August we can cope with scorching streets, breathless gray air from the rivers and the indescribable smell of lightning and humanity that lies in the dead street of the cities. By August it is easier to stay unwilted. But July brings, along with its problematical gillyflowers, an occasional hopeless discouragement to anyone who wants to keep on existing with even a modicum of graciousness.

At the end of a dragging week, when five other pale, exhausted people are coming to pretend to eat some sort of meal together, in a gallant attempt to prove that they are still both civilized and unaffected by the weather, the prospect of preparing food is almost as unbearable as that of eating it. You think longingly of flight—to another country, another year, to a July night in Paris, maybe (in 1935, was it?), when you sat for a long time eating a *pâté maison* from a big terrine, and salad, and drinking cool Walsheimbier from Strasbourg. Remember what a wonderful night it was!

Well, why not? Change of time and place, but that need not make some such lazy, pleasant meal impossible! It can be a gesture, a respectful nostalgic thumbing of the nose, really, at heat and discouragement and the sad truth that neither you nor Paris will ever be the same again.

A Beau Geste in July

PÂTÉ MAISON

SALAD

FRESH BREAD

BEER   COFFEE

To begin at the end, the coffee should, as always, be fresh, hot, and strong, and served in large cups after such a plain supper. The beer, chilled but not too cold, should be fairly light, the kind that can be drunk amply over several hours: a good local brew, or some respectable and widely distributed one. And the bread should be crisp and good, brought home at the last minute from the nearest Italian or French or kosher baker. The shape of the loaves won't matter: round or flat or long, they'll break up into fine morsels, ready in a basket for the pâté to adorn them.

Salad, it seems, is something that often frightens people who are brave as lions about the intricacies of a sauce or soup. They have had one or two failures, due mainly to over-eagerness, and then they are convinced that all lettuce wilts for them, and all vinegar is too sour.

The best approach in a salad, at any time of the year, but more so during the dog days, is one of complete nonchalance. Keep both it and yourself cool, as well as simple!

Paul Reboux insists that a good salad should never have more than three things in it, and this is a pretty good rule to follow. He also says, and most men will agree, that a bowlful of nothing but lettuce is worse than no salad at all, and should be served only to rabbits. Here is a compromise, the kind that I would make for a summer night:

Salad

> chicory (the very curly kind called frisé in France
>   and endive in California)
> tiny spinach leaves
> romaine, watercress, lettuce
> basic French dressing
> pinch of curry powder
> 2 or 3 chopped hard-boiled eggs
> 3 slices broiled crumbled bacon
> 3 tablespoons dry grated Parmesan cheese

Make the dressing of 1 part good vinegar to 3 parts good olive oil, with salt, fresh pepper, and a dry mustard to taste. (No sugar!)

Add a pinch of curry powder, which will give a nutty flavor completely divorced from its own. Mix well and put in bottom of generous bowl.

Have all the greens chilled and thoroughly dry. Pull into eatable pieces. Put the comparatively tougher ones like the spinach and chicory into the bowl and coat lightly with the dressing. Add the tenderer greens, but do not mix. Sprinkle the egg, the bacon, and lastly the cheese over the whole. Serve at once, tossing lightly at the last minute.

This salad can be varied *ad infinitum* but never *ad nauseam*. Small shrimps or anchovies instead of the bacon, shaved nut meats instead of the cheese, this or that, this or that. The trick is quickness, cold, *and* a plain honest dressing.

About the pâté: that is worth much reading and thought, and fun to boot. There will probably never be another exactly like the one you remember from the little restaurant in Paris, so accept that fact without grimness or regret, and see what Escoffier or your favorite headwaiter has to say on the subject. A self-respecting pâté is dependent entirely on the person who makes it, and can be anything between sheepish imitation of the inimitable pâté de foie gras truffé de Strasbourg and a slice of glorified cold meat loaf.

Here, too, compromise is best. It is futile to try to make chicken livers taste like goose livers, and Americans have been assaulted gastronomically by too many church supper or boarding school meat loaves to find even glorified ones really enjoyable.

A pâté to excite any July-weary palate should have all or most of the following attributes: it should be rich and heady, that is, made with plenty of bacon and whatever meat is used, and artfully full of brandy and spices; it should be smooth so that it will spread unctuously on bread or cut neatly with a fork; it should be very cold and served in the terrine it was made in, so that a knife will cut easily down into it, leaving a layer of the savory "butter" at the top; it should keep for several days or more in the refrigerator, improving each day as long as it lasts. Given these qualities, it will probably overshadow that legendary one you ate in 1935, and you can devote the rest of your days to making copies of it and selling them at fabulous prices.

You will need time, first! Then you must have a strong round or oval terrine with a cover. Then you need brandy, fat bacon, boned chicken, and/or rabbit, duck, pheasant, quail—whatever you can find. You need veal and pork to make a forcemeat (look this up in any good cookbook) with the less handsome slice of the game or fowl. You need eggs and salt, and a little powdered thyme and bay. That's all—unless you can find some truffles, which will give the final cachet to the whole!

Put equal parts of the finest pieces of the hare (to simplify things, you are theoretically making a pâté de lièver), and bacon strips, (and truffles!) in a dish and let them marinate in good brandy for an hour. Make a forcemeat in more or less the following proportions: 1 pound of hare (the "scraps"), 6 ounces each of pork and veal, 1½ pounds of bacon. Finish with 1 egg, salt, and 3 tablespoons of brandy for each pound of the forcemeat. Put through a fine sieve.

Line the terrine with the marinated bacon, and then fill it with alternating layers of forcemeat, hare, bacon (and truffles!). Cover with bacon and sprinkle on the thyme and bay and whatever spices you please. Put on the lid, set in a pan of water, and cook in a slow oven. The pâté will be done when the grease that has risen to the top is quite clear; as long as it is cloudy the meat is not cooked. When done take from the oven, let cool well, and put into the refrigerator for at least twenty-four hours before serving.

This is obviously a long, if not tedious, performance. There are two other ways of having a decent pâté to serve: cheating, or buying one from a good restaurant or caterer. The latter is probably the better method, but I have often made a very edible if dishonest terrine by skimping on the almost unprocurable bacon, using good smoked liverwurst in place of forcemeat (which would make Escoffier whirl in his tomb, and rightly), marinating slices of ripe olives instead of truffles, and using nothing more glamorous than a rabbit from my neighbor's hutches. I've been generous with spices, including mustard, and with brandy. And if there hasn't been enough of the bland beautiful "butter" on the top, I have cheated further and added a little of the real thing, melted, before I let the terrine cool. I must admit to success, too—even at the expense of my gastronomical principles, and even in July.

[*House Beautiful*, 1945]

THE DAY FOR INNOCENCE

CHRISTMAS, if it is *right*, is a gay festival, full of generosity and inno-cence, coming as it does between our sober day of Thanksgiving for past rewards and the New Year with its sometimes chilling thoughts upon the future.

To be right, it should be shared, like a proper Chinese feast, by the youngest and the oldest of a family, all eating and drinking and laugh-ing together. Even the toasts to Absent, Lost, and Departed ones should be lifted happily without remorse this day. It should be, and indeed it *can* be if so willed, a fete of intimacy and shared pleasures, no matter how simple.

In my own family, as in many another I am sure, there was a kind of lapse in the birth rate for seven or eight years, and it was astonishing to see how dreary Christmas immediately became. The youngest were too young (if born); the next generation (mine) had passed its first youth and had become embroiled in romances, divorces, and suchlike; the older people were worried and weary; and the oldest, the grandparents and their contemporaries, had quietly and completely vanished.

We went through the familiar motions, decorated the ranch house and the tree and the table as always, and drank more than we wanted, to try to revive some of the old spontaneous gaiety, and ate much less than at such former feasts because of our dreariness. It was dreadful.

Then things changed, and for the better, the *right* way: we all acquired children and shifted our generations, so that mine was now the third or fourth instead of second, really, and our parents were the old ones but mercifully not vanished; and when, upon the green tree, we perched the battered glass bird with its spun-glass tail, the very last of the boxful that Mother had ordered from Germany in 1911, it seemed to sing into the crackling merry air of the living room with notes we all heard in our hearts. And when we drank the last bottle of Father's Tio Pepe, it was *enough*. And when we went to the table, which looked much as it had on Christmas Day for longer than many of us could remember, we ate with a candid hunger that was both enjoyable and strangely solemn, full of thanks for being a family again.

I can easily recount what we ate, for it was as much a ritual as any part of the festival. Now and then, one or another of us has said, not quite meaning it, "For heaven's sake, let's break away this year and not have so-and-so or such-and-such!" We all agree it would be nice, or amusing, or wise. Then we weaken. I suppose every family has its own such patterns, as rigidly held to.

If I were the matriarch, as I may be some day, I might gradually change parts of the menu, as I am conscious that my mother did, to fit the land we lived in, its climate, and most of all, the domestic shift from cook-and-maid to no-help-at-all.

I can imagine, if I lived in a cold country, serving a dinner beginning with a subtle mushroom soup, going on in old-fashioned elegance through chilled celery hearts and suchlike to a roast suckling pig garlanded with holly berries and mistletoe and surrounded by apples roasted on silver skewers and tiny loops of sausages, then perhaps a salad of Belgian endive, then an elaborate frozen pudding, garnished like something for Queen Victoria's sideboard, and silver horns filled with sugared currants and violet petals, a tray of my favorite Russian Fruit Cake, then chilled hothouse grapes—all to the accompaniment of beautiful wines, heavy with honorable renown.

I can imagine that, but it will not come about, for it is a feast for adults, with nothing innocent about it. And even though I never reach the state of matriarchy, my sentimental mind dwells on at times, I already am enough of a mother to know that children—and lots of them—and lots of food *they* can understand, are much more important than any gastronomical sophistications on Christmas Day. My mother knew it, even better than I, which is why her happiest menus for the celebration always went like this:

OYSTERS ON THE HALF SHELL

TURKEY WITH OYSTER STUFFING

CRANBERRY SAUCE

PICKLED FIGS

CLOVERLEAF ROLLS WITH SWEET BUTTER

CREAMED CELERY WITH ALMONDS

UTAH CELERY, CHILLED

HOT MINCE TARTS

PLUM PUDDING WITH HARD SAUCE

SANTOS COFFEE

This sounds peculiar. I suppose it is, but no more so than almost any close-knit family's, I suspect. There were things in it we all loved, and things all of us could eat a little of. The young ones skipped the desserts, and the old ones shunned the fresh celery because of the their dentures. There were two kinds of oysters, two clashing "relishes," two kinds of celery, and no traditional potato dish, two similarly rich ripe sweets! There were *reasons*.

The oysters: That was because we loved fresh ones, so hard to get in hot Southern California, and for Christmas had a big case of them shipped with ice from Maine, with the mollusks still alive and pulling away from us delicately along their edges as we breathed upon them, just opened by one skillful brother-in-law or another. We would come and go in the side garden, where a table was set up with lemon halves, thin buttered black bread, and Grandmother's oyster forks, and the big case and the buckets for shells and the special knife for the shucking on a sturdy bench. We drank the juice from the cold shells, with ale or white wine, as we wished, to go alongside. We took the best oysters into the house for Mother and whoever sat chatting with her and lazily winding the used ribbons from the presents into little balls. Once a cousin found a rather nubby pearl. Once the new minister drifted in to bless us and hurried away, his face as white as his round collar at the prospect of sharing such outlandish food as a Maine oyster on that hot morning.

The turkey, which was always lying grandly upon the giddy sparkling table when the bell rang for dinner, was stuffed to the hilt with oysters, lightly held together by a conservatively flavored bread dressing. My father, who carved it standing up, as was both proper and impressive, remarked once each year and once only (faithful to the ritual), with a familiar melancholy that never failed to make us laugh from one end of the long board to the other, "I suppose that there may perhaps be just a *few* oysters in this, in case *I* might enjoy an *honest* oyster dressing for a change, instead of a mere handful scattered through it."

The cranberry sauce, the kind with the berries still in it, was for my mother. She loved it fervently and would eat it any time of the year and, of course, on Christmas, too. And then later in the day, about dusk, she would go quietly to the kitchen and dig into what was left with a silver soup spoon.

The baked spiced figs were for those who felt, as did I, that they were one of the best things in the world with roast turkey, for some completely unethical reason. They should properly be served with ham, I imagine, or a curry or a Hawaiian roasted pig.

The cloverleaf rolls were tiny, about as big as a silver dollar. They were very rich, but we usually put more butter on them as we ate, to savor their crispness and the smooth cool fat. I can't remember who has made them for us, lately, but when I was a child my mother did, the day before Christmas, to be kept in the icebox for the last-minute baking, and I would help her roll the three little balls of delicious-smelling dough, and enjoy how buttery my fingers could be in this good cause.

Then two kinds of celery! The big shallow casserole of creamed celery with almonds has, for a long time, been one of the things my sisters and cousins and I agree we will *change* this year, or next year. (Once we did and had stuffed onions, which did not seem quite right.) It is a bland dish, in good contrast to the rather heady turkey stuffing, and the crisp almonds in it make a fine change in texture, as in Chinese cookery.

The Utah celery was always important to my mother, perhaps because she had been raised on the prairies where it was a true luxury. She ordered it especially from somewhere near Salt Lake, I believe, and it was wonderful, very full-stalked and like beautiful carved jade. She always had it washed on Christmas Eve, and stood in ice water which had been sweetened generously with white lump-sugar (about six lumps to each quart of water). It was an unwritten family law that to put salt on it at the table would be desecration.

And then dessert!—two heavy, dark, fruitily overpowering ones. There would be a big silver platter with what looked like hundreds of little half-moon mincemeat tarts laid in scallops, overlapping, each stained on its plump top by the brown liquor that had oozed from the fork pricks in it. The pastry was flaky. The mincemeat was of the best, no dehydrated synthetic compound of old cannery rejects. The tarts were hot, but not too hot to pick up and eat in two bites, which was the way we did it. We all preferred them to the plum pudding, but dutifully served it as it should be and nibbled at small portions of it because a dear aunt had made it for us every year for too many to count. (The Hard Sauce, made of good butter and sugar and brandy, and served very cold, was always my job, and I had success with it, except for one year during the last war when I tried to use Australian rum, about one hundred proof, with miserable results.)

Christmas Celery with Almonds

1 quart cooked celery
1 pint cream sauce
½ cup finely grated Parmesan cheese
1 cup blanched slivered almonds

The celery should be of the best quality, the inner but not heart stalks, cut in quarter-inch pieces and parboiled until tender but still firm. Drain well.

The sauce should be well seasoned, very smooth, made of the finest ingredients. Any family has a good recipe, but Escoffier's rule for Béchamel, omitting the veal, cannot be beat.

The cheese should be added to the sauce when it is done; it does not change the flavor of the dish noticeably, but makes a fine golden color to the baked result.

The almonds should be slivered finely, after blanching.

Mix all together, pour into a buttered shallow casserole, and heat at 400° until golden on top and bubbling at the edges.

Lera's Figs

10 pounds figs, preferably purple, not too ripe
5 pounds sugar
2 cups good cider vinegar
whole cloves

Wash figs, and stick one clove in each. Make thick syrup of sugar and vinegar. Pour while hot over figs in uncovered roaster, and leave in slow oven without stirring for two hours. Let stand over-night, untouched. Repeat baking next day. Put in jars, and pour syrup to top of each (10 or 11 pints).

Mushroom Soup
(For a Matriarch)

1 pound fresh mushrooms
2 quarters strong veal or chicken stock
2 tablespoons barley
seasoning to taste
1 cup dry white wine
4 egg yolks
1½ cups rich cream
1 minced black truffle or chopped parsley

Chop the unpeeled mushrooms and simmer in the stock with the barley for one hour. Season to taste, add the wine and strain. Beat the egg yolks and gradually add to them the heated cream. To this add mushroom broth, stirring constantly. Do not allow to boil. Serve at once, garnished with a sprinkle of truffle or parsley.

[*House Beautiful*, 1949]

A FAMILY THANKSGIVING:
AMIABLE IMAGES OF THE PAST

ACCORDING TO the dictionaries, Thanksgiving Day is "appointed for giving thanks for divine goodness and mercies," which is more or less what it was when I was small, whether or not we all knew that. It was ceremonial mostly because my father did not publish his small-town *Daily News* on Thanksgiving. If the weather was good, he played tennis at the public courts, and then we wore Sunday clothes and ate a nice but not special meal, not Sunday noon dinner and yet not an ordinary week-day lunch.

We had a dessert Father liked, instead of stewed fruit...usually a peach or apple pie. He disliked pumpkins, except for our annual jack-o'-lantern, and Mother preferred not to bow to gastronomical traditions that smacked too overtly of the Middle West, where both of them had been born. (She could stomach her homeland most easily between book covers, by Willa Cather et al.)

Usually, after our pleasant lunch with pie because the Pilgrims had once eaten a love feast with their Indian brothers, Father left for an extra set of tennis, Mother took a postprandial snooze to ruminate on the next arrival of a sibling for Anne and me, and we did whatever we felt like that was quiet and amusing, in the backyard. Grandmother Holbrook was in Michigan at Battle Creek, to escape any such gastric and religious threat as a legal holiday or a churchly event.

So basically the day was somewhat solemn, because of the two women, one always there and one almost never. They were at least two poles apart in their religious persuasions, but were led by their genes to consider the feast a spiritual one. Grandmother was a respected Christian or Campbellite. Mother, who could not tolerate the spectacle of total immersion before strangers, even in God's name, had become a good Episcopalian as soon as she was of age, with only one damp sign of the cross on her forehead to prove her faith, and had to keep all us children waiting until Grandmother died, before we could join her church.

In the meantime, we went to the St. Matthas Sunday school, except for an occasional sortie I made into Grandmother's more Pentecostal pews (later I came to prefer good sacramental wine from a silver chalice to grape juice from a little paper cup...). We helped, every autumn, to bank the altar steps with pumpkins and apples and dried ears of corn, to celebrate the "in-gathering" or whatever it was called. (And long before I chose wine over grape juice, I thought the piles of canned foods and knitted coverlets at Grandmother's church were wiser....)

Of course there was a short holiday from school at Thanksgiving, but even it was quiet and perhaps austere, until, when I was seven or eight years old, Father's parents came to live nearby, to celebrate all the great holidays with us, and even plain old Sundays. Then everything became much more ecumenical...more good overt Middle Western. Our gatherings were "religious," but we had a lot more fun. Especially *eating.*

My own enjoyment of the change of our gastronomical pace was partly based on a burgeoning interest in how people feel when they enjoy things they do not want to. For instance, my mother was somewhat abashed by her husband's family, and hid it by professing a genteel resentment of their environmental patterns. They were all raised on the prairies, but she had been sent to schools in Virginia and then Europe, and they had graduated from small religious Iowa colleges.

The Kennedys were no doubt aware of her reasons for seeming uppity, but stayed serenely sure that on Thanksgiving we would all go to church (Campbellite, Methodist, Episcopalian, no matter as long as we could bow our heads), and then sit down to a long, rich "family" feast, with the table covered from start to finish with platters of good things. And when Grandmother Holbrook was not there, which was mostly, tall stemmed glasses were everywhere, with sherries and dark sweet wines for the desserts....

Mother honestly thought that all this accent on food was gross but as a basically sensual person enjoyed it fully. She understood that it was a simplistic offering of thanks, even as she tried to disdain it as one more proof that prairie land traditions were vulgar. I was aware of her as a sensitive person and tried to understand her innate distaste for what she plainly if unwillingly liked, and all the time I loved the overt jolly celebrations, both religious and physical, that my father's family expected and got.

Now every Thanksgiving meant baking and peeling and simmering for days before, and when Grandmother Kennedy helped her husband unload the back of their Model-T, we moaned with delight as we peeked under the napkins and papers on her bowls and pans. She always brought rolls still warm from the oven, a mound of sweet butter, baskets of late figs, jars of her pickles and jams, four or five of Grandfather's pullets roasted and stuffed with wild herbs, pickled mushrooms they had found in the hills...

Never had we seen so much to eat, all at the same time, in our kitchen and then on the table! It was miraculous and sustaining to taste its fine freshness, after we had all assembled and Grandfather had blessed it and us.

It was not that we lived austerely the rest of the year, and certainly not on holidays. We ate three simple but "proper" meals a day, with afternoon tea now and then for visitors from east of the Mississippi. There was always a slavey-of-the-moment to stumble in and out of the kitchen with covered vegetable dishes, platters and tea to set before Mother at lunch, beef hash for Father to serve at night, good silver to use nicely. Conversation was always good too, and children were spoken to, and when Grandmother Holbrook was in Battle Creek we laughed a lot.

But Thanksgiving Dinner, after our Kennedy relatives came, was Bruegelian, Elizabethan, Tolstoian: two vaguely defined courses, no servants except euphoric little handmaidens (my sister, little female cousins and me) who trotted here and there with tidbits for an uncle, the doctor, the sea captain, Aunt Genie. We seemed to sit for hours after the blessing and first satisfactions, nibbling one more little plum turnover, peeling one more honey-sweet grape or guava.

Mother would have excused herself, perhaps to lie upstairs reading in her *Book of Common Prayer* but more probably to snooze happily after the long, amicable meal. Some of the men would walk slowly up to the park, after one last languorous stuffed date and a heel-tap of sweet wine.

The cook-slavey would long since be comatose in her dark sanctum, but somehow the table was finally cleared, except for dishes of fruits and leftover slices of pound cake. We *could* have gone on eating, but we could *not*. Children dozed or talked quietly, under the music of grown-up voices in the twilight. What fun it had been, so strangely peaceful!

The table, twice its usual size, had not been set with proper places for all of us, but the silver and china were on the sideboard, and Mother's longest Irish linen tablecloth was a sea of open dishes and platters, hot, cooling, cold, replaced, emptied, filled again. People took what they wanted, when they wanted, and moved their chairs about as they wished, instead of sitting where they were put and standing up only when their hostess did. Men changed their seats as the long feast went on, and sat now beside a wife, now a girl, now another man.

It was wild and woolly. It was wonderful. When everyone wandered off, after a final sip or nibble, Anne and any other small people and I would causally take a few more nuts or cookies and go out into the backyard, to sit under an orange tree and talk-or-not-talk, eat-or-not-eat, with nobody to say a nay.

Probably few of us, after Grandfather's short solemn blessing, thought about the divinity in the goodness we were then to share, or about God's mercies thus to feed us. But in everyone, that day of amiable communing, there was a latent thankfulness. We ate at the same table, from the same dishes, and felt at ease together, to stand up, sit down in another place, smile here or there without guile. We all gave thanks.

[*The New York Times*, 1983]

SAVORING WINTER

IT SEEMS VERY STRANGE to try to remember the best meal of my whole life, especially one that I ate in the winter.

Of course winter, I think, is better than summer for eating. In summer one picks growing beauties, beans and tomatoes and suchlike; there are all kinds of delicious fruits. But in winter one thinks a bit more about where and what and how to eat.

Another thing about winter, or at least I've found it in my own life, is that I often prefer to eat by myself then. I've been asked about wonderful meals I remember in the wintertime in restaurants, and although I've known a lot of them, I think most of the memorable meals I've eaten have been either with one person besides myself or alone.

I wonder how far back to go. For instance, in about 1945 I was in a restaurant in New York with a very complex man who ordered a strange meal, mostly of kidneys—grilled or simply prepared, I think. Other dishes came before and after, of course, but I noticed that he was watching me as I ate the little nubbins of good tender meat, and I did not learn until about a year later that he himself loathed kidneys in any form, and wondered how I would cope with them. Would I hate them, would I love them, would I swallow them if I hated them, yes or no, would he love me, hate me? He was too complex for me, so finally we parted, but that was a good meal and I liked it, and I liked the people who ran the restaurant he took me to, partly because they were on to his game and never betrayed to him how inwardly amused they were.

And there was another meal farther back. (I've written too much about these things, I find.) Yes, that was one we ate rather late at night or early Easter Sunday in about 1938. I went upstairs to the room of a man whom I later married, because I loved him very much. He had found a big plate of pale butter-yellow, and in the middle was a tin of black-green-gray caviar, with apple blossoms all around it. I remember the blossoms and the yellow plate, and that I was feeling very shy. (They were strong memories, and still are.) I think we drank white wine or maybe some cold gin. But what I really remember most is that after this little meal I went down very prudishly, very quietly and smugly probably, to my own quarters, and I heard him laughing up in the attic, laughing very nicely at my innocence, because it was the most innocent meal I'd ever had, and I was being seduced but I did not know it then. (But I've written about that, I think. Yes, I must have.)

Then I think of a meal—it wasn't a true meal, but none of these really was, with courses and plate-changes and protocol; the caviar with the apple blossoms was not a real *meal*....One time I was hiking, in about 1930, I think. My husband and I were members of the Club Alpin in Dijon, where we were both students. We were taken up as a kind of curiosity by the older members of the Club, because we were naive Americans and yet we had fairly good manners. And every Sunday we used to go out into the hills. We would ride on small local trains for a long time and then pile off, knowing that after we'd walked through the frozen fields and stumbled toward a waterfall or an old château, we'd have a very good dinner in a country hotel that had prepared for our advent for a week at least. Then we would walk some more, very slowly, and finally take the train back to Dijon, everybody soggy and sleepily peevish.

But one day I got away from the people after the long meal. I found myself on a hill, a bare bleak Burgundian hill, probably covered with mustard in the summer, above the vineyards. I was with a tall old man. I think he was a retired general. We had never spoken before. We looked out over the plains toward a place where the Gallic chieftain Vercinge-torix had fought off or fought with or fought for the land, hundreds of years ago.

Suddenly he handed me a piece of chocolate. The day was so cold and so bitter and so mournful, and so beautiful, that I remember that when we bit into the chocolate it snapped off. It was like crumbs of pebbles or crumbs of cement in my mouth, as I stood by the ancient cautious courteous old Frenchman, but it was one of the best communions

I have ever felt with anyone. (And I should not write about that again, because I've already done so, I feel fairly sure.)

How much farther back can I go? I don't know. How about... yes, I think now of the first winter meal that I remember. It was, amusingly enough, rather an early version of a Wine and Food Society dinner today. Very pompous. Very secret. Full of snobbery. Very *important*.

I was about seven, and up Painter Avenue lived a girl named Eleanor Faye, on the same block, so that I could go up there alone. I don't think I went to school yet, so perhaps I was a bit younger. And in the basement of Eleanor's house (she was about eleven, probably), a small select group met, four or five girls older than I and a couple about my age, once a week perhaps. There were two little boys for a while, but we really did not like them. It was strictly a female club, rather like today's Dames d'Escoffier. It was very exclusive, even reclusive.

We met weekly or monthly, as I remember, but probably weekly because time goes so slowly for children. Of course it was a secret meeting. I don't know how the word got around of when to come and on what day. It was always after school, in the basement under Mrs. Faye's kitchen. It was cold down there, very cold, and dark. There was a candle, on a ledge under the glass jars full of jams and tomatoes and suchlike.

Sometimes Caroline Maple was there. Caroline and Eleanor were girlfriends and they both went to the Bailey Street school, which meant that they were in the sixth grade, probably. And then two little girls who lived a few doors up from us, Alice and Lucille, were always there, and now and then I brought my friend Gracie, but she was half Mexican and not too acceptable in our small Quaker community. And the two little boys, Talbert and Garland, were there, but they did not last long with us—then. My little sister Anne was not welcome, because she was two years younger than I and impossibly babyish for that elite older crowd.

The whole project that we were all working on, though we did not really put it in words, was to find out what our parents forbade us to eat, that we most craved and needed and wanted and loved.

One day we would discuss tomatoes. Eleanor called them "tomahtoes" but we said "tomaytoes." We finally decided that sometimes we ate them in the summer, whether we liked them or not, but that they were *out*. We hated them, anytime of the year.

One girl said that her mother and father loathed celery, and that she herself never could swallow it. So we thought about celery. Did she hate it because they did? Should we try it? No. That did not work. We all decided we did not like celery.

The final and best meeting was about one vegetable that we were all forbidden thoroughly to touch: a raw potato. I still wonder about this. Why a *raw* potato? We all liked cooked potatoes in any form. And I don't remember being forbidden to eat it raw, but I agreed completely with the other girls and admitted that I had never tasted one. Why, I do not know, except that people said, "Oh, you wouldn't like it," or "No, don't! It will give you a stomachache," or "People don't *eat* raw potato!"

We were all there that day, which was our peak of attendance. It was in February, I'm sure, because I had valentines on my mind and the cellar was unusually cold. There were two candles, I remember. We whispered, of course, because we didn't want anyone to know we were there, although I . . . well, I don't think Mrs. Faye really did suspect anything. I'll never know about that, because probably most of the people I'm now thinking about are long since tucked away. But we whispered anyway, which added to the excitement and interest of the whole eerie thing.

Somebody, maybe Josephine Maple, who was my peer and the younger sister of Caroline, produced a large potato, and someone else had a knife, a jackknife probably, because old uncles whittled in those long-gone days. We cut the stolen vegetable into little slices. We all squatted on the cold dirt floor very solemnly, six or seven little girls, and nibbled and appraised, and whispered about the flavor, the texture, the wetness, the crunchiness, the grainy taste—or did it taste like clay?

It was very strange, as I look back on it. It was a mirror held up to our futures, to all the solemn seminars and tastings we were preparing for.

We analyzed and guessed and pondered: why did we crave something that our parents, and cooks and whoever was in the kitchen, had absolutely forbidden us to eat? Why were we doing all this?

I knew that I could not give much of a damn then, or ever, about raw potato. I think we all decided that. But it was a great tasting, one of the most satisfying I've ever had, especially in the winter; to be there with those other people, who were looking for what I was looking for, gastronomically.

We found that we had been told never to touch something that we really didn't particularly want to touch anyway, ever again, but we satisfied ourselves. I think we were brave, to keep on crunching and trying and swallowing what we had been told seriously was poisonous or disgusting. We proved a point; we met seriously to do just that, and then arrived at a conclusion and went our own ways. Perhaps that was the best meal I ever ate, at least in company and in the winter, and no matter how much alone each of us really was.

[*The New York Times Magazine,* 1985]

BRING ON WINTER!

JUST REMEMBER what it was like a few short months ago. Toward the end of almost any fall we begin to long, no matter how quietly, for a hint, a tiny suggestion even, of the first nights of chill-before-morning and of cold water in the pipes. We yearn for the untoward thrust and urgency of leaves turning from green to gold and then settling upon the sleepy earth. It is impossible to stay calm and cool and simple when all this begins to happen.

It is the time of year when we feel almost shamefaced about wanting the fine, shockingly bright blue days to end. Finish, be gone, is our silent cry. What we want is for the weather to stop being so damnably desirable; we itch to be uncomfortable again. We think how wonderful it would be to shiver. We clean out the fireplace and almost wickedly lay a little kindle-ish promise of a fire for some night soon, even as we know that we should have the chimney sweep come by before the first match starts a smoky fuming in our neglected flues. We're eager to fall into the cluttered warmth of a stuffy room that has no air currents in it, soundless but for the snowy winds outside the windows and the curtains drawn tightly against even that.

And, of course, along with this unreasonable desire come the almost voluptuous musings, most of them inadvertent and unformed, on cold-weather foods, on *eating*. What will we cook first? What will be most heavenly rich and heavy and thickening?

A stew might be good, the kind that makes the house smell for days, before and then during and finally after it has been eaten. Or a filling soup, made with beans or lentils or something that is a fit complement to whatever satisfying meat or fish may be conjured up, all of it cooked into a gumbo or something that is heady and dark.

Even the need to keep things crisp and fresh seems suddenly undesirable, once this break in the gastronomy of the seasons comes about. Why not start with a kettle of something tonight, and let it sit until morning on the stove in the warm kitchen, without worrying about spoiling as we might in warm weather, and then heat it again after breakfast? Perhaps add a bit of milk, or some leftover pasta, or anything at all to keep it from being forgotten until lunchtime. Then, with any luck, the snow may have stopped, but a sudden cold will have crept into the air, and soup heated again for lunch will smell richer and better than ever it could have the first time around.

Yes—it's time for warm feastings with other refugees from the chill nights of winter, gathered around the board to share with us. Now, we can warm our souls as well as our bodies.

[*Food & Wine*, 1988]

"TOMANE JUNCTION," OR CHRISTMAS 1965

IT IS 1989, and I am in Glen Ellen, where I live now, and I have just found a diary I kept about something that could have been absolutely horrendous. I've called it "Tomane Junction," after the horrible night we all spent on Christmas Eve in 1965. The next morning I found this note pinned on the door of the toilette:

YOU ARE NOW ENTERING

TOMANE JUNCTION

THINK BEFORE YOU ENTER!

The cast of characters consisted of my older girl Anna and Jean-Christophe, her several-months-old son. Then there was Kennedy, my younger daughter who was out from the East where she was going to school. There was Bill Erskine, a very good man. He was the widow of my sister Anne, who had died that year. And Eleanor Friede was there too, the widow of Donald Friede, who had been my husband. He had also died that year, and he was Kennedy's and Anna's father, too. Therefore, I'd lost my younger sister and my former husband, but nobody ever mentioned that, nor did they even seem to realize that the girls had lost their father and their aunt. Anna and Kennedy were fond of my sister Anne, but they were very fond indeed of Donald, in their own peculiar ways. He had not been very close to them when they were growing up, because we got divorced when Kennedy was very young, but the relations were always strong, and Eleanor was a fine stepmother and a good friend to me, too. (That still goes on, thank God.) And I was the devil in the machine, running the whole business.

The place was, of course, our old house on Oak Avenue in St. Helena, where we lived for several more years, until I moved over the Hill to Glen Ellen. It was a good house, three storeys tall. On the main floor of the house were Anna, and little Chris, who had a crib in her bedroom. She had the one real bathroom. Then Eleanor was in the master bedroom, and in between the two rooms there was a little toilette with a washbasin and a toilet. Kennedy and I slept in the attic, where I had a beautiful room, perched there, with a narrow staircase going down to the little toilette. Downstairs, in the basement, there was a bathroom for Bill. They were all used steadily that night.

The log is one of the most futile, and in retrospect anyway, one of the funniest I can imagine. Almost nothing was done as I'd foreseen it. All the plans changed several times. I was right in assuming that the undercurrents of private emotions would make it wise for me to have food always planned well in advance, and in the end that was my downfall. On Christmas Eve we all sat down to a really beautiful turkey Bill had roasted, a pretty feast it was in every way . . . and within three hours most of us might just as well have been dying!

In my reasonable but somewhat unassuming desire to have everything culinary well under control, so that we could sit around and talk and enjoy the baby and forget that both Anne Kelly and Donald Friede had died not long before, I had blandly asked Bill to stuff the turkey late the night of the twenty-third and to roast it early the next morning. (*I knew better. I was not thinking!*) This was dangerous enough, with quantities of raw oysters chopped and packed into the perishable carcass, but to compound my idiocy, the weather turned very balmy during the night while the bird sat on the back porch! It was a perfect prescription for murder, mass murder. . . .

It never occurred to us that the temperature would rise so fast. Still, I didn't think of it in the morning, so Bill and I fixed the oven so that it would hold the damn thing. It was a big bird.

It was delicious. Oh God, it was good. Succulent. Beautiful. Bill is an excellent browner and roaster. He basted it all the time. Wonderful smells. We had a late afternoon dinner that day. It was a *wonderful* turkey! and then, it was *ghastly!*

Before I went to bed, Eleanor asked me for some bicarbonate of soda, saying she felt a little queasy, and I remember that I was vaguely annoyed, for she *had* eaten rather a lot of delicious oyster stuffing. Of course, we all had, except the baby Chris (who fortunately did not get even a bite of it), and me (not much interested in what I had got with some labor and thought onto the table, and only nibbling politely).

Well, total "Tomane Junction" by midnight! Eleanor and Bill were thoroughly sick as was Anna. I listened, up in the attic, to all the toilets being flushed often, and before dawn I saw a towel discreetly near Kennedy's bed, "in case," she said later. I knew there had been poison somewhere in the pot, so I kept samples of *everything*, in case it all got worse, and at daybreak I checked with Dr. Neil. He laughed airily, which seemed heartless to me at the glum moment, and said it was very obvious what had happened. They were purged of everything. They should eat nothing but weak tea and toast until they felt better. No butter, no sweets, no lemon juice even. Very weak tea, and plain, dry toast. This was easy enough to do . . . except that gradually, as they grew better, I began to feel a little queasy myself, and I think I waited until after Bill and Eleanor had left, and then I was quite sick. But that was my nature, and is beside the point, really.

I resolved not to weep and mope with guilt. We all survived. But we might not have. And I shall never be hasty again, in the kitchen anyway.

And it's all rather funny now, but it wasn't then. . . .

[*True Food: Wholefoods for Modern Times,* 1989]

ACKNOWLEDGMENTS

"Legend of Love," *Ladies' Home Journal,* April, 1952; "What Happened to Miss Browning," *The Carleton Miscellany,* summer, 1967; "A Possible Possession," *The New Yorker,* April 17, 1978; "The Ten Most Important Food Books of All Time," *The Chicago Daily News,* December, 1943; "Shall It Be...Eating or Dining?" *House Beautiful,* September, 1944 [reprinted November, 1986]; "Love in a Dish," *House Beautiful,* May, 1948; "Gourmets Are Made—Not Born," *House Beautiful,* June, 1948; "The Great Good Sense and Comfort of the Fork Supper," *House Beautiful,* December, 1949; "Little Meals with Great Implications," *House Beautiful,* March, 1950; "If This Were My Place," *Atlantic Monthly,* April, 1950; "Honest Is Good," *Good Cooking—The Complete Kitchen Companion,* September, 1950; "Made, with Love, By Hand," *McCall's,* September, 1971; "Learn to Touch...to Smell...to Taste," *Vogue,* March, 1972; "How Victoria Set the American Table," *The New York Times Magazine,* September 15, 1974; "Shelf Life," *San Francisco Review of Books,* winter, 1988–1989; "Through a Glass Darkly," *Atlantic Monthly,* November, 1944; "Coffee," *Atlantic Monthly,* May, 1945; "Spoon Bread and Moonlight," *Atlantic Monthly,* April, 1947; "The Taste for Bortsch," *House Beautiful,* March, 1949; "A Hymn to Left-overs," *Pageant,* October, 1950; "The Best Way to Entertain," *Holiday,* March, 1956; "Pasta: Italian-born, American-made," *McCall's,* October, 1956; "Martini-Zheen, Anyone?" *Gourmet,* January, 1957; "The Pleasures of Picnics," *Harper's Bazaar,* July, 1957; "Apéritifs: The Civilizing Influence," *Harper's Bazaar,* March, 1958; "Ode to the Olive," *Travel and Leisure,* September, 1976; "The Midnight Egg and Other Revivers," *Bon Appétit,* May, 1978; "Simple Things," *Bon Appétit,* September, 1979; "Eating Catsup from a Bottle," *True Food: Wholefoods for Modern Times,* summer, 1988; "Travel Notes: Café Olives," *Architectural Digest,* March, 1989; "San Juan Capistrano," *See Your West Program,* 1945 [reprinted in *The Glory of Our West,* 1952, 1958]; "Bonanza Banquets," *The Book Club of California,* 1950; "An Epicure Reviews West Coast Wine Awards," *House Beautiful,* April, 1954; "A Bunch of Wine Buffs Were Rapping It Up, When...," *Golden Gate North,* Fall, 1975; "Napa and Sonoma: The Best of Both Worlds," *Food and Wine,* August, 1979; "The Art of Eating, California Style," *Signature,* September, 1981; "Only in Spots Have We Tamed the California Coast," *Holiday,* November, 1985; "A Mistake," 1989; "Music on Sunday," *Atlantic Monthly,* March, 1944; "Truffles for Weariness," *Vogue,* July, 1948; "All the Food and Wines Were There," *Holiday,* November, 1957; "How to Catch a Sea Monster," *House Beautiful,* April, 1957; "In Nice, Snacking in the Flower Market," *The New York Times Magazine,* October 5, 1986; "Some Other Picnics," *Architectural Digest,* July, 1989; "The Flanners," *San Francisco*

Review of Books, summer, 1990; "The Georgian Sugar Shaker," *Art and Antiques,* February, 1985; "A View of the Delta Queen," 1971; "The Fabled Days of Diamond Jim," *Gourmet,* September, 1992; "On Celebrating a Glorious Fourth in a Free Land," *House Beautiful,* July, 1944; "Hearts and Flowers," *House Beautiful,* February, 1945; "In Honor of Spring," *House Beautiful,* April, 1945; "For Supper...on a Sultry Night," *House Beautiful,* May, 1945; "The Day for Innocence," *House Beautiful,* December, 1949; "A Family Thanksgiving: Amiable Images of the Past," *The New York Times,* November, 1983; "Savoring Winter," *The New York Times Magazine,* October, 1985; "Bring on Winter!" *Food & Wine,* February, 1988; "'Tomane Junction,' or Christmas 1965," *True Food: Wholefoods for Modern Times,* Fall, 1989

INDEX OF RECIPES